# FAST POLICY

## EXPERIMENTAL STATECRAFT AT THE
## THRESHOLDS OF NEOLIBERALISM

JAMIE PECK *and* NIK THEODORE

UNIVERSITY OF MINNESOTA PRESS
MINNEAPOLIS • LONDON

A different version of chapter 1 was published as Jamie Peck, "Geographies of Policy: From Transfer-Diffusion to Mobility-Mutation," *Progress in Human Geography* 35, no. 6 (2011): 773–97; reprinted by permission of Sage Journals. Portions of chapter 2 were published as Jamie Peck and Nik Theodore, "Follow the Policy: A Distended Case Approach," *Environment and Planning A* 44 (2012): 21–30; reprinted by permission of Pion, Ltd. Portions of chapter 3 were published as Jamie Peck and Nik Theodore, "Recombinant Workfare, Across the Americas: Transnationalizing 'Fast' Social Policy," *Geoforum* 41, no. 2 (2010): 195–208; reprinted by permission of Elsevier, Ltd.

Published by the University of Minnesota Press
111 Third Avenue South, Suite 290
Minneapolis, MN 55401-2520
http://www.upress.umn.edu

Library of Congress Cataloging-in-Publication Data

Peck, Jamie.
Fast policy : experimental statecraft at the thresholds of neoliberalism /
Jamie Peck and Nik Theodore.
Includes bibliographical references and index.
ISBN 978-0-8166-7730-6 (hc : alk. paper)
ISBN 978-0-8166-7731-3 (pb : alk. paper)
1. Policy sciences. 2. Neoliberalism.
I. Theodore, Nikolas. II. Title. H97.P43 2015
320.51—dc23
2014025343

Printed in the United States of America on acid-free paper

The University of Minnesota is an equal-opportunity educator and employer.

21  20  19  18  17  16  15        10  9  8  7  6  5  4  3  2  1

*For* BRYONY, HOLLY, *and* HANNAH

*For* MARY BETH, ELISE, *and* KYRA

# Contents

# Preface and Acknowledgments

The origins of this book go back to the mid-1990s, when we both began to work—first independently and later collaboratively—on issues of "policy transfer" in the fields of welfare reform and labor-market programming. Our focus at the time was largely transatlantic because of the issues involved and our own movements and connections in Western Europe and North America. Although we did some writing on this topic a little over a decade ago, several attempts to develop a more sustained focus on these issues were frustrated and delayed over the years—that is, until the Ford Foundation generously provided exploratory funding for a project we called "Policies without Borders," early in 2008. Since the summer of that year, we have been pursuing this project with various degrees of intensity, but its fascination has never receded. Through a combination of planning and opportunism, we have been able to piece together a program of interviews, observations, and site visits far outside our previous methodological (and linguistic) "comfort zones" and well beyond the limits of our original travel budget, including fieldwork in Mexico, Brazil, Indonesia, Bolivia, Spain, Germany, France, Canada, Australia, the Netherlands, Namibia, and South Africa, as well as in the United States and the United Kingdom. We have learned a lot along the way, not least that we are still learning. This book is our attempt to make sense of what we have learned so far.

Our biggest debt of gratitude is to Katherine McFate (now with the Center for Effective Government, then with the Ford Foundation), who saw the potential in this project long before we were able to properly articulate it, who provided what we needed to make it work, and who pointed us toward some promising trails at the start. The large number of policymakers, evaluators, advocates, and observers who took time to talk to us along the way is too long to list here, but we thank them for their time, their insights, and their candor. Especially supportive on our various travels were Sérgio Baierle, Marcos Barcellos, Daniela Coimbra de Souza, Paula Galeano, Badr Khafif, Yibing Li, Elaine Licio, Landy Sanchez, Maureen Turnbull, and Daniela Weiers. We thank Eric Leinberger for his cartographic assistance. Many friends and interlocutors also shaped the ideas, arguments, and approach that we use here, in what has been taking shape as a collective "policy mobilities" project, including Marc Boeckler, Neil Brenner, Allan Cochrane, Catherine Kingfisher, Wendy Larner, Helga Leitner, Rianne Mahon, Eugene McCann, Ananya Roy, Eric Sheppard, Loïc Wacquant, and Kevin Ward. Special thanks are due to Bob Jessop, who in many ways helped initiate this line of work fifteen years ago in a jointly authored paper on fast policy in neoliberal workfare experiments (Jessop and Peck 1999), which never saw the light of day. Various versions of the research reported here benefited from discussion and feedback at presentations at the University of California, Berkeley, the Institute for Applied Economic Research in Brazil, Goethe University Frankfurt, Wilfrid Laurier University, George Mason University, MIT, Open University, the Université du Québec à Montréal, Queen Mary University of London, the University of São Paulo, the National University of the Littoral, the University of Chicago, the National University of Singapore, Stockholm University, the University of Trier, Texas A&M, and the University of Victoria. Finally, we are especially grateful to Jason Weidemann at the University of Minnesota Press for his early interest, repeated encouragement, and abiding confidence that this slower-than-anticipated manuscript on the subject of fast policy would eventually be delivered. For our part, we are also pleased to have made it this far, even though this feels more like the beginning rather than the end of our effort to make sense of the various moving fronts, vectors, and mutual connections in the process of transnational policy development.

J.P., Vancouver
N.T., Chicago

# Abbreviations

| | |
|---|---|
| ABC | Brazilian Cooperation Agency |
| ANSA | World Bank Institute's Affiliated Networks for Social Accountability program |
| BIG | Basic Income Grant (Namibia) |
| BLT | Program Bantuan Tunai (Indonesia) |
| BRASA | Brazil Social Assistance Program |
| CCT | conditional cash transfer |
| CEO | Center for Economic Opportunity (New York City) |
| DfID | Department for International Development (United Kingdom) |
| EITC | Earned Income Tax Credit (United States) |
| EU | European Union |
| FBI | Federal Bureau of Investigation (United States) |
| FLACSO | Facultad Latinoamericana de Ciencias Sociales, or Latin American Faculty of Social Sciences (Mexico) |
| GAIN | Greater Avenues to Independence (United States) |
| GDP | gross domestic product |
| GRET | Groupe de recherche et d'échanges technologiques |
| IDB | Inter-American Development Bank |
| IFPRI | International Food Policy Research Institute |
| ILO | International Labour Organization |
| IMF | International Monetary Fund |
| IOPD | International Observatory on Participatory Democracy |
| LSG | Local Solidarity Governance (Porto Alegre, Brazil) |

| | |
|---|---|
| MDS | Ministry of Social Development (Brazil) |
| NAFTA | North American Free Trade Agreement |
| NGO | nongovernmental organization |
| NYC | New York City |
| OECD | Organization for Economic Cooperation and Development |
| ONYC | Opportunity NYC |
| PB | participatory budgeting |
| PETI | Programa de Erradicacao do Trabalho Infantil, or Child Labor Eradication Program (Brazil) |
| PGU-ALC | UN Urban Management Programme for Latin America |
| PKH | Program Keluarga Harapan, or Hopeful Family Program (Indonesia) |
| PNPM | Program Nasional Pemberdayaan Masyarakat, or National Program for Community Empowerment (Indonesia) |
| PRI | Partido Revolucionario Institucional, or Institutional Revolutionary Party (Mexico) |
| PROCAMPO | Programa de Apoyos Directos al Campo, or Farmers Direct Support Program (Mexico) |
| PROGRESA | Programa Nacional de Educación, Salud y Alimentación (Mexico) |
| PROSANOL | Programa Nacional de Solidaridad, or National Solidarity Program (Mexico) |
| PT | Partido dos Trabalhadores, or Workers' Party (Brazil) |
| RCT | randomized control trial |
| Red FAL | Forum of Local Authorities for Social Inclusion and Participatory Democracy |
| SA | Social Accountability (World Bank) |
| SIF | Social Innovation Fund (United States) |
| TANF | Temporary Assistance to Needy Families (United States) |
| UAMPA | União das Associações de Moradores de Porto Alegre, or Union of Neighborhood Associations |
| UCLG | United Cities and Local Governments |
| UN | United Nations |
| UNDP | United Nations Development Program |

| | |
|---|---|
| UNESCO | United Nations Educational, Scientific, and Cultural Organization |
| UN-Habitat | United Nations Human Settlements Program |
| UN-UMP | United Nations Urban Management Program |
| URB-AL | European Commission's Urban Regional Aid Programme |
| USAID | United States Agency for International Development (United States) |
| W-2 | Wisconsin Works (United States) |
| WDR | World Development Report (World Bank) |
| WSF | World Social Forum |
| WTO | World Trade Organization |

# Introduction

## Policies without Borders

It is often observed, in this self-conscious age of globalization, that we live in a perpetually accelerating and ever-more interconnected world. New ideas, fads, and fashions, in particular, seem to be moving at social-media speed. And new *policy* ideas, especially those highly sought-after "ideas that work," are apparently now able to find not only a worldwide audience but transnational *salience* in remarkably short order. The rapid ascendency of silver-bullet policies in fields like microcredit programming and urban "creativity" strategies certainly seem to fit this profile, the various traces of which are not entirely ubiquitous, of course, but they are undeniably far flung.[1] The acceleration in cross-border policy traffic is also reflected, if not enabled, by the veritable industry—"social infrastructure" might be a better term—that has sprung up around "best practice" codification, practitioner conferences, learning exchanges, knowledge transfer, and communities of practice, a world that is populated by a mobile class of policy gurus, entrepreneurs, consultants, bloggers, evaluator-advocates, and model peddlers.

The sense that "no policymaker is an island" anymore, that policymaking now routinely occurs in knowingly comparative terms, and that best practices from elsewhere pervade so much of the policymaking conversation is clearly not an entirely imagined condition. Systematic studies of the rate and reach of policy diffusion seem to affirm this increased interconnectivity and cross-referential intensity,[2] but the increasingly reflexive, transnational consciousness that characterizes many policymaking communities surely has effects of its own, in any case. Policymaking imaginaries have been "debordered," even if the connections are highly selective and the balance of "trade" remains just as uneven, and even if the achievement of policy outcomes remains a stubbornly localized, context-specific process. Learning from, and "referencing," distant models and practices is now commonplace, even as literal replication never really happens. And learning curves can be shortened—sometimes dramatically—if local reform efforts are framed, from the get-go, by a reading of the best-practice literature, by borrowing from a well-known model, or by the importation of authorized designs, expertise, and formulations. It is a widely acknowledged feature of policymaking common sense, in many parts of the world today, that shorthand processes like these, and the various forms of "speed-up" they imply, have become normalized. "Traveling policy, like globalization, is nothing new," Catherine Kingfisher writes,[3] "nevertheless, it has been accelerating in recent decades to such an extent that it is now ubiquitous, almost mundane."

None of this is to stake the questionable claim, it must be emphasized, that policymaking worlds are racing toward convergence—unilaterally driven by steamroller models of best practice, or "flattened" into a neoliberalized monoculture—but it is to make the more subtle point that those policy-making worlds are becoming more intimately and deeply interconnected than ever before. Furthermore, a related proposition is that this condition of interconnectivity is itself subject to historically distinctive forms of acceleration and intensification. Continuous monitoring and learning, continuous promotion of best-practice models, continuous inter-referencing of policies, especially at moments of path-altering "reform"—all these are features of reconstituted policy worlds. And in the terms we are exploring here, they are reconstituted *fast* policy worlds.

Our point, then, is not to declare that "fast policy" represents a new and totalizing global condition, or some new-age ontology of policy formation, as if to entail an existential revolution across what were once-parochial and hitherto-slow worlds of policymaking, and their absorption into a seamless and ultimately featureless space of policymaking flows. All the world is a blur: fast policy as the new paradigm! This is not the case we are making here. Rather, we seek to *problematize* fast policy, both as a phenomenon (or "condition") that is real and consequential, as well as one that is routinely prone to misrepresentation, not to say exaggeration. We are interested, above all, in the social and political practices that *enable* fast-policy mobilities, in the ideological and institutional alignments that facilitate (or otherwise) their diverse travels and interconnections, and in their frailties and limits, as well as their incipient functionalities and logics. Speed does indeed seem to be of the essence here, but it is a kind of speed that is manifest in the intensification of long-distance (inter)connections, one that is revealed in the fortified reach and extended range of "mobile" policy frames, routines, and models, and one that takes account of the heightened immediacy, saliency, and indeed urgency of what have apparently become increasingly *compressed* policymaking moments.

These forms of transnational intensification and compression, it should be reiterated, do not necessarily imply perfectly lubricated convergence or one-way global isomorphism. Instead, *Fast Policy* is concerned with those social practices and infrastructures that enable and sustain policy "mobility," which enable the complex folding of policy lessons derived from one place into reformed and transformed arrangements elsewhere. It is concerned with friction as well as flow. After all, while some aspects of the policymaking process, like the generation of codified institutional designs and models, seem to be built for travel, there is much that cannot be so easily bottled for export, including charismatic leadership, propitious local circumstances, and the presence of supportive partners. Consequently, the book's seemingly oxymoronic objectives are to explore the social embeddedness of policy mobility, the institutionalization of fast-traveling practices, the grounded processes that enable accelerated cross-border learning, and the often prosaic lives of cosmopolitan actors.

Drawing on a geographical sensibility, this will involve an examination of the tensions between fixity and motion in contemporary policymaking practice: while the policymaking imagination may be globalizing, and while transnational circuits of expertise and practice are proliferating, the stubborn reality is that *making policies work* very often remains a hands-on, messy, and very much "local" affair. It follows that one-sided celebrations of unconstrained policy mobility will not do, but neither should it be assumed that institutional idiosyncrasy and geographical inertia are destined to prevail forever. The purpose of *problematizing* fast policy is consequently to explore both the connections and the contradictions between the smooth spaces imagined and made by global policy models and the more mundane and "sticky" reality of day-to-day delivery, between the apparently limitless world of the business-class policy guru and peripatetic consultant on the one hand, and the more circumscribed spheres inhabited by local administrators, stakeholders, and frontline workers on the other.

Our approach to these questions, from an empirical standpoint, has been to spend the past five years jumping on and off the jet streams of two conspicuously transnational currents in contemporary policymaking: first, in the social-policy realm, conditional cash transfers (CCTs) can now be found in almost fifty countries; second, in the arena of municipal governance, participatory budgeting (PB) has diffused to thousands of local jurisdictions. Much more on these later, but in a nutshell, CCTs "condition" cash payments to poor households, making them comply with a range of rules concerning school attendance, family health and nutrition, and so forth, the conventional rationale for which is intergenerational human-capital building. The best known of the CCT models was developed in Mexico (as PROGRESA, later renamed Oportunidades) in the second half of the 1990s, though these cash-transfer schemes have since spread across nearly all of South America and considerably beyond. This will be our first case study of fast policy. Our second, participatory budgeting, is another Latin American "invention." PB is a model of citizens' engagement in the prioritization of local-government spending that has been paradigmatically associated with Porto Alegre, Brazil, but that likewise is now encountered all over the world. Both of these policies, PB and CCTs, have been advocated by multilateral organizations, including United Nations' agencies and the World Bank, but neither are entirely creatures of these rarified worlds, having been variously "made," shaped, and propagated by a wide range of national and local government agencies, in some cases by social movements, and by sundry other actors, intermediaries, and entrepreneurs. Each exists, in other words, in a complex and multilayered social field, social fields that we have been exploring for the past five years.

The original rationale for focusing on these two policy domains was that, first, they have been proliferating rapidly (if diffusion processes usually describe a forward-leaning S-shaped trajectory, both have been on a steep upslope for well over a decade); second, they each have displayed a precociously global reach while at the same time traveling "uphill," as well as laterally, from sites of origination in the southern hemisphere (although the question of where such policies "come from" is invariably contested, their geographical locus, in both instances, is Latin America); and third, the journeys these policies have made, and the institutional footprints they have left behind, have often crossed partisan and ideological lines, recruiting a heterodox band of supporters, promoters, and interlocutors, while also crossing national borders (even as CCTs have carried with them a flavor of neoliberal reformism, while PB retains a certain spirit of insurgent localism). And a final, more methodological, reason for considering two policy fields was that this would at least temper any temptation to "read off" from a single case, or to extrapolate in a singular fashion; perhaps the "shape" and dynamics of fast policy would be qualitatively different in the two fields.

The exploration that follows is comparative in scope in a double sense, although not really in the conventional sense. First, it is cross-national, spanning empirical fieldwork on six continents and in fifteen countries, even if it was never intended to be a methodologically symmetrical, side-by-side comparison of policy regimes. This has been, in other words, a multisited investigation, involving an exploratory mapping of nodes, networks, and netherworlds in the two policy fields. It has entailed extensive travels (or transects) across the moving landscapes of PB and CCTs, while recognizing that the goal of truly comprehensive, encyclopedic coverage is not a remotely realizable one. Second, the analysis is comparative in the sense that it culminates in a series of "lateral" reflections across these two policy fields. This has allowed us to think across the two domains, identifying commonalities and contrasts in the dynamics of change, in their overall "arcs" of innovation (and degradation), in dominant strategies and policy technologies, and in the cast of characters (institutional and individual) engaged in different aspects of the reform process.

Of course, it must be acknowledged at the outset that this kind of analysis is indicative, not exhaustive, given the sheer impossibility of reaching a methodological saturation point in the pursuit of two such far-flung and literally borderless phenomena. There was a practical limitation here, since we were both present for all of the interviews and observations (though a few were conducted solo). If the analysis was not exactly exhaustive, then certainly in other ways our capacities were exhausted! Our (almost) realistic goal was to execute a series of transects across the two policy fields, cutting through some of their more important nodes and translation centers, while also pushing out to some of their sites of contestation or failure. Our hope was that this double-handed effort to "follow the policy," across two fast-mutating fields, might expose some unpredictable twists, turns, openings, and dead ends—and at the very least it would take us in some unexpected directions. Crucially, we had nothing approaching a "map" of the two fields to start with. What we did have was an idea of some of the "hot spots" and key coordination points; beyond that, we were hoping to pick up (better) directions along the way. Fortunately (and as it turned out, fascinatingly), this is exactly what happened. We encountered more than a few surprises, and in fact did not really anticipate even some of the more important *directions* of change at the outset. Predictability is not a defining characteristic of either of these policy worlds.

In fact, to anticipate some of our more substantive conclusions for a moment, rather surprising degrees of institutional *and political* indeterminacy were evident in both of the policy fields that we will explore in this book, PB and CCTs. Rather than an orderly and predictable diffusion path, both are marked by complex and splintering trajectories, neither of which could have been predicted at the outset. This is not merely to make the claim that (original) "designs" rarely hold, and that the institutional and technical character of policies evolves, mutates, and often degrades as "travel" occurs, even as this is certainly part of the story. More than this, the *politics* of this process turn out to be complex, multidirectional, and unpredictable too. In both of the cases that we studied, the policies were transformed in ways that not only exceeded the visions and predilections of their original architects but that in significant respects confounded and even contradicted them. One of these divergences, perhaps, could be said to confirm a pessimistic reading of the disciplining effects of neoliberalism: PB was born as a radicalizing project of deep democracy in Brazil, a longtime policy of choice among left advocates, but as it has been increasingly mainstreamed by agencies like the World Bank, or borrowed for merely tokenistic purposes by calculating politicians, it has lost a great deal of its "edge." True, some quarters of the PB advocacy movement have retained their faith in the project's potential, as a disruptive technology of open-ended political change. But genuinely progressive political experiments are now vastly outnumbered by the hollow adaptations and pale imitations. Now, while this might be interpreted, soberly, as an(other) illustration of the limits of radical localism in a neoliberalizing world, or of the corrosive effects of ideologically imposed norms and constraints, the complex trajectories of CCTs seem to call for a different interpretation. Here, a policy initiative that rose to prominence with the implicit, and later very explicit, support of the "Washington Consensus" agencies—since it strictly "conditioned" social assistance on human-capital building behaviors, based on the close monitoring of a narrowly targeted population of low-income families—would later take on a more complex character, merging with "neowelfarist" currents in some settings while in others opening up a complementary space of experimentation within the basic income movement. In some cases, CCTs have even threatened to evolve into the kind of no-strings-attached, unconditional cash transfers to the poor that are anathema to neoliberal policymakers.

This is not the place, yet, to dive into the tangled weeds of these policy fields, and all of their intriguing specificities. Rather, it is to underscore the claim that interconnected processes of policy *making, mobility, and mutation* deserve attention in their own right, not least because they are more unpredictable than one might initially think. Crucially, they are subject to neither design determinism nor political foreclosure. The sphere of fast policy is not simply a domain for the reproduction of dominant practices, but neither is it an arena in which anything goes. New, or only hazily understood, dynamics seem to be at work here, dynamics that also seem to vary from one policy field to another. While we genuinely did not know, at the outset, in which directions our investigations would take us, it was this sense that there was important action (and actors) to be revealed in the shadowlands of policy making, selling, borrowing, and learning that drove the project. It called for a methodology that did not itself lead to foreclosure or preemptive judgment, but which was instead open and exploratory.

This necessarily somewhat improvised methodology—based on interviews, observations, and documentary analysis—was not expected to reveal prototypical patterns, though our hope was that it would draw attention to emergent processes and practices. While extended immersion in each and every individual location was not a realistic option, a degree of "network immersion" in the two transnational policy fields might be achieved. Our approach involved some degree of going with the policymaking flow, in order to see what this might reveal, though we were also keenly aware that passively floating downstream, along with the strongest currents, could also create misleading impressions of unity and unidirectionality. The persistent challenge was to avoid slipping into a form of sampling, as it were, on the dependent variable, and merely affirming some anticipated account of policy hypermobility, as articulated by the most powerful players (many of whom had interests in promoting such narratives). We had to avoid becoming dupes of the policy networks themselves, getting hooked on the catchiest policymaking tunes, or becoming enrolled into the choral societies that tend to form around favored programs of reform. These challenges are compounded, of course, by the fact that many of the most successful intermediaries and interlocutors in these fast-policy worlds are themselves charismatic actors and savvy entrepreneurs. They are successful in part *because* they are engaging and eloquent cosmopolitans. They are armed with well-polished scripts and a surfeit of supporting evidence; they are accomplished persuaders. While this was, in part, the very world we wanted to understand, it also necessitated at least a measure of contrarian skepticism; a willingness, periodically, to step off the global matrix, sometimes in the company of local critics or with others in a position to provide different kinds of alternative-reality checks; and a sensitivity to contradictory and countervailing evidence. Clearly, these explorations would need to venture out beyond the policy-making equivalent of the airport shop.

## Following Policies

The research strategy that we have adopted here—of following policies across mutating fields of reform and innovation, first separately, and then in comparison—was self-consciously pursued as a means of exposing new temporalities and spatialities of policymaking. The research design itself was consequently emergent and exploratory, rather than prescribed and preformulated, thereby opening up the potential for a considerable degree of inductive learning en route. Our desire to try something different, methodologically speaking, reflected the nature of the rapidly mutating policy fields in question, into which we would have to become "embedded" before figuring out a travel itinerary, before developing a program of interviews through referrals and "snowball" techniques, and before deciding which particular programs and which institutional sites should be prioritized. Going with the policy-making flow, to a certain degree, seemed to make more sense in this context. But the other reason to try something different was that the more traditional approaches to what has usually been styled as "policy transfer" between bounded institutional spaces seemed to have been associated with diminishing analytical returns.

The tradition of research on policy transfer and diffusion mostly stems from work in the field of political science. This approach, the roots of which can be traced to the 1960s, but which experienced something of a revival in the 1990s, takes as its object of analysis the conspicuous diffusion of innovative policy designs and legislative devices across jurisdictional boundaries, at first intranationally and later internationally.[4] In large measure, rational action (or bounded rationality) on the part of decision-makers is assumed, or held as a (universal) yardstick against the observed behaviors of policy actors. These rational decision-makers, who sit at the center of an often de-contextualized and depoliticized story, are seen to be scanning the horizon for effective policy solutions to identified problems, variously learning or borrowing from "better" or more effective practices.

Orthodox analyses of policy transfer tend to be normatively positive and methodologically positivist; they are principally concerned with the legible design features of "successful" policies, with the patterns of diffusion that they describe (typically "outward," from singular places of invention), and with the decision-making and learning behaviors that facilitate these transfer processes. Conventionally, little attention is paid to the social and ideological contexts of the policymaking process, to the politics of policy knowledge production, or to the more indeterminate zones of policy implementation and practice.[5] Policies themselves are likewise reified, usually in terms of specific design features, and they are seen to travel, more or less intact, across generally inert institutional landscapes populated by knowing and relatively rational actors.

This rational-choice approach to policy transfer has been productive in its own terms, but it has shed little light on the social and institutional fields that are our concern here. The style of analysis of policy transfer studies, on which we reflect further in chapter 3, tends to be somewhat arid, and indeed rather paradoxically depoliticized. Little is revealed of the "social lives" of policies and those of their various advocates and audiences—a principal concern in the research we report here. Far more promising and productive, from our perspective, is the still-emergent interdisciplinary field of "critical policy studies," with its diverse connections to anthropology, development studies, political sociology, geography, organizational theory, and comparative political economy, which in various ways seeks to problematize the socio-institutional character of policy-*making* processes, and the capacities *and limits* of cosmopolitan policy projects, transnational governance processes, practices of peripatetic expertise, and the shaping of globalizing norms.[6] In our own fields of political-economic geography and critical urban studies, this line of work is closely complemented by the burgeoning program of "policy mobilities" research, much of which is directly concerned with trans-local and cross-scalar movements in policy discourses and technologies of the kind that we problematize here.[7]

These alternative approaches to the problematic of policy movement are grounded in a range of critical epistemologies, conceptualizing the policy-making field as a socially structured and discursively constituted space, marked by institutional heterogeneity and contending forces. Rational, learning behaviors are not assumed to prevail. Instead, policy actors and actions are understood to be politically constituted and sociologically complex. As such, the beliefs and behaviors of policy actors are *constitutively* embedded within networks of knowledge/expertise (many of which are translocal and transscalar), as well as within more "localized" socioinstitutional milieux. Policy designs, technologies, and frames are likewise to be seen as complex and evolving social constructions rather than as concretely fixed objects. In fact, these are very often the means and the media through which relations between distant policymaking sites are actively made and remade. A policy "model," for example, can only exist as a model once it has enrolled an "audience" of interlocutors and would-be emulators, this field of reception itself representing more than some passive hinterland, but an active zone of adaptation and transformation, not to say dialogic and joint constitution. The admiring gaze—a necessary condition for all models—is a social product, not just a matter of unilateral projection.

The audiences of received policy models have roles to play in the (social) production of these models, the extralocal salience of which can only be achieved through the enrollment of "followers."[8] Influential models are rarely, if ever, the work of a single architect. Policy "designs," in this respect, will tend to evolve *across* fields of social mediation and interaction, themselves marked by institutional difference and uneven development. It may be commonplace to *represent* policy models as rational abstractions—essentializing some supposedly definitive cluster of design features or packaging some programmatic philosophy—but in fact these are co-constituted through the networks, and across the landscapes, through and over which they travel. In their acquisition of extralocal salience, policy models reveal their character as "relational" constructions; they do not simply travel, intact, from sites of invention to sites of emulation, like some superior export product, or to borrow the parlance of the field, as "silver bullets." Instead, through their very movement they (re)make connections between these sites, evolving in form and effect as they go. Fast-traveling policy models, like PB and CCTs, do not simply drop from the sky, yielding "impacts" here and there; their reach and influence are constructed through policy networks, each of which possesses specific institutional, ideational, and ideological characteristics. In this sense, policy models do not simply fly across patterned institutional landscapes, somewhere down below; they have become enmeshed in the transformation of these moving landscapes. And they are not "transferred" intact, as complete packages. As Noemi Lendvai and Paul Stubbs have persuasively argued, *translation* is a more appropriate metaphor.[9]

Exploring the social lives of globalizing policy models necessitates the embrace of a range of methodological strategies, many of which are located outside the conventional, positivist canon. Genealogical and discourse analyses have indispensible roles to play in the deconstruction of traveling policy technologies and texts, and the lineages and networks with which they are associated. And judicious combinations of ethnographic observation and depth interviewing are essential to any adequate understanding of the inescapably social nature of those *continuous* processes of translation, intermediation, and contextualization/decontextualization/recontextualization, through which various forms of policy mobility are realized. Continuing methodological development and experimentation is consequently necessary.

This is a far cry, however, from taking policy designs at face value and then analyzing their diffusion and emulation within a positivist, rational-actor framework, in the manner of the orthodox policy-transfer literature; it necessitates critical investigations of those multisited *social* processes through which policy rationales, rationalities, and routines are constructed and reconstructed. Rather than a machinic process of replication, policy mobility is inescapably associated with policy mutation: if the form and effects of policies vary with context and shift while in transit, becoming embedded in both networks and within multiple "local" milieux, the "thing" that is being followed is evidently not itself an immutable object.[10] In practical methodological terms, this means connecting the (rarely pristine) places of policy invention not only with spaces of circulation and centers of translation but also with the prosaic netherworlds of policy implementation, in all their diversity. The latter are persistently overlooked (or downplayed) in those orthodox approaches that variously rationalize or scientize the policymaking process, but as the sphere in which policies and programs "become real," they are in fact crucial to the manner in which the conjoined process of policy mobility/mutation occurs.

This calls for a methodological approach sensitive both to movement (for instance, transnationalizing policy models, peripatetic modes of expertise) and to those variable experiences of embedding and transformation under-way in "downstream" sites of adoption/emulation. Together, these constitute distended policy "fields," the uneven development of which routinely acts as a spur to further experimentation and adaptation. The methodological problematic, then, is not simply one of accounting for transactions or trans-fers, but encompasses the origination and reproduction of multisite policy networks, which as "transnational policy communities" may become social worlds in their own right. Among other things, this undoes traditional under-standings of the (policy) field "as a single and (relatively) geographically bounded place," as Janine Wedel and colleagues have emphasized, because, increasingly, this "consists of loosely connected actors with varying degrees of institutional leverage located in multiple 'sites' that are not always even geographically fixed."[11] Researching policy mobility/mutation need not always and necessarily be a multisite endeavor,[12] but "following the policy" will often entail methodological travel, along the paths carved and through the spaces made by the policies themselves.

The critical approach to policy mobility/mutation sketched here is not associated with a fixed methodological repertoire, but gives license to an open-ended embrace of methodological experimentation and reflexivity, ranging from policy ethnographies to genealogical analyses and social-constructivist diffusion studies.[13] "Following the policy" is therefore, by defi-nition, an exploratory method. Crucially, while this approach seeks to take the translocal relativization and mutability of policy seriously, indeed as a problematic, it is also important to draw lessons from the rich traditions of multisite ethnography and the extended case method.[14] Focusing on flows and connections must not come at the expense of leaching out "local" socio-institutional context. It is also important that even when working mostly in a "lateral" dimension—through networks and across multiple sites—this does not iron out or obfuscate the role of power relations. We must never lose sight of hierarchical and nodal sources of power, and of patterned asym-metries in capacities and resources, even when deep in the weeds of local implementation issues. There is undeniably a risk that fixing the analytical gaze too tightly on mobile policy objects themselves might simply reproduce, in a different form, the kind of reification typical of orthodox approaches to policy transfer. The charge (not to say challenge) of developing a *textured* appreciation of the social lives of global policy models can therefore be seen as a guard against any temptation to fetishize mobility itself. Mobility must not be understood as an "extraterrestrial" process, detached from context. In connecting often distant policymaking sites, it may, however, be changing how "context" matters, as the norms and practices of policymaking seem to be increasingly shaped, jointly and simultaneously, by those mobile frames of reference invoked by traveling models and by the shifting mosaic of local translations.

Our goal is certainly not to make the case for a critical variant of policy diffusion studies, but instead to think in terms of continuous and often contradictory processes-cum-practices of *translation*.[15] One reason to be skeptical of diffusionist optics is that they invoke a universe of "radiating" policies, traveling out unidirectionally from places of invention and control, as opposed to a more dialogic and multisited understanding proposed here. In this latter view, power and control still matter, but they are more often exercised multilaterally, while there is no clear separation between the sphere of policy design (which is often understood to be more theoretical) and fields of experimentation (conventionally regarded as more practical), as the two increasingly become mutually interdependent. What happens "locally" is therefore much more than a second-order or downstream concern, or merely a contingent matter of implementation. It is very much part and parcel of what has become a distended and multipolar process of policymaking, in which experimental or best-practice sites have become intricately connected to centers of advocacy and persuasion, both as symbols of real-world credibility and as a new kind of currency: "policies that *work*." The questions of how policies-from-elsewhere are put to work by local actors, and how they are translated, circulated, contextualized, and embedded, must always be on the table, as must those relating to the purposive "disembedding" of positive policy lessons from the sanctified sites of "success." The attendant "ethnographic question," David Mosse has argued, "is not whether but *how* [policy] projects work; not whether a project succeeds, but how success is produced."[16]

## The Journey Ahead . . .

It should be evident by now that the fieldwork for *Fast Policy* began with, and was animated by, a methodological sensibility and a broad sense of direction, as opposed to an empirical investigation of a "known" terrain. It is for this reason that we have introduced the book by discussing how the problematic of fast policy was approached, rather than to anticipate our conclusions per se. Prior to this project, we had both worked extensively on issues of urban governance, as well as on social and labor-market policy, albeit mainly in Europe and North America. The Policies without Borders project that is the basis of this book presented an opportunity to explore some of the spaces "in between" the kinds of sites that we have typically studied, as well as to work in some very different settings, including Latin America, southern Africa, and Asia. Our hope was that this would yield some fresh perspectives on what for us has been an issue of longstanding concern—the changing geographies of policy—in a way that might be revealing in methodological as well as substantive terms. Certainly, it was a different kind of journey for us . . .

The research for this book was not undertaken according to a fixed theoretical schema, or indeed according to determinate positions in the policy fields in question. Rather, particular nodes in the moving landscape of participatory budgeting and conditional cash transfer programming were selected as points of departure, after which a series of journeys were undertaken, out to sites of latest-generation innovation, as well as to some of the places where problems were encountered, or where mid-path adjustments were effected. Our travels also took us to some of the principal coordination and distribution centers, like the World Bank and various government ministries, in additional to various venues of "intermediation," such as evaluation houses and practitioner conferences. We have chosen to organize this book in a corresponding fashion, while also seeking to stay close to practice and close to the cases.

This book is divided into three parts. Part 1 outlines our approach to fast policy more systematically, making the case for the kind of geographically sensitive, socially constructivist perspective that has shaped the approach here. Chapter 1, "Geographies of Policy," begins by critically reviewing the literatures on policy learning, transfer, and diffusion, with an eye toward understanding the contributions and limits of orthodox approaches to understanding policy mobility. Here, the false choice between, on the one hand, highly stylized, rational-choice conceptions of policy transfer, which conventionally invoke idealized forms of policymaking behavior while abstracting from political and social context, and descriptively parochial, place-specific accounts, on the other, is rejected in favor of a social-constructivist approach that problematizes the inherent tensions between local specificity and global interconnectedness, and the continuous processes of embeddeding and disembedding, (mis)translation and mutation that this entails. This is followed by a short chapter, the first in a series of reflections that close each section of the book, where we anticipate some of the methodological and interpretative challenges of this critical and reflexive approach to policy mobility. Here, in conversation with the extended case study method, we characterize our strategy for researching a far-flung selection of interconnected fieldwork sites, which we provisionally style as a distended case study approach.

While part 1 establishes, in a provisional way, a theoretical and methodological framework for the book, it follows from the social-constructivist approach that we advocate, sensitive to institutionalized power geometries and to the complex localization of "global" policies, that this is more a matter of sensibility and orientation. Ultimately, explanatory traction is to be found within the contextualized cases; it is not really a matter of theoretical adjudication or methodological surety. It is the cases that expose the institutional indeterminacies, the roles of (distributed) social agency, the unanticipated political turns. Hence the need to delve deeply into the *distinctive* social worlds of PB and CCTs, in parts 2 and 3 of the book. Both of these extended case studies open with chapters concerned with iconic locations on what are fast-moving maps of policy innovation and adaptation. This is then followed, for each of the two policy fields, by a complementary analysis of some of the extralocal dimensions and drivers of the policymaking landscape, their characteristic modes of organization and morphology, and their emergent dynamics. Parts 2 and 3 of the book close with reflections chapters, which range across the cases in more abstract terms, picking up some of the analytical threads introduced in part 1.

In part 2, "Social Policy as Practical Science," we explore the world of conditional cash transfers, beginning where we began in the project itself, with New York City's bold attempt to fashion a version of Mexico's Oportunidades program. Chapter 3, "New Ideas for New York City," explores Mayor Bloomberg's experiment in South-North policy learning, his ultimately frustrated attempt to replicate the well-publicized successes of Oportunidades. New York City's struggling CCT program is a sobering reminder of the challenges of "off-the-shelf" policy borrowing, even under generally favorable institutional and political circumstances, but it also illustrates the continuing, persuasive power of "scientized" evaluation methods and compelling invention narratives. Following this, chapter 4 adopts a more global perspective on the fast-moving field of CCT policy development, considering the roles played by multilateral agencies and a series of more "lateral" networks, and concluding with a discussion of potentially divergent currents in the continuing evolution of this policy field. In one sense, this is a story of the formidable power of organizations like the World Bank as "knowledge managers," reflecting the premium that is increasingly placed on international expertise and verifiable evaluation evidence, in addition to the more politicized processes of message management. On the other hand, the limits and uncertainties of the Bank's hegemonic reach are also revealed: domestic politics continue to exert a major influence on project design and implementation, permitting second- and third-generation mutations to occur, "in the wild," which often contradict preferred paths of policy development, and which sometimes even open the door to alternatives. Our second reflections chapter, "Tailwinds, Turning Points," first calls attention to the enormous momentum generated behind the "paradigm positive" policy program that is CCTs, which has been powerfully steered, most notably by the World Bank, through a combination of financial incentives and technocratic persuasion. But it would be premature to characterize this as a process of hegemonic diffusion, because even with these strong following winds CCTs have morphed and mutated in some surprising ways, in some cases diverging significantly from the orthodox path. We invoke the metaphor of "transduction" here to capture this sense of continuing mutation under conditions of viral networking.

Part 3, "Propagating Progressive Practice," engages with the case of participatory budgeting. Rather than begin with an instance of mature-stage adaptation, as we did with the example of the New York CCT program, here we begin in a place that has become almost synonymous with participatory budgeting, Porto Alegre, Brazil. The Porto Alegre story, which is the focus of chapter 6, turns out to be much more, however, than a narrative of heroic invention. Yes, this is the acknowledged site of what has become a hallowed, original experiment, and (still) a space of inspiration for many, but Porto Alegre also illustrates the political slipperiness of the PB concept, which under more conservative administrations has become a hollowed out version of its former self. Policy models are consequently not always what they seem, even in their places of supposed authenticity. Chapter 7 takes up this theme in more transnational terms, examining the extensive "repurposing" of participatory-budgeting routines in the context of generally more mainstream experiments in inclusive local governance, arenas in which multilateral banks and purposive policymaking networks have assumed an increased significance. The "synthesized" or "pasteurized" version of PB favored by the multilateral agencies, which ironically seeks to facilitate public participation in a largely depoliticized manner, is seen to have traveled far and fast, but the transformative potential of the original seems to have been lost along the way. Our third reflections chapter, "Headwinds, Hollowing Out," contrasts an "organic" phase of PB propagation, during which the original Porto Alegre model traveled in a fashion that retained its political integrity, with the currently prevailing "synthetic" phase, in which a stripped-down version of this bundle of participatory practices is put to work more as a tool of urban management than as a prelude to ever-deeper forms of transformative democratization. We also emphasize the vital role of policy networks, of various kinds, in the transnational (re)construction of the PB field, concluding that these are nevertheless invariably connected to centers of political power, as one might think of sinews being connected to policymaking "muscle."

The principal objective of the book's conclusion is to reflect on some of the analytical lessons have been learned *across* the two case studies. While the burden of our argument will be that there is important explanatory "action" to be found in the contextualized specificities of these cases, where the dynamics and even directions of change prove to be somewhat unpredictable, we must also learn through the reflexive and reconstructive maneuvers of theorizing across cases—not least to ask whether there are recurrent patterns in their very unpredictability. The condition of accelerating and intensifying multipolar policy change is a compelling feature of both cases, as are phenomena like deliberative policy "modeling," in which policies are built for extralocal projection, and the crucial intermediating roles played by a range of peripatetic actors and entrepreneurs. At the same time, we conclude that there is evidence that qualitatively different forms of fast policy are at work in each of the sprawling fields of practice that are PB and CCTs, before going on to consider what this might mean for the politics of policy "translation." Fast policy refers to a condition of deepening transnational interconnectedness, in which local policy experiments exist *in relation to* near and far relatives, to traveling models and technocratic designs, and to a host of financial, technical, social, and symbolic networks that invariably loop through centers of power and persuasion. The policymaking process accelerates under these conditions, as local policymaking increasingly begins with imported or borrowed designs, from which new permutations and adaptations are repeatedly worked. This creates shortcut alternatives to more deliberative, developmental modes of policy formation, and tends to favor the kinds of technocratic strategies pushed by well-resourced multilateral agencies and validated by evaluation science over organically grown, endogenous approaches to policy innovation. Many of these shortcuts, furthermore, also short-circuit processes of democratic deliberation and control, one of the most ironic instances of which must surely be that of hollowed-out, formulaic forms of participatory budgeting that are now rapidly traveling the globe. Fast policy remains an inescapably political process, and indeed even a social condition, but some of its strongest currents have been marked by a kind of networked technopolitics that is largely disconnected from democratic deliberation and popular control.

# PART I

## In Pursuit of Fast Policy

# 1

# Geographies of Policy

The modern policymaking process may still be focused on centers of political authority, but networks of policy advocacy and activism now exhibit a precociously transnational reach; policy decisions made in one jurisdiction increasingly echo and influence those made elsewhere; and global policy "models" often exert normative power across significant distances. Today, sources, channels, and sites of policy advice encompass sprawling networks of human and nonhuman actors/actants, including consultants, web sites, practitioner communities, norm-setting models, conferences, guru performances, evaluation scientists, think tanks, blogs, global policy institutes, and best-practice peddlers, not to mention the more "hierarchical" influence of multilateral agencies, international development funds, powerful trading partners, and occupying powers. That traveling policy ideas are heavily mediated, of course, is nothing new. What does appear to have changed, though, is the intensity of that mediation, along with the velocity of policy transfer, learning, and modeling. Indeed, it is increasingly argued that the apparatus of policy diffusion and development has transnationalized in such a profound and irreversible way as to render anachronistic the notion of independent, "domestic" decision-making.[1]

Contemporary policymaking processes have promiscuously spilled over jurisdictional boundaries, both "horizontally" (between national and local political entities) and "vertically" (between hierarchically scaled institutions and domains). They also seem to be accelerating. In this book, we argue that these developments should be seen as key characteristics of emergent fast-policy regimes, marked by the pragmatic borrowing of "policies that work," by compressed development and implementation horizons, by iterative forms of deference to best practice and paradigmatic models, by enlarged roles for intermediaries as advocates of specific policy routines and technologies, and by a growing reliance on prescriptively coded forms of front-loaded advice and evaluation science.[2] The advent of fast policy, Bob Jessop has observed, has been marked by "the shortening of policy-development cycles, fast-tracking decision-making, rapid programme rollout, continuing policy experimentation, institutional and policy Darwinism, and relentless revision of guidelines and benchmarks."[3] These, in turn, characterize new postures of policymaking, based on experimentality, crisis-driven opportunism, and heightened reflexivity. Jessop goes on to note that these conditions tend to privilege those who are able to "operate within compressed time scales, narrow[ing] the range of participants in the policy process, and limit[ing] the scope for deliberation, consultation, and negotiation."[4]

On the face of it, at least, policy ideas and techniques do seem to have become mobile in entirely new ways—exhibiting an extended reach, as well as a diversity of registers. These phenomena have been variously captured in terms of the relational rescaling of governance systems, the construction of mobile modes of neoliberal governmentality, and the uneven transnationalization of policy knowledge and expertise.[5] Yet while it is now widely acknowledged that the boundaries between jurisdictions and policymaking sites are becoming more porous,[6] that policy learning and transfer have become continuous (if not endemic) processes,[7] and that the rate of transnational policy diffusion is accelerating,[8] there are unresolved debates around whether these processes are driving "convergence" in policy regimes; whether they imply a fundamental challenge to, or a reconstruction of, conventional sources of (national) political authority; and whether they are most appropriately understood in terms of "network" or "restructuring" ontologies. There is a sprawling literature on these questions, mostly in political science, but also extending into sociology, anthropology, and comparative institutionalism, together, more recently, with a growing body of work in geography. While it has only been intermittently theorized as such, the phenomenon of "policy transfer" is of course an intrinsically geographical one.

This chapter engages with the problematic of policy movement from a geographical perspective. It does so by exploring the distinction between rationalist-formalist traditions of research on policy *transfer,* most clearly illustrated in the orthodox political science literature, and social-constructivist approaches to policy *mobility and mutation,* an emergent project with diverse roots in the interdisciplinary zone of "critical policy studies."[9] This latter approach, it must be said, remains somewhat inchoate, though it draws upon an increasingly interconnected body of work, from across the heterodox social sciences, which is variously committed to postpositivist and socially contextualized analyses of policymaking processes. If the orthodox policy transfer literature tends to be preoccupied with accounts of rationally selected best (or better) practices moving across jurisdictional lines, the new generation of social constructivist work is considerably more attentive to the sociospatial context of policymaking activities, and to the hybrid mutations of policy techniques and practices across dynamic institutional landscapes. Here, the movement of policy is more than merely a transaction or transfer, but entails the relational interpenetration and mutual interdependency of policymaking sites and actors, spawning phenomena such as global policy "models," transnational knowledge networks, and innovatory forms of audit, evaluation, and advocacy.

The mobilities approach resembles a rolling conversation rather than a coherent paradigm, though the distinctions with rational-choice political science are usually quite sharp. In a stylized form, these are summarized for heuristic purposes in Figure 1. Here, we engage critically with three extant literatures on policy transfer and transformation, drawn mainly from political science, comparative institutionalism, and political sociology, with a view to elaborating, in dialogue with this work, the basis for a distinctively geographical and social-constructivist approach to the problematic of policy mobility-mutation. The first of these literatures is the wave of diffusion studies, beginning in the 1960s, which focused attention on the spatial sequencing of policy choices, deploying a rational-actor approach that would later evolve into more elaborate models of policy learning. This is followed by an examination of more structurally oriented theories of transition, in which ruptural or crisis-driven processes of policy transformation are privileged over the incrementalism of the diffusion studies. Finally, the emergence of a more recent, neodiffusionist approach is considered, in which various forms of induced and coerced policy mobility are evaluated against choice-based models. Across this critical commentary, particular emphasis is placed on the ideological, ideational, and institutional *environments* within which policy-mobility processes operate—a passive backdrop in the original diffusion paradigm, but which is more often understood to be *co-constitutive* of policy

|                              | *Policy transfer*                                              | *Policy mobilities*                                                                                                                  |
| ---------------------------- | ------------------------------------------------------------- | ----------------------------------------------------------------------------------------------------------------------------------- |
| Origins                      | Disciplinary: political science                               | Transdisciplinary: anthropology, geography, heterodox political science, comparative political economy, sociology, urban planning    |
| Privileged analytical object | "Successful" transfers: conspicuous jurisdictional border-crossing | Policies in motion/interconnection: continuous transformation and mutation                                                     |
| Social action                | Instrumental: bounded rationality                             | Strategic: embedded calculation                                                                                                     |
| Dynamic                      | Frustrated replication of best (or better) practices          | Contradictory reproduction of connected but unevenly developing policy regimes                                                      |
| Spatiality                   | Sequential diffusion                                          | Relational connection                                                                                                               |
| Epistemology                 | Positivist/rationalist                                        | Postpositivist/constructivist                                                                                                       |
| Explanation                  | Reification of essentialized design features                  | Contextually sensitive analysis of emergent capacities                                                                             |
| Approach                     | Abstracts from politics of knowledge and practice             | Problematizes politics of knowledge and practice                                                                                   |

Figure 1. Policy transfer versus policy mobilities.

transfer and transformation in more recent social-constructivist work. The account also draws attention to the (often implicit) methodological *scaling* of the three approaches in question: the original diffusion studies were classically modeled on "horizontal" transfers within federal systems like the United States; theories of transition have been typically concerned with national-level adjustments in the face of international pressures and incentives; and the neodiffusionist approach grapples with the transnational reconstitution of (fast) policy networks and regimes, as near-continuous processes of policy change begin to operate across more porous and open systems.

These arguments anticipate two broad conclusions, relating to the spatiality of contemporary policy development processes, which in turn underpin the approach that we are operationalizing in this book. First, context matters deeply, in the sense that policy regimes and landscapes are more than empty spaces within and between which borrowing and learning take place; they comprise socioinstitutional landscapes that are dynamically remade through the traffic in policy norms and practices, the flows of which reflect (and remake) particular policy regimes, rather than simply being isolated vectors of post hoc transformation. There are, in fact, no clear lines between policy innovations *in motion* and the fixity of policy regimes *awaiting reform*, but these are two sides of the same dialectical process. Second, beyond the transfer ontology, in which policies diffuse unidirectionally from the capitals of innovation to hinterlands of emulation, it will be suggested that policy mobility represents one of many ways in which policy regimes have become *relationally* interconnected. Laggards are no longer simply following leaders, but rather, policy development processes are operating across a multipolar universe within which *relative* positions become more and more mutually referential and interdependent—as new generations of fast-policy "models" and "best practices" are being forged *across* transnational expert networks and communities of practice, and *between* co-evolving governance regimes.

## From Diffusion to Learning

Orthodox conceptions of policy transfer typically invoke a rational universe in which decision-makers more or less freely choose between policy models-cum-options, albeit with varying degrees of knowledge and uncertainty. There is a long tradition of exploring patterns of policy diffusion and motives for policy adoption in the political science literature. The most influential strands of this work draw on historical data from the U.S. states, modeling adoptive behavior in a fashion consistent with the precepts of neoclassical economics and orthodox communications theory.[10] These diffusion studies developed explanations of the spread of phenomena like Progressive Era policy innovations, from their heartlands in the Midwest of the United States to sometimes even contiguous "catching up" states. So was born the enduring notion of the policymaker as an optimizing, rational actor, scanning the "market" for potential policy products, along with the modernist conception of effective or superior policies diffusing (first, furthest, and fastest) across jurisdictional spaces.

In the market for policy innovations, apparently, there are producers and there are consumers. And the U.S. model of "competitive federalism," it has been argued, established the basis for a kind of natural experiment in the functioning of policy markets. The Founding Fathers had placed their faith in competition between the states to restrain the growth of government, over and above the "parchment barriers" of constitutional restrictions, on the understanding that this would exert downward pressure on taxes while promoting efficiency. In the resulting marketplace for public services, it is "[c]ompetition among governments [that] promotes policy innovation."[11] In his classic study of "horizontal" policy diffusion between the states, Jack Walker remarked that the "process of competition and emulation, or cuetaking, is an important phenomenon which determines in large part the pace and direction of social and political change in the American states."[12]

Drawing on advances in communication, decision, and diffusion theory,[13] Walker sought to develop a choice-based model of the policy diffusion process. His account, in essence, was one of technocratic modernization and increasing efficiency: policy innovation was being driven by the most sophisticated buyers—larger, resource-rich states, endowed with the most advanced organizational capacities (such as New York, Massachusetts, and California)—the downstream benefits of which would eventually trickle toward the laggard states (like Mississippi, Nevada, and Wyoming). Moreover, the *rate* of innovation was shown to be accelerating markedly over time, as the gap between innovator-pioneers and emulator-adopters was consistently reduced between the 1870s and the 1960s, as the early tendency of states to follow their geographical neighbors progressively gave way to a more nationally integrated system with its "specialized set of communication channels through which flow new ideas, information and policy cues."[14] Viewed from a "system" perspective, rather than from the vantage point of subnational policy actors, this can be seen as an early manifestation of an "infrastructural" policymaking network.

The policy diffusion studies affirmed one of the stylized facts of innovation theory—the presence of an S-shaped curve in cumulative rates of adoption, in which a small cluster of policy pioneers is subsequently joined by a larger group of mainstream adopters, after which there is a leveling off around a higher-stage norm.[15] In the U.S. case, the reformist state governments of the Progressive Era—such as Illinois, Michigan, Minnesota, New York, Ohio, and Wisconsin—constituted a dynamic regional cluster of legislative and policy innovators, effectively coproducing rounds of policy reform in fields like railroad and health regulation, and minimum wage and workers' compensation laws, which rippled out to the other states.[16] Shared political values, needless to say, enabled and lubricated these early rounds of adoption,[17] just as, at the international scale a century later, they would facilitate the early diffusion of neoliberal policy measures like privatization and financial liberalization,[18] the beginning of another S-shaped curve in cross-jurisdictional policy innovation.

The politics of this process, however, did not much detain the first generation of diffusion analysts, who were less concerned with "the circumstances under which new ideas or programs [were] conceived or developed" than with the strength of the connections between state policymaking systems, pertinent communication channels, and the geographical distribution of "competent staff, superior clerical facilities, and supporting services."[19] In explanatory terms, the decision rules of state policymakers were seen to hold the key to explaining the rate and distribution of policy diffusion, above and beyond issues of ideology or power. And policy "innovations" themselves were little more than inert data units, explicitly named in statutes, and traveling across a landscape marked only by formal jurisdictional boundaries.

The first wave of diffusion studies seems to have succumbed to its own S-shaped innovation trajectory, petering out during the 1980s. This was also the decade, perhaps not coincidentally, in which the apparently optimizing and modernizing trends toward "good governance," transmitted downward (or perhaps "backward") from the most administratively efficient organizations by way of nationally integrated communication channels, were seriously disrupted. In fact, some of the old regional patterns in policy diffusion reasserted themselves, almost in reverse, as many of the pioneers of the Progressive Era were abruptly redesignated as "rustbelt" states. Here, the new dynamic was one of competitive emulation born of economic distress, as deindustrializing states rushed to implement new programs for industrial retention and attraction, and as often unseemly and sometimes apparently unthinking races to the deregulated bottom were joined.[20] The logic of diffusion now seemed to have less to do with noble notions of optimal decision-making or the "emulation of virtue"; it was more about the prosaically impelled "spread of necessity."[21] Competitive pressures and economic insecurities seemed to be inducing the adoption of a narrow repertoire of local economic development policies, the very prevalence of which eroded what marginal effectiveness they might have had, in the zero-sum scramble for jobs and investment.[22]

Maybe the figure of the policymaker under duress was an incongruous one for rational-choice analysts. Soon, attention was shifting toward a new form of deliberative policy development, based on a conception of the policymaker as a learning agent, working within the constraints of *bounded* rationality. A new generation of policy learning studies would subsequently be developed. "A policymaker is not a theorist," Richard Rose flatly insisted, "but a social engineer seeking knowledge instrumentally," while the process of lesson drawing is ultimately about "whether programmes can transfer from one place to another; it is not about what politicians think ought to be done."[23] Motivated to solve a policy problem (or at least to minimize electoral dissatisfaction), this idealized policy actor finds herself in a state of ignorance at $t = 0$. Her subsequent, purposeful steps include scanning the program evaluation evidence from jurisdictions that have addressed similar problems, followed by the construction of conceptual models of programs in order, essentially, to isolate those design features that make them "effective" from those contextual or "idiographic details of foreign practice [that] can distract attention from essentials, and confuse what is generic and potentially transferable with what is specific to time and place."[24] Within this approach, differentiated search costs and capacity constraints induce policymakers to pursue lines of least resistance in their search behavior, and in making adoption decisions they are satisficers, doing what is necessary to minimize local dissatisfaction rather than searching endlessly for "ideal" policy solutions.[25]

Lesson drawing, for Rose, has become a normalized and routinized aspect of contemporary policy development, whose rather more jaded, instrumentalist policy actors engage in trial-and-error muddling through, finding "short cuts" and acceptable compromises where they can.[26] Here, policy learning is a continuous, gradualist process, in contrast to the kind of tectonic shift implied by the notion of a transition between policy paradigms.[27] Such quick-fix policy lessons are not even, in this sense, "innovations," since they represent selective, piecemeal borrowings from other jurisdictions. The concern, instead, is with policymaking *behavior*, conceived mostly in instrumentalist and voluntaristic terms, in which the lesson represents "an action-oriented conclusion about a programme or programmes in operation elsewhere."[28] As such, the policy learning approach can be distinguished from earlier diffusion studies, which were more concerned with the sequential dynamics of the diffusion process itself, "presuppos[ing] a kind of technocratic determinism."[29]

The diffusion studies, Wolman pointed out, had merely inferred—essentially from patterns in policy adoption data—how and why particular policies were traveling, with the result that "we know almost nothing about the *process* by which such policy transfer occurs."[30] His worldly and revealing tale of the transfer of urban-policy practices and philosophies between the Reagan administration and the Thatcher government—which had been animated by the British riots of 1981, but which also reflected an ideological preference for devolved, business-led strategies—was hardly consistent with the notion of rational, systematic information gathering and cold-eyed evaluation:

> Visiting ministers, civil servants and fact-finding groups see what they are shown. They are, perhaps inevitably, exposed much more to the views of advocates—those who administer programs or receive benefits from them—than the views of critics or neutral observers. They tend to be shown "showcase" examples rather than average situations. . . . They will rely more on verbal information than on written material and rarely on analytical written material.[31]

In this case, itineraries organized by consultants, in which visiting British delegations were handed off between political appointees in federal offices, operatives in conservative think tanks like the Heritage Foundation, and guided tours of carefully selected "exemplary projects," seem to have been designed to purposefully *sell* rather than to merely *tell* stories of policy innovation. (And the Thatcherite customers were eager to buy.) Meanwhile, it was conceded to be "extremely unlikely . . . that dissident voices or critiques" would even be encountered, on such tours of best-practice sites/sights.[32] If there was "lesson drawing" at work here, it was occurring within ideologically prescribed parameters, if not blinders, while the emphasis on favored programs effectively served as a form of advocacy by proxy. In such contexts, "models" were used knowingly, as "political weapons," while the stylized rendering of technical novelties and far-off success stories effectively served as a ruse for wrong-footing or neutralizing political opponents.[33] In this sense, the search for a new policy "solution" is not only a rigged "lesson," but represents a moment in a politically insulated and practically self-fulfilling decision-making cycle: the political proclivities of the supposed "learners" are conveniently affirmed in a selective search process, while the consideration of potential alternatives is effectively precluded, especially if these are somehow countercultural or the products of competing political parties. This is hardly a process of open-minded "learning," but one of incrementally extending policy practice within ideologically determined parameters, and therefore within ideologically circumscribed fields of vision and practice.

In contrast to the bits-and-pieces, instrumentalist, and incrementalist conception of policy learning presented by Rose, Wolman maintained that there was more interest among policymakers in "concepts and approaches, rather than specific policy designs."[34] Indeed, in contrast to the situation in which objectified policy "problems" somehow called forth appropriate "solutions," politicized *opportunities* for intervention seem to have been actively sought. It was to become increasingly clear that periodic crises and strategically selected targets presented the *means to enact* preferred strategies—like privatization, public-private partnerships, the mobilization of "little platoons," or deregulation.[35] Policy "learning," such that it was in evidence, was being normatively prefiltered. As Robertson argued, "Lessons from other polities are more likely to be used to attack the status quo with evidence that feasible and potentially superior alternatives exist elsewhere."[36] His deft analysis of conservative and liberal labor-market policies (respectively, right-to-work legislation, "man in the house" welfare regulations, and workfare demonstration projects as archetypal conservative policies; plant-closure pre-notification legislation, state-enacted minimum wages, and extended welfare provisions as typical liberal policies), demonstrated that learning and diffusion are politically channeled, rather than "open" processes. In other words, policy transfers tend to be "ideologically exclusive," while "[f]ar from being a mere technical exercise, lesson-drawing is intensely political."[37]

Wolman's case study of urban policy transfer, in what would later be understood as the early stages of transatlantic neoliberalization, reluctantly embraced a similar conclusion, though here the ghost of the rational actor was never fully exorcized.[38] He concluded (rather disapprovingly) that the information gathering process is "unsystematic and highly anecdotal," noting that the "level of analysis [was] not highly sophisticated," being dedicated less to revelatory, incremental learning than to effecting "major, discontinuous change," which in some cases represented the very "rationale for looking at other countries' policies."[39] The policy transfer and learning process, one might more forthrightly conclude, was constitutively politicized.

This is a conclusion that Dolowitz and Marsh were more willing to confront in their influential review of the policy transfer literature.[40] Questioning the idealized portrayal of policymakers as rational, calculating subjects engaged in "voluntaristic" forms of policy learning, Dolowitz and Marsh enlarged the frame of reference to include "coerced" transfers executed in the context of asymmetrical power relations. Their attendant conception of the policymaking process takes account of ideological predispositions, strategic orientations, and the "messy" realities of what Kingdon once called the "policy primordial soup,"[41] yielding the following often-quoted definition of policy transfer as

> a process in which knowledge about policies, administrative arrangements, institutions etc. in one time and/or place is used in the development of policies, administrative arrangements and institutions in another time and/or place.[42]

Dolowitz and Marsh were concerned to stretch the concept of policy transfer (which they contrasted with intentional "learning") beyond its pluralist origins, subsequently elaborating their classificatory framework to encompass a broader array of non-state actors (such as consultants, advocacy networks, think tanks, and NGOs), while confronting the ways in which "policy entrepreneurs 'sell' policies around the world."[43] They continued, however, to position notions of coercive or "push" transfer (involving direct imposition) in an axial relationship with a still-idealized conception of the rational policy actor, freely choosing between well-documented alternatives, with the boundedly rational, learning actor located somewhere in between. In effect, this locates "cases" of policy transfer, which themselves become distinct analytical units, on a choice-coercion continuum. Through the addition of a second dimension, running from immunity to transfer through to isomorphic convergence, these cases can then be located within a two-dimensional policy space.[44] In the political science literature, such analytical routines have enabled the continued elaboration of taxonomic frameworks, the aim of which is, apparently, to exhaustively classify the full range of empirically observed policy transfers. The explanatory potential of these approaches, however, remains limited.[45] They are, for the most part, post hoc classifications of different forms of conspicuous policy mobility.

The orthodox literatures on policy transfer, diffusion, and learning have been constrained by varying degrees of adherence to optimizing "logics of choice," in which "imitation, copying and adaptation are [understood to be] the consequences of rational decisions by policy-makers."[46] The attendant conception of the policymaking process tends to be highly mechanistic and focused on the formal attributes (or underlying rationalities) of policies and programs.[47] Meanwhile, the analytical gaze is fixed, in effect, on policies in transit, willed into motion by searching and learning subjects. What is more, these searching and learning practices tend to be evaluated in terms of universalistic models of rational or satisficing behavior, abstracted from their respective social and institutional contexts. Policy transfers, the objects of analysis, are likewise typically visualized in disembedded and asocial terms, floating in abstract analytical spaces, or boxed inside descriptive taxonomies.

For all the empirical evidence that various forms of policy transfer, particularly in the transnational domain, are on the increase, it remains the case that in this tradition there has been "little conceptual work on the process."[48] Moreover, the self-limiting character of this work is reflected in the statement from Dolowitz and Marsh that "few scholars look at how the definitions of problems or solutions are socially constructed."[49] Notwithstanding the achievements of the political-science literature in opening up the field of policy-transfer studies, these questions of social construction call for a different point of departure from the idealized universe of rational-actor models, in which atomized agents operate in the bright sunlight of information-rich policy markets. Rather than examining these issues of social and institutional construction in purely abstract terms, we take some cues here from innovative work on policymaking under conditions of political stress, in this case in the Central and Eastern European "transition" economies. We do this not only in order to start from somewhere, rather than nowhere, but also to denaturalize the "environment" of the policy-transfer and mutation process. Starting in a different place, more heavily shrouded in the shadows of uncertainty, need not (and indeed *should* not) imply the replacement of one normalized "policy environment" with another. Rather, in the following section, it serves, first, as a disruptive jolt to the smoothly functioning conceptions of diffusion learning models under supposedly business-as-usual conditions, and second, as a way to call attention to the constitutive role of "context." This is more, as it so happens, than mere background scenery to the policy actors' performance.

## Between Crisis-Driven Reform and Variegated Policy Mobility

If the fifty U.S. states provided the testbed, maybe even an inadvertently naturalized setting, for orthodox theories of policy diffusion, learning, and transfer, where might one begin to look for different, maybe more radical and disruptive accounts? Beginning with a different (conjunctural) context can be a device to call attention to some of the historical and geographical specificities of ostensibly universal processes of rational transfer and learning. Why not Central and Eastern Europe, the dramatic "market transition" of which, more than two decades ago, did much to spur recent interest in the protagonists and practices, causes and consequences of "policy transfer"? As a place to start, this does not immediately invoke, of course, the idea of the rational monitoring of policy options and unhurried processes of learning, or indeed incremental and orderly notions of policy adjustment by way of targeted transfer, freely chosen from a universal menu. Instead, this was an externally mediated "transition," realized under pressure. But the point is not to position this "abnormal" geographical case against a normalized portrayal of rational, crisis-free learning. Rather, it is to underline the claim that policy transfer is an inherently political, in fact *geo*political, process, one that is impossible to abstract from sociospatial and historical context.

This claim hardly needs laboring in the case of the postcommunist "transition," but for this very reason the example is heuristically valuable. Central and Eastern Europe is a location in which a wholesale and historic process of institutional reconstruction occurred, as it were, under duress. Awash with imported "solutions," never perfectly replicated, it is a region in which hybrid and "recombined" policy forms have been produced with almost tectonic intensity. These crisis-driven processes of "market-friendly" policy transfer/transformation have been occurring in the shadow of a range of powerful interests and agencies—some domestic, some external; some public, some private; some invited, some imposed. In the sense that the U.S. states famously constituted a kind of "laboratory" for policy experimentation, ostensibly reflecting an underlying rationality of competitive federalism,[50] the postcommunist countries of Central and Eastern Europe found themselves in a "learning environment" marked by almost critical urgency, if not outright vulnerability. Some lessons from abroad would have to be learned the hard way, and very quickly. This was not orderly learning but "shock treatment."

The postcommunist countries were each confronted with a unique set of conjunctural challenges, prompted by systemic failures across the ideological and institutional realms, to which they responded in ways that reflected both their historically accreted capacities and their shifting positions within transnational policy networks. Their daunting task, which was likened to "rebuilding the ship at sea," entailed a series of transformations in policy rationales, instruments, and rules. As such, they not only provide a stark counterpoint to portrayals of policy transfer and diffusion processes in supposedly "normal" times and places, they also throw into sharp relief the question of the normative and practical *geographical* origins of mobile policy fixes. Do these diffuse, intact, from hegemonic capitals to global peripheries, or are new dialogic *connections* being forged in these circumstances of often asymmetrical power relations?

Reflecting on the Central and Eastern European experience, Claus Offe later argued that a hyperrational "logic of consequentiality" was at work in which expert-advocates claimed unimpeachable legitimacy for policies that had allegedly "worked elsewhere," effectively transplanting these *onto* other jurisdictions "irrespective of whether they meet with ideas, traditions, and mentalities that prevail in these societies."[51] Privatization was duly installed as a programmatic logic. Performative deference to these ideologically singular external "models" of market-based reform would prove to be compatible with the political interests of reformers in many of these situations, even if the practices in which they were engaged bore little resemblance to rational emulation. By purposefully misconstruing the process of policymaking, as an imagined process of total supersession, social dislocations were reframed in terms of costs of "adjustment"—a temporary period of pain in anticipation of a longer-term gain. And since the imported systems came complete with supposedly guaranteed results, any failures of performance must have been due to mistakes made during their local (re)assembly.

What was practically "inevitable" here, of course, was not the guarantee of sure-fire results from the imported policies—often hyped by consultants and advisors, and enforced through loan conditionalities—but their prosaic *failure* to meet these very expectations. Yet ironically, the serial inability of "imposed" policies to deliver the expected results typically led to even more hectic, if not drastic, rounds of institutional re-engineering.[52] Policy failure would often be excused by domestic political conditions (necessarily bold reforms had been diluted by political concessions) or by implementation problems (since the policies "work" elsewhere, local delivery systems must be at fault). Paradoxically, such forms of policy failure would often result in redoubled reform efforts. Policies were spreading, in this sense, by failing, as the underperformance of first-round reform efforts became the rationale for more stringent measures.[53] If the first rounds of shock treatment did not work, the dosage had to be increased.

What is at stake here is not the "efficiency" of the policy transfer process, the efficacy of different forms of learning, or even the size of the "replication gap" between the original model and its flawed copy. Rather, experiences like these open up a series of deeper questions concerning the politics of institutional transformation in radically relativized contexts, both in place and between places. Under conditions of radical uncertainty, if not crisis, appeals to "lessons from abroad" and the accompanying performative deference to "learning from successful models" effectively relieves (or displaces) some of the burden of responsibility from the local architects of reform, helping, in Offe's words, "to create a deceptive clarity about some evidently and easily superior solution, to mobilize support, and to disguise the creative alterations that the supposed 'imitation' is likely to involve."[54] Declarative expressions of lesson learning therefore comprise a recurrent theme in what might be described as the vernacular theorization of policy transfer. "It is a common theoretical gambit to claim that the elements proposed for diffusion are actually found somewhere," Strang and Meyer have observed, the buried rationale being that the operative process is not so much "faithful copying as theoretically mediated diffusion or disguised diffusion."[55]

Even if the notion of perfect institutional replication is a fantasy, the fiction of imitation can, in such circumstances, be a productive one. The pressurized implementation of shock-treatment measures in the postcommunist countries was not simply a matter of imposing imported designs, it was also about the preemptive capture of policy design as a *political* process. As Offe put it:

It is as if the man-made and hence contingent nature of institutional change must be denied and artificially "forgotten." Otherwise, the example of the designer will invite others to attempt a different design. . . . [If] newly designed institutions can be depicted as being not so new after all, but rooted in some respectable past . . . trust in their capacity for performing the functions that they are supposed to perform can be strengthened by the pretense that they are just replicas of demonstrably successful models imported from elsewhere. . . . [R]eflexive discourses about the origin of institutions seem to avoid the notion of intentional creation. Instead, they rely on subjectless categories. . . . [In this way,] institutions just "evolve," "develop," "emerge," are "discovered," or "spread" . . . all of which is to obscure their origin in intentional action.[56]

Here, a transition between policy paradigms was being effectively "automated," in a postpolitical fashion; there was one destination—the market economy—and the journey would (have to) be an irreversible one.

Above all, perhaps, the postcommunist experience clearly calls attention to the institutional and political *contexts* within which such allegedly universal processes operate. "Proven models," in such cases, are ideologically situated constructs, and they come from *somewhere*. More than this, the postcommunist transitions highlight the ways in which certain modes and manifestations of policy transfer might be seen, in a more than trivial sense, as "creatures" of context. Patterns and processes of policy transfer and diffusion are not only institutionally *mediated*,[57] but institutionally *embedded*. They are embedded in, while at the same time being mechanisms of, historically and geographically specific experiences of (state) restructuring. And the postcommunist case, rather than an aberrant exception, can be seen as a specific manifestation of an incipient transnationalization of the policymaking process, accompanied by the hard and soft selling of "global solutions."[58] This has not, it is important to emphasize, been a prelude to homogenization, notwithstanding the fact that widespread processes of neoliberalization can be seen to be at work "across cases."[59] In other words, policy mobility and mutation would appear to be simultaneous processes. Policies may be crossing borders ever more "freely," but this does not beckon a flat earth of standardized outcomes or some socioinstitutional monoculture.

The crisis of the postcommunist states was also, historically speaking, a paradigm-breaching moment. As such, it can be seen as a preeminent example of what Peter Hall has called, in a different historical and geographical context, "third-order" policy change. This entails a wholesale movement from one paradigm to another, along with simultaneous adjustments of a second- and first-order nature, in Hall's terms, including changes in key policy instruments, their settings, and the hierarchy of goals that underpin them.[60] Third-order paradigm shifts, in this sense, involve a phase-shift in the *Gestalt* of the policy process, as one framework of policy ideas, standards, procedures, and practices is (unevenly) displaced by another. In the course of such a structural shift, the very ontology of the policymakers' world undergoes a fundamental reconstruction. As Bockman and Eyal have persuasively argued with respect to the Eastern European case, the power of policy discourse in such contexts is to make, and then reproduce, alternative regimes of truth, the tenacious influence of which stems not from the fact that "they are taken for granted, not because actors do not think about them, but because they think *with* them."[61]

Hall also emphasizes how discursive formations that work to stabilize "framework[s] of ideas and standards that [specify] not only the goals of policy but also the very nature of the problems they are meant to be addressing."[62] Policy paradigms, like Keynesianism or neoliberalism for example, comprise their own social ontologies, their own hierarchies of goals and preferred instruments, constituting what Mark Blyth has called a "prism" through which policymakers read, interpret, and act on the world.[63] It follows that phase-shifts, from one paradigm to another, involve much more than the adoption of new policy measures and mechanisms, or even completely transformed material conditions. The "policy world" is undergoing dramatic environmental change, to be sure, but the means through which this world is understood and acted on are also changing. As Peter Hall explains,

> [T]he process whereby one policy paradigm comes to replace another is likely to be more sociological than scientific. . . . The movement from one paradigm to another will ultimately entail a set of judgments that is more political in tone, and the outcome will depend, not only on the arguments of competing factions, but on their positional advantages within a broader institutional framework, on the ancillary resources they can command in the relevant conflicts, and on exogenous factors affecting the power of one set of actors to impose its paradigm over others. . . . [The] movement from one paradigm to another is likely to be preceded by significant shifts in the locus of authority over policy. [It will likely also] involve the accumulation of anomalies, experimentation with new forms of policy, and policy failures that precipitate a shift in the locus of authority over policy and initiate a wider contest between competing paradigms.[64]

The meticulously documented case that Hall uses to explicate these arguments is the turbulent transition from Keynesianism to monetarism in British macroeconomic policy—the petri dish, incidentally, out of which some of the earliest privatization initiatives would grow. This was not simply an instance of externally induced "structural adjustment," though powerful external players like the IMF were involved; nor was it a case of first- and second-order policy change culminating in third-order change, as if through escalation. In the final analysis, it was a disjunctive process, as much *realized through* as animated by crisis, and a very particular crisis at that. Here, the shift between policy paradigms was a jarringly orthogonal one, rather than a process of smooth succession, involving the effective *overlayering* of one political-economic ontology on top of another, one ideational order on top of another, and one set of policy diagnoses and policy logics on top of another. The layer beneath was never obliterated, but new reform ontologies and new rounds of policy formation were antagonistically oriented to their predecessors, and both sought and (partly) achieved a root-and-branch reconstruction of the prevailing policy rationality.

And, as it turned out, certain policy instruments that had been developed in one conjunctural crisis—like the privatization of state-owned enterprises in the UK—could be refashioned later, for a quite different context, such as the postsocialist transition in Eastern Europe. The "family" of neoliberal reform measures consequently comprises a range of decontextualized and recontextualized instruments, which are always associated with local ratio-nalizations and effects, but which also acquire some of their salience and legitimacy from their (near and far) "relatives." This calls attention to some of the ways in which contemporary policymaking has become a polycentric and relational process—rendering increasingly anachronistic the notion of strictly endogenous, "domestic" policymaking—since nominally "external" influences have become, in effect, constitutive. And, in turn, each new addi-tion to an evolving family of mutually referential policies changes the fam-ily itself, sometimes incrementally, sometimes more fundamentally. Highly mobile policies, in particular, are in a sense not only creatures of their fields of reference and influence, they meld into these fields, co-evolving in an iter-ative fashion.

## Rethinking "Diffusion"

What is notable about the previous examples of rapid policy change in the context of paradigm shifts and/or conjunctural crises, in Eastern Europe and in the UK on the cusp of neoliberalization, is that the process of policy change itself is socially, geographically and historically embedded; it is not abstracted, idealized, or decontextualized. Policy instruments and routines are being (re)used across different contexts, but as this happens the meaning and consequences of these policies also change. So we have adaptation and mutation, but also interconnection and mutual referencing. The "insides" of policymaking worlds therefore become inseparable from their "outsides," yet the outcomes are more likely to take the form of tangled, relational complexity than simple convergence toward a dominant form.[65] Building on these insights, Garrett, Dobbin, and Simmons have revisited the question of policy diffusion and transfer from a social-constructivist perspective, one that is sensitive to historically distinctive forms of ideological mediation and institutional interdependence.[66] In a fashion that is in many ways complementary to the approach we develop here, they seek to transcend the conventional tropes of (unilinear) global convergence, one-way transition models, and (static) path dependency by way of a neodiffusionist emphasis on mutually dependent transformation. Theirs is a critique *both* of the "underlying meta-model of political and policy change [in the form] of unconnected domestic processes," *and* of the exaggerated reaction to this orthodoxy in contemporary concepts of exogenously driven global convergence.

Framed against the null hypothesis that policy-formation processes remain essentially endogenous to nation-states, Garrett and his colleagues set out to test the efficacy of four causal mechanisms of international policy diffusion—emulation, learning, competition, and coercion. The first of these mechanisms, emulation, is in many respects the most familiar. With roots in the orthodox diffusion literature, emulation refers to the voluntary adoption of new policies in contexts of less-than-perfect knowledge, albeit through channels, and across terrains, that are socially constructed. This elaborated approach is a more sociological one insofar as "understanding how public policies become socially accepted is the key to understanding why they diffuse."[67] Minimally, this calls for an intersubjective understanding of the means and ends of policy, implying that the very bases on which policy transfers occur are socially constructed. And policymakers, from this perspective, typically inhabit murky and confusing worlds, such that even "the most rational of decision makers can rarely find incontrovertible evidence of the effectiveness of a prospective policy," with the result that "theory and rhetoric" inevitably play a major role in search and emulation processes.[68] Forms of emulation include "follow the leader" models, where wannabe policymakers copy the strategies of powerful or successful actors/institutions, which become viewed as a kind of standard practice for improved performance;[69] "expert theorization," where epistemic communities coalesce around favored policy solutions that are subsequently "sold" through various channels;[70] and learning from peers, where emulators borrow from those countries with whom they share political or cultural affinities, or what Rose called, reflecting the methodologically individualist bent of this approach, "psychological proximity."[71] Much of the work in this vein operates at a high level of abstraction, however, tracing the broadest outlines of diffusion-via-emulation within social constructivist frameworks like the Weberian notion of a "world polity."[72] More promising are those approaches that trace the cultures and practices of epistemic communities, such as free-market economists and neoliberal technocrats, demonstrating their formative roles in both articulating policy (often literally) and in codifying and circulating knowledge concerning its enactment.[73]

Learning models of policy diffusion are predicated on the understanding that intelligence concerning "success or failure of policy change in other countries is expected to influence the probability of policy change in the country under analysis."[74] In orthodox treatments, the learning process is effectively individualized, as information on policies is continuously accumulated and updated in a Bayesian fashion, with subsequent adoptions representing a form of optimization. But learning is itself "social," and will often tend to be quite narrowly circumscribed or "channeled."[75] And if learning is more prevalent among ideological peers, then it can be difficult to isolate deliberative learning from other forms of emulation and transfer. While learning models presuppose that "successful" policies are more likely to be replicated, and that "failures" may likewise serve as potent warning signs, the near impossibility of rationally determining "success" or "failure" outside the framework of particular policy paradigms and belief systems means that learning behavior is, more often than not, in the eye of the beholder. Merely observing that some countries follow the lead of others is not the same as demonstrating the presence of deliberative learning, while formal deference to evidence-based policy likewise does not account for the ways in which evidence-based systems are themselves often embedded in ideological or theoretical regimes.[76] Learning is therefore a (situated) social construct.

Competition models, in contrast, explain the diffusion of (characteristically neoliberal) modes of governance in terms of their complementarity with unevenly distributed competitive pressures: "Governments have strong incentives to choose 'market-friendly' policies that make their jurisdiction an attractive place for global investment, and to remain competitive in product markets by minimizing costs."[77] Here, the policy choices of competitors, where they are understood to be conducive to private investment, incentivize diffusion among those jurisdictions most closely linked through market relations, manifestations of which include smokestack chasing or courting talent workers, and races to the bottom in environmental regulation or welfare provision, at the interurban and international scales. David Harvey's influential analysis of urban entrepreneurialism echoes some of these themes,[78] as do those accounts that emphasize the role of accelerating capital mobility as a "primordial threat" to local jurisdictions, or as an inducement to preemptively lower taxes.[79] Here, the diffusion process tends to be manifest in "horizontal" styles of competitively induced contagion, mostly explicitly among jurisdictions competing for scarce-but-mobile resources, assets, or market advantages. However, the evidence for competitively driven convergence is often circumstantial, and there is a paucity of work that documents specific mechanisms of competitive policy transfer, or which establishes how these phenomena are co-constituted through policy paradigms and ideational fields.

Finally, coercion involves "the (usually conscious) manipulation of incentives by powerful actors to encourage others to implement policy change."[80] Strong actors in this case might be powerful nation-states, multilateral agencies, and possibly even NGOs, who are able to impose their will by inducing subordinate actors to implement policy change, for example, through the threat of military force or political sanction, through conditionalities attached to loans or aid, through forms of political or public (relations) pressure, or through the monopolization of expertise and ideational channels. The diffusion process here tends to be hierarchical, with policy imperatives emanating out (or "down") from powerful centers. Policy coercion may exhibit a concrete institutional, legal or regulatory form (such as IMF loan conditionalities, EU law, WTO sanctions, or NAFTA regulations), or it may take the less tangible form of hegemonic power, adherence to particular policy paradigms, or normative isomorphism. But clean lines of cause and effect are invariably difficult to establish, even where power asymmetries are extreme (for example, if local cadres work to realize sectional interests through the adoption of nominally "coerced" policy shifts, thereby exploiting the perception of external imposition). Characteristic of work in this vein is Gill's analysis of the embedding of "disciplinary" neoliberalism in constitutional conventions and hegemonic institutions at the global scale,[81] and Gilardi's deconstruction of the "vertical diffusion" of regulatory practices within the European Union.[82] Recurrent themes in the policy coercion literature include an emphasis on exogenous influences and actors, together with the productive exploitation of power asymmetries.

Garrett and his colleagues reach the conclusion that, even as international policy diffusion appears to have become an endemic and entrenched phenomenon, there is little evidence that direct forms of coercion have been especially prevalent, and neither, where they are found, have they been effective. Furthermore, voluntaristic modes of policy learning are, in reality, even more rare. On the other hand, various forms of economic competition and social emulation, often acting in concert or combination, seem to be the dominant mechanisms of policy diffusion, many of them operating through power-soaked epistemic networks. The very reach and complexity of these networks apparently outruns the controlling capacity of crudely coercive efforts, but this is more of a commentary on the form than the fact of hegemony. Diffusion processes, in this context, do not necessarily reproduce more "efficient" forms of governance, neither are they spontaneously animated by the rational decisions of well-informed policymakers. Indeed, Garrett and colleagues reckon that the plethora of new policy networks and circuits is more likely to spawn "'unreasoned' mimicry" than deliberative learning,[83] enlarging the repertoire of isomorphic practices identified in the influential work of DiMaggio and Powell. Institutional isomorphism, according to this position, denotes not simple convergence, but a tendency for *conformity* between a community or group of organizations on the one hand, and the environment, or "field" in which they are located, on the other.[84]

DiMaggio and Powell identified three principal forms of isomorphism: coercive isomorphism, which may take the form of persuasion or collusion, as well as force; mimetic isomorphism, driven by uncertainty, in which institutions "model" themselves on influential peers, either through deliberate emulation or through less discriminate styles of policy borrowing from conspicuous sites and sources; and normative isomorphism, through proliferating professional networks, with their distinctive forms of socialization, organizational vocabularies, and codes of conduct, the most powerful of which channel through various kinds of "central organizations."[85] While DiMaggio and Powell initially illustrated their claims concerning normative isomorphism with reference to professional and managerial organizations, subsequent attention has focused on the role of expert and technocratic networks, many of which have been instrumental in the propagation of neoliberal reason, practice, and rule.[86] Kogut and Macpherson, for example, demonstrated that the presence of Chicago-trained economists exerted a quantifiably measurable influence on governments' subsequent decisions to privatize, the blunt instrument of coercion having been rendered largely moot by *preceding* involvement in the "shared construction of an ontology of knowledge."[87] These processes of shared construction, however, were not handed down on tablets of stone, or rendered *in toto* in Chicago School workshops, but were produced in *and between* networked institutional sites. Although, in this case, "the transmission of ideas [may have occurred] through a global network of experts" with Chicago affiliations, this was not an unmoored or floating network, but one "whose efficacy [was] dependent upon local political conditions and the control over the exercise of state power."[88]

And while nodal centers of one kind or another tend to play key roles in managing such networks, deepening relations of interdependence seem to have been associated with a trend away from simple monocentricity. Even under conditions of marked power asymmetries, policy networks are inescapably relational constructs. And the policy "objects" that pass through these networks are not only transformed on the journey, they are also transform*ing of* both the network and its nodes. Contra the original diffusionist paradigm, in which policy innovations travel unidirectionally across an essentially inert landscape, mobile policies also reorganize the institutional geographies and regulatory relations—what DiMaggio and Powell call the "structured field"—in which they are embedded. As Bockman and Eyal explain, "Institutional models are not simply passed along, copied and imitated via transnational networks [, they] are put together and reproduced through them."[89] This underlines the need to probe the institutional, sociological, and economic factors that "structure" such fields, the flexible architectures of the networks that provide their (inter)connective tissue, and the variably "mobile" policy designs and techniques that both reflect and reconstitute them.

The policy process that DiMaggio and Powell describe as *modeling* involves more than one architect, more than one site of invention—it involves an extensive web of intermediaries, audiences, resistance movements, advocates, interlocutors, spaces of translation and mediation, and, not least, sites of repeated recalibration and reinvention. The project of privatization, for example, was in one sense clearly a "traveling technology" of government, but at the same time was also a polycentric and polyvalent phenomenon. Even though the pattern of privatization initiatives around the world exhibits the classic S-shaped form,[90] its complex diffusion was initiated, energized, and reproduced by a wide range of actors and institutions, drawing variously on territorial and transnational networks, including the diasporic community of

Chicago School economists, management consultants, ideologically attuned technocrats in countries like Chile and New Zealand, members of the Mont Pelerin Society, vanguardist politicians like Reagan and Thatcher, and think tanks in London, Washington, D.C., and elsewhere. The project evolved simultaneously, not sequentially, across these multiple sites and networks.[91] The production of policy innovations and "models," in the context of late neoliberalization, would therefore be mischaracterized as a diffusionist model, beginning with an immaculate moment of local invention and ending in diffuse forms of emulation and adaption. It more closely resembles a multipolar regime of continuous (re)mobilization, which is animated and reanimated as much by the failures of earlier waves of misintervention and malregulation as it is by "blue-sky" strategic visions.

## Policies in Space

It is circumstances such as these, often encountered in real time, which confront the new generation of critical policy studies. This heterodox body of work is beginning to forge distinctive approaches to the problematics of policy mobility and mutation. In this chapter, we have engaged with three literatures concerned with issues of policy transfer and development in order to develop an orientation and build a theoretical vocabulary for the task ahead. Orthodox approaches to tracking policy diffusion, transfer, and learning tend to assume a rationalist search for solutions—or new cures for existing ailments. Although recent work in this vein has taken account of a wider range of policy actors, from management consultants to think-tank advocates, while embracing more prosaic and worldly understandings of the realpolitik of policy transfer,[92] the residual effects of rational-choice thinking linger in what are often narrowly actor-centric, mechanistic, and decontextualized accounts. For the most part, this tradition begins with formal jurisdictional geographies as its naturalized units of analysis, while conceiving policy transfers as literal shifts of policy packages or rationalities between these preconstituted entities. However, the environments in which policies are variously borrowed, formed, and implemented are not inert backdrops to policymaking, but are both ideologically and sociologically structured; they are shaped by competing projects and marked by contestation. Here, an array of institutionally situated policy actors draws upon a range of positional resources and capacities to mobilize their variously conflicting and complementary projects for institutional transformation, wielding alternate "models" in ways understood to advance strategic interests. In this context, "policy transfer" denotes not so much an interconnected web of behavioral practices, or a zone of rational decision-making, but more an arena of contest and struggle—and a strand of mutual *connection* between policymaking sites. Rather than preformed *and replicable* rational condensates (mobile "solutions"), received models are iteratively remade through their imperfect actualization across multiple sites. They define, in effect, zones of evolutionary policy development, constructed across dispersed communities of practice and expertise, and realized through always-uneven power relations and often in moments of crisis.

What might be called the "objects" of policy transfer—policy ideas, innovations, technologies, and models—do not float freely in some unstructured universe, to be picked over selectively by a designated community of continuously learning policy*makers*. Rather, the field of policy transfer is itself socially and institutionally constructed; it is sharply contoured and striated, in the form of shifting landscapes of conjunctural openings and preferred channels; it is structured by relatively enduring policy paradigms, which establish intersubjective frames of reference and institutionalized centers of authority; and, perhaps above all, it is saturated by political calculations and power relations. These intensely contested and deeply constitutive contexts, which have their own histories and geographies, shape what is seen, what is (seriously) considered, and what *counts,* in terms of policy innovations, preferred models, and best practices. They also frame those narratives of "policy failure" that establish the premises and preconditions for policy experimentation, and which variously animate and constrain the search for new institutional fixes. In such situations, discursive frames and institutional frameworks perform a "preceptorial" function, licensing some cognitive and political behaviors, shaping policymaking imaginaries, and enabling certain patterns of "learning," while disciplining or even excluding others. Yet such phenomena do not simply exist, as it were, behind the backs (or above the heads) of policy actors. Regularized patterns of policy action and moments of innovation are constitutive elements of the institutionalized circulatory systems (with their own expert networks, sedimented styles of practice, structures of authority, and so forth) that tend to stabilize along with different policy paradigms.

If there is a defining feature of social-constructivist approaches to the problematic of policy mobility, in this regard, it lies with the recognition of an analytical necessity to *contextualize* policymaking behaviors, and not to abstract inappropriately from power relations, social practices, institutional rules, or political conjunctures. None of this, of course, lends itself to an easily codified, one-size-fits-all methodology, and indeed one of the hallmarks of this style of critical policy studies is the maintenance of heterodox variety in terms of analytical practices. Exemplary social-constructivist studies can be constructed in a variety of methodological registers,[93] and there will surely be a premium in maintaining constructive conversations across these different approaches. It must be recognized, however, that there is an inherent tension involved in the social-constructivist study of globalizing policy models and technocratic practices, which on the face of it resembles the paradoxical pursuit of socially decontextualizing phenomena through socially contextualized means. The challenge, in many ways, is to render this tension a constructive one, to expose the work involved in the construction and circulation of global models and to reveal the social lives of technocratic systems. This calls for an exploration of the social fields within which policy mobility occurs, indeed which make it possible. Since, in practice, these are hardly zones of friction-free replication, it is clear that there is something to explain.

The mobilization of favored models and preferred practices presupposes, and in fact requires, fields of ongoing "experimentation." And the nonreplicating character of this two-way process—the absence of *actual* laboratory conditions—means that networks of policy development tend to exhibit the distinctly nonlinear qualities of (often erratic) distension, by virtue of their proliferation and dialectical interaction. A particularly apt illustration of this is the mutually dependent *co-evolution* of neoliberal "theories," such as those associated with Chicago School economics, and those spaces of practice and reformulation in Eastern Europe and Latin America that were instrumental in the actualization, construction, and reconstruction of those theories. These were not simply implementation zones for neoliberal practices honed in the hegemon. Rather, there were complex, iterative, and "dialogic" interactions across what became a multilocale, experimental regime. Neoliberal policy knowledge was not unilaterally fabricated in command centers like Washington, D.C., or ideational hubs like Chicago, to be subsequently shipped out to sites of reassembly in more "peripheral" locations; neither did it spontaneously "trickle down" through the metropolitan hierarchy. Rather, it was constructed through *reciprocal interactions* between sites of theoretical production and zones of creative realization, evolving along a decidedly nonlinear and somewhat haphazard path. In a sense, this was a "learning system," though much of the learning in question involved learning from policy failures, learning to exploit opportunistic openings, and learning to remake policy rationalities on the hoof.

The policy transfer process, for all its trappings of "disembedded" policy development, must itself be understood as an institutionally produced and embedded phenomenon, the character, causes, and consequences of which are more likely to be recovered in the realms of conjunctural specificity and network relations than in the idealized universe of rational-actor models. Ultimately, the nascent mobility-mutations approach invoked in Figure 1 is being constructed upon quite different epistemological and ontological foundations from those of the orthodox transfer-diffusion paradigm. Policies are not, after all, merely being *transferred* over space; their form and their effects are *transformed* by these journeys, which also serve continuously to remake relational connections across an intensely variegated and dynamic socioinstitutional landscape. This implies that contemporary phenomena like global policy models and peripatetic best practices, while they may be methodologically and politically eye-catching, should not be fetishized by virtue of their evident mobility per se. Policy mobility is but one moment in a wider, transformative process, involving the ongoing *mutation* of policies and policy regimes in a manner that seems to be more deeply cross-referential and relativized than ever before. As a result, there is a need to problematize not only movement itself—the transferred innovations, the emulated best practices, the mobile policy technologies—but also the restructured institutional and social *relations* that such movements necessarily entail. If transfer ontologies typically imply the unidirectional diffusion of policy innovations, and buyers only connecting with sellers for an impersonal transaction, the kinds of relational ontologies alluded to here should instead call attention to the dialectical reconstruction of policy landscapes, crosscut by a host of mobile policy ideas and projects, and overlaid by a web of intermediary actors and connective circuits. "Mobile" policies, in this sense, dynamically reconstitute the terrains across which they travel, at the same time as being embedded within, if not products of, extralocal regimes and circuits.

# 2

# Reflections

## Pursuing Projects, Following Policies

How might the social-constructivist intuitions explored in the previous chapter inform a methodological strategy? As we have indicated, the methodological repertoire for critical policy studies in this area ideally ought to be an open and reflexive one, though roles must be reserved for those approaches that call attention to, and elucidate, the social content and context of policymaking processes and practices, at every stage from conception to execution. There will be a place for street-level implementation studies, for in-depth interviews with policymakers and takers, for textual and genealogical analysis, for ethnographic investigations of policymaking sites and arenas, and more. We discussed some of these questions of method in the introduction. Here, in the first of three reflections chapters, which are intended to engage with underlying theoretical and methodological themes at the close of each section of the book, we delve further into questions of research design and method, first in terms of the general orientation of the Policies without Borders project, from which the book derives, and next by addressing some issues of case-study formulation and design, and the elaboration of the extended case method that we provisionally style here as a "distended case" approach. We end this reflection with a comment on where this approach came from, and where it might go.

### Methodological Departures

Broadly speaking, our approach has been to build upon the rich tradition of research in geographical political economy, especially where this has involved the concrete, situated analysis of various kinds of "policies in motion," largely in the service of understanding the political economy of regulatory transformation, moving landscapes of institutional change, and social dynamics of policy advocacy and opposition.[1] Some of this work has been concerned with the contemporary dynamics of neoliberalization, or market-oriented state transformation, understood not as a monolithic program of unidirectional change, but as a contradiction-riven and context-embedded mode of restructuring.[2] In various ways, this work represents the backdrop to the explorations of fast policy contained in this book, but we have opted not to frame the analysis explicitly in these terms. In large measure, this is because we wanted to see where fast policy might take us, rather than starting out with a particular theoretical map, or indeed a particular destination.

Our approach in this book, then, has been informed by this previous work, but it also represents something of a departure, in a number of ways. First, we wanted to concentrate on processes of policy formation and reproduction at the scale of particular policy projects and their respective fields of operation, not in isolation but comparatively. This reflected a desire to focus, in a socially grounded way, on the mechanics and practices of (fast) policy development, but we also wanted to create an opportunity to approach mid-level theoretical questions. Thinking across (and extrapolating beyond) individual policy fields seemed to be one way to do this. Such an approach would provide a way of staying "close to policy," to policy actors and their material and discursive practices, at the same time abstracting, to some degree, from some of the particularities and idiosyncrasies of each policy field. So we prioritize exploration and explanation at the level of particular policy fields, understood here as distinctive social worlds, but also try, by the end of the book, to think across these domains.

Second, we wanted to explore policy fields that were neither paradigmatically neoliberal nor especially easy to classify as neoliberalism's "other." CCTs certainly have strong connections to Washington Consensus institutions and interests, and even to strands in Chicago School thinking,[3] but they also represent distinctly "social" interventions with welfarist undercurrents, which in Brazil and elsewhere have been embraced as part of a social-rights agenda. Some see potential in this approach for the transcendence of neoliberal modes of governmentality, though others see it as a leading edge of late neoliberalization.[4] Participatory budgeting, on the other hand, was initially positioned as an incubator of grassroots alternatives to orthodox economic policies and authoritarian state structures, although once its associated policy field began to internationalize so too it became increasingly colonized (not to say compromised) by neoliberal actors and interests. While it retains radical currents and potentialities,[5] PB is no longer necessarily seen as an exclusively (or even predominantly) left technology of government, its more technocratic and depoliticized forms having been co-opted, most benignly, as a mainstream strategy of urban governance, and more cynically, as a device for the self-management of municipal cutbacks and devolved austerity programs. Both policy fields, PB and CCTs, consequently display an orthogonal and (at the very least) contingent relationship with the principal dynamics of neoliberalization. They are difficult, in other words, to "tag" in these terms, and their confounding quality makes them interesting for both theoretical and political reasons.

Third, it follows that the relations between PB, CCTs, and broad fronts of neoliberal transformation, and to the hegemonic power centers of neoliberalism as an ideological program, are complex and perhaps contradictory rather than entirely predictable, and that the dominant direction, and maybe even the ultimate fate, of the two policy projects must remain intriguingly open questions. Candidly, our starting hunches, that CCTs would prove to be the locus for ameliorative neoliberal reformism (or "flanking"), while PB would be a space for constrained and uneven but nevertheless determined contestation of this evolving orthodoxy, proved to be somewhat wide of the mark, though in an ultimately revealing way: the progressive potential of CCTs exceeded our expectations, while the radicalizing capacities of PB seem to have been almost exhausted in practical terms. If nothing else, this measure of unpredictability at the policy-field level suggests that there are (social) dynamics here worthy of serious attention, beyond what might be deduced from "reading off" more generic models of neoliberalization, while echoes and connections across the two fields call attention to what might prove to be more generalized features of fast policy, beyond the specificities of the fields themselves.

Fourth and finally, the cases themselves posed methodological challenges, at least relative to traditional approaches to system-specific or in situ policy analysis. As polycentric policy fields characterized by a complex cartography of multiple fronts of reform and zones of inertia, PB and CCTs seemed to require a research strategy that was not only multisited but which also endeavored to *move with and across* these dynamic and fluid landscapes. This could not simply be a matter of buying a business-class ticket to the capitals of cosmopolitan policymaking, or riding the well-lubricated circuits between them. It had to involve situated and connected investigations across a variety of sites and along various channels, which took account of frictions and backwash effects in addition to the dominant currents and tides. It would also have to be sensitive to the real risk of sliding into affirmative (or even celebratory) accounts of cosmopolitan "spaces of flows," peopled by all-knowing global policy elites, or resorting to "impact model" explanations of the overdetermination of local outcomes by "up-there" global forces.[6] Susan Wright has formulated the resulting methodological imperative particularly well: it entails the development of "research strategies for investigating how the small details of social change that are observable in particular locations connect to wider processes of social, economic and political transformation. . . . The challenge is to find ways of studying *through* the specificities of particular sites and their relationship to events in other sites to grasp large-scale processes of change and track the emergence of new systems of governing and forms of power."[7] This is more than a matter, clearly, of selecting the correct methodological technique; it speaks to the broader concerns of case-study formulation and research design.

## Mapping Methods

Our approach here, as we have indicated, has been necessarily exploratory rather than definitive. But in developing a framework for the Policies without Borders project we sought to learn from (as well as take some cues from) recently reinvigorated discussions around the extended case method (ECM). This has a long lineage, reaching back at least as far as the Manchester School ethnographies that were developed after the Second World War under the influence of Max Gluckman; but the most notable recent engagement with this approach has come from Michael Burawoy and his students at the University of California, Berkeley.[8] We have attempted to work in this spirit, modifying the approach in light of the specific demands of studying transnationalizing policy networks. This has involved the extensive tracking of mutating policies across countries, dwelling less with individual cases but instead attempting to span crucibles of "invention" and multiple sites of adaptation and mutation. Four exploratory extensions of the ECM were envisaged in the project, following the methodological axioms outlined by Burawoy, each of which represents an adaptation prompted by the particular challenge of tracking global policy models across far-flung sites and through distended networks that are heavily mediated by powerful institutions and elite actors.

This is indicative of how we have sought to connect and work with the loose web of "distended" case studies that comprise the study.

First, according to Burawoy, ECM seeks to *extend the observer to the participant*, beyond the established ethnographic tradition of passive observation by way of co-location, by adopting a more self-consciously disruptive posture. This is justified on the grounds that social orders are often more effectively observed in a state of disturbance, rather than in what might be presumed to be their "natural" state. The distended case approach adopted here works in this vein, in its use of a judicious combination of observations, documentary analysis, and depth interviews, as a means of probing, interrogating, and triangulating issues around the functioning of global policy networks, the reconstruction of policy models, and the adaptation of policy practice—spanning an expansive "causal group" of policy actors, advocates, and critics. We tried, as far as we could, to inhabit these policymaking networks, arenas, and fields, in an experience-near fashion. It would have been naive and counterproductive, however, for this to be "disruptive" from the very outset. The recurrent problem of accessing policy elites in particular, and maintaining network access in general, necessitates a degree of strategic circumspection, if not bounded conformity.[9] Researching policy mobilities typically involves "studying out," to distant sites where the density of pre-existing contacts and readily accessible informants may be sparse. And it will typically also involve "studying up," in situations in which "conducting interviews is often the only means of gaining entrée to difficult-to-access 'fields,' such as individuals in powerful institutions."[10]

To be sure, there are some limitations of interviews, in comparison with ethnographic saturation,[11] as these are somewhat staged and often rather scripted encounters, especially when they involve urbane and articulate policy elites. Penetrating below the official line, to the "hidden transcripts" beneath can be a demanding feat. And conversations with demonstrably powerful policy actors may often yield exaggerated accounts of foresight, rationality, worldly connectivity, or creative entrepreneurism—what might be called "agent inflation." Unrealistically high degrees of intentionality and indeed authorial originality were quite routinely claimed by many of the people that we interviewed: successful policies, as the saying might go, have "many fathers." As a result, interview encounters always have to involve a measure of critical distance, while the resulting transcripts must be subject to varying degrees of textual deconstruction.

On the other hand, interviews should not always be relegated to the status of ethnography's poor relation, for they have distinctive strengths and can serve particular purposes, not least when attempting to speak to power.[12] When they work well, interviews should be interactive, dynamic encounters, not merely extractive, fact/opinion-gathering exercises; they entail dialogue as much as digging. Depth interviews enable researchers to probe contending accounts and evaluate protoexplanations among a range of knowing interlocutors; they provide opportunities to excavate the social and political context of decision-making, to delve into the "reasons for reasons," and perhaps most importantly, to pass back and recirculate narratives and emergent explanations for verification, qualification, or rejection. In other words, interviews enable the *purposeful* coproduction of social data, at the nexus of interviewee worldviews, in all their variety, and the evolving bundle of questions actively pursued by researchers. And when "studying up," they can be used in situations in which opportunities for (non)participant observation are otherwise inherently limited, by the "black-boxing" of elite decision-making and often by resource constraints.[13] Of course, interview programs cannot begin and end with the inhabitants of corner offices, but should seek to capture a range of opinions and perspectives (including dissident views), outsider as well as insider interpretations, together with some understanding of prosaic bureaucratic practice and "street-level" relations, in order to minimize the ever-present danger of becoming "trapped in the echo-chamber of policy talk."[14]

A posture of constructive engagement, rather than disruptive intervention, seemed more appropriate in the context of the Policies without Borders project, nudging interlocutors toward reflexive and comparative assessments through the juxtaposition of alternate interpretations and experiences from other sites. In the process, researchers become active participants in the exchange and evaluation of cosmopolitan policy knowledge and practice, albeit in the context of a reflexive and critical orientation, rather than as advocates of favored models or "network dupes." In this respect, liminal or "outsider" status can be a methodological asset of sorts: some understandings of network sociology may be shared with participants, but the fact that all such perspectives must also be situational and relational means that some degree of multiperspectival triangulation can be achieved with these actors, even before going "off the grid" to engage with critics and outside observers. Despite outward appearances to the contrary, global policy knowledge is almost never "settled," and global models are typically quite "frail"[15]—the trick is to figure out *how*. So, in principle there is always the potential, not to mention the need, for deeper and more candid conversations, cutting beneath the "official transcript."

A second strategic goal of ECM, in the Berkeley reformulation, has been to extend ethnographic practice across space and time, "road testing" hunches, hypotheses, and theories-in-reconstruction across a cumulative sequence of multisite investigations or "experiments."[16] While broadly sympathetic to this approach, Gillian Hart suggests that it sometimes merely "gestures to concepts of spatiality without fully engaging them."[17] We attempted to respond to this challenge by reconceiving the spatial and scalar relations between research sites as conjunctural nodes within three-dimensional webs of relations (scalar × spatial), *across which* transformative processes operate, evolve, break down, trigger countervailing forces, and so on, rather than as experimental settings in which "global" imperatives/theories/powers are somehow unilaterally "implemented." This involved dispensing with preconceived assumptions regarding the (linear, radial, or top-down) sequencing of policy invention and emulation in favor of an understanding of policy "reinvention" as a continuous, multisite, and cross-scalar process—it meant searching for meaningful discrepancies and significant exceptions (and then holding these against dominant narratives) and tracing networks of innovation in multiple directions, many of which were quite unanticipated prior to the interviews themselves. For example, in the CCT case, "distant" iterations of the policy, across southern Africa, proved to be potentially more consequential than the more loudly trumpeted, hotspot experiments in New York City or Santiago. Having visited southern Africa, these more "disruptive" tales from the policymaking field could be passed back, for comment and elaboration, in subsequent interviews in Brasilia or Washington, D.C.

This more open-ended methodological stance entails thinking beyond and outside the "incorporation" model of global networks,[18] and questioning pervasive assumptions of linear transformation, top-down imposition, and center-periphery diffusion. In the realm of critical policy analysis, however, it certainly must not lead to an inappropriate "flattening out" of power hierarchies, or to an underestimation of the roles of significant institutional mediators, translation sites, and centers of authority, but it does at least render these as questions for empirical investigation, rather than pre-given "realities." And this approach also opens up a much wider horizon for investigating the ways in which processes of policy formation and failure not only "play out" across hinterlands, but are effectively constituted *across* multiscalar and multisite fields, in sometimes surprising ways.[19] To characterize these as simply "global" is insufficient, while also signaling logics of all-encompassing incorporation and top-down impact that may or may not be operative in particular circumstances.

Our application of the distended case approach does, however, call attention to the inescapable tradeoff between the situational depth (and connectivity with subjects and settings) achievable in long-duration, single-site studies, and those "low-flying" (but flying nevertheless) network-centric perspectives that privilege cross-conjunctural reach over sustained, in situ engagement, and traveling over dwelling. The approach advocated here seeks to exploit the potential of the latter without entirely sacrificing the explanatory traction of the former, given that an additive, best-of-both-worlds position (local depth + transnational reach) is not practically attainable. Clearly, it is not always possible to "be there," when in the study of global policy networks there is a constant imperative to also "be" somewhere else. But moving between sites and folding back lessons from each of them allows for a different kind of triangulation and verification from that associated with extended copresence; it provides a means of exploring meaningful geographical and institutional variations, and tensions and tears in the policy-making consensus.

The challenge here is one of traveling within cosmopolitan policy networks without becoming another creature of those networks; of making sense of fast-moving "best practices" without losing sight of prosaic practice; of taking account of phenomena like policy tradeshows without succumbing to explanatory dilettantism, or some kind of methodological "tourism, [just] tripping around from site to site."[20] If the demanding objective of policy ethnographies—and other forms of "close-up," qualitative research on policy processes and practices—is to penetrate the "assumptive worlds" of policy actors, "to watch and interact with people on their own 'territory' and using their own language,"[21] while not taking everything that is said or seen at face value, or falling prey to textual literalism or "inside dopester" credulity, then the challenges are multiplied when the time spent "dwelling" in individual research sites must be circumscribed. The mobilities researcher may prioritize moving with translocal policy networks, projects, organizations, and agents, but the conventional requirements of fact-checking, contextualization, and triangulation are nonetheless ever-present, as is the risk of being taken for a "network dopester"—not least after spending extended amounts of time in the company of charismatic cosmopolitans and global policy entrepreneurs.

It would be going too far to suggest that this kind of policy travel might actually narrow the mind, in the sense of only registering those practices that are flashing brightly on the "global grid," or of reducing local deviations, mutations, and adaptations to the status of minor disruptions in an otherwise inevitable rollout of a universal model. A minimum methodological requirement, however, must be the adoption of a restlessly critical posture in relation to these risks of overreading global success stories, not least because there are communities of policy actors that, understandably, have much to gain from the circulation *and valorization* of such polished scripts. Our approach to dealing with this challenge has been to marry a commitment to following fast-traveling policies, and their associated network-communities, with a determination to position these within the moving landscapes with which they are recursively connected. (The often-exaggerated talk of world-transforming models must be brought to earth.) This has meant taking account of moving fronts and "hot spots," but also being on the lookout for (often unreported) failures, divergences, and sources of opposition and alternatives.

Extending interview programs over time and space, over several years and several continents, inevitably leads to some degree of redundancy, but even this can be productive. Following movements in the two policy fields led us down a number of blind alleys. There were some cases that we studied, and indeed some countries that we visited, that have not ultimately found any place in the discussion here, but even these superficially unproductive visits—and the sometimes low-return interviews we conducted there—informed the analysis in other ways. For example, we explored several PB sites, and even some advocacy networks, that we concluded were engaged in shallow and largely symbolic policy borrowing. The details of the specific cases may not have warranted extensive discussion, but the existence of such forms of hollow, formulaic repetition proved to be quite significant, as a generalized phenomenon. "Negative cases," weak signals, and unused interviews therefore shaped the overall explanation, even if as "data" they are absent, or only obliquely referenced, in the pages that follow. This is not, we should emphasize, a remit for cherry-picking or for placing disproportionate attention on a few "extreme" cases; it speaks to the need to generate an explanatory "surplus" in projects of this kind, which seek to convey a sense of the policymaking landscape within which individual cases, models, or experiments are conjuncturally located. The situational context of particular cases is not, then, an inert backdrop to action on the main stage, but actively and jointly constitutes the stage itself. Beyond merely "locating" cases, this means embedding them, both relationally (in relation to one another) and theoretically (in relation to evolving explanations).[22]

A third form of extension envisaged in the ECM involves extensions "outward" from micro processes to macro forces, delving deeply into part-whole connectivities between observed, local phenomena and their extralocal relations, and reaching out, in explanatory terms, from immediate (site-specific) contexts to translocal linkages, interrelations, and domains.[23] This cannot mean granting an explanatory trump card to "external causes," but it does necessitate the careful interrogation (and weighing) of extralocal determinations, sometimes with the aid of the methodological device of "divergent cases"—those that display diverse or discrepant outcomes, even as they are connected by common causative processes or power relations. Again, this is an invitation to explore "global forces" as contestable and contradictory phenomena, not as iron laws, the diverse "localizations" of which are always potential incubators for path-changing mutations and alternatives.

In this vein, distended case approaches to the study of global policy networks set out to explore a range of sites variously connected to particular communities of policy practice or philosophy, or heterogeneous networks of innovators, emulators, adaptors, and circulators,[24] probing their frayed edges and zones of dissipation, as well as their centers of authority, sampling sites of policy "failure" as well as "success," accounting for contestations and alternatives, and periodically stepping off the cosmopolitan grid so as to position network nodes within a more expansive reading of "local" institutional and social milieux. Following the policy, in this context, cannot be reduced to the relatively straightforward task of tracking norms, practices, and agents "downstream" from sources of conspicuous (or claimed) authority, or outward from dominant centers of calculation; it must be multidirectional and it must span not only the spaces of intensive exchange but also those of contingent connection, marginalization, and exclusion. And it must also encompass not only the immediate local context of policy adoption-adaption-implementation, but the "context of context,"[25] the positioning of experiments, failures, and alternatives within an understanding of the wider

patterning of policy transformation. Similarly, the "framing" of policy rationalities is much more than a discursive process, since it also reflects the
extralocal rules and norms of different policymaking games, the role of norm-
shaping institutions and innovation managers, institutional incentives, fiscal
constraints, and so forth.[26]

The connections between micro practices and macro forces were also
explored in the Policies without Borders project by taking full account of
meso-scale influences—indeed this is the intermediate analytical scale at
which the emergent concept of fast policy is pitched. Between the generalized dynamics of neoliberal transformation and institutional restructuring,
on the one hand, and the local contingencies of particular policy initiatives,
on the other, fast policy occupies a social space that is organized around
phenomena like practitioner networks, conferences, blogs and web sites,
evaluation programs, new and fading models of reform, experts and advocates, critics and opponents, and such. This was the terrain on which we
worked, in a methodological register located somewhere between that of the
low-flying or close-focus ethnographer and that of the applied state theorist
or synoptic policy analyst.

Finally, perhaps the most distinctive feature of Berkeley-style ECM is the
express commitment that is made to *reconstruct* theory, not merely to apply
or even to "test" it.[27] This means that, beyond mere confirmation, extending
the case should be an occasion for theoretical extension and reconstruction,
not theoretical dejection. There are, in this respect, especially important implications for the selection of case-study sites, because these cannot simply
be spaces in which traveling theories are realized or affirmed in some frictionless sense;[28] research sites should be identified with a view to troubling
theory, placing stress on its basic premises and foundational claims, while
exploiting the potential of such engaged, critical accounts to *disturb* received
understandings and conventional wisdom.[29] What Burawoy initially characterized as a "kamikaze" approach to theory development may have been only
inconsistently achieved in practice,[30] but the dual concern with acknowledging the importance of theory (as opposed to free-form inductivism), while
also emphasizing its essential plasticity, remains a defining characteristic of
the ECM.

Turning, one last time, to our exploration of distended policy networks,
there is certainly a shared sense of the significance of open-ended theory
development, but in this case "theory" itself is rather more tentative, indeed

intrinsically exploratory. Beyond the skepticism concerning rationalist diffusion models and a willingness to embrace network-oriented methods
while remaining agnostic about network-centric explanations,[31] it must be
acknowledged that alternative theoretical formulations are not available "off
the shelf," and so prototheories must be reflexively developed among and
across the cases. "Process tracing" can be an effective first step in this direction.[32] As a result, this is a project closer to explanatory prototyping than
to hypothesis testing, and more akin to provisional theoretical construction
than to full-service reconstruction. It is a journey on the emergent pathways
of fast policy, not a means to confirm a preformed theory.

## Mancunians Abroad

The distant origins of this book, and the Policies without Borders project
that preceded it, lay in a moment of methodological happenstance. This was
when one of the authors, on research leave from the University of Manchester
in the UK and trying to make sense of the febrile geopolitics of the U.S.
"welfare reform" process, interviewed the other, at the time ensconced in
the research department of a civil-rights organization, the Chicago Urban
League. Back in the mid-1990s, the American welfare state was experiencing
a domestic form of fast-policy transformation, as local models of workfare
like the GAIN program in Riverside, California, and W-2 in Wisconsin were
being promoted as models for system-wide reform. In the final analysis, not
only did these state and local prototypes anticipate key aspects of what
would become the federal reform (or "welfare repeal") of 1996, the cumulative weight of emulative reforms in just about every corner of the country
rendered national-level change practically inevitable.[33] The radical "model"
of U.S. welfare reform—combining strict work incentives with time-limited
benefits and devolved delivery—would duly reshape the coordinates for reform debates in other countries, and among the international development
agencies and think tanks, the politics of welfare reform having become not
only transnationalized but truly multiscalar.

These conversations would continue back in Manchester, courtesy of a
reciprocal fellowship program, as we moved on to carry out collaborative
research on American influences on the Blair government's welfare reforms
of the late 1990s.[34] This was the beginning of exploratory theoretical work on
the process known as "policy transfer," although attempts to initiate comparative case-study work were initially frustrated. It was out of discussions

with Bob Jessop—also on a visiting appointment at Manchester at the time— that preliminary ideas about fast policy were first sketched.[35] In this respect, the concept was emergent in a theoretical program around neoliberal restructuring and elaborations of the regulation approach, as well as in the preceding decade of empirical work on welfare reform.[36] It was never a purely abstract formulation. It was shaped by research programs that were anchored in (variable) local experiences and (generally) national reform efforts, but which only secondarily and latterly took account of international dimensions, at first as "external" influences. The research design for this book, on the other hand, problematizes this transnational dimension much more explicitly, even if we have not sought (or wanted) to lose some our old habits of taking local differences and national specificities seriously. Like fast policy itself, it would be necessary to work across these scales.

Just as policies seem to be mutable across space—varying in both form and effect, even as they articulate in diverse ways with globalizing norms, fixes, and paradigms—so too it would seem that *explanations* for these phenomena need to be especially sensitive to what is evidently a fast-changing, relational context. "Following the policy" may not immediately generate determinant and generalizable explanations, yet it may lead to surprising encounters, unexpected turns, and unforeseen conclusions. In this respect, the journeys that policies make are worth following because neither their direction nor their outcomes can be known in advance. Their cross-border travels and localized effects certainly cannot be simply "read off" from the orientations and goals of sponsoring institutions in the global power centers or, for that matter, from received theories. Above all, perhaps, this calls for a reflexive methodology, tracing emergent policy mobilities across distended networks of relationally connected sites, and accounting for dominant patterns and trajectories of transformation, as well as for unscripted deviations and alternative mutations. It is tempting to think that there might be echoes here of that earlier, Mancunian incarnation of the ECM: the "cloth-cap ethnographers" of the Manchester School were exhorted to deploy a somewhat improvisational, "abductive method," or as Max Gluckman liked to put it, to enter the field and then "follow their noses."[37] Half a century later, perhaps "following the policy" can provide a basis for a different kind of methodological exploration.

# PART II

## Social Policy as Practical Science

# 3

# New Ideas for New York City

Ｎew York City is a place of big ideas. During the Progressive Era, at the turn of the twentieth century, the city was a beacon for social-policy reform, forging innovations in public education and housing. By the end of the century, however, it had secured quite a different reputation, as a bastion of conservative and neoliberal experimentation around new forms of social control and regulation, such as zero-tolerance policing and work-based welfare reform, or workfare.[1] The city that had helped to construct the American welfare state, and the country's liberal-urban settlement, was by the 1990s leading the way in doing away with these very legacies. New York's uncompromising version of workfare, in particular, was promoted by Mayor Rudy Giuliani as the antidote to "welfare dependency" and ill-discipline among the urban poor. The solution would no longer be to compensate the poor for the absence of work, but to enforce employment as a means of strengthening their work ethic, while combating those "dependency lifestyles" that were now seen, in the neoliberal critique, as the root cause of poverty.[2] Giuliani's successor, Michael Bloomberg, demonstrated a marked preference for businesslike pragmatism over ideological saber-rattling, though he was arguably no less inclined to regard New York City as the center of the (policymaking) universe. He was consequently playing to type, though maybe a little out of character too, when he announced that the centerpiece of his second term in office would be an ambitious effort to combat the stubborn problem of urban poverty—recognizing that what the City had been doing had failed, in the increasingly fraught policy sphere of "welfare," and pledging to learn from better practices, wherever these might be found.

In the spring of 2006, Bloomberg had established a blue-ribbon Commission for Economic Opportunity—linked to a new innovation unit in city hall, the Center for Economic Opportunity, with which it shared the businesslike acronym "CEO"—in order to examine the character of twenty-first century poverty in the city and to scan the horizon for the most effective solutions. Few doubted the seriousness of the problem, given that one in five New Yorkers lived below the poverty line, but the mayor also sought to instill a new sense of urgency. Bloomberg's time in office was term-limited (a constitutional inconvenience that he would later remove), so measurable and meaningful action was required in short order. One of the commissioners recalled that when the mayor addressed the group in the spring of 2006 he was insistent that "'Labor Day, I want answers. I'm announcing what we're doing after Labor Day because there's only three years [of my second term] left . . . No contemplating the navel, please.' That very results-oriented approach affected the spirit of the deliberations."[3] The commission did not quite meet this demanding deadline (missing it by a few weeks), but its galloping, global review of more than sixty antipoverty strategies ultimately focused, as charged, on those "actions that can produce quick results," while maintaining a "commitment to make deeper investments for the longer term," in education and skills development, and in "making work pay."[4] The commission had worked with breakneck speed, but apparently the mayor was determined to remain one step ahead.

Bloomberg welcomed the commission's findings, but practically in the same breath proclaimed his enthusiastic support for an audacious experiment that, while on the radar of one of the CEO working groups, had not been featured anywhere in the final version of the fifty-page report. Conditional cash transfers, or CCTs—the scheme pioneered in Latin America that "conditions" payments to poor families on the maintenance of human-capital building behaviors like school attendance and regular health screening—would be adopted on a trial basis in New York, the first city in the Global North to consider such a move. As Bloomberg explained:

> If you're serious about tackling poverty, an entrenched problem that has proven resistant to conventional government programs, you have to be serious about trying new things, taking a new tack. That's what we're here to do. . . .
> Conditional cash transfer programs have proven effective in countries around the world and, frankly, we need some new ideas here in New York City to fight poverty.[5]

Provocatively styled by the mayor himself as a "controversial pilot program," New York's CCT would be "modeled on programs that have succeeded in Mexico and other countries but haven't yet been tried in the United States."[6] Opportunity NYC was to be "modeled" on the Mexican program Oportuni- dades, ostensibly because it was the most intensively evaluated of this new generation of antipoverty schemes—but also because, in a phrase that the mayor and his staff took to repeating, "it works." This $50 million experi- ment would be funded primarily from private sources,[7] and it would rigor- ously evaluated—"just as a business would," as Bloomberg put it—by the leading project-demonstration and evaluation house, MDRC.

New York City may have been flamboyantly "borrowing" this idea, but its mayor certainly knew how to make the most of the limelight. Widely admired for his managerial competence and ideological dexterity, Bloomberg received widespread praise for a maneuver portrayed as simultaneously pragmatic and courageous.[8] The largely inert world of "post-welfare" policymaking— which, following more than a decade of frantic experimentation, had settled, in the wake of the federal reform of 1996, into an incrementalist temper—was suddenly reanimated. Bloomberg traveled to Washington, D.C., to promote his new program at the Brookings Institution, prompting the venerable think tank's president, Strobe Talbott, to describe New York City's antipoverty effort, which included more than thirty other new initiatives alongside the flagship CCT experiment, as "among the most ambitious, extensive, and innovative in the country."[9] Before long, the *New York Times* editorial page was trum- peting Opportunity NYC as a model for other U.S. cities, several of which were already actively exploring similar strategies.[10]

Opportunity NYC was garnering international attention as well. An event jointly organized by UNICEF, the World Bank, and the United Nation Development Fund's Special Unit for South-South Cooperation, called Eyes on the South as a Knowledge Hub, lauded the Bloomberg administration's CCT initiative as a pioneering example for those "[r]ich countries [that] are learning from 'the south' in customizing these innovative schemes that have shown clear results," insisting that "no nation has the monopoly on the best ideas." As the World Bank's vice president for Latin America and the Carib- bean, Pamela Cox, commented:

> We are meeting to learn what works and why, and how the experiences and lessons drawn from some of our partners such as Brazil [and] Mexico, have transformed themselves into emblematic programs leading to new nationally

endorsed social policy and an example for the world. . . . This is globalization at its best, bringing development solutions to twenty-first century challenges.[11]

The epitome of the World Bank's "knowledge bank" strategy, CCTs were benefiting from a $2 billion funding pipeline by late 2007, with a strong emphasis on technical expertise results-driven emulation: "Independently conducted impact evaluations have been an integral part of CCT programs and [have] provided the basis for making decisions regarding program continuity and expansion worldwide." The Bank has been the central actor in

| Program size/target: | Conditions | |
| --- | --- | --- |
| | *Education +* | *Education only* |
| Nationwide | Bolsa Família (Brazil) Oportunidades (Mexico) Bono de Desarrollo Humano (Ecuador) Familias en Acción (Colombia) Program of Advancement through Health and Education (Jamaica) | Bolsa Escola (Brazil) Jaring Pengamanan Sosial (Indonesia) |
| Niche (regional or narrow target population) | Chile Solidario Social Risk Mitigation Project (Turkey) | Female Secondary School Assistance Program (Bangladesh) Japan Fund for Poverty Reduction (Cambodia) Education Sector Support Project (Cambodia) Basic Education Development Project (Yemen) |
| Small scale/pilot | Programa de Asignación Familiar (Honduras) Cash Transfer for Orphans and Vulnerable Children (Kenya) Atención a Crisis (Nicaragua) Red de Protección Social (Nicaragua) Opportunity NYC (USA) | Subsidio Condicionado a la Asistencia Escolar–Bogotá (Colombia) Punjab Education Sector Reform Program (Pakistan) |

Figure 2. The expanding universe of CCT experimentation. Source: Adapted from Fiszbein et al. 2009.

an expanding universe of CCT experimentation (see Figure 2). On this scientifically leveled playing field, the Bank continued, lessons would no longer
only travel in the traditional direction, "out" and "down" from centers of
northern expertise; as the New York case had precociously demonstrated,
"this time the knowledge flow has gone the other way around."[12]

The startlingly rapid ascendancy of Opportunity NYC may have impressed more distant observers, but closer to home many were decidedly
more skeptical. Some were dismayed over what they saw as presentational
flash over policy substance, despite the vaguely Orwellian claims to the contrary, concerning fearless and unyielding long-term commitments, learning
scrupulously from what works, and so forth. The mayor's high-profile new
unit, CEO, one longtime social advocate complained, had more to do with
attention seeking than solution finding, predicting that "at the end of CEO,
[Bloomberg will have] a poverty strategy where there's more poverty, a
homelessness strategy in which there is more homeless, and a hunger strategy in which there is more hunger. And he's the brilliant changer of all antipoverty thought!"[13] A colleague from a prominent community organization,
which had attempted to engage constructively with both the work of the
commission and with the task of establishing the new CCT program, also
complained about the headline-grabbing rush, and the sense of "frustration,
about people not being at the table and not being approached about the
[Opportunity NYC] policy." And these frustrations were not only the pre-
serve of those on the outside, looking in:

> Interestingly, a lot of the commission members didn't even know that [the
> CCT] announcement was going to happen. . . . I remember speaking to one
> of the commission members really soon after the release and he said, "I can't
> even believe that Bloomberg mentioned the Opportunity NYC program in his
> initial statement, because it wasn't in our report and he must have known that
> would take the light away from everything else. It would be the thing every-
> body would talk about and everything else would be forgotten."[14]

> When [the proposal] first came out we tried to get involved in a dialogue about
> it [Opportunity NYC], but it was already a done deal at that point. So it's
> not like it came out and we're now open for discussion. . . . It was more like,
> here's what we're doing and your voice can just be in opposition or in support.
> And of course, if you are in really vocal opposition then it's, "What, don't you

believe in experimenting and trying to do things that are new and different?"
So it was a very sensitive space to be in.[15]

The speed of policy development around New York City's CCT program,
in these early stages at least, was clearly outrunning not only conventional
channels of consultation (including with some of the "targeted" communities) but also the very processes of deliberation that the mayor had entrusted
to the commission. The speed with which the mayor acted left many in the
local policy community (and even some of his own appointed advisors) in a
"sensitive space": borrowing an imported design, along with some of its projected legitimacy, enabled the mayor to move decisively. On the advice of a
handful of peripatetic policy experts—some of whom worked for the World
Bank, some of whom were operating more independently—the mayor and
his deputy, Linda Gibbs, had been convinced that the CCT policy design was
both practically importable and ultimately workable. They would soon be
scheduling a mayoral visit to Mexico City, flanked by a high-level delegation
of policy managers and evaluators, with the ostensible objective of "look[ing]
under the hood," but evidently also to cement the political legitimacy of the
planned replication.[16] For those located outside this tight circle, Opportunity NYC was effectively a "done deal" on the day that the mayor publicly
declared his interest in the program.

Following the Bloomberg delegation's journey "upstream" to the source
of what one in the inner circle called their "inspiration"—the Mexican
Oportunidades program—this chapter seeks to open up questions around
the geographical and institutional sourcing of CCT policies. As will become
increasingly apparent, it is not merely an oversimplification but a misrepresentation to describe this as a simple transfer—or one-way transaction—
between policy elites in Manhattan and Mexico City. The New York CCT
was never going to be a replica of Oportunidades (for all the earnest shows
of learning and the performative deference to social-policymaking colleagues from the South), even if the Mexican model did provide a template
of sorts, and a technocratic frame of reference. The course-cum-cause of
CCT programming would *itself* evolve and mutate by virtue of the New York
experiment. Moreover, the cross-border relationship manifest in the Opportunity NYC / Oportunidades connection, while asymmetrical, would soon
evolve into a complex and dialogic one, and from an early stage it would
involve a number of interested parties. The roles of these actors are further

explored in chapter 3, which examines the proliferation of knowledge and practice networks around CCT development from a more global perspective. Here, we begin somewhat closer to the ground, albeit in two locations, delving into the circumstances surrounding the (re)birth of the New York CCT program before moving out (and back) to consider the program's alleged "origins" in Mexico.

## Bloomberg Looks Down

Michael Bloomberg began his second term in office on a high. He had just been reelected by a resounding nineteen-point margin, the City's bond rating was the envy of its peers, unemployment was falling as economic growth picked up, and the welfare rolls had been driven to a forty-year low. Quietly cultivating speculation about a possible presidential bid, the mayor was tempted to think big. His 2006 State of the City address set out the nature of the challenge:

> Even though we have become a national leader in promoting welfare-to-work, our great city remains home to the nation's poorest congressional district—the sixteenth in the South Bronx. And that has been true for too long. Men and women struggling to get out of poverty deserve our help—and so do their children. Our nation has learned by experience that we cannot eliminate poverty by throwing money at the problem. But our city has shown that problems once thought to be beyond hope: dangerous streets, failing schools, chronic homelessness—can be turned around, if we target our resources where they are needed most, if we set measurable goals, and if we hold ourselves accountable.[17]

He went on to promise a "major reduction" in the number of New Yorkers living in poverty, engineered by way of an innovative package of "self-sufficiency" measures, safely ensconced within the prevailing ideological frame of "hard work and personal responsibility." Creating a hostage to fortune, the mayor informed the public, and his staff, that he would simply "refuse to accept failure."

The newly launched Center for Economic Opportunity, with an annual budget of $150 million, had a charge to experiment boldly in poverty-reduction programming "on a private sector model," as a cross between a philanthropic foundation and a venture-capital fund.[18] It was to act as a "catalyst . . . to test and evaluate innovative new strategies" for tackling poverty.[19]

The role of the Commission for Economic Opportunity, in this context, had been to explicate a "core set of shared values" within which CEO would work, establishing a "post-ideological blueprint" for the new agency.[20] Premised on an expectation of no-more-than-incremental increases in public funding, these values were defined as follows:

- Hard work and personal responsibility fuel our economy;
- All New Yorkers should share in the rewards of economic growth and prosperity;
- Wherever possible, government and the private sector must work together to reward work and support working families;
- Context is critical—poverty cannot be reduced outside the network of families, religious institutions, schools, and other community organizations.[21]

Hewing close to the ideological mainstream, the commission maintained that "although the [federal] welfare reform [of 1996] has been successful on a number of fronts, an increasing number of working families still cannot earn their way out of poverty."[22] Its "success," presumably, was accounted for by the reduction of the welfare rolls, as the alleged cure for welfare dependency; its failure could be measured by the intensification of working poverty. The first iteration of workfare had propelled the poor into jobs,[23] but it had failed to lower the poverty rate. Having dipped in the late 1990s, the city's poverty rate had been rising since 2000, even as the work participation rate among the poor climbed from 38 percent in 2000 to 46 percent in 2005.[24] The poor were working, evidently, but the policy was not. There was more to the problem of poverty than "welfare dependency."

It seems to have been the manifest failure of mainstream policies to move the needle on urban poverty, no doubt coupled with a desire to substantiate the rhetorical commitment to thinking "outside the box," that prompted Bloomberg to reach beyond the commission's package of recommendations. In choosing to headline the CCT measure, the mayor publicly committed his administration to what he called a "bold step," that of

implementing a strategy not previously tried in this nation, and not directly recommended by the Commission. Historically, the rest of the world has often looked to America for leadership in social policy—but there is no reason that we cannot also learn from the experience of others. And I think New York can take the lead in this regard. This policy is called "conditional cash transfers," and it is designed to address the simple fact that the stress of poverty often causes people to make decisions—to skip a doctor's appointment, or to neglect other basic tasks—that often only worsen their long-term prospects. Conditional cash transfers give them an incentive to make sound decisions instead.[25]

The CCT proposal had not been among the commission's specific recommendations, though it was on the agenda during its deliberations. One of the speakers invited to the commission's conference, held at the City University of New York in June 2006, was Laura Rawlings, an evaluation specialist at the World Bank, with responsibility for human-development programming in Latin America and the Caribbean. Rawlings had been task manager for Colombia's cash-transfer program, Familias en Acción, launched in 2000, and for several years she had been leveraging the programming and evaluation lessons of CCT programs, through a range of international events, forums, and channels.[26] CCTs, according to Rawlings, represent "perhaps the clearest manifestation of [the] new thinking on social assistance," as the goals of short-term poverty alleviation have given way to a strategic emphasis on economic growth, human-capital development, and labor market flexibility, though she cautions that "it should not be assumed from positive evaluation results from a number of countries that similar success can be achieved in other countries in different contexts."[27] At the time, Rawlings was primarily concerned with the challenge of transferring the lessons of CCT programming from middle-income countries like Mexico to very poor nations with limited institutional and fiscal capacity, though soon she would engage with the distinctive task of tailoring the strategy for deployment in one of the world's wealthiest cities.

Rawlings's interlocutor on the Commission for Economic Opportunity was a distinguished professor of applied psychology at New York University, Lawrence Aber, a longtime champion of incentives-based antipoverty programs. Aber had pressed the CCT idea in the commission's deliberations, but later reflected that "the idea just seemed too foreign to the majority of commission members." Nevertheless, this had struck a chord with Deputy Mayor Linda Gibbs, who had found, Aber recalled,

CCTs intriguing and of great potential interest to the Mayor. What commanded attention was their innovation, evidence of effectiveness, value-orientation

and their appeal to political leaders on the right and on the left of the political spectrum. . . . [D]espite the fact that they were not recommended by the
Commission on Economic Opportunity, the Administration decided to adapt
them to the needs of New York City and rigorously test them as a pilot. If
proven efficacious, the plan was to bring them to scale in New York. In short,
the local demand for ideologically balanced, evidence-based, antipoverty strategies could be supplied by the emerging movement for CCTs.[28]

New York's CCT experiment was constructed on the basis of both practical
knowledge and evaluation evidence from south of the border. A "learning
exchange" was established between the Bloomberg administration and Mexican authorities late in 2006. With the backing of the Rockefeller Foundation, which provided "research and development capital" for Opportunity
NYC, the first stage of this learning exchange brought Mexican officials to
New York City in January 2007, followed by a reciprocal visit by a mayoral
delegation to Toluca and Mexico City three months later. The Mexican ex-
cursion enabled the New York team to observe the Oportunidades program
"first hand," including cash-distribution methods and other aspects of implementation, while contemplating how these might be "tailored to New York
City's needs and circumstances."[29]

The design of the New York program—which was outsourced to the evaluation house, MDRC, in partnership with the community development
agency, Seedco—was finalized in the weeks following the Mexican delegation's visit to city hall. In its incentives-based philosophy, and in its emphasis
on an integrated, targeted approach, Opportunity NYC closely resembled
the Oportunidades model (see Figure 3). Opportunity NYC would "incentivize" approved forms of personal and family decision-making for designated participants—like maintaining unblemished school-attendance records,
working full time, opening bank accounts, and attending parent-teacher
conferences—by way of an elaborate schedule of direct cash payments. Following the CCT philosophy, it combined the immediate objective of relieving
material hardship with the short-term goal of encouraging and rewarding
"positive actions," as the foundation of a longer-term strategy for breaking the
intergenerational cycle of poverty through reorganized behaviors and human-
capital formation. Slated to run for three years, the pilot program conditioned payments on a schedule of incentivized activities across three realms:
(1) children's education efforts and performance, (2) family's preventive health

care practices, and (3) parents' workforce efforts. Below is a description of Opportunity NYC program characteristics.

Opportunity NYC consists of three pilot programs, based on incentive schedules developed by the City's Departments of Health and Mental Hygiene, Education, Consumer Affairs, Housing Preservation and Development, and Small Business Services; the City's Housing Authority and Human Resources Administration; and the "support of international, national and local experts and community leaders."[30]

Opportunity NYC: Family provides monetary incentives to families in the following areas:

*Education incentives* to promote school attendance, parental engagement, achievement, and improved performance on standardized tests;

*Health incentives* for maintaining adequate health coverage for all children and adults in participant households as well as age-appropriate medical and dental visits for each family member;

*Employment and training incentives* to promote increased employment and earnings, or combine work activities with job training and education.

Participating families may earn $4,000–$6,000 per year, depending on family size and the number of activities that are completed successfully. Participants will report their completion of incentivized activities and receive their earned cash transfers every two months.

Began September 2007: 2,550 qualifying families were selected to participate in this program. Families must (a) have a household income of 130 percent or less of the federal poverty level (approximately $22,000 per year for a family of three), (b) have at least one child entering the fourth, seventh, or ninth grade in September 2007, and (c) live in one of the six target community districts.

*Opportunity NYC: Adults* provides monetary incentives to adult Section 8 voucher holders for maintaining full-time employment and completing job training and education programs. *Employment and training incentives* will promote increased employment and earnings, or combine work activities with job training and education. Participating adults may earn up to $3,000 per year. Participants will report completion of incentivized activities and receive their earned cash transfers every two months.

Began December 2007: 2,400 qualifying adults were selected to participate in this program. Qualifying adults must (a) be the recipient of Section 8 voucher services, (b) be eligible for the FSS program, and (c) live in one of the five NYC boroughs.

*Opportunity NYC: Child* offers small monetary incentives to children in fourth and seventh grade classes throughout the city, for effort and performance on standardized tests taken during the academic year. The program was designed and administered by Harvard University economist Dr. Roland Fryer, in collaboration with the NYC Department of Education.

Participating students in the fourth grade will receive up to $25 for a perfect score on each of 10 interim assessment tests taken throughout the school year, up to an annual total of $250. Seventh graders can earn up to $50 per test, for a maximum payment of $500 per year. Each is based on a scaled incentive.

Began September 2007: involving 20 fourth grade and 20 seventh grade schools, or approximately 9,000 students. Schools can volunteer to participate.

The Opportunity NYC experiment enrolled 4,800 families (half of whom were allocated to a control group, for evaluation purposes, and therefore ineligible for the program's financial incentives), drawn from six high-poverty neighborhoods—Central and East Harlem in Manhattan, Brownsville and East New York in Brooklyn, and Morris Heights / Mount Hope and East Tremont / Belmont in the Bronx. The original plan was that on-program families could receive up to $5,000 per year, comprising individual payments of $50–$300 attached to an elaborate range of designated activities and targets (see Figure 3). All of the initial funding came from nongovernmental sources, a device apparently designed, according to some observers, to "take some of the sting out of the criticism."[31] The architects of the program concluded that it was politically infeasible to direct public dollars to the experiment, at least during the trial stage.

If this was the plan, it was only partially successful. Criticism came as much from the right as from the left. The design feature that attracted the most attention was the emphasis on behavioral incentives, which some conservatives questioned on the grounds that this amounted to paying the poor for things they should be doing anyway, while some advocates for the poor complained that the approach effectively assumed behavioral deficiencies and was therefore "belittling."[32] The carefully modulated objection from the Manhattan Institute, the free-market think tank that had championed

| Activity | Reward amount |
| --- | --- |
| **Workforce incentives** | |
| Sustained full-time employment | $150 per month |
| Education and training while employed at least 10 hours per week *(employment requirement discontinued after Year 2)* | Amount varies by length of course, up to a maximum of $3,000 over 3 years |
| **Education incentives** | |
| *Elementary and middle school students* | |
| Attends 95% of scheduled school days *(discontinued after Year 2)* | $25 per month |
| Scores at proficiency level (or improves) on annual math and English language arts (ELA) tests | |
| Elementary school students | $300 per math test; $300 per ELA test |
| Middle school students | $350 per math test; $350 per ELA test |
| Parent reviews low-stakes interim tests *(discontinued after Year 1)* | $25 for parents to download, print, and review results (up to 5/year) |
| Parent discusses annual math and ELA test results with teachers *(discontinued after Year 2)* | $25 (up to 2 tests per year) |
| *High school students* | |
| Attends 95% of scheduled school days | $50 per month |
| Accumulates 11 course credits per year | $600 |
| Passes Regents exams | $600 per exam passed (up to 5 exams) |
| Takes PSAT test | $50 for taking the test (up to 2 times) |
| Graduates from high school | $400 bonus |
| *All grades* | |
| Parent attends parent-teacher conferences | $25 per conference (up to 2/year) |
| Child obtains library card (discontinued *after Year 2*) | $50 once during program |

Figure 3. Opportunity NYC Family Rewards Program: Schedule of Incentives. Source: Riccio et al. 2010. Opportunity NYC Family Rewards Program: Schedule of Incentives. Source: Riccio et al. 2010.

| Activity | Reward amount |
|---|---|
| *Health incentives* | |
| Maintaining public or private health insurance *(discontinued after Year 2)* | |
|    For each parent covered | Per month: $20 (public); $50 (private) |
|    If all children are covered | Per month: $20 (public); $50 (private) |
| Annual medical checkup | $200 per family member (once per year) |
| Doctor-recommended follow-up visit *(discontinued after Year 2)* | $100 per family member (once per year) |
| Early-intervention evaluation for child under 30 months old, if advised by pediatrician | $200 per child (once per year) |
| Preventive dental care (cleaning/checkup) | $100 per family member (once per year for children 1–5 years old; twice per year for family members 6 years of age and older) |

Figure 3. (*Continued*)

Giuliani's workfare program was that "New York is a different universe . . . [l]eaving aside whether Mexican poverty policy cries out for emulation," although behind this lay a grave concern that cash transfers to the poor would surely incubate new forms of dependency.[33] In contrast, criticisms from the left were somewhat restrained, possibly reflecting the pragmatic turn that some social-advocacy organizations took in the wake of the 1996 welfare reform, coupled with an increased reliance on (fragile) funding sources, many of them channeled through city hall. The Temporary Assistance for Needy Families (TANF) program, the product of the federal workfare reform of 1996, not only conditioned welfare claims on job-search efforts, it also established a climate of unforgiving behavioral requirements, while decentralizing delivery to states and localities. Correspondingly, reform politics have subsequently tended to be muted, administratively specific, and localized;

for all intents and purposes, they have become postideological and pragmatic. This was the programming vacuum into which Opportunity NYC
was launched.

The buzz around the Bloomberg experiment was attributable to the way
it had been cleverly positioned to leverage "next stage" reforms in the United
States, not as a critique of the postwelfare consensus, but as a reanimation
and rejuvenation of its reforming spirit. Unlike Latin American CCTs, Opportunity NYC would incentivize *work,* alongside the staple conditions regarding education and family health. Even though work enforcement had a mixed
record, at best, as a poverty-alleviation measure, and even though rates of
employment participation among the city's low-income populations were
already high, this (evidently) was seen as an ideological necessity. As one of
the commission members bluntly put it, "You weren't going to do CCTs in
America if you didn't incentivize work," while a colleague similarly conceded, "There was no way this was going forward without something related
to adults' labor-market participation or job training; that was the nature
of doing it in this political environment."[34] Yet even as the New York City
CCT experiment was embedded in, and adapted to, this orthodoxy of work-
oriented reform, its emphasis on positive incentives (as opposed to punitive
sanctions) was regarded as subtly revolutionary. As another commission
member emphasized, if the experiment worked, the postwelfare consensus
might be incrementally realigned, an interpretation that one of the program's
architects endorsed:

> People have very strong feelings about whether incentives work or not [, but]
> most people understand that helping to make work pay is a good thing. . . . So
> the notion that you are building around that wage appeals to lots of different
> people.[35]

> With food stamps, the more I need the more I get. Here, it depends on what
> I do. That's really different [from] conditioning on need. Even with EITC
> [Earned Income Tax Credit], in fact, the lower my income, the less I earn, the
> more EITC I get. This is really turning cash transfers of various kinds totally
> on its head. This is no longer conditioning on need in one form or another . . .
> you are conditioning on behavior, on your *positive* behavior. The underlying
> theory is this is going to reduce your long-term dependence. In the postwelfare

world, we're heading more and more in that direction. I'm not sure you could have done this ten years ago.[36]

Opportunity NYC was therefore launched with high expectations that it might somehow catch—and maybe even epitomize—the next wave of reform, and that a model at least *remade* in New York might spur new rounds of experimental programming in the United States and beyond. As one of the program's designers explained,

> [Bloomberg] has said on many occasions in public, "I have no idea if this is going to work, but shame on us if we don't try." So he wasn't going to put public dollars into it, [but] instead he put his own dollar down first and he was able to say to every other funder . . . "Won't you join me? We're going to do this seriously. It's going to be evaluated, we will learn from this, it has the potential to change public policy here in the US, but I have no idea if it is going to work."[37]

In fashioning their bold experiment, the New York redesign team had no shortage of out-of-town technical assistance at their disposal, not least from the World Bank. But the reservoir of local expertise in program design and delivery was a deep one too. MDRC had been the foremost organization in the evaluation of welfare-to-work demonstration projects in the long lead up to the federal welfare reform of 1996, which in many ways had been propelled by state- and local-level experiments.[38] The large nonprofit agency, Seedco, was likewise a seasoned manager of social programs in the city, with a large and experienced staff and an intimate knowledge of the local political and institutional terrain.

Opportunity NYC officials talked of taking "inspiration" from Mexico, and learning from the CCT "concept," but they were also clear that something rather distinctive was being fashioned in New York. The retooling of the program and its customization to local conditions, however, had to occur within a highly compressed time frame. The mayor wanted to see results quickly, after all. As two of those who worked on the accelerated roll-out of the program explained,

> What we've ultimately designed . . . is our own, unique New York City version of this that takes a great deal of inspiration from what happened [in Mexico]. But it is by no means what you might call a real replication.[39]

The beauty of this is [that] we've taken a concept, a conceptual framework that has worked elsewhere, and tweaked it and applied it to the realities of New York City. Obviously the realities of Mexico and Chile and many other countries that apply this model don't fit in with the realities here. That was our job for a good part of the year, to figure out what those changes should be and how they were going to be implemented. In ten months [it went] from an idea on some piece of paper, on the back of a napkin—*what if?*—to last Friday we made the first payments to over 1,400 families. It's been an *intense project!*[40]

A colleague noted that there were limits to what could be learned, either from program-administration counterparts in Mexico or from technical-assistance experts at the World Bank, due to the fact that "their expertise comes from their experience abroad. They were the go-to people in terms of information gathering, what models are abroad, and what might be tried here. But they are not experts in the types of poverty we face here."[41]

Addressing this would be New York City's very own "intense project," to reiterate the words of one of the local program managers. Even if Opportunity NYC was somewhat insulated from "outside" influences, from the multilayered advocacy community in the city, its rapid-fire design process nevertheless did fall prey to political maneuvering across the various departments of city hall. As one program manager put it, "Every Tom, Dick, and Harry came out of the woodwork with a conditionality. So we ended up with all these conditionalities—it was a political process."[42] It was a political process, in fact, that burdened the program early on with an administratively complex incentive structure—reflected in the long and finely targeted schedule of qualifying payments (see Figure 3)—which caused many of the professional evaluators involved to "worry privately that ONYC [was] too complicated."[43] Some of the lessons of this multivariate experiment, they feared, might be lost, especially as these were soon being compounded by the program's "extraordinarily rapid start-up and early administrative challenges."[44] These concerns were echoed by a World Bank official closely involved in the early development of the program:

There is the potential of learning a lot from New York. . . . My only concern . . . is that there are *so many* domains, and they are incentivizing *so many* things, that it's going to be very hard to disentangle what was behind the results that were observed. . . . If I could wave a magic wand I would give them another

year and more breathing room. So many eyes are on New York right now, and
it's a complicated program. . . . There is going to be a lot of pressure on them to
come out with results quickly.[45]

What would transform Opportunity NYC from an intriguing experiment to
a next-generation CCT model, many believed, would be compelling evaluation results. "[C]lear, positive results would give the policy a clear boost,"
Lawrence Aber speculated.[46] Not only would this generate the momentum
for this pioneering urban CCT to leapfrog to other jurisdictions, it would
also pave the way for taking the initiative "to scale"—as a full-fledged antipoverty effort, rather than a pilot program aimed at a few thousand families.
As a commission member commented, "If we can collectively prove that
certain strategies work, it makes it harder to ignore them. That can help the
funding stream continue."[47]

One reason why there were "so many eyes on New York" was that the
results of its CCT experiment might be parlayed into a number of emerging
policy discussions. One involved other cities in the United States, especially
as speculation began to build about new initiatives in urban, social, health
care, and education policy by the first-term Obama administration.[48] The
Rockefeller Foundation, which had been investing in a number of dissemination initiatives around Opportunity NYC, had established a "learning network" involving a number of interested cities from across the United States,
including Los Angeles, Chicago, and Washington, D.C., in parallel with the
rollout of the pilot. And the multilateral agencies, along with CCT policy
networks in Latin America and elsewhere, were especially attuned to what
the New York experiment might reveal about the viability of these programs
in big cities. As a leading World Bank policy advocate observed,

> When we brought New York City in, it was really about "What can we learn
> from the New York program vis-à-vis operating in urban centers with multiple
> programs?" . . . A lot of the programs in Latin America started in rural areas
> and are now moving into urban areas, and it's a completely different dynamic.
> Labor-market dimensions are very different, the targeting is different, what
> might be reasonably required [is] different . . . [as are] benefit levels. So that's
> one of the new frontiers. New York is interesting to a lot of people not only
> with this urban question but also because they have a labor-market dimension
> to their program.[49]

New York City therefore occupied a dual position in the moving landscape of CCT policy innovation. In some respects, it was a "late adaptor," riding the coattails of a policy movement that had been (hyper)active in Latin America for more than a decade. At the same time, New York was being styled, as the "new frontier," as a test site for the extension of the program into the field of employment incentives, into administratively congested, "service-rich" urban areas, and into the Global North.

Even before Opportunity NYC's first operational year was complete— as an experimental pilot program, it must be remembered—New York was showing signs of growing into this immodest role, as a next-generation model. This was on display when the inaugural meeting of the Inter-American Social Protection Network was held in New York City, in September 2009. The event's keynote panel featured contributions from U.S. secretary of state Hillary Clinton, Chilean president Michelle Bachelet, president of the Inter-American Development Bank Alberto Moreno, and Mayor Bloomberg, in front of an audience of senior officials, evaluators, and policy advocates from all of the major multilateral agencies with an interest in the region, from most of its national governments, and from the private and nonprofit sectors. Secretary Clinton was appropriately diplomatic in spreading the credit, but also took the opportunity to single out New York's potentially scene-stealing contribution:

> New York City, of course, is a crossroads for the entire world. And the first conditional cash transfer program in the United States was launched by Mayor Bloomberg after he saw for himself the results in Mexico. Millions of Mexican families have gotten a boost toward better education, health, nutrition, long-term stability. Opportunity NYC intends to do the same for the poor within our own city. . . . If you look at what has been happening in the social development arena in Latin America, we have a story to tell. . . . We've seen, in remote villages and big cities alike, governments experimenting with innovative approaches to fighting poverty. Conditional cash transfer programs are one example of this wave of innovation right here in our hemisphere. . . . Now we know these are not, as they say, a silver bullet. They don't work in every country, in every community, on every count. But in many places, they are working. . . . I'm very proud that it's New York City which is pioneering this approach in our country. I had eight wonderful years representing this city and this state. And if it can make it here, it can make it anywhere, Mr. Mayor.[50]

Mayor Bloomberg's response was no less gracious, in the company of such distinguished visitors from the Global South, reiterating his conviction that only results would make the difference, no matter how appealing the business case. The studied posture here was that of the rigorous experimenter:

> When we studied the program that met with so much success in rural Mexico, we asked ourselves: How could we adapt it to work in an urban setting like New York City? To find out, we raised private funding and began a . . . pilot program [that will] enable us to have a more robust picture of the long-term viability of Conditional Cash Transfers for cities in the United States. . . . Opportunity NYC is just one of 40 new poverty-fighting strategies that our Administration has launched over the past three years. But it's one of our boldest and many people are anxious to see how we do. . . . Not every new program that we try is going to be successful, but if we are serious about breaking the cycle of poverty and reducing the disparity between rich and poor that, unfortunately, is wider in our hemisphere than in any other place on Earth, we must be unafraid to test new approaches rigorously, fully prepared to discard those that don't do the job, and willing to share with our neighbors the ones that do.[51]

Bloomberg was able to share with his audience the earliest of early findings from the five-year evaluation of Opportunity NYC, which he interpreted as promising, indeed "positive trends." School attendance was marginally up amongst the treatment group in MDRC's randomized trial, as was enrollment for statewide examinations. On a panel presentation later in the day, in the session "Sharing experience: same goal, different realities," Deputy Mayor Linda Gibbs elaborated on this cautiously optimistic line, crediting her Mexican colleagues with "establish[ing] the empirical foundation to support replication" of CCT programs, the contribution of the "learning exchange" that they had subsequently constructed, and the inputs of experts at the World Bank and elsewhere. The long-range goal, however, continued to be that of taking the program to fully operational scale in the United States—very much a domestic challenge. "If [the] early evaluation results are promising, CEO will advocate for federal policy change and promote program changes that reflect lessons learned from the Opportunity NYC experiment."[52] To meet this challenge, New York officials would have to continue, studiously, to measure and market their bold experiment. Opportunity NYC may have been "modeled on [the] Mexican experience," as the glossy report on the event observed on its front page,[53] but a model, as yet, it was not. Neither was it attached to sustainable local, state, or federal funding supply lines, though Bloomberg's wager was that this might change should Oportunidades North capture enough limelight, emerging as a second-generation model in its own right.

## Maquila Social Policy?

Mexico's *maquila* zone is a wide belt of export-processing factories, located mostly in the north of the country. The *maquila* factories enjoy tax- and duty-free status, enabling them to import raw materials, intermediate products, and machinery, taking advantage of low labor costs to process and assemble final products, often in combination with "imported" managerial and technical expertise. Originally, *maquilas* mainly served export (or re-export) markets in the United States, but since NAFTA they have been allowed to service domestic markets in Mexico. A policymaking analogy, borrowing the *maquila* metaphor, would likewise call attention to such "reassembly" functions locating individual sites within extended chains (or webs) of production.[54] Should PROGRESA/Oportunidades be understood in such terms, or does it instead represent an endogenous development, a Mexican "original," as much of the official discourse around CCTs would suggest?

The origins of the Mexican CCT program lay in the turbulent events of 1994—the year that began with the passage of NAFTA and the ascendancy of the Zapatistas, witnessed the assassination of two of the most senior politicians from the governing Institutional Revolutionary Party (PRI), and which culminated in the "December mistake," a dramatic devaluation of the peso by the incoming Zedillo administration, plunging the country into economic crisis. A $50 billion aid package, brokered by the Clinton administration, eventually averted Mexico's precipitous economic slide, but not before 6 percent had been removed from the country's GDP during 1995, as the "Tequilla effect" reverberated through the economies of the Southern Cone. In Mexico, the crisis brought sustained reductions in real wages, together with sharp increases in unemployment and informality, as well as a structural expansion of poverty—engulfing more than half the population.[55]

The country's antipoverty programs, known to be flawed and faltering long before the peso crisis, were suddenly the focus of urgent attention. Despite the siege-like atmosphere gripping the new government, one of the cooler heads ultimately prevailed. Santiago Levy, a U.S.-trained econo-mist and newly appointed deputy minister of finance, saw that there was an opportunity "to use the crisis as a motivation for change."[56] Mexico was relying on a rudimentary package of food-subsidy programs to underwrite consumption in low-income households, supplemented by a patchwork of temporary employment, retraining, microcredit, income-transfer, and social-development initiatives. Most notorious among the latter were PRONASOL and PROCAMPO, both of which were marred by corruption, mismanage-ment, and clientelism. These programs were a legacy of the PRI's botched attempt to counterbalance a neoliberal restructuring of the economy, from the mid-1980s onward, with a makeshift form of "welfare machine" politics.[57] PRONASOL was a poorly designed and mistargeted program, which oper-ated as a vehicle for government patronage and as a "social tranquilizer" for the most egregious effects of neoliberal restructuring.[58]

In the wake of the peso crisis, the Zedillo administration faced the chal-lenge of implementing a harsh austerity program in the context of soaring inequality and deepening poverty, and doing so with a package of inherited policies clearly unequal to the task. The country's antipoverty effort had long been underresourced and mismanaged, languishing in disarray in the cities, while barely maintaining "an increasingly miserable status quo in the coun-tryside"; meanwhile, a tokenistic set of labor-market policies had achieved nothing beyond "chip[ping] at the margins."[59] Acknowledging that the "eco-nomic crisis created the immediate motivation for change," Levy neverthe-less maintained that the debate in Zedillo's cabinet paid due attention to the "accumulation of empirical evidence, administrative experience, and ana-lytical arguments" in steering a course toward a step-change reform in anti-poverty policy.[60] The experts were about to take charge. The increasingly technocratic style of decision-making that had accompanied Mexico's neo-liberalization had been further centralized under the economist-president, such that "policy making [became] more efficient, but not more account-able."[61] From the outset, a self-consciously technocratic approach was deemed of "paramount importance" to the advocates of Mexico's CCT program,[62] in order to shield the initiative from political "interference."

Finance Ministry economists had long been critical of the inherited regime of food subsidies for their high administrative costs; for their failure to reach the geographically dispersed, rural poor; and for wastefully underwriting the consumption of the nonpoor, especially in cities.[63] Meanwhile, they were increasingly drawn to a new line of research in behavioral economics, which was moving beyond critiques of welfare dependency and into the realm of household decision-making and the microeconomics of human-capital development. In its explorations of the interaction effects between nutrition, health, family size, education, and economic status, this work had concluded that the explanation for the intergenerational persistence of poverty lay in the risk adversity and truncated planning horizons of poor households. Levy, who had been involved in this work both as an academic economist and as a consultant to various multilateral agencies, was convinced that this called for a new approach, one that would reorganize the incentive structure confronting poor families, encouraging investments in long-term human-capital formation (especially the health and education of children), as opposed to the established pattern of "cling[ing] to small parcels of land."[64] Economist-reformers within the Zedillo administration therefore mobilized more than a compelling institutional rationale for a paradigm shift in antipoverty policy. They also were able to provide what Levy called "the analytical backbone" for their bold reform proposals, drawing on the latest research evidence and a complementary reading of emergent "best practice."[65] This in turn was keyed into the leading front of the "intellectual consensus" among senior economists at the World Bank, IMF, and the Inter-American Development Bank (IDB), with whom top Mexican officials had long enjoyed close professional relationships.[66]

Meanwhile, the urgent social reality was that the Mexican economy had slumped into a crisis-induced recession in a situation in which "there were no effective safety nets in place."[67] And a series of sobering external assessments were concluding that, in the aftermath of the peso crisis, "distributional conflicts have escalated to the extent that they now pose a serious threat to the reform process itself."[68] The Zedillo administration's short-term response was to combine austerity measures with emergency income maintenance for the very poor. Meanwhile, the Finance Ministry worked assiduously on the other side of the "neoliberal equation"—a CCT-style policy package, focused on human-capital development, designed to "boost along the adjustment process."[69] As the principal architect of the reforms explained, "The challenge was to design a rapid short-term response to the crisis with the existing instruments while setting a course toward a medium-term strategy that, aside from protecting the poor from the transitory shock, could foster a sustained increase in their standard of living."[70] This "radical departure from the status quo" may have represented a paradigm shift for Mexico, but it was also a calculated claim to vanguard status within the nascent policy orthodoxy of the multilateral banks.[71] It would seek to crystallize an emergent orthodoxy, based on the principles of conditionality and human-capital development.

The path-breaking CCT program, PROGRESA, launched in 1997, certainly marked a departure. (The program was later renamed Oportunidades, by which it is now generally known.) Replacing, rather than augmenting, the previous package of food-subsidy programs, PROGRESA concretized a qualitative shift in both the means and ends of antipoverty policy. In-kind income subsidies were replaced by direct cash transfers, conditioned on specific behaviors deemed to increase investments in human capital. The microeconomic rationale was that this would restructure opportunity costs for poor families, prone to underinvestment in human capital, without increasing dependency or reducing work effort. There was tacit recognition, in fact, of the limits of pure work enforcement in (rural) poverty alleviation, since evidence showed that the scope to respond to economic stress at the household level was constrained when "all employable family members are already working [such that] their ability to increase their hours worked in hard times is limited."[72] In theory, stabilizing the incomes of such families should allow them to pull their children *out* of the labor market, returning them to school— thus securing long-term growth in human capital. Or so the theory went.

In order to incentivize such rational investments, the program sought to extend freedoms of choice around consumption to poor families, but there was also a neopaternalist gloss: according to PROGRESA's architect, Santiago Levy, "If you want the poor to behave like adults, then you must treat them like adults."[73] As Miguel Székely (Mexico's undersecretary for social development and himself a former IDB economist-researcher) explained, the introduction of PROGRESA had entailed a series of "paradigm shifts," for policymakers, politicians, and program participants. The idea of direct cash transfers to the poor had "scandalized" many observers, Székely recalled,[74] given the country's sordid history of corruption and clientelism. But by outsourcing the cash payment system to banks and telegraph companies, by establishing a lean central administration,[75] insulated from immediate political pressures, and by maintaining a high degree of transparency with respect to financial transfers and program rules, PROGRESA sought explicitly to break with past practice.

A defining feature of PROGRESA, consistent with its performatively experimental status, was a quite unprecedented commitment to "independent evaluation," from the earliest stages of the program's implementation.[76] Robust evaluation findings, it was claimed, would place the program on a firm footing, but crucially, as a form of systematization it would also facilitate the "travel" of lessons from the putatively model program. Arguably a calculated risk, this marked a radical departure for the country, for the wider region, and in some respects for social policy in global terms. The new program was pitched as a beneficiary of the latest research evidence, to which it would reciprocally contribute by way of a state-of-the-art randomized trial evaluation. The program rollout and evaluation design were designed in tandem, with a view to securing the integrity of latter, and the process was contracted out to the leading Washington-based evaluation house, the International Food Policy Research Institute (IFPRI). Others, though, have been less inclined to anoint this as a rarified moment in the progression of evaluation science. Critics of PROGRESA called attention to the close ties between the IFPRI researchers and Finance Ministry officials in Mexico City, who are reported to have actively discouraged dissemination of evaluation results within the country itself.[77] Notably, the first presentation of the evaluation results took place not in Mexico, but in Washington, D.C. In some respects, the knowingly leading-edge design and evaluation-cum-promotion of the program were transnational accomplishments from the start.

It was largely on the basis of the extensive and widely disseminated evaluation effort that Oportunidades later secured its reputation as an exemplary and "pioneering" policy, indeed the concrete expression of a "new generation of social programs."[78] According to IFPRI, the program's evaluators, its distinctive features would be stylized as:

- The direct provision of cash benefits (as opposed to the indirect method of food subsidies), paid to mothers rather than through intermediaries or bureaucracies;
- Avoiding "welfare dependency" through a human capital–based method of tackling the intergenerational transmission of poverty;
- Conditioning income transfers on unambiguous and strictly enforced behavioral requirements, applied to all beneficiary households—concerning school attendance; uptake of primary health services; training in nutrition,

hygiene, and family health; compliance with vaccination schedules and nutritional interventions;

- The meticulous targeting and monitoring of households in extreme poverty;
- The integration, from the time of the program's earliest planning, of a state-of-the-art, control-group evaluation.[79]

Often-retold histories of the program celebrate the bold vision and determined leadership of those involved in its original design and authorization, especially Santiago Levy. This said, the initial rollout was cautious. There was a need for political as well as institutional reassurance that the program would work. The real-world validation of PROGRESA's "operational hypothesis," involved discreet field-testing with 31,000 households in the state of Campeche, a location sufficiently isolated from the capital to ensure insulation both from the prying eyes of journalists and from competing interests within the government bureaucracy itself (including opposition from the ministry of social development). Levy recalls that the pilot program for PROGRESA was never publicly announced, its quiet rollout "relatively far from Mexico City" having been intended "not [to] attract too much political attention."[80] As a senior official from the World Bank later reflected,

> Yes, [Levy] was bold and it was also something that he was able to get away with, because it was these remote rural areas! . . . Often when CCTs are introduced today they are huge programs, immediately reaching a lot of people, and rolled out very quickly. They were able—intelligently—in Mexico to start at a pilot level and then to [realize the subsequent] program expansion by building on the evaluation.[81]

Following positive evaluation reports from the field sites, the program was gradually taken to scale. While program delivery was effectively devolved to the community level,[82] its management was strictly centralized, ensuring the standardization of operational rules and consistent treatment of eligible participants, rather like "a kind of social security program."[83] This form of technocratic centralism was vigorously defended by the program's architects, including in the face of concerted opposition from community groups, seeking a wider role in the program's design, development, and governance.[84]

PROGRESA comprised three components. Its educational provisions included monetary grants for each child enrolled in school, conditional on the maintenance of a stable attendance record. (In order to deter premature exits to the labor market, grants were pegged to the child's age and set at a higher rate for girls than boys.) The health component covered basic health care for all members of beneficiary households, with an emphasis on health education and preventive interventions. Finally, the nutrition component comprised a fixed monetary transfer, intended for food consumption, together with nutritional supplements for children and mothers. The total size of cash grants was capped at around US$90 for families with children in primary or secondary school, and US$160 for those with children in high school. Transfers were to be paid directly to women on the grounds that they were deemed more likely to make responsible investments, especially concerning children.

At its peak, 90 percent of PROGRESA funding went to rural areas, compared to 31 percent of equivalent subsidies in 1994, "match[ing] more closely the geographical distribution of poverty."[85] The Zedillo administration's US$1 billion annual budget for PROGRESA was therefore essentially a redistributive transfer to high-poverty rural areas, enabling cash transfers to reach 40 percent of the country's nonurban population. In the short term, this represented a massive—indeed almost certainly crisis-averting—injection into the incomes of millions of rural families. Meanwhile, the negative consequences of this did not go unnoticed in the cities: the withdrawal of tortilla and milk subsidies triggered a series of urban riots in the late 1990s, and marked unease among the political leaders of middle-income states. But despite "some tense times," Zedillo urged his Finance Ministry to "stay the course" with the phase out of food subsidies and the rollout of PROGRESA.[86]

Remarkably, the election of Vicente Fox in December 2000, which ended the seventy-one-year political monopoly of the PRI, did not adversely affect the program. On the contrary, PROGRESA was expanded, including a commitment to serve urban areas. In March 2002, the Fox administration assumed political ownership of the program, renaming it Oportunidades. The program has since become a cornerstone of the social protection system in Mexico, having been sustained through two more presidential transitions (to Felipe Calderón and the Partido Acción Nacional, 2006–2012, followed by a return to the PRI under Enrique Peña Nieto since 2012). Today, the program serves more than 6.5 million families (approaching one third of whom are in cities), which is equivalent to one in three of the national population. The program's US$5.3 billion annual budget accounts for around half of federal antipoverty spending in Mexico.

Crucially, the Fox administration's decision to retain, and indeed to expand, the program was reportedly influenced by the "extremely positive" conclusions from the first phase of evaluations.[87] These claimed:

- Increased school enrollments at all stages, particularly for girls;
- Improved grade progression and lower drop-out rates;
- Significant reductions in child labor;
- Marked improvements in nutrition and preventative health care, especially for young children;
- Improvements in child growth rates and reductions in stunting;
- Improvements in the quality and quantity of food consumed;
- No reduction in adult labor-force participation;
- An enhanced role for women in household decision-making, but also increasing demands on women's time;
- Low administrative costs, by historical and international standards.[88]

Even at this early stage, PROGRESA had "acquir[ed] some international visibility," having been praised by the IDB and the World Bank, and drawing early imitators in Colombia, Jamaica, Honduras, and Argentina, both in terms of program design-cum-philosophy and its accompanying evaluation strategy.[89] The rebranded *Oportunidades* would soon be enjoying the status of the world's "flagship" CCT program, the object of "international acclaim."[90] A model had apparently been made.

## Oportunidades as Joint Venture

When James Wolfensohn stood down as president of the World Bank in July 2006, he followed the well-trodden path to the Brookings Institution, to head the Wolfensohn Center for Development. The Center's mission was to "focus on impact, scaling-up and sustainability of development interventions," by commissioning "rigorous, independent research" and by attempting to bridge "the gap between development theory and practice."[91] One of Wolfensohn's first acts was to appoint Santiago Levy, whom he had previously dispatched on World Bank consulting assignments to Brazil and Egypt, as a visiting fellow of the Center, with a brief to write a book on the PROGRESA/Oportunidades story. In the foreword to the book, Wolfensohn enthused about the potential of this "homegrown" Mexican program as an international development model:

I was . . . very excited when I first encountered [this] innovative program in Mexico [, which] met many of the expectations that I had nurtured regarding successful poverty reduction initiatives: it was homegrown, based on solid economic and social analysis, comprehensive in approach, and sensitive to the institutional and political realities of the country.[92]

Wolfensohn went on to say that the World Bank and other international organizations had "made use of this very impressive and successful Mexican initiative" in assisting other nations, such that more than twenty developing countries had since emulated "programs like Progresa," with many more on the way.

This was a theme that Levy echoed in his moderately candid account of the origins and development of PROGRESA/Oportunidades. Only toward the end of this paean to endogenous policy development does Levy remark, almost in passing, that "[d]uring 1995 and 1996," the World Bank and the IDB "generously provided technical advice on different aspects of the program," going on to explain that

during the initial years of the program, it was not deemed convenient to obtain international funding for the program. In 1996–97 such financing would have added yet one more controversial aspect to what was already a fairly significant change in poverty policy, perhaps giving the impression that the program was the result of a mandate or an adjustment program agreed upon with international financial institutions.[93]

Levy's reticence was well founded. Knowing full well how closely the PROGRESA philosophy reflected ascendant currents in international development orthodoxy, especially among the multilateral banks, his presentation of the program as "homegrown," rather than an "import," had more to do with political calculation than misplaced immodesty. If PROGRESA had been perceived as (just) another chapter in Mexico's "structural adjustment" by multilateral agencies, its fate would surely have been sealed.

Yet Levy and other key officials had maintained a discreet but continuing dialogue with the IDB from the beginning,[94] the bank having provided funds for the evaluation of PROGRESA by way of IFPRI in Washington, D.C. Since 1999, Levy had also been assiduously pursuing a major loan for the program from the IDB, the technocratic culture of which matched that of the Finance Ministry. By cultivating this potential source of financing, and by ensuring that early evaluation results were made available to incoming Fox administration officials, Levy assured the fledgling program's "lock in." The Fox team's initial skepticism was soon converted to active support. In March 2002, the IDB approved the transfer of US$1 billion in development financing for the rebadged Oportunidades over a period of three years—and at the time, the largest poverty-related loan in the bank's history.

A year later, Oportunidades featured as one of the most enthusiastically touted programs at a major World Bank / International Bank for Reconstruction and Development conference on the "scaling up" of poverty alleviation measures.[95] The manual of case studies that established both the inspiration and the coordinates for the conference's "global learning" philosophy affirmed the received origin-story of Oportunidades as a program "conceived and staffed by a group of experienced and highly credentialed government officials [in Mexico]" while crediting its subsequent diffusion to a "rigorous, ongoing evaluation process."[96] The billion-dollar "prize" from the IDB came at the *end* of this sequential success story, the earlier entanglements with multilateral institutions having been conveniently forgotten.

Later that year, Oportunidades was featured as a cover story in the IDB's house magazine, *IDBAmérica,* where the genealogy of this "homegrown" program was once again affirmed: "If the paternity of a social program as large and complex as PROGRESA—now called Oportunidades—could be easily attributed, its fathers would be Santiago Levy and José Gómez de Léon."[97] Gómez de Léon, a demographer and former advisor to President Zedillo, had been PROGRESA's first national coordinator, working closely with Levy on the design and implementation of the program, until his premature death in 2000. It was Gómez de Léon who had perfected the "poverty mapping" system that was a technical prerequisite for the close social and geographical targeting of the program, while Levy controlled the purse strings. Together, these "renowned social scientists were the chief architects of what many observers consider one of the most successful poverty-alleviation programs in Latin American history."[98]

Others, though, have questioned the Mexican paternity of CCT programs. A "systematic review" by economists at the IDB concluded that "CCT programs began a decade ago with the Bolsa Escola program in the outskirts of Brasilia."[99] Delivered by municipal authorities and beginning in 1995, Bolsa Escola had transferred modest cash allowances to low-income families living around Brazil's federal capital, conditional on school attendance of children under sixteen.[100] Later expanded to other urban areas, and eventually federalized in 2001, Bolsa Escola exhibited the dual rationale that would become a defining characteristic of CCT programs—short-term cash assistance together with longer-term human-capital formation.[101] Another Brazilian CCT program, PETI, was established the following year, also conditioning payments on school attendance, but in this case targeted on the displacement of egregious forms of child labor.[102] Subsequently, these and other localized CCT-style programs were consolidated by the Lula administration in 2003 into Bolsa Família, the flagship social program in Brazil's "Zero Hunger" initiative. The World Bank was closely involved in the redesign and reorganization of this program throughout this somewhat turbulent transitional phase, providing "high-level dialogue [together with] analytic and advisory support," along with a targeted loan of US$6.2 billion, setting another record.[103] The sprawling network of Brazilian CCT programs was initially beset by implementation and management problems, in contrast to the relatively surefooted and centrally coordinated rollout of PROGRESA. More positive evaluations, however, have followed the consolidation and rationalization of Bolsa Família.[104]

Having started out "hesitatingly and somewhat chaotically," CCT development has occurred at a galloping pace since the consolidation of Bolsa Família in 2003.[105] Now the largest CCT program in the world, Bolsa Família was reaching nine million families by 2006, rising to twelve million in 2009, and then to almost fifteen million in 2013, at which point it was well over twice the size of Oportunidades. In comparison with the pristine reputation of Oportunidades, however, Bolsa Família has long been seen by evaluators and advocates as something of a Cinderella program. World Bank documentation on Bolsa Família frequently cites lessons from PROGRESA/Oportunidades, noting that the Bank has "acquired considerable technical expertise around the world in strengthening targeting systems, developing monitoring and evaluation systems for conditional cash transfers, and in promoting the types of institutional innovations envisaged for the [program]."[106]

In marked contrast, the official history of PROGRESA/Oportunidades makes light, quite deliberately, of both international experiences and historical precedents; political sensitivities around loan conditionalities and Washington expertise meant that these outside influences were only acknowledged belatedly.[107] During the period when it was deemed politically "inconvenient" to be seen to be drawing on multilateral financing for Mexico's antipoverty programs (1995–2001), channels of expert communication remained open to the World Bank and the IDB, reflecting "personal relations" and "trust" with key figures in both the Zedillo and Fox administrations.[108] Neither is there any mention, in the otherwise-exhaustive accounts of the origins of PROGRESA,[109] of the Mexican government delegation that visited Brazil in 1996 on a fact-finding tour of municipal Bolsa Escola programs.[110] This early sighting has been airbrushed out of received accounts of the program's "invention" in Mexico.

There is consequently some justice in the *Economist*'s decision to share the credit for the invention of CCTs, which it hailed in a lead article as an "idea [that] seems to work," between the two countries: "CCTs are a Brazilian invention[, though] the first large-scale program began in Mexico."[111] Nevertheless, while Santiago Levy and his colleagues may have had to travel to Brazil to witness the first operational CCT program, they certainly did not discover its philosophy in the backstreets of Brasilia. In fact, Levy's advocacy of CCT-like policies can be traced back at least as far as those of his fellow economists, Cristovam Buarque and José Márcio Camargo, in Brazil. Camargo first set out the case for a CCT program late in 1991. But earlier that same year, Levy—then on the faculty at Boston University—had produced a report for the Latin American and Caribbean Operations Department of the World Bank, which praised the "impressive changes" in the management of Mexican macroeconomic policy since the mid-1980s (liberalization of trade and foreign direct investment, privatization, tax reform, deregulating swathes of the domestic economy), while outlining a

> strong case for direct targeting of benefits only to the extremely poor. Such benefits should be administered under a single program that simultaneously delivers food (through coupons rather than price subsidies), preventive health services, and education hygiene, birth control, and food preparation and conservation. Food pricing policies should be divorced from poverty considerations. A poverty program for the extremely poor should direct its efforts at reducing fertility, morbidity, undernutrition, and infant mortality.[112]

Making the case for CCTs in all but name, the report attacked the inherent "urban bias" in existing social policy and subsidy programs, countering that the "root cause of poverty in Mexico lies in the rural areas," where a series of distortions in labor markets and dysfunctional behavioral responses on the part of the (extremely) poor were entrenching poverty and impeding human-capital formation.[113]

Correspondingly, Levy argued that an appropriate policy response must be carefully calibrated and tightly targeted, so as to minimize the risk of governmental overreach and the "leakage" of benefits to the nonpoor (including the "moderately poor"), while "avoid[ing] the creation of a class of 'welfare dependents.'" More than six years before the launch of PROGRESA, this less-than-game-changing approach was already understood, by Levy himself, to be "congruent with the overall direction that economic policy has taken over the last few years." At this early stage, it was clearly understood that the economic *and political* rationale for "a high-visibility program [was that of] strengthening the social consensus behind other structural changes [while] showing that such changes will not be allowed to *increase* poverty."[114]

More particularly, Levy's analysis was congruent with the emergent consensus on the role and rationale of antipoverty efforts across the multilateral agencies, where the 1980s' concern with compensatory "safety net" provisions was evolving into a more developmental "social protection" model, albeit with a continuing emphasis on human capital.[115] Levy himself had spent most of the 1980s in this milieu, having periodically worked as a consultant and technical expert for the IDB, OECD, ILO, and UNDP, culminating in two extended spells as a visiting researcher at the World Bank between 1990 and 1992. This was, in many ways, a watershed period for the "Washington Consensus" agencies,[116] marked by a growing awareness that an evolving package of neoliberal reform measures had coalesced into a de facto policy consensus,[117] albeit with a mounting recognition that, too often, the favored macroeconomic recipe was associated with worrisome social externalities, including the intensification of inequality and poverty.[118] These themes, which animated Levy's work at, and for, the World Bank in the first half of the 1990s,[119] would be portrayed as "state of the art" thinking by the time of the planning stage for PROGRESA.[120] In analytical terms, this reflected the positive impact of Amartya Sen's "capabilities" approach, coupled with an acknowledgement of overreach in neoliberal critiques of antipoverty efforts during the 1980s.[121] It also found expression in the World Bank's embrace of the dual objectives of market-oriented growth and "enabling" investments in the human capital of the poor.[122]

The "consensus" in antipoverty policymaking and development economics to which Levy would later refer can be seen to have established the preconditions, if not the very terms, for PROGRESA and the new generation of

CCT-style programs that followed in its wake.[123] Such "adjustments to adjustment" thinking within the Washington Consensus institutions *prefigured* the ostensibly endogenous growth of CCT programming in the mid-1990s, no matter what later rounds of revisionist historiography have asserted. Certainly, there are strong indigenous currents in such policymaking, but both the broad philosophical direction and many of the specific programming routines reflect what—from its origins—was a project embedded in *transnational* policy networks and circuits. The CCT policy paradigm itself, in fact, should be regarded as a transnational phenomenon. As Yaschine aptly puts it, PROGRESA may have been "the outcome of national design, but [it] was also influenced by the ideological ties that its designer had with the World Bank."[124] Indeed, a cadre of Mexican economist-technocrats were active coproducers of the policy consensus at the multilateral agencies.

In light of the false starts and tangled history of the Brazilian CCT programs, in the final analysis it is Mexico's PROGRESA/Oportunidades that stands alone as the most pristine and celebrated case of CCT policy formation. Thanks, above all, to its "technically rigorous impact evaluation," the Mexican program defines the point of origin for what has since been characterized by the World Bank as a "widespread social experiment."[125] The experimental evaluation design that enveloped PROGRESA at the start was conceived in such a way that the program could be scaled up (serving several million families through a lean administrative structure) and scaled out (first to Mexican cities, and then beyond). This transnational experiment in social policymaking has been a joint venture all along. It was "made" neither in Washington, D.C., nor in Mexico City, in a unilateral sense, but emerged dialogically between these and other sites, as currents in (late) "Consensus" thinking cross-pollinated with facilitated experiments. It would be to oversimplify to describe the Mexican CCT experiment as multilateral policymaking by proxy, because propitious conditions and enabling capacities on the ground were essential to the continuing legitimacy of these efforts, just as the evidence of a *working* model would reciprocally shape the course of policy development.

PROGRESA/Oportunidades now stands as the most prominent member of a large and growing family of CCT programs, which have not only family resemblances but also family *connections,* often facilitated by the expert networks, financial relationships, and practitioner communities of the multilateral agencies. The "social experiment" having been duly propagated, the received view in Washington is that, according to the World Bank's Laura Rawlings, while the challenges of "translat[ing] the initial successful experience of a handful of programs ... into generalizable lessons, applicable under a variety of circumstances" are certainly very real, the seductive, technocratic possibility remains that "much of the success of CCT programs [is] not intrinsic to the [specific] program model, but [is] instead attributable to sound technical design and creative innovations that could easily be incorporated into other programs."[126] This, in other words, is a *generalizable* model. Less than two years later, this same World Bank official would be pressing the case for CCTs in New York City. But would "success" itself travel too? Hillary Clinton's quip "if it can make it here, it can make it anywhere,"[127] would come to have an ironic echo, as Mayor Bloomberg's heavily bankrolled experiment began to yield some unexpected results. This can be read as a confirmation that there are no hard-and-fast rules governing the reproduction of traveling policy models, even when these are sanctioned by the most powerful global agencies. Opportunity NYC would prove to be a(nother) conjuncturally specific moment in the ongoing reconstruction of a social-policy consensus, realized not through fiat but on the uncertain terrain of transnational "experimentality."[128]

## New York Learns a Lesson

When Mayor Bloomberg went out to BronxWorks, one of the nonprofit agencies charged with the delivery of Opportunity NYC, to speak at the launch of MDRC's first major evaluation report on the program, there was anticipation in the air. After all, it was only a few months before that the mayor had been touting preliminary indicators of the scheme's success with Secretary of State Clinton and fellow leaders of what was then being styled as something like a hemispheric social-policy pact. But soon the mood was to become decidedly subdued. The evaluation results were underwhelming. The silver bullet may not have been a blank, but there certainly had been some misfiring. To the surprise of many observers, the mayor announced what amounted to a fast-policy failure:

> If you never fail, I can tell you, you've never tried new, innovative things. And I don't know that this is a failure. I think it is, some things worked, and some things didn't, and some things the jury is still out on. And anything new you're going to have that diversity of results. . . . You always hope you'll come across a

magic silver bullet, and you never do. If these were simple solutions, somebody would have found them a long time ago. And you make progress incrementally, particularly if you're trying to focus on some of society's biggest problems.[129]

MDRC's evaluation report had revealed outcomes that were mixed, but largely within the parameters typically associated with CCT programs. What had been rebranded the Opportunity NYC Family Rewards program had dispersed $14 million to 2,400 families, at an average of around $6,000 per household over the first two years. These payments had a significant impact on immediate poverty alleviation, with "treatment" families being measurably better off than control-group families, and 33 percent less likely to report food insecurity. Poverty, in other words, had actually been reduced, albeit by way of the commonsensical means of transferring money to poor households, but crucially, the needle was not significantly moved on many of the incentive domains on which so much store had been set and which defined this, practically, as a *conditional* cash transfer and, symbolically, as a social-policy innovation. There had been improvements in the uptake of preventive health services, but most of the educational and employment incentives fell flat. Schooling outcomes were not improved, undermining the program's human-capital building rationale, while treatment-group parents were somewhat *less* likely to be in work, and more likely to be in poorly paid work, than the controls.

For its part, MDRC—an organization that had been in similar situations many times before, through its evaluations of U.S. workfare experiments in the 1990s—was at pains to emphasize that these were only *early* findings from a program barely twenty-four months old, half of which was "a 'start-up' phase during which operational 'kinks' were being worked out." The "extraordinarily rapid" rollout of the program, which was beset by the "challenges of recruiting so many families so quickly," had evidently been driven in accordance with the mayor's political timetable, rather than more practical or operational concerns. As a result, MDRC remained of the view that it was "too soon to draw firm conclusions about the full potential of Family Rewards."[130] The political conclusions, however, had apparently already been drawn, and the administration was clearly backing away from the program. A potential champion of evidence-based policy development had apparently become one of its villains, Bloomberg having set a dubious standard for "how *not* to react to rigorous evaluation," in the words of one commentator.[131]

This said, a wider reading of the program's financial fundamentals suggested that it was unlikely to be sustainable, let alone "scalable."[132] The administrative cost of delivering $14 million in rewards to low-income families had been $10.2 million. The evaluation itself would cost an additional $9.6 million. And there was no sign of significant governmental resources flowing to any scaled-up, and very costly, version of the program.

What was clearly an expensive experiment had failed to deliver the results anticipated by its nongovernmental paymasters. This reawakened concerns that the original design of the intervention may have been at fault, not in the shape of the Mexican prototype but in the circumstances of New York's adaptation. The program's champion in the administration, Linda Gibbs, confessed that far from sharpening and refocusing the incentive structure confronted by poor families, the administratively complex schedule of rewards and requirements concocted in New York may have overwhelmed it: "Too many things, too many details, more to manage in the lives of burdened, busy households. Big lesson for the future? Got to make it a lot more simple."[133] Those that had been here before, like NYU's Lawrence Aber, who had been working on the design of model CCT programs in South Africa, had feared this from the beginning:

> New York was building the aeroplane while flying it. Due to the political imperative of getting the initiative off the ground in time for some short-term results to be ready before Bloomberg left office after his second term, the process of preliminary research to inform the design [of] the intervention before it was evaluated was short-circuited. Some architects [also] admit that ONYC is too complicated.... These shortcomings were NOT the results of stupidity or carelessness: they were the product of rushing to design and mount the effort in real political time and facing real logistical and financial constraints.[134]

Few, if any, policy experiments enjoy the liberty of operating outside of real political time, of course, or in circumstances unburdened by logistical or financial constraints. Fewer still can draw on more than a decade of meticulous evaluation data and carefully codified practice, supplied free of charge. The prospect of Opportunity NYC being revived when the results of its five-year evaluation emerged seemed remote, to say the least, even before Bloomberg's exit from office in late 2013. Having bought himself a third term, Bloomberg had run out of political time. His successor, Bill de Blasio, is unlikely to adopt a "controversial" program, the overhyped potential and subsequent underperformance of which were both very much "owned" by the billionaire mayor.

The forward progress of the CCT experiment in the United States may have been impeded by Bloomberg's inadvertently negative demonstration project, but various forms of lateral diffusion may still be possible. Its post-welfare patina still holds some appeal for Third Way Democrats, even as the Republican Party beats an accelerating retreat from both redistribution and reason. The American CCT experiment lives on, in a modest way, in a series of local experiments, while what is left of the energy from New York has been parlayed into a federally funded demonstration project, the Social Innovation Fund (SIF), the goals of which resonate in various ways with the governing philosophy of the Obama administration—including the embrace of "nudging" interventions and the propagation of market-friendly social-policy prototypes.[135]

The mixed and mediocre evaluation results announced at the BronxWorks press conference cast something of a cloud over the final months of the program, which reached the end of its three-year operational phase in August 2010 (although the MDRC evaluation continued tracking families for an additional two years). The spirits of some program staff were lifted, however, by the award of a federally funded SIF grant in the summer of 2010, in support of the "replication" of five CEO initiatives in partner cities across the United States.[136] Family Rewards, the traveling name for New York's tarnished CCT experiment, would be one of the five programs, to be tested in modified form with six hundred families in Memphis, Tennessee, and with the same number in the Bronx. MDRC would again conduct a five-year randomized evaluation, recruiting a further six hundred families to control groups in the two cities. The pursuit of more positive evaluation results in the Bronx and Memphis could yet confirm a prediction of the original architects of the New York experiment, made at the time of the program's launch: "If this works in New York, it is as likely that it will travel somewhere else as it is that it will be sustained in New York. [Bloomberg] might become a transmitter in other ways."[137]

Mark II of the U.S. variant of the program is utilizing a more streamlined incentive structure, coupled with a Chilean-style adaptation touted by the World Bank, the addition of caseworker support: "Families struggling to achieve the outcomes that earn reward payments [will be able to] get help from staff to try to improve their achievement."[138] In this way, the process of policy bricolage continues: PROGRESA/Oportunidades had been an amalgam of multilateral programming theory and rudimentary experiments from elsewhere, including Brazil; New York had reconstructed the Mexican model to suit local circumstances, but made the mistake of overelaborating the imported model and rushing its implementation; now New York and Memphis would collaborate in stripping down the Opportunity NYC model, augmented with World Bank–approved adaptations from Chile. It is not clear that there ever was a pure "original" here, and neither has there been a singular vector of reform, for all the efforts to fix that through the promotion of Oportunidades. Located at one of many fringes of this experimental web, the SIF program represented yet another hybrid. As the program's documentation sought to (re)explain the policy lineage:

> The original Opportunity NYC *Family Rewards* program was launched in New York City in September 2007 as a special research demonstration project inspired by evidence from a pioneering CCT program in Mexico and a growing number of programs around the world. . . . [The] program . . . produced a number of positive impacts across a range of education, health, and workforce measures, and had some success in reducing current poverty and material hardship. *This suggests that the model, with some strengthening, has the potential to be an important poverty-fighting tool.* In the new SIF initiative, participating cities will test a common program model that builds on the initial New York City experience, while accommodating local variation in the characteristics of the low-income population, the local social service environment, and the local income-support and benefit systems. . . . In contrast to the original [Opportunity NYC] model, the replication will be simpler and offers fewer incentives, making it easier for families to understand. It will also . . . provide families with more proactive staff support and guidance.[139]

Announcing the startup of the program, Memphis mayor A. C. Wharton Jr. praised this "goal-oriented, data-driven initiative," which he hoped would address "the lack of economic empowerment felt by so many people in our city," while Bloomberg welcomed this "new way for New York City's Center for Economic Opportunity to share its most successful pilots with other cities. . . . Great initiatives like Family Rewards in Memphis can benefit from what we've learned in New York, and cities across the country can improve their programs based on Memphis' experience."[140] Having lobbied aggressively to join the multicity experiment, Mayor Wharton was credited for taking a chance on this "daring program," portrayed locally as a "dangling-carrot approach to social ills," in the service of the long-established objective of enabling families to "pull themselves out of poverty."[141] In Memphis, there was certainly a familiar undercurrent of skepticism—about paying the poor for what they should already be doing. Yet perhaps some measure of assurance came with the program's big-city credentials: "Bloomberg said the program is working in his city and should be emulated elsewhere," the local newspaper reported, though its metro columnist may have captured the mood best: "Yes, it's a gimmick, but let's just try it."[142]

# 4

## Globalizing Social-Policy Practice

B efitting Mexico's symbolic status as the anointed birthplace of CCTs, as well as the country's complex entanglement with multilateral policymaking circuits, the city of Puebla was the location for the inaugural international summit for this new generation of antipoverty programs, "the first of its kind to focus on operational and implementation issues related to CCTs."[1] Funded by the World Bank, the 2002 conference brought together program managers and evaluators from eight countries with pioneering CCT programs—Brazil, Columbia, Costa Rica, Honduras, Jamaica, Nicaragua, Turkey, and Mexico. It featured a day-long study tour of two Oportunidades facilities—in effect, a pilgrimage to what was billed as "one of the most successful CCTs in Latin America"—followed by two days of presentations, workshops, and expert dialogue. One of the organizers of the event recalled that "it was only about fifty people and it was really basic [but] we brought some people in who were quite captivated by the idea [of CCTs]."[2] While the focus was pragmatically placed on operational issues pertaining to administrative concerns like accurate beneficiary targeting and the maintenance of payment systems, it was also an early rallying point for the true believers, founding members of what would become the CCT *movement*.

The refinement *and diffusion* of "positive operational practices" was the rationale for the Puebla event, such that delegates were charged with "learn[ing] from one another with the final goal of improving the operation of their programs."[3] Clearly, the principal bankrollers of these experiments, the World Bank and the IDB, had an active interest in this effort, since in one way or another they had provided support—financial and otherwise—to all of the programs represented at the meeting. These were among the first steps in the construction of a transnational community of practice around CCTs—a heterogeneous but nonetheless purposive alliance of funders, evaluators, practitioners, consultants, and political overseers. These CCT pioneers had been learning by doing, with a helping hand from the multilateral agencies, and they were now beginning to learn by sharing, but there was no mistaking the concerted political impetus behind the reform effort. Operational innovations and positive evaluation results were being deployed strategically to spur new thinking around design issues, but the real momentum was coming from above, from national governments in conjunction with the multilateral banks. And more often than not, the imperative (indeed urgency) derived from a social, economic, or food-supply crisis. Acting quickly required readiness, readiness to roll out new (and preapproved) programs with considerable speed. The delegates from Colombia and Jamaica, for example, reported that for their new programs

> it was not possible to complete the pilot phases and to test all of the processes [before the roll out]. Some processes could not be tested completely but had to be implemented at the national level anyway.[4]

At the same time, great store was being set by the need to insulate fledging CCT programs from (partisan) politics of a more disruptive nature. The optimal operating environment was presented as one in which efficient institutional coordination and streamlined procedures for monitoring and sanctioning clients established, in effect, a technocratic shell around the programs—as it had previously in Mexico. Meanwhile, as the conference report stated, "[p]olitics should not be allowed to influence the targeting processes or the registration of beneficiaries, nor should the party in power use the program in its political campaigns."[5] Such is the curiously depoliticized character of post–Washington Consensus social policymaking, in which an approved mode of ameliorative programming is advanced in a highly technocratic manner.[6]

These themes were echoed in the second international conference on CCTs, which took place in São Paulo, Brazil, in 2004, with the support of the World Bank, development agencies from the UK and Germany, and the Washington-based evaluation house, IFPRI. The local hosts were keen to showcase their newly launched Bolsa Família program, which had consolidated a number of earlier schemes into what was being promoted as the centerpiece of President Luiz Inácio Lula da Silva's antipoverty effort. In its first year of operation, Bolsa Família had recruited more than 3.6 million families—in terms of operational scale, already at the shoulder of Oportunidades, which served 4.2 million families at the time—on an expansion path that would soon make it the world's largest CCT program. What had already become clear, however, was that the Brazilians would not be sticking to the World Bank–approved game plan. The information packet circulated to the more than one hundred delegates, which included candid summaries of the vital indicators of seventeen national programs, observed that the decentralized delivery of Bolsa Família may have "made it possible to put into execution a large program in a record time," but this had pushed those municipalities with limited institutional capacity to the point of "collapse," while targeting and eligibility monitoring had not been "applied rigorously."[7] This clearly ran against the grain of World Bank advice, epitomized in the "model" rollout of Oportunidades, to apply targeting and conditionality measures strictly in the context of tight technocratic control in accordance with the protocols of randomized trials.

This orthodox message was reiterated by a Brazilian economist based at the World Bank, Francisco H. G. Ferreira, in the opening session of the conference, whose paean to Oportunidades was organized around the refrain "Complacency is to be avoided." Avoiding complacency meant deliberate targeting, in order to avert the "excessive leakage" of cash transfers to the less-than-extremely poor; it meant the maintenance of a "steady flow of orderly and expected exits" by way of the unstinting application of conditionalities, means-testing, and targeting, so as to preempt a "culture of dependency;" and it meant putting in place a "credible evaluation [as] a program's best advertisement," one based on the preferred method of the randomized trial, which had been shown to "ensure continuity across political cycles."[8] The rapporteurs' summary of the conference recorded that the next presenter, Eduardo Fagnani of the heterodox economics department at the University of Campinas, "did not agree with all of Mr. Ferreira's points." Revealing some of the key lines of dispute in the preceding Brazilian debate around CCTs, Professor Fagnani countered that supply-side incentives would likely make little difference in the absence of sustained economic growth and increased labor demand; with one half of the country's population in poverty, as measured by the minimum wage, the rationale for scrupulous (and costly) targeting was questionable on ethical, let alone technical, grounds, as was the case for policing the boundaries of social programs, which were manifestly too small relative to the scale of the poverty problem; as a result, "CCTs must be seen as part of a broader strategy . . . [including] some universal policies."[9]

These debates—between universal and targeted programs, over degrees of conditionality, and between centralized management and devolved delivery—reverberated through the twenty-five national delegations represented at the conference, most of whom were now operating CCT programs of their own, or were planning to do so. The majority was hewing to the orthodox line of tight management and strict conditionalities, as articulated by the World Bank and IDB, and concretized in the Mexican approach. The Palestinians, for example, had recruited World Bank consultants to design the conditionality and targeting regime for their time-limited safety-net program in the West Bank of Gaza. The Mozambicans, on the other hand, were taking advantage of both aid and technical assistance from the Brazilian agency for international cooperation, ABC, an arrangement that reflected not only Lusophone affinities but the pragmatic and logistical challenges involved in delivering social assistance to a scattered and deeply impoverished population with desperately overstretched services and institutional resources.[10] In fact, both the World Bank and IFPRI had been active in Mozambique since the 1990s, conducting evaluation work that resulted in a major overhaul of the country's rudimentary cash-transfer system.[11] While CCT programming had since expanded, the Mozambican government reportedly remained "ambivalent" about this approach,[12] due to concerns that it might lead to dependency among beneficiaries and also might induce governmental reliance on fickle flows of donor income, given that such programs themselves might become permanent. In this context, the advice that was forthcoming from Brazil was clearly different from that received from the World Bank and its affiliates. As two senior policymakers from Brasilia with experience of these exchanges reflected:

> For a country such as Mozambique, I'm a lot more scared, because . . . they don't have the same capacity . . . sometimes even a sense of inferiority. Things have been shoved down their throat ever since the World Bank came into existence. . . . I would rather not be shoving Bolsa Família down people's throats [as well].[13]

[African policymakers] listened carefully to our way of thinking on condition-alities, but I don't know if they are going to change the way that they are doing it. Things are very different when you talk about Brazil or Chile, and when you think about Mozambique or Zambia. . . . You can't just take this [program] and move it to another place. You have your [own] infrastructure and your way of thinking [about] problems. . . . [Much] depends on where people put the blame [for] poverty.[14]

Warming to the theme of the root causes of poverty, this well-traveled social-policy expert, now based in Brasilia, recalled a residential retreat that he had attended with the architects of Opportunity NYC. What he char-acterized as the American perspective, of individualizing both the causes of poverty and the rationale of policy interventions, was contrasted to the social-rights approach of the Lula Administration: "There are different political cultures in the countries. Who is responsible for poverty? The indi-vidual or the social structure? In Brazil, you have a more European view of this—[poverty is caused by] the lack of opportunities and not just individual choices."[15]

No wonder, then, that it has been the first C of CCTs that has tended to do the dividing, politically speaking. Even though the majority of those attending the Third International Conference on CCTs, in Istanbul in 2006, may have made up their minds on this score, "the dilemma of whether to condition" found its way into the program in the form of a debate between Miguel Székely, an undersecretary for social development in the Mexican government on the pro-CCT side, and Michael Samson, a South African economist, making the case against conditional and targeted programs. Sam-son's skepticism on the principle of conditionality earned a sympathetic hear-ing from some in the audience—including representatives of several of the European development agencies, delegates from several leading international NGOs, and those with affinities to centrist strands in the International Labour Organisation (ILO) and the United Nations Development Program (UNDP). But the majority of delegates, especially those from government agencies and evaluation units in the large number of countries that were implement-ing CCTs, were more concerned with operational, "how-to" questions than such issues of underlying principle. For his part, Samson would later reflect that the jury remained out on the question of conditionalities, even at the end of the Istanbul conference, not least on the grounds that the lopsided

evidence base (which had mostly measured forms and degrees of conditionality, not its presence/absence) remained "insufficient" and inconclusive:

> Conditionalities aim to reinforce the human capital development impact of
> cash transfers, helping to break the inter-generational transmission of poverty
> by improving the child's likelihood of growing up and finding decent work.
> [But they may also] compromise the poverty reduction objective—at least
> in the short run—by penalising the households with reductions in their ben-
> efits. Conditionalities can deprive the poor of freedom to choose appropriate
> services—and to freely make decisions to improve household welfare. Condi-
> tionalities can be expensive, inflexible, and inefficient—in the worst of cases,
> screening out the poorest and most vulnerable. Often the burden of complying
> with conditionalities falls disproportionately on women. Conditionalities can
> undermine the dignity of participants as well as the poverty-reducing impact
> of the programme, and they are potentially stigmatising. Conditionalities can
> also compromise a rights-based approach to social protection.[16]

But even if the majority of the almost four hundred delegates at the Istanbul
conference had (already) bought into the principle of conditionality, there
remained significant differences—both operational and philosophical—
about what it was that the conditions really *meant*, both for program managers and for recipient families. The World Bank's "lessons learned" document
from the meeting called attention to divergent approaches to the "*enforcement* of conditionalities: non-compliance triggers more care from social
workers (Brazil) or quickly causes termination of benefits (Mexico)."[17]

This observation captures what had already become a rather deeply embedded geographical cleavage within the fast-growing world of CCT programming—between soft-conditionalities-with-social-rights under the Brazilian
approach and hard-conditionalities-with-social-obligations as epitomized by
the Mexican model. The World Bank, for its part, continued to favor the latter, sometimes supplemented by the adoption of case-management systems,
as pioneered in Chile. The organization's near omnipresent role, as a source
both of program funding and technical advice, meant that these principles
were echoed in the majority of newly commissioned CCTs. Technocratic
momentum had been achieved. There would not be another international
conference, and therefore no rematch of the Székely/Samson debate, but in
many ways this reflected the success of the World Bank's diffusion project,

certainly not its failure. As one of the conveners of the conference reflected, "It's *so big*! . . . We're not doing [the international conference] any more, largely because it's become so unwieldy. . . . It's so big now that getting everyone together seems almost impossible. . . . But it really does have its own momentum now."[18]

In this chapter, we explore some of the dimensions of this process, of CCTs "going big." While the movement of CCT principles and programming techniques has been extremely fast, while paradigmatic models like Oportunidades have continued to exert various forms of long-distance influence, and while the World Bank and its allies have been proactive, if not hyperactive, in promoting their versions of "best practice" in this field of new-generation social policies, there have been some surprising turns in this less-than-perfect case of globalizing diffusion. We begin, as it were, at the notional "center" of this process, with the World Bank and its strategies for propagating CCTs. We then move to Brazil, where the giant CCT program, Bolsa Família, has been influenced by the World Bank playbook while also departing from it in rather heretical ways. And then we step into the field of South-South policy translations, where the diverse manifestations of cash-transfer programming in locations like Indonesia, Chile, and Namibia tend to resemble patterned—but far from uniform—mutation, rather than diffusion-replication. The chapter ends by returning to the question of the evolving global "compact" on social policy, in which the issue of conditionality remains at the same time hegemonically axial and the subject of insurgent contestation.

## World Bank as Wave Machine

By the time that the World Bank published its "bible" on conditional cash transfers in 2009, it was clear that what the report called "the CCT wave" had acquired truly global proportions. Present in only three countries as recently as 1997 (Mexico, Brazil, and Bangladesh), CCTs would soon be found in more than forty nations, cumulatively reaching tens of millions of beneficiary families (see Figure 4). As the World Bank report proclaimed,

> Countries have been adopting or considering adoption of CCT programs at a
> prodigious rate. Virtually every country in Latin America has such a program.
> Elsewhere, there are large-scale programs in Bangladesh, Indonesia, and Tur-
> key, and pilot programs in Cambodia, Malawi, Morocco, Pakistan, and South

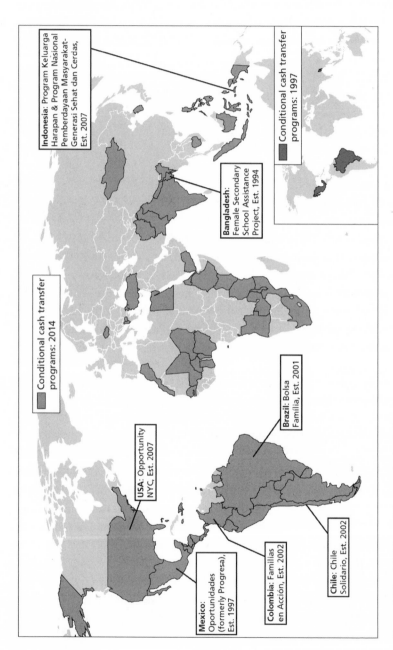

**Indonesia:** Program Keluarga Harapan & Program Nasional Pemberdayaan Masyarakat-Generasi Sehat dan Cerdas, Est. 2007

**Bangladesh:** Female Secondary School Assistance Project, Est. 1994

Conditional cash transfer programs: 1997

Conditional cash transfer programs: 2014

**USA:** Opportunity NYC, Est. 2007

**Mexico:** Oportunidades (formerly Progresa), Est. 1997

**Colombia:** Familias en Acción, Est. 2002

**Brazil:** Bolsa Família, Est. 2001

**Chile:** Chile Solidario, Est. 2002

Figure 4. The CCT "wave." Source: Author's data.

Africa, among others. Interest in programs that seek to use cash to incentivize household investments in child schooling has spread from developing to developed countries—most recently to programs in New York City and Washington, D.C. . . . Interest in and the scope of CCT programs have grown enormously in the last 10 years.[19]

The World Bank has had a hand in CCT experiments in practically every country in which they are found today. If this role was an indirect one at the (politically sensitive) time of the planning of PROGRESA in Mexico,[20] it has been front and center ever since. Indeed, the Bank now positions itself at the "threshold of the global policy debate" on CCTs, summarizing the "consensus" on the theory and practice of antipoverty interventions in the following way.[21] First, CCTs reflect the Bank's recognition that *active* safety-net programs have a legitimate and significant role in "protecting and developing human capital," while opening up pathways out of poverty for "activated" individuals and families. Second, CCTs operationalize the notion that behavioral interventions must be a cornerstone of "postwelfare" social policy, be these positive incentives or corrective nudges. And third, as the most intensively evaluated social programs in history, CCTs epitomize what has been a truly "systemic push to build a strong evidence base on the performance of safety net programs." CCTs, in other words, first anticipated and now crystalize the elite consensus on poverty alleviation. And having first seeded the ideational and technical "supply side" of the CCT concept, the World Bank could now pursue its policy agenda indirectly, through the demonstration effects of such programs, including direct financing.

Santiago Levy's stewardship of the PROGRESA/Oportunidades experiment has acquired almost mythical status in this respect, as the pristine exemplification of these principles constructed, as it were, avant la lettre. The gold standard experimental design of the Mexican CCT intervention is widely credited with not only "bullet proofing" the program with respect to political "interference" but also preparing the ground for the program's scientized marketing and extrajurisdictional replication. In a world of serial underperformance and ambiguous outcomes, PROGRESA proved to be a game-changing intervention. The narrative of a senior economist at the World Bank, summarized below in three episodes, captures the essence of the received account (itself frequently reiterated), and the source of its potency as a "learnable moment" for other policymakers:

It was certainly a very brave decision by Santiago [Levy] and others with him to have this external evaluation. I mean, we're talking about randomized control trials . . . [in 1997]! Nobody was talking about that in the development literature or in the labor literature in the U.S. . . . "We're going to have this nationwide program, and we're going to randomize, and we're going to hire an external [evaluation] firm, and we, the government, are not going to do it." This is just really, just really brave. . . . The Mexican example was hugely influential in that sense.[22]

In this respect, the fact that the infant program survived the transfer of presidential control from the Zedillo to the Fox administration in 2000, which of course represented a momentous transition in political leadership after decades of single-party rule under the PRI, attests both to the power of (positive) evaluation and to the integrity of the original intervention. In the midst of the transition, World Bank economists were summoned to

a high-level briefing with Fox [along with] a handful of other people who had been involved from the beginning in the evaluation of PROGRESA. [The World Bank economist] said, "Look, you'd be crazy to shut this thing down, *it works*! You have no idea about anything else, whether it works or not. This *actually works*." And then Fox said, "OK, let's keep it, [but] rename it and then expand it." Now, I'm sure the story's gotten embellished over time, but I don't think it's entirely apocryphal.[23]

Whether apocryphal or not, the fact that the Fox administration did actually retain, rename, and then ambitiously expand the program, assuming full political ownership of what was to become a permanent feature of the social-policy landscape, does indeed speak volumes—especially to that class of elite decision-makers, in other countries and in the multilateral agencies, that are in a position to greenlight (or otherwise) similar interventions. In an uncertain and unforgiving world, an expert-certified assurance that "it works" can carry considerable weight:

At the [World] Bank, we jump on any evidence there is that something is actually working. . . . For too long we just haven't had any idea of what's working and what isn't, and we've supported things nevertheless. So now we have something, some evidence that it's working. So I think that's part of the explanation [for the rapid diffusion of CCTs]. And countries themselves . . . they're saying, "Gee, this thing seems to be working, seems to be a good idea. Why don't we finance it, let's just borrow money from the Bank." So that seems to be part of what's going on there. [But it's also] one of those development fads. You know how much these things take on a life of their own.[24]

The manner in which CCTs took on "a life of their own," in the wake of the mold-shaping Mexican experiment speaks to the sometimes less-than-edifying *Realpolitik* of transnational policy mobility. Here, the fact that a favored policy model was able to travel with affirmative evaluation evidence had the effect of elevating what often are inescapably political decisions about the design and financing of antipoverty interventions to the heady heights of scientific progress. The programs were also eminently "bankable" in that multilateral funding was almost assured, as long as approved design standards were met.

As the previous chapter revealed, it was *political* decision-makers in New York City that immediately saw the potential of the CCT concept as a policy idea that stood out from the array of shopworn and often blighted alternatives. As a seasoned program evaluator who played a leading role in the PROGRESA experiment from the beginning recalled, "If you just describe it, it just sounds like a really cool idea! [Maybe] it doesn't sound so cool or innovative now, [but back then] we thought, 'Hey, this is genuinely different,' in a way that really caught people's attention."[25] In the final analysis, it was the marriage of this "cool idea" and the adoption of an uncompromising experimental design and positive outcomes that created the foundations for a globalizing "demonstration effect," as this informant continued:

With PROGRESA, not only was the program innovative, but because the Mexicans on the whole did a decent job of implementing it, and the evaluation work was carefully done, you actually created this demonstration effect. . . . There's a very strong demonstration effect, just like with things like microcredit, the Grameen Bank, and others. It's partly the demonstration effect, you know: this doesn't solve all the world's problems but it *works*, it has a demonstrably good effect. There is that element to PROGRESA, and CCTs more generally, which in part explains the dissemination. Part of it is the conceptual idea, but it's also, less glamorously, the demonstration effect in terms of the actual ability to implement the program. . . . Now, in Africa, where you have lots of really poor

people, you have low human-capital outcomes, you have a continent littered
with good intentions but failed interventions of all sorts, there's considerable
interest in actually seeing whether or not these programs can be applied.[26]

What really added to the allure of the CCT model, in this context, is that its
rationale was provocatively positioned, as Aber and Rawlings later put it, at
the very "threshold" of orthodox discourse, both defining and "pushing the
boundaries of the new thinking."[27] While clearly demarcated from welfare-
style interventions, pejoratively styled as mere "handouts" (see Figure 5),
CCTs nevertheless represented a disruptive programming technology in
the sense that they both affirmed and unsettled the received wisdom. The
neoliberal naysayers would complain that cash transfers were bound to sap
the work effort of the poor (already presumed to be lacking), while the redis-
tributed funds would surely be misused (within households already seen to
be prone to dysfunctional decision-making). Typical objections to the logic
of CCT programs reveal something about the grip of such conventional
thinking:

> At the time [of the early discussions around PROGRESA], there was a very
> strong presumption that people would basically drink and smoke away the
> money, and would just sit around under trees and not actually work. If you
> think of that sort of mindset, fifteen years ago, then in fact it was an open ques-
> tion whether or not these cash transfers linked to [specific] behaviors would
> actually have a genuinely positive effect.[28]

> The kinds of things that the people have worried a lot about in the U.S. [con-
> cerned] reductions in adult labor-market participation. . . . But as best as we
> can tell, . . . basically you give people money, and they seem to do sensible
> things with the money. They don't seem to all run off and drink and smoke
> and whatever. And in addition to that, they keep on working much as they
> were before.[29]

With CCTs, policymakers could experiment "safely," without fear of social
pathology or financial overreach. Operating, quite self-consciously, on the
cusp of acceptable thinking, the CCT philosophy effectively agitates the ortho-
doxies of social-assistance and development policy, inducing decision-makers
to engage in what continues to be portrayed as "bold experimentation," while

offering the reassurance of World Bank, and even scientific, approval. And the Bank's formidable research-and-promotion effort clearly demarcates where the innovative frontier is located, both incentivizing and *providing direction to* the transnational reform process.

This explains why the World Bank's urtext on CCTs, which came on the heels of a decade of active program and community building, coupled with billions of dollars of underwriting, should have to take a tortuous detour into post hoc theoretical rationalization, awkwardly attuned to what "[e]conomists might think."[30] This attempt to (re)construct, effectively after the fact, an "economic rationale for conditional cash transfers" plunges into theories of imperfect markets, explores the microfoundations of paternalism and merit goods, confronts the thorny issues of principal-agent problems and suboptimal parenting, and free rides on the legitimacy from Chicago economist and Nobel laureate, James Heckman, before reaching the conclusion that in the less-than-ideal worlds inhabited by the poor, the public, and policymaking elites, the case for CCTs stands:

> Although market-driven economic growth is likely to be the main driver of poverty reduction in most countries, markets cannot do it alone. . . . Although direct cash transfers have opportunity costs (in terms of foregone alternative public investments) and may have some perverse incentive effects on recipients, there is a growing body of evidence to suggest that some such transfers may be both equitable and efficient.

|  | Temporal dimension | Philosophy | Tools | Perceived barriers | Goals |
| --- | --- | --- | --- | --- | --- |
| Traditional | Assistance in times of need | Social responsibility for the poor— "handouts" | Transfers | Culture, dependency | Alleviating poverty, redistribution |
| New | Dynamic, tailored support | Partnership with the poor— "hand up" | Incentive-based transfers | Access to information, incentives | Moving out of poverty, growth, human capital |

Figure 5. Views on social assistance, before and after CCTs. Source: Aber and Rawlings 2011.

> The cash transfer programs that have been growing most rapidly across the developing world over the last decade or so are CCTs. . . . Because attaching a constraint on the behavior of those you are trying to help is an unorthodox idea for economists, [we have] reviewed the conceptual arguments for making cash transfers conditionally.
>
> Essentially, there are two broad sets of arguments for attaching conditions to cash transfers. The first argument applies if private investment in children's human capital is thought to be too low. The second argument applies if political economy reasons mean that there is little [public] support for redistribution, unless it is seen to be conditioned on "good behavior" by the "deserving poor."[31]

The attraction of *conditional* cash transfers, following this logic, is that they mandate human-capital building behavior on the part of poor families, thereby pump priming the economic independence of the rising generation, while sending a clear signal to politicians and to the taxpaying public that social assistance implies a targeted and temporary social contract, in which poor families reciprocate by actively investing in their own long-term advancement out of poverty rather than accepting "something for nothing."

This rendering of the microeconomics of paternalism strongly echoes the original rationale for PROGRESA/Oportunidades,[32] which in a circular fashion is repeatedly invoked by the World Bank as a source of real-world verification. So while an orthodox economist might be expected to blanch at the thought of the state intervening to direct households how to spend their money—even poor households—this might be forgiven if the status quo was deemed even less defensible: "Proponents of the pioneering Oportunidades CCT program explicitly couched the initiative as an alternative to the electricity and tortilla subsidies, in a way that would be both more equitable (by reaching the poor) and more efficient (by eliminating the price distortions generated by the subsidies)."[33] Oportunidades was also credited with the innovation of operationalizing the concept of "coresponsibility," both as a means of legitimating the program among taxpayers wary of "handouts" to the "lazy or careless" and as a way to target those among the "deserving poor" prepared to take the necessary steps to "improve their lives."[34] Again, the World Bank's economists cited Santiago Levy as the authoritative source of this insight: "Shared responsibility and respect inevitably imply a reciprocal effort by the poor families to link the benefits they receive to concrete actions on their part," Levy and Rodríguez had earlier argued, maintaining that "independently of technical considerations . . . it was considered vital that PROGRESA benefits go directly to poor families and be conditioned on direct action by them to improve their own nutrition, health and education, and that such support complement but not substitute for their day-to-day efforts."[35]

These formulations position CCTs, and especially the paradigm-defining Mexican program, at the heart of an emergent postwelfare orthodoxy. They open up the space for discussing social safety nets and certain kinds of (targeted) redistributive spending, but do so on the terrain of active, targeted, human-capital oriented interventions. The World Bank circulates a decision tree, reproduced at Figure 6, designed to enable policymakers to respond rapidly to circumstances where cash-transfer interventions may be needed, connecting key decisions to basic design features, the logic of which reproduces

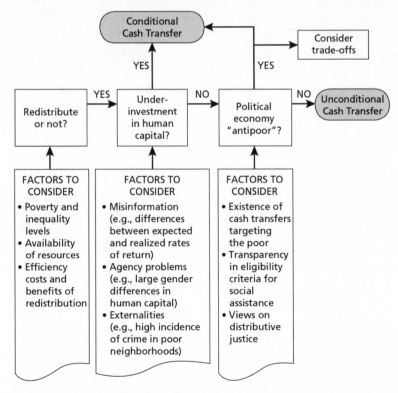

Figure 6. Conditionality first: a World Bank decision tree. Source: Fiszbein et al. 2009.

a preference for conditional over unconditional programs. The pattern of program-evaluation evidence also tends to favor conditional interventions, which at the same time tend to be the locus of World Bank "advice." As Figure 7 illustrates, the evaluation optic of the Bank, as well as its resource commitments, have been trained on CCTs. These programs have duly become part of standard governmental repertoires in the context of crisis situations.

No recent event has tested the strength of this would-be programming orthodoxy as sternly as the 2008–2009 global financial crisis. The World Bank's position has been that countries that had comprehensive CCT programs in place were, on balance, better prepared to weather the effects of the crisis than those without them, even though these "instruments [were designed] to address long-term, structural poverty rather than sudden income shocks," and as such were "not an ideal instrument for dealing with transient poverty."[36] Administratively complex CCTs, the Bank's economists pointed out, were not designed either to enroll or to discharge beneficiaries quickly, as short-term economic conditions changed, and their rationale was not simply to alleviate immediate poverty by way of cash transfers, but to realign behavior around long-term investments. (For these reasons, they averred, temporary workfare programs represented the most appropriate policy response to cyclical downturns.) On the other hand, the technical capacity embedded in CCT staff and systems could be of considerable value

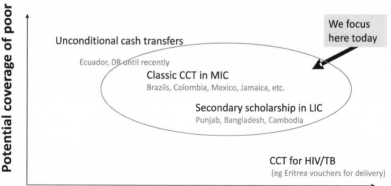

Figure 7. The World Bank's evaluation optic. Source: Grosh 2011.

in "risk management," as long as it was made quite clear that any increases in benefits or in coverage were only temporary, and that they would be scaled back to "pre-crisis levels" as soon as economic conditions improved.[37]

What was sacrosanct, in other words, was the anti-dependency logic enshrined in CCTs, a philosophy that Mexican president Felipe Calderón was to impeccably echo as his administration struggled to manage the effects of the global downturn on the Oportunidades program. The crisis would not, he insisted, be used as an excuse to abandon the country's poor to their fate, but those who had "managed to improve their levels of well-being" had earned the right to continuing support, even at a time of extreme budgetary pressure:

> The path we have followed in social policy, under equal conditions, ceteris paribus, as the scientists say, is the right social policy. . . . [Oportunidades] is a program that is a long way from being either paternalistic or welfare-based. The point is not to give away money, particularly not in exchange for electoral support, but rather to support income, accompanied by the responsibility of the beneficiary family to take its children to school and the doctor, and to attend courses on nutrition and improving family life.[38]

There had been some speculation that the economic crisis would force the Mexican authorities to relax the program's (signature) emphasis on strict conditionalities in the interest of rapid enrollment and short-term poverty alleviation, but the Calderón administration's cool-headed technocrats stayed the course. This apparently came, however, at the expense of the *country's* dependency, as an additional injection of $1.25 billion was to be approved by the World Bank (taking the agency's total stake in Oportunidades to $3 billion), ostensibly as a counter-cyclical measure. In approving the loan, the Bank's executive directors commended the "demonstrated measurable development impact" of the program, and the "importance of Bank support to facilitate South-South and South-North learning opportunities presented by the project."[39]

## "We Did Not Make an Experiment"

Brazil is different. In the world of CCT programming, the country manages, simultaneously, to be globally conspicuous and something of an outlier. One of the more undisciplined CCT programs, Bolsa Família bends the rules. This is a story less of technocratic surefootedness, more of social urgency and institutional improvisation. As a well-traveled ministerial advisor explained, the fundamental difference between his country's experience with conditional cash transfers and those of Mexico or New York City was that, "We did not make an experiment. We did not wait for the good conditions. We had an issue—which was extreme poverty and hunger—and the political choice was to make [Bolsa Família] happen as soon as it can. So it happened, on a large scale."[40]

While there is no single narrative of Bolsa Família in Brazil, this observation is not untypical of the tenor of discussions around the program. In the words of a senior administrator in the federal government, "It is a program still 'in dispute,' even inside the Ministry [of Social Development]. We have at least three different views on what the program is, and on what the program should evolve to be."[41] Within this plurality of views—in which some see Bolsa Família as a stepping stone to a basic income, while others press for its "Mexicanization" through the tightening of conditionalities; then there are those who dismiss the initiative as little more than vote-buying on the part of the ruling Workers' Party (PT), while others promote it as a platform for transformative social change—there is, however, at least one notable silence. While among the program's many advocates and supporters there is certainly pride in what has been accomplished both with and by Bolsa Família, there is very little of the technocratic triumphalism that surrounds Oportunidades, and not much of the managerialist hubris that has been associated with some of its transplants.

An apt illustration of this distinctive policymaking culture is that (even) the World Bank's definitive report on Bolsa Família studiously avoided either overselling or oversimplifying the program, an attitude conveyed in the unassuming title, "The Nuts and Bolts of Brazil's Bolsa Família Program: Implementing Conditional Cash Transfers in a Decentralized Context."[42] As one of the key figures in the CCT evaluation scene reflected, "'Nuts and bolts' was kind of self-effacing. 'We're just putting the thing together, and this is how it basically works.' There was no Model, *capital-M*, selling of it."[43] The usual deference to the technical integrity of CCTs as a mobile social-policy intervention is almost entirely absent from this telling, which instead takes full account of Bolsa Família's endogenous roots, which stretch back as far as national debates in the late 1980s and a subsequent crop of municipal initiatives, while accounting for its subsequent, sometimes scrappy development in terms of an unfolding "*reform* program."

Rather than some pristine experiment, rolled out in the context of technical supervision and meticulous monitoring, the launch of Bolsa Família involved the absorption and integration of a series of preexisting schemes at the federal and municipal levels,[44] establishing an administrative and financial framework under which these could be reorganized and expanded into a national program. It would be necessary to strike joint management agreements with every one of Brazil's 5,564 autonomous municipalities, while building (and then managing) a vast household registration system (the *cadastro único*), all at a speed determined more by political imperative than by administrative feasibility.[45] This was a process that the World Bank's technical assistance team, for all their expertise in accelerated system building, found themselves following rather than leading:

> The World Bank is honored to have had the opportunity to serve as partners to the Bolsa Família Program, and the team would like to acknowledge our appreciation of the long-standing support and collaboration provided by officials in Brazil's Ministry of Social Development (MDS). We are consistently impressed by their dedication, professionalism and technical excellence. They have truly been "running a marathon at a sprinter's pace" in the design and implementation of the [Bolsa Família program], and we appreciate their patience in helping us try to "keep up" with them.[46]

Keeping up with the Brazilians, however, was really only part of the story. It is indisputably true that Bolsa Família was driven to scale at breakneck speed—"expansion, expansion, expansion, expansion," was how one close observer characterized the rollout.[47] It rapidly became the largest program in the world, more than doubling in size again soon after that, and eventually reaching almost fifteen million families.

It is not to question the competence of Brazilian policymakers to observe that it was reassuring to have the World Bank at their back (and with their own interest in seeing the program succeed) during this challenging time. But there was much more to this relationship than political hand-holding and technical assurance. Clearly, Brazil did not need to go to the World Bank or the other multilateral agencies to learn how CCTs work, because in their own way they had pioneered these very interventions. Nevertheless, the policy conversation has in many respects become *increasingly* symbiotic and truly dialogic over time, as the World Bank has had to acknowledge Brazil's achievement, even as it has diverged from Mexico's paradigmatic path, and as Brazil has also sought to place its homegrown model into international circulation. One of the architects of Bolsa Família described an iterative process of multiscalar development, which only later in its evolution had moved towards "coherence":

> The story of the CCT in Brazil [is different from] the story of the CCT coming from outside Brazil. You have these two streams, which united from the mid-1990s on. The story really began here in the early 1990s with the minimum income discussion, [so first] you have the state and local experiences in Brazil [that] inspired the federal government to do the same thing. . . . Then you had the role of the international organizations diffusing this idea all over the world. . . . This model has been translated in Brazil in a way that is particular, because we have our context. From 2006 on, that's when the program really arrived. The program has coherence with the [generic] CCT model [now], but it has been built in Brazil.[48]

Claims to exceptionalism, of course, should not all be taken at face value. "The Brazilians would say they had their program before the Mexicans, [but] it just didn't get the publicity," a U.S.-based program evaluator commented,[49] albeit with an important qualifier: "I'm not sure the Brazilians would be willing to admit that they learned from PROGRESA." It is a poorly kept secret that Santiago Levy was present at a high-level meeting between President Lula and World Bank president James Wolfensohn, on the eve of the announcement that Bolsa Família would become Brazil's flagship social-policy program.[50] The Bank, by all accounts, was keen to see some variant of the CCT model adopted as the framework for Lula's antipoverty program, urging him to work with the inheritance of the Bolsa schemes and the earlier wave of municipal efforts. It was also keen to have a presence in Brazil, as a senior Bank official candidly recalled, "We played a very behind-the-scenes, technical role. . . . We provided support in a very quiet, behind-the-scenes way. And we always were careful. If we ever interacted with the press we did it with respect. It's their program, you know. It's *their* program. It's not a World Bank program. . . . That was an important part of our partnership [, which involved the] building of trust and respect over time."[51]

The idea of a scaled-up Bolsa Família as a "unifying" program had been a current in Brazilian discussions for some years, although it must also have been tempting for the Lula Administration to underline the distinctiveness of the defining zero-hunger commitment by making a clean break with a "new" and baggage-free initiative. A close observer of this process maintained that the multilateral agencies "have never been influential in the decision-making" in Brasilia, not least because "the local [CCT] programs were created without even the knowledge of the World Bank," but the political calculus was soon to change:

> Once it came to the federal level, of course the World Bank had a dialogue with the Brazilian government.... Once Bolsa Família was created ... somebody said, "Look, we're a leftist government. We're going to get criticized for doing this ... So let's see if we can get them on board to give us more legitimacy." And the World Bank was very anxious to get in on this, because by that time CCTs were a big thing, and the Brazilian CCT was going to be the biggest on the planet.... There was some discomfort in the beginning. They were strange bedfellows: a rightist multilateral organization [and] a leftist government, but it was a partnership that worked well for both. The World Bank could say that it was involved in Bolsa Família, and in a few things they did help out, in the sense of giving advice that was taken. And the Lula Government managed to get the World Bank stamp that says, "Look, this is not some leftist delirium here! The World Bank, they are supporting this. They think it's good."[52]

This interpretation—calculated "legitimacy sharing" informed by mutual expedience—was reiterated by another senior policy analyst, who explained that while loan funds advanced by the World Bank and the IDB for Bolsa Família were motivated by political, and not budgetary, concerns: "Brazil didn't need it [financial support], but they wanted to do it for the government to be able to say, 'We have the backing of the IDB. We have the backing of the World Bank.' It was also good for [the multilateral agencies] to say, 'Look: we're supporting the biggest CCT program in Latin America.' I think it was a political game."[53]

There was little inclination, however, to share the credit for CCTs with Mexico. Santiago Levy's presence at the Lula-Wolfensohn meeting was not publicly acknowledged—reciprocation, perhaps, for the fact that Levy's own fact-finding tour of municipal Bolsa Escola programs in the mid-1990s, in the company of a Mexican government delegation, also later disappeared from Oportunidades own "creation myth."[54] Beyond the political score-settling and disputed paternity claims, however, lessons from Mexico were being filtered through the "policy dialogue" that was established between the Bank and the federal authorities in Brasilia. The Brazil Social Assistance program, or BRASA, grew out of the World Bank's analytic and advisory service, taking the form of policy notes, "a series of comparator cross-country case studies," and a rolling program of technical analysis and advice, interlaced with the Bolsa Família rollout itself.[55] Both parties confirmed that, at the level of practice, this was very much a "horizontal relationship," the Bank's contribution being welcomed at the level of "technical support. It was not a to-do list, but a dialogue."[56] By the same token, this respondent—a participant in this dialogue at the ministerial level—confirmed that "a lot changed when [the Bank] arrived here; they arrived here thinking about the international experience, but we have the local experience."[57]

The World Bank, for its part, was also learning from this local experience, although perhaps not in the usual way. The Brazilian authorities insisted that the contract negotiations with the World Bank were to be conducted in Portuguese, not in English, as would have typically been the case. The Bank's negotiator, who reportedly learned much more than the language itself in the course of these negotiations, which extended over several months, and who went on to lead the project team in Brazil for five years, earned the widespread respect and trust of her Brazilian counterparts, not least as "a very good interlocutor."[58] In fact, this was but one side of a carefully choreographed relationship between the Bank and the Brazilian government, in which there were no heavy-handed attempts to claim the credit for Bolsa Família but instead a more subtle process of mutual ideological alignment. This is illustrated in the following observations from two senior policymakers in Brasilia:

> They [the officials at the World Bank] have a model, as mainstream economists, [they have] a typical model of CCT in their minds. On the other hand, the World Bank is a political player. If you look at the actions of the local World Bank office here, you are going to see that they are more pro-government than anything else you can find in this country! They really praise Bolsa Família. . . . In this paper, "The Nuts and Bolts of Bolsa Família," you have a bit of the ideology, the wishful thinking of the World Bank, in the sense of what they wish the Bolsa Família to be, but it's pretty much [a product of] the legislation and the rules and whatever. . . . They also commissioned research on how the media

reacted to Bolsa Família. I am pretty sure they did that to please the government. . . . The World Bank came here, and they tried to change [Brazil] and
they saw that they had no chance, and they joined them![59]

[Some say that the World Bank] didn't impose their agenda but they assimi-
lated ours! . . . It was not a matter of money. We did not need the money to do
this, as some countries in Africa [do].[60]

And what the Brazilians chose to do with "their model" would depart from
World Bank orthodoxy in at least one crucial respect—conditionalities.
Here, the first C of CCTs has a rather different (local) meaning. In practical terms, conditionalities do not bite especially hard in Brazil. "It's quite
hard to be kicked out of Bolsa Família," a federal program evaluator candidly
observed. "They say that at the local level, a social worker goes to meet
the family, but we're not sure in how many municipalities this thing takes
place. . . . There is a discourse, in the law, and then there is a procedure that
is completely different."[61] As a member of the World Bank team in Brasília
explained the underlying philosophy,

In Brazil, . . . the poor are poor because of a historical process of social exclusion, and we owe them a debt. That's fundamental in Brazilian thinking: they
have citizens' rights [but] have not always had access to those rights, and we
have to pay this debt back to the poor. This is one of the most unequal countries on the planet. That permeates even into the conditionalities. Their view
is, wait a minute, if I have a child not attending school [but on the] program,
are we going to take it away? Is my first response a penalty or a punishment?
No, our response should be to go and investigate, *to use it as a flag—use it as a
flag for more care.* For them, they would say that the C, as in CCT, is for care.
[The idea is] not condition right away, it's not a contract right away."[62]

As the *Nuts and Bolts* report carefully explained—in effect, to a Washington
audience—individualistic and behavioral accounts of the causes of poverty
were the exception, rather than the rule in Brazil (even though these have
had a growing purchase in the conservative media), and it followed that the
perception of appropriate policy interventions was quite different. According to World Values Survey data, 76 percent of Brazilians believe that the
poor are poor because "society is unjust," while 70 percent reckon that the

poor have "very little chance" of escaping poverty; the corresponding figures for the United States are 39 percent and 29 percent, respectively.[63] In contrast, the belief that the poor are lazy was held by 61 percent of Americans, but only 20 percent of Brazilians. CCTs, in this light, were not generally seen as tools for behavioral correction in Brazil but as "a social policy instrument that seeks to integrate . . . 'rights' to education, health and social assistance [understood] as a way for society to pay its 'historical debt to the poor.'"[64] As one of the program's advocates in the Lula administration put it, "It is a program that reaffirms rights."[65]

Consequently, even though conditionalities were part of the Brazilian approach from the start—they are "in the DNA" of this local model, as one insider put it[66]—the *meaning* of this component of what would become an omnibus CCT design is different in Brazil. The World Bank's stylized definition of Bolsa Família clearly places the program in the CCT family, affirming two of its most important traits, but goes on to add a third—"local" programming characteristics concerning client empowerment and complementary services:

> Like other conditional cash transfers (CCTs), the BFP [Bolsa Família program] seeks to help (a) reduce current poverty and inequality, by providing a minimum level of income for extremely poor families; and (b) break the inter-generational transmission of poverty by conditioning these transfers on beneficiary compliance with human capital requirements (school attendance, vaccines, pre-natal visits). *The BFP also seeks to help empower BFP beneficiaries by linking them to complementary services.*[67]

Or as the World Bank's CCT manual describes it, in rather understated terms, Bolsa Família "takes a softer, more gradual tack on conditions; and puts a shade more emphasis on redistribution than on human capital formation."[68]

Rather than seeing Bolsa Família as being "soft" on conditionalities, taking a "looser tack," or somehow as an equivocal version of the ostensibly definitive, Mexican approach, it is more appropriate to recognize these as aspects of the program's genuinely endogenous character. Bolsa Família internalizes a different philosophy, not simply divergent practice; it occupies a distinctive position in the evolving universe of CCT programs, rather than merely being an idiosyncratic outlier to a putative global norm. Reflecting this, as Bolsa Família has increasingly been drawn into the international dialogue about CCTs, this has often reinforced the sense of the program's distinctiveness; it may have been relativized, in other words, but it has not been normalized. So, it is common to hear a gentle pushback from senior officials in Brasília against what is portrayed as the more singularly econo-mistic philosophy of Oportunidades, and the human-capital emphasis characteristic of the Washington consensus on CCTs:

> The emphasis on human capital is not as strong here as in Mexico. . . . Here, you don't hear much about human capital. . . . Here, you hear about social inclusion, social emancipation. *It's not just a question of semantics,* you have a complex of meanings associated with those things. . . . In Mexico, you have a more unifying discourse about [human capital]. You have documents from the government talking about that . . . from very early on you have a high [level of] consistency in thinking about the program. In Brazil, . . . the differences between the views [of the program] are much bigger than in Mexico: in the constitution you have a vision, in the Ministry [of Social Development] you have lots of perspectives, in the media you have another one, and in the municipalities you have a different one. You do not have this unified line of thinking. . . . The [overall] idea in Brazil is to support the family to improve their condition.[69]

Speaking for the Ministry of Social Development, this respondent was insistent that "the conditions are not punitive, they are not meant to punish these families. The idea is to use these conditions to reinforce their rights, to reinforce their universal rights of access to health and education. This is the heart of the model. . . . [We] use conditionalities not as a way to punish families, but to create conditions for them to exercise their rights."[70]

These are more than pious statements of ministerial intent. They are reflected in local practice too, itself quite variable. So when midlevel program managers began to participate in the CCT practitioner network for Latin America and the Caribbean—which is convened as a means of cross-fertilizing administrative practice between countries—the Lusophone delegation stood out in more ways than one. As one of the World Bank officials involved in the program recalled of a week spent with a delegation of Brazilian administrators in Mexico, "We saw it at the local level, just to exchange and talk through how do you guys do the penalties [et cetera] and that's when the Brazilians are like, 'We're not the national police on this program! This immediate contract penalty stuff is not for us!' . . . The Mexicans [on the other hand] love the penalty approach, they're like '*Boom*! It's a *contract!*'"[71]

These differences in programming cultures should not be naturalized, however, even if they are performed repeatedly. In some respects, the debate around conditionalities has been quite turbulent, especially when the Brazilian media began to focus critically on this, Lula's flagship initiative, during his presidential reelection campaign of 2006. Prior to that time, an insider recalled, the implicit position of the ministry had been, "We have them [conditionalities], but we're not going to be especially worried about them," but this began to change—or had to *be seen to* change—once the philosophy and performance of the program became mainstream political issues:

> The media really started banging Bolsa Família because of conditionalities, very, very strongly. They were saying, "What is this? You're not [delivering] what you sold to Brazilian society." So . . . the Ministry has made an effort to go after conditionalities. Of course, they are still going after them in a way that's more humane, in the sense that, say, if someone has stopped going to school, they get five letters before their scholarship is cut. They get a letter, and then they get another one, and another one; the municipality gets a letter. . . . The idea is [still] that the [program] should not be punishing but more enabling in relation to conditionalities: "Look, municipality, are you offering schools? Why is this kid not going to school?" . . . In the end, what ends up happening is that you send off the five letters over a one-year period, and if they still don't show up you cut them off. The bottom line is that. [But] the numbers are pretty small. Very few people have been cut [from Bolsa Família].[72]

Far from undermining the program, this trial by media fire only served to reaffirm its political resilience. When a member of the World Bank's Brasília team reflected on this episode, it was taken as a lesson in the *politics* of conditional social programs:

> What is the purpose of the conditionality? My feeling all along is that it certainly has a developmental impact, but it also has a political-legitimacy impact. And that legitimacy, or credibility, can be questioned if people don't think you're taking it seriously. So, the monitoring and the consequences [i.e., program sanctions] also play into the political credibility of the government, and of the program. . . . Let's look at these conditionalities: they are appealing to the

right and to the left. On the right, they don't want handouts for nothing, this is a contract: "We're going to at least make the poor do something to get their benefits. We don't want welfare dependency." On the left: "This is empowering! We're helping the poor take up their citizens' rights." *Same instrument!* The conditionality is a credibility-enhancing function, which would not be the case with just a pure cash transfer. So my theory is, it's politically appealing . . . because those line up so well. And it doesn't take a lot of GDP. For a really small share of GDP, you can get a pretty good impact. And the way you do it is pretty much politically popular across the spectrum, left and right.[73]

The political optics of programs like Bolsa Família will often diverge from how they actually operate at street level, or deep in the administrative weeds, where much can be lost, or never seen. The vast scale and decentralized delivery of Bolsa Família only adds to this kaleidoscopic complexity. This clearly also impedes the evaluation process, introducing the kind of institutional and sociological indeterminacy that is anathema to the purified research designs necessary for randomized trials. As a World Bank economist said, in slightly exasperated tones, "Maybe the Brazilians have a point [about their different approach to conditionalities]. It would be nice if they evaluated their damn program and we could actually demonstrate that, right?"[74]

### Between South and South

Some would say that playing the card of Latin American exceptionalism is something of a Brazilian habit.[75] But at the same time, a perception of Bolsa Família as the overgrown stepchild of the CCT family certainly has a wider currency. "My impression is that the World Bank and the IDB, they never liked Bolsa Família that much," a Brazilian policy analyst commented, "So Brazil was never the big example that they wanted to disseminate in Latin America. Whenever they have [an event] they invite the Mexicans or the Chileans! [And] when they thought that the Mexican model became a bit worn out, hard to sell, at least in Latin America, they tried to sell the Chilean model, Chile Solidario."[76]

Chile Solidario is a modestly scaled program by Latin American standards—targeting around 250,000 families in extreme poverty—but it is distinctive for its strictly time-limited, intensive style of intervention, its deployment of social workers to actively engage with families, and its strictly contractualized nature.[77] Something of a World Bank favorite—"very compelling" is how one of its many advocates in the Bank's Washington headquarters described it[78]—Chile Solidario is "thus far a model unto itself, although other programs are moving to emulate it to a degree."[79] The view from Brasilia, on the other hand, was that while Mexico may have *earned* the "iconic" status conferred upon PROGRESA/Oportunidades by the World Bank and the evaluation-science community,[80] the favoritism shown to the Chilean upstart by the multilateral agencies was galling, even if the "marketing" success of such programs did reflect, by implication, a degree of Brazilian complacency:

> Like the U.S., we're a big a country. We look at ourselves. We don't worry about marketing beyond our borders. PROGRESA did a spectacular marketing thing, technically well done, so I can give them credit for being the model. What irritates me is Chile Solidario, which was never well evaluated technically. They didn't do anything like PROGRESA did. And when they did evaluate it recently they found out it doesn't work! But now they are the big model, [more so] even than PROGRESA. Most countries are following the Chile Solidario model. Maybe it's because it's more palatable to a more conservative public to say we're only going to help [poor families] for two years and then they are going to leave them to their own means. The Colombia program is along those lines, the Paraguayan program is along those lines, most of what you have seen in terms of replication [recently] has been Chile Solidario style, not PROGRESA style.[81]

Again, different aspects of Chile Solidario tend to appeal to different audiences. In the United States, it finds echoes in Mark II of the Family Rewards program, for example. In contexts in which more individualistic analyses of the causes of poverty hold sway, and where CCT interventions are embedded in a high-capacity, often program-rich environment, "the Chilean model is very compelling . . . probably the one that would be the most attractive in the higher-income countries. It's the case-worker idea, and they can afford that kind of intervention."[82] The Chilean model, in this respect, can also be seen to resonate with the Bank's ideological preference for crisply structured, highly contractualized, narrowly targeted, and instrumentally focused programs, which time limit benefits rather than opening the door to long-term support.

The fact that Chile Solidario is a time-limited intervention is also crucial. In this sense, the program can be seen as a Southern companion to TANF in the United States, the paradigmatic example of time-limited welfare. In its embrace of time limits, however, the United States remains something of an outlier among the advanced industrial nations, even if, to varying degrees, many of these have embarked on their own journeys of workfare-style reform.[83] Strictly time-limited welfare, with no second chances or fallback programs, is still regarded as ideologically severe in countries with relatively well-established welfare-state settlements. The notion of time-limited assistance, on the other hand, can play differently in less-developed countries, where social safety nets are no more than weakly institutionalized and sparsely funded. A Brazilian social-policy analyst explained the appeal:

> Many Latin American countries can't *afford* a program that supports the same family for ten years, twelve years. The beauty, the *sole* beauty, of the Chilean model is [that] the families stay in the program for two years and they have this psychosocial support [system], they have this social worker that goes into the household. They have to sign this contract: "there are seven dimensions that I'm going to work on with you," including, for example, domestic violence, planning the budget, health, education, work opportunities, [obtaining official] ID.... Only when the family signs the [contract], do they start receiving the transfer . . . and then the benefit decreases every six months. . . .
>
> Colombia was the first country to try to emulate that [with] a five-year limit . . . but [in the end] they haven't graduated any families at all. . . . [In contrast], in countries like Paraguay, they have a three-year limit and they really need to graduate the families [for] budgetary reasons. . . . They have to phase out some families. But it's difficult for them to have a good argument to graduate families, because if you graduate them from the program you [should] have graduated them from poverty. . . . To tackle that they have emulated a lot of Chile Solidario.[84]

"Graduation from poverty," however, has become an increasingly elusive operational goal in the years since the global financial crisis, as severe spikes in poverty and unemployment have placed significant strains on many CCTs, and on social-protection systems more generally. The coincidence of increased social need and budgetary stringency establishes almost impossible tradeoffs for social-policy planners, who may wish to target and time limit interventions in the interests of financial discipline, or to minimize the threat of "dependency," but who at the same time must (be seen to) be moving to alleviate material hardship for no-less-pressing social and/or political reasons. What different countries decide to do is, in the final analysis, always conditioned by domestic politics, but many are now exercising this discretion within the policy matrix of CCTs.

An escalating series of food, fuel, and financial shocks since 2007 led to sharp increases in global commodity prices, which in turn significantly eroded the purchasing power of the world's poorest households. In response, many countries moved to rapidly create, restart, or expand cash-transfer programs—some imposing conditionalities and others not—in order to safeguard living standards and protect future human-capital investments.[85] In Brazil and Mexico, for example, the number of families receiving Bolsa Família and Oportunidades was expanded and benefits levels were topped up. More unexpectedly perhaps, in Chile, an *unconditional* cash transfer (UCT) was added to the mix of social-protection programs centered on the flagship Chile Solidario, but now repositioned as part of an Ethical Family Income initiative. Enacted in May 2012, Ethical Family Income establishes "three pillars" of social assistance—dignity, duties, and achievements—each with a corresponding conditional or unconditional cash transfer.[86] Households living in extreme poverty are targeted by the first two pillars, with the principle of dignity being equated with a time-limited unconditional cash transfer based solely on financial need, while the principle of duty carries with it a conditional cash transfer awarded to those families that maintain school attendance and regularly access health care checkups for children. The third pillar, achievements, targets conditional cash transfers to low-income families whose children are ranked in the top 15 percent of their class.[87]

Increasingly, cash-transfer schemes are being deployed as vehicles for achieving multiple social-assistance objectives, from mitigating the impacts transient economic shocks on poor households, to incentivizing investments in human capital, to undertaking infrastructure projects with a community-development ethos. In this context, there has been a dramatic acceleration in South-South social-policy exchanges. While Mexican and Chilean policy models, among others, have an elevated presence in these exchanges, they are rarely adopted *in toto,* but instead tend to exert a pervasive and often preemptive influence in shaping policymaking frames of reference, the coordinates of reform deliberations, and the repertoire of program options. The reach of hegemonic policy models is therefore extensive, even if this does not translate into literal replication. In Indonesia, for example, the direct adoption of CCTs has proved to be impractical, even as the model continues to influence the overall course of reform. What the Indonesian case shows, in fact, is that the sanctioned orthodoxy of CCTs will often provide the "frame" for reform processes, particularly (although not only) under conditions of political or social stress, but the dynamics of reform will oftentimes stretch or even breach the design parameters associated with such off-the-shelf solutions. No sooner, then, will countries like Indonesia join the transnational policymaking grid of CCTs than the shape of this grid will begin reciprocally to change. Sometimes, there will be relatively little "backwash" to other jurisdictions, while on other occasions new coordinates and currents for transnational reform will be established.

For Indonesia, the 1997 Asian financial crisis brought to an abrupt halt a quarter century of sustained economic growth, generalized reductions in poverty, and broadly improving education and health standards. Over the course of a single, tumultuous year, the value of the rupiah tumbled by 85 percent, domestic prices soared by 78 percent, food prices trebled, the economy contracted by nearly 14 percent, and the poverty rate more than doubled to 33 percent (further entrenching chronic poverty).[88] The mass protests that followed led to the fall of the authoritarian Suharto regime and spurred the creation of numerous social-protection programs on what essentially was a blank slate, given the absence of such programs in the country prior to that time.[89]

Successive presidential administrations have endeavored to construct a comprehensive system of social assistance in Indonesia by implementing, with varying degrees of success, a number of cash-transfer and price-subsidy programs, though as a proportion of GDP the budgetary allocations associated with these programs remain the lowest in Southeast Asia.[90] The first moves involved the introduction of commodity-subsidy measures, such as a fuel subsidy and the rice-for-the-poor program, *Raskin*, which have been roundly criticized for their loose targeting, high costs of administration, and other operating inefficiencies.[91] In the wake of these criticisms, cash-transfer programs have become an increasingly important component of "responsible" poverty-alleviation efforts in Indonesia, often with the direct financial and technical support of the World Bank, along with other international-development agencies. Indonesia's first cash-transfer initiative comprised a set of cash-for-work programs that made temporary income available to residents of disadvantaged communities who take up employment on public works projects. Cash for work was, for all intents and purposes, a form of emergency relief that was issued to help impoverished residents weather the Asian financial crisis. In the post-crisis period, cash-transfer programs have become an enduring feature of the Indonesian social-policy scene, and the locus of collaborative policy-development efforts by the government and multilateral development agencies. The World Bank recommended the launching of a CCT in early 2005, as a way to ease the transition away from fuel subsidies, arguing that the Latin American experience suggested that a conditional transfer could be effective in Indonesia.[92]

The path from a subsidy approach to CCTs would not, however, be as direct and rapid as had been the case in Mexico. In 2005, President Susilo Bambang Yudhoyono authorized the rapid implementation of Bantuan Langsung Tunai (BLT), a temporary, unconditional cash transfer that was delivered to a quarter of all households to mitigate the impact of reductions in fuel subsidies.[93] The BLT was hastily reintroduced in 2008 during the global financial crisis, reaching more than nineteen million households, and it stands as the largest UCT implemented to date. A senior World Bank policy analyst recalled the stressed debates over the relative merits of various social assistance mechanisms—including subsidies, UCTs and CCTs—as the government sought to rapidly implement new programs amid economic instability and acute material hardship:

> During the first unconditional cash transfer, which was rolled out very fast in the space of five months . . . there was talk about setting up a CCT at that time. In Indonesia . . . they are sort of like phoenix programs. In the middle of a crisis, there is a program that the government rolls out relatively quickly, and it generally becomes a permanent feature of social assistance. . . . The notorious example is the subsidized rice program, which was born in [the late 1990s] and at that time was supposed to be special distributions of below market-price rice, but ended up being a regular yearly transfer, and it still exists today. It ended up being, by budget expenditure, the largest social assistance program in Indonesia. So UCTs and CCTs were being debated as potential crisis responses, part of the next generation of social-assistance programs in Indonesia.[94]

The introduction of a large-scale UCT proved to be politically controversial, however, both within Indonesia and among the international financial institutions that were becoming increasingly involved in assisting the government with the design of social-assistance programs.

Concerns centered first on the implementation and rollout of Indonesia's UCT program, and then on its design features, particularly the decision not to impose conditionalities on benefit receipt. A senior government administrator recalled that in the first weeks of the program, "we had serious protests from all over the country: mistargeting, misconception of the program, misinformation, every kind of 'mis' you can think of!" [95] With the assistance of the World Bank, a rapid (re)assessment was conducted, resulting in modifications to the verification, targeting, and monitoring regime, after which "the protests were much reduced." With regard to the absence of conditionalities, concerns that "people will become lazy and dependent" were commonly voiced in top policymaking circles, even as there was little or no evidence to support such assertions. As a senior development-agency manager stationed in Indonesia observed, "It doesn't happen, the transfer size is too small, and if anything it goes the other way; it helps people have the resources to find jobs."[96] A subsequent World Bank evaluation of BLT, published in 2012, supported this assessment, and might yet signal a shift in the terms of the wider debate around the uses and merits of unconditional cash transfer programs.[97] The evaluation found that the cash transfer was primarily used for "essential items," such as food, school fees, and transport costs; it reduced the incidence of child labor; it was responsible for an increase in health care utilization; and it had indeed catalyzed a move by recipients into employment.[98] A senior policy analyst at the World Bank conceded, "If the dire prediction was that this would make people fat and lazy—a sort of 'welfare mom' hypothesis—actually, it was the other way around."[99]

Notwithstanding these encouraging signs, in the wake of Indonesia's unorthodox foray into unconditional cash-transfer programming, policymaking would soon be taking a more conventional path. With the aid of the World Bank, Indonesia's first CCT, the Program Keluarga Harapan (PKH), was introduced in 2007. Following the classic pattern, the PKH pilot program was delivered to eight hundred thousand severely disadvantaged households in seven of the country's thirty-four provinces, the cash transfer being conditioned on the requirement that beneficiary households send children to school and obtain preventive health-care services. The rollout of PKH, however, exposed a range of long-standing supply-side deficiencies within the health and education sectors, so much so that, in many parts of the country, it was not possible to adequately deliver the very services upon which the PKH conditionalities are based. Perversely, this meant that the program itself was not deliverable where it was urgently needed, in the most remote locations, despite the extreme poverty and diminished life chances of their residents. Uneven institutional capacities, unmet basic infrastructure needs, and chronic service gaps, though, had long been a concern of planners in Indonesia. To better meet the needs of impoverished neighborhoods and villages, government planners proposed an inversion of the logic that pervades most development spending—let the affected communities determine development priorities.

Several high-ranking officials within the Indonesian government received their graduate degrees in urban planning at U.S. universities, where the tenets of *community development*—that within any community there is a wealth of knowledge and experience that can be channeled into collective action to achieve shared goals—deeply informed the curriculum. Concerned that macroeconomic shocks create disproportionate hardships among the poor in under-resourced parts of the country, including urban neighborhoods, some of these government planners moved to put "community . . . in the driver's seat," so that "if there is another shock . . . the community [is] able to deal with the poverty issues, the economic shocks."[100] Putting community in the "driver's seat" meant instituting new decision-making processes through which infrastructure and services needs would be identified and addressed. However, the process orientation necessitated by a community-development approach, one involving public deliberation and collective decision-making, clashed with the World Bank's preference for targeted programs designed to efficiently transfer funds to poor households. A government planner recalled the debate at the time, and his insistence that the experience of previous cash-transfer policies, as well as the scope to build upon community capacities, pointed to a modification of the World Bank's preferred approach:

> I was arguing with [the World Bank official], we have so much experience with cash transfer programs, with cash for work. It didn't give us good results. I want to have a project with procedures, processes to enable the people to deal with problems themselves . . . and when the money from the government comes in, to materialize the plans, *they* decide what they want to do. The task manager from the World Bank didn't like the idea, because this will not disburse money in a fast way. Because when you talk about community, of course, you need a process, and this takes a lot of time.[101]

In this instance, the World Bank was eventually persuaded, and the Urban Poverty Program was launched to improve conditions in impoverished urban neighborhoods through block grants available to improve basic infrastructure by employing area residents in public-works projects. The World Bank provided a $335 million loan to build roads, improve drainage systems, repair houses, rehabilitate schools, and build more than 1,600 health clinics.[102] The Urban Poverty Program was the precursor of a larger, more ambitious mutation of the CCT approach, the Program Nasional Pemberdayaan Masyarakat (PNPM). This program seeks to hybridize two (often conflicting) principles of economic development and social assistance—participatory planning and conditionalities. Under PNPM, villages receive a block grant each year. Residents undertake a participatory planning exercise to determine how best to use the funds to meet a set of health and education targets. The amount of the subsequent block grant is determined, in part, by the progress the village makes towards achieving the targets. Thus, what some policymakers in Jakarta characterize as "community-based CCTs"[103] marry bottom-up planning and decision-making with the type of performance standards that have been a hallmark of CCTs elsewhere.

The Indonesian experience with constructing a comprehensive system of social protection in the wake of the Suharto regime's long-term neglect of antipoverty programming reveals some less-than-predictable lessons about the ways in which cash-transfer programs are being adapted, implemented, and debated outside their "home" region of Latin America. Here, policy experimentation has been guided by the prevailing practices and received wisdom from early adopters abroad, mostly as interpreted by the multilateral development agencies, and in many ways this received CCT experience establishes a preconstitutive "frame" for the reform process. Crucially, however, even as the accompanying flows of expertise and financing shape what might be considered to be more or less expedient pathways for reform, they are not determinate of the reform process. There is no tabula rasa. And adoption invariably entails adaptation. Social-policy dialogues may have been transnationalized to a significant degree, and they may often be conducted under the long shadows cast by favored global models, but at the same time they are inescapably demarcated and animated by domestic political pressures, discursive representations of "the problem," and policy precedents. The experimental field that has been established around CCTs is a multiactor space, and just as favored models tend to come and go, so also does the editing of the approved policymaking script tend to become a continuous process. The big development banks are nearly always in a strong position in these situations, but they do not always get their way.

This said, adaptations are not all born equally. While the incorporation of community-based decision-making into the prioritization of education and health targets, à la Indonesia's PNPM, might be considered to be a broadly complementary elaboration of the centralized, technocratic CCT model, the country's extensive dabbling with unconditional programs crosses a more fundamental line. The conspicuous silence on the question UCTs in the World Bank's otherwise exhaustive handbook on cash transfers left little doubt as to the Washington position on social policy. But the stresses caused by the global economic crisis, coupled with the sometimes-unruly evolution of cash-transfer schemes in locations as diverse as Brazil, Indonesia, and southern Africa, opened the door to a range of less (or "differently") conditional approaches. Notably, the World Bank's position on conditionalities in Brasilia or Jakarta has been anything but doctrinaire and inflexible; here, the policymaking process around CCTs was characterized by pragmatic negotiation. While it may be accurate to say that there is still no "strong, coherent Bank position" on the question of the circumstances under which UCTs might be seen as an acceptable policy intervention, as officials in the Jakarta office maintained,[104] some of their interlocutors in government planning offices were advancing the rather more robust claim that CCTs and UCTs "serve completely different purposes."[105] This positions UCTs as a potentially useful form of "short-term shock mitigation" in the event of sudden economic downturn, currency devaluation or financial crisis, "a short- to medium-term poverty-alleviation approach" that can be activated or rescinded on short notice.[106] This need not be not an anti-CCT position as such, as some of the same officials emphasized the positive role of conditional cash transfers as a more "responsible" policy, appropriate—where political circumstances and planning horizons allowed—to the long-run challenge of developing human capital while tackling the intergenerational transmission of poverty. This might be read as a form of incorporation into the newly established CCT consensus, even if the number of card-carrying advocates is relatively small. This said, it remains notable that, despite the apparent openness of some within the Bank to consider the applicability of UCTs, the Bank has stopped well short of endorsing the principle of unconditionality.

But is conditionality necessary to ensure program effectiveness? After nearly two decades of policy experimentation with a range of cash-transfer schemes, as well as countless evaluation studies and policy reports, this question—in so many ways the definitive one in the design of CCTs—remains curiously underexplored. Not for the first time, however, this has been an occasion for potentially heretical questions to be raised at the margins, in this case at the margins of the globalizing field of CCT experimentation. Though largely ignored in the global debate about cash-transfer programs, the most direct evidence concerning the efficacy of UCTs can be found in a two-year pilot program undertaken by a coalition of civil society organizations in Namibia. In 2001, the Namibian government appointed a commission to offer reform proposals for the country's tax system. The commission noted vast income disparities within the country, as well as deeply entrenched poverty. Key among its recommendations was a basic income grant (BIG) to address these problems. Although the government went on to implement many of the commission's recommendations, the basic income grant proposal stalled. Prime Minister Nahas Angula initially expressed support for the BIG, until the IMF entered the debate.[107] The IMF advised the government to reject the UCT proposal, arguing by way of a faulty analysis that the BIG would be financially ruinous for the country.[108] Although advocates working with civil society organizations showed that the IMF had grossly overstated the fiscal impact of the BIG in making the elementary mistake of confusing gross and net costs—"We were able to prove them wrong in five minutes," one analyst remarked—the damage had been done.[109] The government dropped the proposal, contending that the economic case for the BIG had been refuted.[110]

Confronted with this setback, a coalition of civil-society organizations launched a pilot program to test the feasibility and efficacy of a UCT. A basic income grant of 100 Namibian dollars per month (equivalent to approximately US$9) was distributed to 930 residents of the Otjivero-Omitara settlement in the form of a universal, cash-based allowance. Otjivero-Omitara is a village located about one hundred kilometers east of Windhoek, where 86 percent of residents were "severely poor" (based on the official poverty threshold), unemployment exceeded 70 percent, and more than four in ten children suffered from malnourishment.[111] With a randomized trial ruled out as "ethically problematic" on the grounds that residents should not be denied social protection for the sake of research purposes, a nonrandomized evaluation of the two-year BIG pilot project was conducted, following the collection of baseline data in the year prior to program implementation. The evaluation revealed promising results: malnutrition plummeted, children's school attendance and health clinic visits rose, the unemployment rate declined, and residents increasingly sought employment opportunities in outlying areas—outcomes that were all achieved without the imposition of conditionalities.[112]

Coalition members anticipated that, should the experiment prove successful, the Namibian government would adopt some version of the BIG UCT as a national policy. Evaluation findings revealed measureable improvements in resident well-being, results that were manifestly on par with those of CCTs. Still, the Namibian government has been slow to act. One coalition member lamented, "The question that they always confront us with is, 'Has it been done anywhere else?' It hasn't been. We are the first example. But why should we always wait for someone else to do things? If the World Bank came in and said 'do it,' they would do it immediately."[113] But the BIG pilot has garnered little attention from the World Bank or from other multilateral development agencies, and the Namibian program remains something of an anomaly, if not an ideological orphan, in international debates regarding the future of social-protection policy. Largely overlooked in orthodox circles, the BIG stands as a case of largely unrequited model building, the relative isolation of which stems not from inferior performance, but because it contradicts the expert consensus in cash-transfer policy, which remains rooted in technocratic approaches to policy design predicated on means testing, targeting, and, of course, conditionalities.

## Social Targeting or Social Protection?

When World Bank president Robert Zoellick took questions after his opening address at the 2012 joint meetings of the Bank and the IMF, the former Goldman Sachs man was reportedly in a reflective mood, now entering his final few months in what had been an economically turbulent period in office. Asked a leading question about how low-income countries should be expected to cope with widespread reductions in development assistance, in the context of continuing macroeconomic instability and the rise of social-protest movements around the world, from Tahrir Square to Wall Street, his response was understandably oblique, but nonetheless revealing. Reiterating his recent theme, that it was necessary "to move beyond a kind of charity model,"[114] Zoellick reminded his audience that while the market could not be bucked, new models of social assistance had fortunately begun to displace the discredited approaches of the past:

> The world is an unpredictable place. We are not going to change that. So people who believe they can control this price or that price, I wish them—well, I don't wish them good luck—but anyway, it is not going to work. What we should be doing, however, is making sure that every country has an effective social safety net, and . . . we have learned a lot from developing countries about how to do this in a cost-effective way. The Bolsa Família Program in Brazil, the Oportunidades in Mexico—these are done for half of one percent of GDP. Trust me, if the U.S. Congress could get their entitlement programs down to any remote degree of that, they would be pretty happy; and yet they cover 15 to 20 percent of the people, and they provide a ladder up. . . . We at the Bank have helped extend conditional cash transfer programs to about 40 other countries.[115]

The global conversation on social policy had indeed started to shift, but the World Bank was not getting it all its own way. CCTs have remained an important part—and in many ways a locus—of this conversation, as a centerpiece of the post (or late) Washington Consensus, but the economic and political dislocations prompted by the global financial crisis seemed to have widened the ideological bandwidth on a host of issues in the long-neglected field of social security. It is true that as a silver-bullet policy in waiting, the CCT model caught the attention of an even wider audience in the wake of the global crisis. Helena Ribe, manager of the World Bank's Latin American region, went on U.S. television to endorse the conspicuous achievements of CCTs: "The evidence is very compelling. And on my many years of experience working in development in all regions of the world with the World Bank, I have never seen one program that receives so much interest and that has been replicated in as many countries as this model of conditional cash transfers."[116] There had been time to add in some discussion of the crisis to the Bank's long-planned manual on CCTs, before it went to the printers, although this had emphasized that these were not universal panaceas but part of a long-term commitment. While the case for CCTs might be evaluated, alongside workfare and UCTs in "rapid appraisal" situations, there were "ample reasons to be cautious and to avoid transforming their obvious virtues into a blind advocacy of CCT programs."[117] Meanwhile, the *Economist* magazine, known for its long-standing commitment to market-based approaches, but also for its worldly skepticism, was prepared to anoint CCTs as the "world's favourite new anti-poverty device."[118]

Not the entire world. Joseph Hanlon and colleagues at the University of Manchester certainly see things differently, bluntly observing that the World Bank's signature report on the new generation of social-assistance programs "is called *Conditional Cash Transfers,* and hardly mentions South Africa because cash transfers there are unconditional."[119] Their reading of the big six cash-transfer programs in the world—in Brazil, Mexico, South Africa, China, Indonesia, and India—is that, while it can be safely concluded that such large-scale interventions are both administratively practical and financially feasible, their coexistence demonstrates "just how varied such programs can be. They are unconditional, soft conditional, and hard conditional; are targeted narrowly and broadly; and vary greatly in what proportion of household income they provide."[120] These countries, in fact, had all faced political and economic crises of their own in the 1990s and had developed responses that were as notable for their variety as for their singularity. Their *shared* demonstration effect, that cash transfer schemes apparently work—both in immediate poverty alleviation and in some longer-term measures of human development—had in turn

> triggered an avalanche of other cash transfer programs in the South, ranging from small pilot projects to nationwide schemes. . . . At least 45 countries in the Global South now give cash transfers to more than 110 million families. This policy revolution has swept the South in the past decade and is challenging attitudes in the North.[121]

The lessons from this "avalanche" of experimentation with cash-transfer schemes were indeed beginning to run in some unpredictable ways.

The ILO, which has been fighting a (mostly) losing battle to extend social-protection and employment rights on a global basis while campaigning for "decent work," had been making little headway on its signature program of "social security for all,"[122] until evidence of the wave of cash-transfer experiments started to come in. (The fact that many of these had been funded, evaluated, and promoted by the ILO's more conservative neighbors in the community of multilateral agencies, like the World Bank and the IDB, was a boon on this occasion.) Suddenly, there was both evaluation evidence and real-world experience to back up the claim that limited welfare payments need not—as neoliberal and conservative critiques had long asserted—cause debilitating "dependency" on the part of the poor or drive sinkholes into government finances. And when the arrival of the global financial crisis further shifted the political and social calculus, necessitating some kind of action in the face of rising poverty and social insecurity, it seemed that the tide was finally turning. As senior ILO officials portrayed what they hoped might be the beginning of a sea change against the neoliberal consensus:

> The demonstration that a basic set of social security benefits is affordable, also for developing countries, first broke the spell that had beset the social security development debate [, but] it took a global financial and economic crisis to push social security to the top of the international agenda.[123]

Thanks in part to the CCT experiments, some of the largest of which operate at a cost of less than 1 percent of GDP, the question of whether low-income countries could afford basic social security could now be answered affirmatively.[124] Received readings of the evaluation literature also revealed few worries over work-disincentive effects (except for children, of course), unintentionally providing practical support for some arguments in favor of basic incomes.[125] Casting a deliberately wide net, the ILO suggestively repositioned the international cluster of CCT programs within the larger family of cash transfer programs of all kinds, listing UCT experiments, rather provocatively, at the top (see Figure 8).

Along with strategic allies in the multilateral community (in particular, various branches of the United Nations system), and in alignment with Brazil, Argentina, and some donor countries, the ILO made concerted efforts to build an international coalition around what would become known as its social protection floor initiative. In collaboration with the World Health Organization, the ILO convened a high-level advisory group under the auspices of the UN (and including, as "cooperating agencies," the IMF and the World Bank), whose report of 2011, *Social Protection Floor for a Fair and Inclusive Globalization,* pressed the case for an unprecedented global commitment to social protection. Framed, needless to say, in diplomatic terms, the Bachelet report acknowledged the "responsibility of each country to design and implement social floors shaped within a framework of nationally specific institutional structures, economic constraints, political dynamics and

| Type of cash transfers | Countries | Number |
|---|---|---|
| *Unconditional* | | |
| Household income support | Chile, China, Indonesia (until 2007), Mozambique, Pakistan, Zambia | 6 |
| Social pension | Argentina, Bolivia, Bangladesh, Brazil, Botswana, Chile, Costa Rica, India, Kiribati, Lesotho, Mauritius, Namibia, Nepal, Samoa, South Africa, Uruguay | 16 |
| Child/family benefits | Mozambique, South Africa | 2 |
| *Conditional* | | |
| Cash for work | Argentina, Ethiopia, India, Republic of Korea, Malawi, South Africa | 6 |
| Cash for human development | Bangladesh, Brazil, Colombia, Ecuador, Indonesia, Honduras, Jamaica, Mexico, Nicaragua | 9 |
| *Total number of countries with at least one program* | | 30 |

Figure 8. The landscape of cash-transfer experiments, as seen by the ILO. Source: ILO 2009.

social aspirations," recommending that "a number of principles and modalities [must] be taken into account" in the articulation of an international framework for social protection:

- Combining the objectives of preventing poverty and protecting against social risks, thus empowering individuals to seize opportunities for decent employment and entrepreneurship.
- A gradual and progressive phasing-in process, building on already existing schemes, according to national priorities and fiscal constraints.
- Coordination and coherence between social programmes. In particular, and within a perspective treating human development on a life cycle basis, the floor should address vulnerabilities affecting people of different ages and socio-economic conditions, and should be regarded as a framework for coordinated interventions at the household level, addressing multidimensional causes of poverty and social exclusion and aiming to unlock productive capacity.

- Combining income transfers with educational, nutritional and health objectives, to promote human development.
- Combining income replacement functions with active labour market policies as well as assistance and incentives that promote participation in the formal labour market.
- Minimizing disincentives to labour market participation.
- Ensuring economic affordability and long-term fiscal sustainability, which should be anchored in predictable and sustainable domestic funding sources; while noting that international solidarity in the form of cost-sharing may be needed to help to start the process in some low-income countries.
- Coherence between social, employment, environmental and macroeconomic policies as part of a long-term sustainable development strategy.
- Maintaining an effective legal and normative framework, so as to establish clear rights and responsibilities for all parties involved.
- An adequate institutional framework with sufficient budgetary resources, well-trained professionals and effective governance rules with participation of the social partners and other stakeholders.
- Ensuring mechanisms to promote gender equality and support the empowerment of women.
- Effective health-financing systems to ensure access to needed health services of good quality.[126]

Beneath this veneer of inclusivity, however, it is not difficult to discern that the Bachelet report was attempting to stake out a position quite distinct from what Rianne Mahon has characterized as the "liberal-residualist" approach to social-policy characteristic of the World Bank, based on the principles of targeting and conditionality, while at the same time transcending the marginally more progressive (or perhaps simply accommodationalist) "capabilities" or "social investment" paradigm favored by the OECD, based on human-capital development.[127]

The diagnostically salient issue here remains that of conditionality. The Bachelet report gave plenty of airtime to CCTs, including discussions of Bolsa Família, Oportunidades, and Chile Solidario, but it only did so in the context of what is portrayed as an "ongoing debate" over conditionalities: in light of the "diversity of opinions and mixed evidence" on CCTs, the report concluded that the conditionality "debate remain[ed] open," a position that was echoed on the progressive flank of OECD deliberations on social assistance.[128] What the Bachalet report was really doing, however, was attempting to *reopen* a mainstream debate around conditionalities, one that had been subject to a form of technocratic foreclosure, fast-policy style.

By necessity, the Bachelet group deferred the issue of the resolution of this debate to the realm of interagency coordination, international agreements, and technical assistance—the global netherworld where many such initiatives are destined to drift—backed up by a (shared) commitment to "experimental approaches to social protection," "rigorous evaluation," and "knowledge sharing."[129] Here, the newly launched Global Social Protection Floor Advisory Network would work with the phalanx of technical-assistance programs at the national and regional levels, including the development assistance frameworks (UN), the decent work country programs (ILO), and the poverty reduction strategy papers and accelerated growth strategies (favored by the IMF, the World Bank, and various donor agencies). Much was ultimately lost in this multilateral shuffle, where it must be said that UN and ILO interests rarely have the upper hand on questions of economic policy and fiscal commitments. On the other hand, Social Protection Floor commitments do travel with the moral authority of the Universal Declaration of Human Rights, as did the Millennium Development Goals before them,[130] which suggests that they may continue to evade ultimate sacrifice on the altars of neoliberal ideology or evaluation science, at least not without a protracted struggle. In this respect, the rather unvarnished take on CCTs found on the Global Social Protection floor website is instructive. Here, it is (re)asserted that "*human rights are unconditional,* and as social security is a human right, it is therefore unacceptable to deny it through the enforcement of conditions."[131] An exception is granted in those instances where conditions are applied in a rights-based context, where the conditions do not merely bind beneficiaries, but commit the state to the comprehensive delivery of education, health, and social services—effectively an endorsement of the Bolsa Família approach. In this context, "countries with less developed infrastructure," both in terms of administrative capacity and the reach of services, are likely to find that they unable to uphold the supply side of the CCT bargain, while redirecting resources into the monitoring and management of conditionalities can be perverse in such a context. After all, even the most technocratically advanced of these programs divert substantial resources to the monitoring function itself. It has been calculated that for the relatively efficient Mexican CCT, for example, "only" 9 percent of total program costs are absorbed by administration, surveillance, and management functions, but if family conditionalities and household targeting were to be abandoned, these costs would fall by more than half.[132] (In New York, as the previous chapter showed, where the bloated administration budget consumed over 42 percent of total program costs, even setting aside the cost of the experimental evaluation, which almost doubled the overall management budget, the "nonconditionality" dividend would be considerably higher.)

It can be concluded, therefore, that there may yet be some surprising twists and turns in the global paths of CCT experimentation. For all of the financial, institutional, and scientific weight placed behind this effort by the World Bank and its allies, for all the attributions of silver-bullet status by experts and advocates,[133] for all the work of practitioner networks and technical assistance programs, the ambiguities, questions, and controversies about CCTs stubbornly remain. Even though only a tiny fraction of this evaluation-driven and financially incentivized effort has been devoted to testing the viability and effectiveness of the progressive alternatives to CCTs—unconditional social transfers and basic-income initiatives—one of the more perverse consequences of the conditional cash transfer "avalanche" may have been to keep open, even to animate, a contra-conditionalities position on the moving terrain of social-protection policy. Whatever the long-term fate of the ILO's post-crisis efforts on this front, the lingering questions around UCTs call attention to the fact that "policy transfer" remains an inescapably political process. Attempts at technocratic (fore)closure will doubtless continue, and they will also continue to shape both the contours of domestic reform projects and the formation of globalizing social-policy norms; but these are *always* incomplete processes, no matter how asymmetrical the accompanying power relations. So narrowly formulated, technocratic experimentation in the spirit of Oportunidades, Chile Solidario, and their favored successors will continue, with the enthusiastic imprimatur of the World Bank, but so will the seductive "social policy diplomacy" of countries like Brazil,[134] and the relatively progressive coalition-building efforts of the ILO, various UN development agencies, and international NGOs. Fast-policy failures, as in New York City, or the kinds of rule-bending workarounds fashioned in Brazil, may yet shape the trajectories of (conditional) cash-transfer programming in quite unexpected ways.

# 5

## Reflections

### Tailwinds, Turning Points

What does the transnational field of CCT experimentation reveal about the logics and limits of fast policy? This interlude takes the form of a reflection on the preceding case study, with a view to teasing out issues of analytical pertinence, at least one step removed from the empirical details themselves. As such, it stands as a provisional and deliberately schematic conclusion to part 2 of this book, at the same time as it anticipates the comparative analysis *across* the globalizing policy fields of conditional cash transfers and participatory budgeting in this book's conclusion.

At the outset, it must be acknowledged that the sprawling geography of CCTs represents a conspicuous case of "model power," one in which the reach and efficacy of the model, which is hardly self-propelled, seems to be strongly related to a multidimensional program of prospective financing and evaluation-driven endorsement by powerful agencies like the World Bank. At the same time, the CCT case speaks to some of the limits (and uncertainties) associated with the exercise of this increasingly pervasive form of technocratic influence, since the journeys of cash-transfer programs "in the wild" have proven to be rather more unruly than a literal reading of the centrally scripted story—drafted and redrafted in Washington, D.C., in conjunction with an array of collaborators in Mexico and elsewhere—might have suggested. In this context, it is notable that the defining characteristic of CCTs—their conditionality—has yet to be stabilized. Consider this posting from a senior economist and featured blogger, Berk Ozler, on one of the World Bank's evaluation sites, in response to the rhetorical question, "What do [we] mean by a conditional (or unconditional) cash transfer program?"

[T]here are a myriad of ways to design and run a cash transfer program. You can identify a behavioral condition related to your outcome of interest (visit health clinics, test negative for drugs, get children vaccinated, keep daughters in school, etc.) and then be vigilant in announcing it (so that everyone understands the rules), monitoring it, and enforcing it. Alternatively, you can treat these dimensions of announcement, monitoring, and enforcement as continuous variables and vary your effort in each of them: this means you can have a "conditional" program that is monitored but not enforced, monitored but enforced only after many warnings and delays, not monitored at all, etc. You can also have programs that are announced to be conditional even when there was never any intention to monitor or enforce the condition. Similarly, you can announce a cash transfer program and have a social marketing campaign that encourages the beneficiaries to invest in their children's (or their own) human capital. You can have an unconditional cash transfer program for poverty reduction that is run by the Ministry of Finance . . . or to reduce dropouts by the Ministry of Education . . . they are not the same thing. Again, the list goes on.[1]

In the technocratic terms of the post–Washington Consensus, such questions of how to define *and design* a CCT-style intervention must be detached from the philosophical principle of conditionality itself and instead rendered technical. "[I]f you're a donor or a policymaker," Ozler continues, "it is important *not* to frame your question to be about the relative effectiveness of 'conditional' vs. 'unconditional' cash transfer programs [, because] the line between these concepts is too blurry." The expert advice from the World Bank, rather predictably, is that "your question needs to be much more precise than that. It is better to define the feasible range of options available to you first (politically, ethically, etc.), and then go after evidence of relative effectiveness of design options along the continuum from a pure UCT to a heavy-handed CCT."[2]

The World Bank has clearly been extremely effective in its attempts to animate the terrain of CCT experimentation, not least in cultivating, manufacturing, and distributing favored models. As a social-policy actor, in fact, the World Bank can be seen to be in the business, increasingly, of producing "demonstration effects." Despite appearances to the contrary, however, this is proving to be more of an art than a science. Here, we reflect on this experience, in light of what remains only a sampling of the global diversity exhibited by the CCT field, according to three broad themes—mobility, mutability, and momentum. More expansively, we also consider the possibility that "experimentality,"[3] understood as the flipside of recurring policy failure and serial underperformance, might be seen as an adaptive mode of governance, one that appears to be playing an increasingly important role in the contradictory reproduction of neoliberalism.

## Mobility

Conditional cash transfers are an especially vivid example of fast-traveling, if not hypermobile, policies. The earliest operational models, to be found in a handful of Brazilian municipalities in the mid-1990s, at first seemed to have little future. They appeared to be working—albeit on a modest scale—but were hardly being championed, even at the federal level, in their country of birth, while the attention of the multilateral agencies was also focused elsewhere. The arrival at the time of a Mexican government delegation, on a pre-PROGRESA fact-finding tour, must therefore have seemed somewhat incongruous. But the Santiago Levy team was piecing together an experiment with much more grandiose goals. The peso crisis had provided a conjunctural opening for a paradigm shift in Mexican social-assistance policy, an opportunity to dismantle the regime of food subsidies, along with its clientalist relations, and to install PROGRESA as the carrier of a new approach, based on the incentivization of human-capital investments at the household level and targeted to the rural poor. Santiago Levy's immaculate design drew on the latest currents of orthodox thinking in development economics, operationalizing principles that the multilateral agencies had been honing for some time, and encasing these in a state-of-the-art evaluation strategy intended to forestall political interference with the program. The gamble paid off, in that positive, short-term evaluation results quickly transformed this bold experiment into a mobile model, securing its domestic longevity while setting the stage for an unprecedented wave of international emulation.

Although it suited all of the actors involved, both in Mexico City and in Washington, D.C., to present this as an indigenous invention, in truth PROGRESA/Oportunidades was actively *coproduced* by a cluster of Mexican policy entrepreneurs (around Levy, as well as with José Gómez de Léon, and others), along with policy experts at the multilateral agencies—the latter organizations having taken an indulgent, strategic interest in this cleverly designed experiment from the start, and which were soon pouring billions of dollars into a transnational propagation effort reaching into every continent. None of this, notably, was achieved through the heavy-handed techniques of structural adjustment or prescriptive policy-based lending; for the most part, the global diffusion of CCT policies has been accomplished by way of a telling marriage of financial incentivization and technocratic persuasion. Stylized as models, working CCT programs have duly become concrete proxies for, as well as practical condensates of, orthodox policy preferences. More than this, they have come to symbolize the reformist "front" for a globalizing pattern of social-policy development.

Here, the fact that CCTs have also been carriers for the emergent orthodoxy of evaluation science, the randomized control trial (RCT), has been crucial. Positive evaluation results, established first by PROGRESA/Oportunidades and affirmed by a series of second- and third-generation experiments, have secured the status of CCTs as programs "that work," even as the entire process has been ideologically framed all along. (So experimental designs were to remain largely premised on the desirability of *some kind* of conditional programming, the preferred norm around which technocratic testing and refinement occurred, while sacrilegious questions concerning the *fact* of conditions rather than merely their *form* were ruled mostly out of bounds, at least as questions for scientific testing on Washington's dime.) CCT policy norms have mostly traveled through the technocratic medium of evaluation science and the parallel rationalities of neoclassical-cum-new behavioralist economics, validated in the concrete form of actually existing models, subsequently promoted as "models."

This has also facilitated the construction of a "postpolitical" veneer around CCTs, the somewhat bipartisan appeal of which can be traced to their intriguingly kaleidoscopic character: conservatives see in them a rejection of the something-for-nothing welfare ethos, while liberals place value on the realization of social rights for marginalized populations. These political valences, coupled with the formidable resources (in both dollars and expertise) of the multilateral agencies, mean that the CCT wave has had the benefit of a strong ideological tailwind, and hardly any inconvenient political baggage, meeting relatively few serious obstacles in its rapid transnational spread. Needless to say, perhaps, the policy would never have been likely to surge from just two or three to over forty countries in the space of a little over a decade had it been ideologically countercultural or somehow politically disruptive. As a relatively low-cost form of poverty alleviation with few negative side effects, which has earned both popular appeal and expert approval, this remarkable rate of uptake has clearly been warranted to a substantial degree.

Yet it would be wrong to assume that CCTs have been remaking the social-policy world entirely in their own image, in a unilateral and unmediated fashion. In fact, the sheer size and speed of the CCT wave has generated its own "backwash" effects. The nagging and still largely unanswered question of *unconditional* cash assistance has refused to go away, and indeed its mostly progressive advocates have found unexpected openings in a policy dialogue newly responsive to evidence and rational experimentation rather than innuendo and prejudice. The modest costs and positive effects of large-scale cash-assistance programs have disarmed some antiwelfare warriors. At the same time, the principle of behaviorally focused interventions, which at least at some level presumes that "corrective" action is both required and legitimate, has been consolidated as a postwelfare axiom across the political mainstream. Advocates and opponents of CCTs, as a result, are likely to have somewhat mixed feelings about the current state of play. The well-resourced and organized pro-conditionality forces may be making most of the running, but the contingencies of practice and, to some degree, consideration of ethical principles, continue to mitigate against the complete "closure" of this policy debate.

In this context, fast-moving policy models like CCTs also exert more subtle forms of normative influence: they cast very long shadows over policy debates, above and beyond their expanding operational footprint. In some cases, as in New York City, their propensity to arrive on the scene almost fully formed, as "policies that work" (albeit somewhere else), can have the effect of forestalling, foreshortening, or completely circumventing local deliberation, debate, and consensus building around reform efforts. The local advocates of imported models may be relieved of some of the responsibility for the process of policy design; they may be able to use these off-the-shelf solutions to leverage or accelerate institutional change or to preempt what might have been difficult local struggles around reform (and beginning with the articulation of basic principles rather than the borrowing of best practice). These features are crucial to the mobile efficacy of fast policies.

Even in those cases where imported policy models do not directly "format" local responses, they will often exert indirect effects, shaping the terms (and terminology) of debate if not the actual technologies of intervention.

Brazil may have been pursuing a *relatively* autonomous course as the archi-tect and manager of its own regime of not-really-conditional cash transfers, but at the same time its approach has been "relativized," not least by the purveyors of authorized CCT expertise at the World Bank. Bolsa Família duly becomes the least-loved corner of a triangular intervention space, with the "iconic" Oportunidades and the "compelling" Chile Solidario occupying the more favored corners for advocates of the newfound policy orthodoxy. The effect of this triangulation strategy is not simply to lift the relatively modest Solidario program into a status of implied equivalence with the big-league players in Mexico and Brazil, it also tilts the field in favor of the two more strictly conditional schemes, while projecting into circulation the kind of case-management practices and time-limited programs favored not only in Chile but also among key constituencies in the multilateral agencies. If the process of model building is ultimately founded on a certain design fetishism (coupled with the replication fantasy that superior designs secure superior outcomes), these acts of positioning and relativization can be seen as interventions in the space of policy design.

## Mutation

The conceit that (good) policy design secures (positive) policy outcomes implies that the designs themselves are immutable, that they travel as com-plete, prefabricated entities ripe for replication. Worldly policymakers, of course, know better. At least they understand perfectly well that there must always be some degree of accommodation to local circumstances, and indeed domestic political "realities," in that some retrofitting or customization is in-variably required. But for a model to be a model there must be a certain degree of functional integrity, a moderately predictable relationship that holds between (policy) inputs and (policy) outputs. Mayor Bloomberg's staff readily appreciated that the operating environment of the Oportunidades delivery site they visited in rural Mexico was radically different from that in their target neighborhoods in inner-city New York, yet there was also faith that the essence of the model could be reproduced, and that—to borrow the medical language of randomized trials—that the poor patients would respond to the intervention in an analogous manner.

The inescapable facts, however, that the treatment regimen itself can never be perfectly replicated, and that local conditions in the borrowing regions will always diverge, sometimes radically, mean that every "transfer" is a frustrated and incomplete one. In fact, all manner of contaminations and mutations can be expected—and not as the exception but as the rule. "Scaling up poverty reduction does not imply . . . mere 'replication,'" World Bank researchers have rather reluctantly concluded. "Country and context specificity appear to be intrinsic in all experiences."[4] The impossibility of replication and the inevitability of contamination mean that no policy is ever literally "transferred." Instead, a more appropriate metaphor might be that of "transduction." Transduction is a term in genetics referring to the process in which viral vectors introduce foreign DNA into a receiving cell, leading to genetic mutation. If policy models can be seen, correspondingly, to establish webs of viral connection, they do so through processes of always-imperfect translation that nevertheless result in transformative change and continuous adaptation. As carriers of policy DNA, models need not follow a pattern of radial or sequential diffusion, but may make all manner of lateral and nonlinear connections, spawning multiple and often cumulative adaptations in a rolling process of "infection" and continuous mutation. Imagined in this way, policy mobility comes to resemble not so much a series of bilateral transactions, or a unidirectional process of centrifugal diffusion, but rather a mutually interacting network, a moving landscape, or an evolving ecosystem. Particularly potent models, moreover, can be expected to accelerate and animate this adaptive process in an intensive manner, catalyzing waves of nonlinear and cumulative adaptation.

The adaptive field of CCT policy development, as we have seen, originated with an unevenly matched pair of early experiments—at the municipal scale in Brazil, as the product of domestic currents and influences, and at the national scale in Mexico, at the nexus of transnational expertise and pressing political imperatives. If what would become Bolsa Família was to evolve slowly, and in many ways uncertainly, over subsequent years, before achieving its consolidated national form, PROGRESA/Oportunidades was constructed quite purposively with the intention of rapidly growing to scale, to become an institutionalized fixture, and, indeed, to *travel*. Immodestly imagined as a demonstration project from the start, the evaluation-science echo chamber that was built around the program, administered by an off-shore research institute, effectively ensured that positive programming messages would pass quickly into the fast-developing transnational circuits of evidence-based reform. These were the circuits into which New York and other would-be emulators would later tap. The meticulous codification of

PROGRESA/Oportunidades—both in its design and in its effects—was sufficient to ensure the technocratic legitimacy of the program,[5] even in this context-hopping context, although it is notable that the visit by New York City's mayoral delegation was still deemed necessary to secure the effort's *practical* political credibility. Bloomberg still had to kick the tires himself. In turn, this enabled the rapid reassembly of the CCT in a manner customized to the circumstances of this "advanced" urban location, establishing Opportunity NYC as a clearly related experiment (but a nonreplica), on what proved to be an aggressively short time scale.

The policy connection that was duly established between New York and Mexico neatly illustrates one of the characteristics of these globalizing fast-policy regimes: even if marked by certain power centers, they are polycentric in form, with the result that "local" experiments acquire their salience, meaning, and potency *in relation* to one another. Almost immediately, the upstart New York program was being watched—not least by Mexico—for potentially translatable lessons on how to implement CCTs in densely populated and service-rich urban areas, lessons that would later be folded back into earlier-generation CCT programs across Latin America. Opportunity NYC was also positioned at the experimental edge of attempts to prod the next generation of CCT programs toward more "performance-based" human-capital conditionalities, by way of monetary incentives for educational achievement and workforce participation. Soon joined by a parallel initiative in the Washington, D.C., school district, also subject to randomized-trial evaluation, "[a]dministrators of CCT programs in the developing world now could benefit from the experimentation in U.S. programs," World Bank researchers observed, including "paying students for learning outcomes [and] performance on standardized tests."[6]

But if these were some of the trajectories of experimentation in the World Bank orbit, themselves advancing on multiple, simultaneous fronts and crosscut by all manner of reflexive connections, they were certainly not alone. Initially located at the fringes of this scientifically sanctified policy-development circuit, Bolsa Família retained both a distinctive culture (based on a somewhat muted social-rights approach) and its own dynamics of development (based on progressive integration across a decentralized delivery system and the "loose" administration of conditionalities that would define the program's quasi-exceptional status). If Opportunity NYC could be described as a refinement or elaboration of the PROGRESA/Oportunidades rationality, extending the operational logic and guiding philosophy of that model, Bolsa Família represented a more radical, orthogonal development. Functioning somewhat autonomously from the neoliberal ideological matrix projected by the World Bank, the unruly, "nuts and bolts" experiment that is Bolsa Família retains the potential to inspire new rounds of emulative policy development outside the frame of the now-orthodox CCT model,[7] with the latter's emphasis on surgical targeting, behavioral modification, and techno-cratic administration. For all the attentions of the World Bank, Bolsa Família has remained resistant to complete absorption into this evolving neoliberal grid, thereby symbolizing the continuing potential for more-than-reformist divergence from this still-nascent paradigm. Its countercultural message, of "soft" conditionalities in a social-rights context, is a potentially appealing one for many policy audiences, even as its prejudicial portrayal as an unaf-fordable, unconditional "handout" violates the strict principles of neoliberal governmentality.

## Momentum

The orthodox pattern of CCT innovation, closer to the experimental poles concretized by Oportunidades and Chile Solidario, can be considered to be "paradigm positive" in the sense that it defines a zone of active reproduction for what aspire to be, or have become, hegemonic policy models. Indeed, this form of ideologically and fiscally restrained policy experimentation must be recognized as one of the more significant contemporary domains for the practical reproduction of hegemony itself; it is part of an ongoing war of position conducted through technocratic means, in which models serve as condensates and carriers of neoliberal hegemony—not in the static "ten commandments" form of the Washington Consensus, but as an always-adaptive but variably deliberative, reactive, purposeful, opportunistic, and crisis-induced mode of policy development.[8] The World Bank's far-reaching efforts in knowledge banking and practice networking seek to advance this process through deliberative-technocratic means, codifying and advertis-ing designated forms of best practice, financing and evaluating sanctioned forms of policy experimentation, and stylizing models as object lessons and demonstration projects that might steer and incentivize favored pathways of reform. The World Bank's CCT "bible" exemplifies this process.[9] It defines, in effect, the shape of the orthodox "front" of reform, even if the underlying facts on the ground remain much more messy and multidirectional.

This amounts to a concerted effort to channel and canalize the ongoing process of social-policy transformation by way of a strategy of "permanent persuasion,"[10] rather than through the application of blunt force—for example, through neoimperial diktat or structural adjustment. (In this respect there is an echo of the behavioral-modification logic of CCTs themselves, in the way that they aspire to remake the incentive structure for poor families, as model power is mobilized with a view to "nudging" desired responses on the part of potentially unruly actors—in this case, policy actors.) This offensive may be formidable—operating as it does with the benefit of the following winds of ideological reinforcement, institutional capacity building, evaluation-scientific justification, and financial facilitation—but it also is one beset by frailties, limits, and contradictions. The adoption of an experimental ethos, in this sense, reflects more than a positive embrace of deliberative, pragmatic, evidenced-based, and results-oriented methods; more prosaically, it reflects the state of serial policy failure and systematic underperformance that is one of the defining characteristics of neoliberal interventions. In such a context, fast-policy practices become necessary as a means for churning and reanimating continually adaptive processes of experimentation, as past failures (re)create both a "market" for future fixes and a receptive space-cum-audience for next-generation interventions.

New York City's meandering path is a case in point: from attacks on the New Deal welfare settlement in the 1970s and 1980s, through experiments with workfare programming married with systemic reform in the 1990s, to recent attempts to propagate postwelfare policy innovation by way of a new generation of CCTs, this zigzagging pattern of cumulative reconstruction has occurred almost entirely on the terrain of neoliberal "solutions," while at the same time awkwardly demonstrating the inadequacy of these solutions. The mediocre performance of Bloomberg's CCT experiment is consequently not an unfortunate exception, but just another manifestation of neoliberal (mis)rule. The way that this has lent itself to new rounds of experimentation, between New York and Memphis and elsewhere, even in the context of apparent failure, illustrates how such flawed neoliberal interventions tend to "fail forward."[11] The measure of hegemony, they say, is never having to pay the price for one's mistakes.

The resurrection of the Family Rewards program, predictably labeled Family Rewards 2.0, in yet another round of evaluation-drenched experimentation in Memphis and New York, is testimony to the strength and persistence of the ideological following wind that accompanies such paradigm-positive interventions. As one of the lead evaluators of the Opportunity NYC program explained, the (rapid) response to the fact that "early findings point[ed] to toward a mix of results," was to "develop a stronger version of the model," in effect while the experiment was still in motion.[12] Failure rarely takes the form of a permanent roadblock on the path of neoliberal reform; more often than not it is an occasion for creative workarounds and rerouting efforts that are nevertheless committed to the same strategic direction. Continued mutation at the level of policy and practice—"experimentality"—is therefore necessary for the contradictory reproduction of neoliberal rule, marked as this is by the nonavailability of truly sustainable institutional fixes. The creative dynamism of neoliberal governance, in this respect, reflects an entrenched pattern of routine policy failure, on the one hand, and the continued grip of this adaptive mode of market-oriented hegemony, on the other. One of the ways in which this contemporary form of hegemonic reproduction works is to steer processes of fast-policy experimentation toward an ideologically constrained "solution space." So as orthodox variants of the CCT model jumped—or, perhaps more accurately, were *pushed*—from three to more than three dozen countries in little more than a decade, the model itself has largely evolved in a paradigm-reinforcing fashion.

But this is never the end of the story. Even though there is enormous momentum behind this pro-neoliberal pattern of transformation, a momentum that gathers more force each time a new program is enlisted into the orthodox family, as a member of the rising (second, third . . .) generation, it would be a mistake to characterize this as an "automated" or friction-free process of self-reinforcing reproduction. As the Brazilian and Indonesian cases demonstrate, the reach of this expanding family of programs continues to exceed even the World Bank's powerful grasp, as the politically contested and socioinstitutionally complex character of these interventions "in the wild" means that their potential to jump the neoliberal grid is an ever-present one, at least in principle.[13] What happens in practice, in turn, will reflect the balance of social forces in different locations, the configuration of institutional architectures, and a host of conjunctural political-economic conditions. Like Polanyian "double movements"—social and institutional reflexes that variously exceed (neo)liberal tolerances, both flanking market failures and establishing a seedbed for alternatives—their precise form is unpredictable even if their tendential presence is not.

In the case of CCTs, "internal" limitations of the orthodox model may not, as yet, have seriously slowed the program's international rollout or incremental evolution. Most conspicuously, some of these limitations pertain not to incidental but to fundamental, "designed-in" objectives of the orthodox model. First, the efficacy of the conditions themselves has been difficult to isolate in a conclusive way, with Hanlon et al. noting in their review of the evaluation literature that "[i]t is very difficult to distinguish between the effects of conditions and those of the grant itself."[14] Second, the supply-side faith that improvements in human capital will drive increases in employability and ultimately "exits," both from the program and from poverty, has also been called into question, even in Mexico, where Oportunidades has encountered the "limits of what cash transfer programs can achieve on their own . . . highlight[ing] the fact that their gains can be sustainable only if they are implemented within a social policy strategy . . . that generates growth, creates employment, and gives incentives for pro-poor growth."[15] This, coupled with the just-as-notable *absence* of evidence that cash transfers promote welfare dependency, has (inadvertently) contributed to reanimating discussions around unconditional programs and their role in wider social-protection strategies.[16] The sheer scale and speed of the CCT "avalanche" has paradoxically (re)opened a space for the consideration of alternatives, in the form of their ideological alter ego, unconditional cash transfers. To some extent, this space was actively reopened by a handful of countercultural experiments, such as Namibia's BIG UCT, with the support of a select group of NGOs and international funders hoping to rebalance the field of experimentation itself in favor of more progressive models. But there is also a sense in which the stubborn question of UCTs has lingered, as the unexplained residual, in the massive experimental-design evaluation effort that has been constructed around CCTs. The deployment of expensively conducted randomized trials may have the effect of consolidating incremental reform trajectories around a tight cluster of "official" questions—concerning how to calibrate conditionalities—but these efforts at technocratic closure are never hermetically sealed or operationally complete.

The possibility of a progressive or anti-neoliberal reflex in the trajectory of antipoverty policy at the transnational scale did not arise spontaneously, of course. There has been concerted pressure from progressive policy advocates and from more liberal development agencies, often with the active assistance of organizations like the ILO and UNDP, pressure that was later reinforced by the damaging effects of the global economic crisis and its protracted aftermath. It must be acknowledged that these countertendencies remain relatively weak in comparison with the still-dominant orthodox trajectory, that they are for the most part reformist and (themselves) incremental rather than radically counterhegemonic, and that their presence "on the ground," as actually existing alternative experiments, remains somewhat sparse. Yet the apparent momentum generated by the wave of CCT experiments continues to beg searching and disruptive questions about approaches located outside, or on the fringes of, the dominant paradigm. And the impetus that was generated behind social-protection floor initiatives in the immediate wake of the global economic crisis—even if it has yet to bring about a strategic reorientation of the global compact on social policy—underscores the more general point that policy mobility is rarely, if ever, a predictable process. And it is never a one-way street.

# PART III

# Propagating
# Progressive Practice

# 6

## Porto Alegre as Participatory Laboratory

The Brazilian city of Porto Alegre has become synonymous with both the cause and the practice of progressive policymaking. The site, since the late 1980s, of a radical experiment in participatory democracy, Porto Alegre would subsequently become the principal host city—and spiritual home—of the World Social Forum.[1] Porto Alegre has come to be seen, in this latter sense, as a kind of anti-Davos, a paradoxical capital of the global justice movement, which as a "network of networks" of course eschews the very notion of coordinated control or hierarchical power. As Michael Hardt and Antonio Negri wrote, during the initial ascendancy of this progressive "movement of movements," it was in many ways appropriate that Porto Alegre had "appeared as a nomad point or, rather, a transitive space" for the peripatetic global left: "The World Social Forum at Porto Alegre has already become a myth, one of those positive myths that define our political compass."[2] The geographical signifiers were impossible to miss. Davos, the invitation-only gathering of the world's economic oligarchy, epitomized the privatized detachment of corporate and state elites, plotting their globalization schemes inside a militarized security bubble. Porto Alegre was instead an open space of exchange and debate for the sprawling ecology of progressive networks, located on the boundless, sweltering plains of Rio Grande do Sul, broadly aligned around an array of progressive causes, including anti-imperialism, environmentalism, gender rights, economic democracy, and antiracism, but united (at least) in their opposition to the project of neoliberal globalization.

Rather more prosaically, Porto Alegre had earned this status as the ideal(ized) home of the global justice movement by virtue, of all things, of its remarkable record of achievement in municipal governance. Rarely a domain of heroic achievement, the experiment in what would be known as "participatory budgeting" (PB) had been established, during the 1990s, as an inspirational model both for grassroots democratization and progressively oriented "good governance." The Orçamento Participativo was in many ways the defining program of Brazil's Workers' Party (Partido dos Trabalhadores, or PT), both reflecting and shaping the politics of the decade in which Brazil emerged from the shadows of military dictatorship. By directly involving local residents in the determination of municipal investment priorities, PB had not only opened up entirely new spaces of public deliberation, it had pioneered a creative form of "redistributive democracy."[3] According to Boaventura de Sousa Santos, the PT's "popular administration" of Porto Alegre inaugurated what amounted to a "new modality of municipal government," installing a model of intensely local democratization that managed to be, at the same time, rooted and real, but also aspirational and even utopian:

> The Porto Alegre democratic experiment is one of the best known worldwide, acclaimed for both the efficient and the highly democratic management of urban resources. . . . The participatory budget promoted by the Prefeitura of Porto Alegre is a form of public government that tries to break away from the authoritarian and patrimonialist tradition of public policies, resorting to direct participation of the population in the different phases of budget preparation and administration, with special concern for the definition of priorities for the distribution of investment resources.[4]

According to Fisher and Ponniah, it was the "success of this innovative participatory budget process [that] made Porto Alegre the ideal home for a movement searching for alternatives to the neoliberal world order."[5]

What most excited the left, both within Brazil and abroad, was that an emergent, revitalized politics was being developed not from the top down but by grassroots social movements, which in a variety of ways had been cultivating practices of deep democracy at the street level. In the waning days of the dictatorship, extreme levels of socioeconomic inequality and the excesses of authoritarian rule had undermined the very legitimacy of the Brazilian state. The disenfranchised urban and rural poor began to mobilize in opposition to state-sanctioned injustices and dispossessions, and against their exclusion from (local) decision-making around the allocation of public resources.

Throughout Brazil, an upsurge in popular participation in voluntary organizations, most notably among the poor, had been accelerating with Brazil's democratization, particularly during the 1980s.[6] In Porto Alegre and elsewhere, these organizations promoted continuous experimentation with forms of direct and representative democracy in an effort to resolve what Santos and Avritzer have termed "the crisis of double pathology: the pathology of participation, especially in view of the dramatic increase in levels of abstention; and the pathology of representation—the fact that citizens themselves feel less and less represented by those they have elected."[7] The drive was for a recuperated politics coupled with a radical renewal of state–society relations, ultimately paving the way toward a new social contract based on the Arendtian formulation, the "right to have rights."[8] The Orçamento Participativo was in many respects the result of these emergent political demands, as well as a codification of the push to reanimate and democratize the Brazilian body politic. This reflected the historical imperatives, first, to dismantle and replace authoritarian decision-making structures, while second, constructing new modalities of pro-poor policymaking as a means of redressing enduring inequities.

The Porto Alegre experiment rapidly acquired a symbolically significant place in the intellectual imaginary of the global left, which was seeking to decolonize its own traditional thinking, to learn from the Global South and from bottom-up-initiatives, and to marry global social justice with "global cognitive justice."[9] Such lessons from Brazil, in this context, represented much more than exotic "alternatives," they seemed to stand for distinctly Southern forms of theory-practice, drawing on radically different praxiological traditions.[10] These included long histories of popular education, liberation theology, and varieties of associationalism, as well as sundry precursors to what would later be known as *horizontalidad*. Participatory approaches held the promise, in fact, of Southern policy operating on different registers altogether from their jaded counterparts in the Global North. More than a new policy design, PB crystallized a new policy *process,* breathing new life and drawing new participants into policymaking practices. Participatory budgeting thus became an exemplar for the Real Utopias project, where in its stylized form as "empowered participatory governance" it came to represent one of the pathways toward a transformative *deepening* of democracy.[11]

Meanwhile, in much more orthodox circles, PB had also acquired model status for international audiences of a quite different kind, including urban-policy consultants, functionaries of the Washington Consensus organizations, and public-sector accountants. Porto Alegre's model of urban governance had received praise by the World Bank in the early 1990s as an exemplar, not so much for radical democratization, but for efficient service delivery and transparent financial management, and the city later received loans both from the World Bank and the IDB.[12] The program was soon to be propelled into the international spotlight when it was featured as one of forty-two "best practices" in good urban governance at the UN-Habitat II conference, convened in Istanbul in 1996.[13] Technocratic translations of PB have since been implemented in an extraordinarily wide array of locations, numbering hundreds and on some counts thousands of municipal administrations worldwide—indeed, "from Albania to Zambia," according to an encyclopedic World Bank assessment.[14]

In effect, while it retains a distinctly progressive patina, PB has been simultaneously traveling through mainstream and alternative policy circuits. These two faces of PB—as a relatively orthodox urban-governance fix and as an open-ended means of radical democratization—were brought into increasingly sharp contrast, if not contradiction, in the first decade of the World Social Forums. When the newly elected president Luis Inácio Lula da Silva addressed a crowd estimated at over one hundred thousand, at the third World Social Forum in Porto Alegre, he underlined the need "to demonstrate that another world is possible; Davos must listen to Porto Alegre."[15] The PT's long political ascendancy, which culminated in Lula's election in 2002, had been predicated on an unprecedented alliance between labor and social movements on the one hand, and a network of municipal and state governments on the other.[16] What became known as the *modo petista de governar* (the "PT way of governing") had in fact been constructed *through* PB, as an open-ended and evolving system of "co-government" with civil society.[17] It was largely on this basis that the PT secured its reputation as the "party of sound municipal policies"; indeed, the PT way of governing would become strongly associated, during the 1990s, with clean, corruption-free governance, one opinion poll in Porto Alegre revealing that 89 percent of the city's population regarded the PT administration to be honest.[18]

Lula's election to national office, however, was to represent something of a rupture with, even a reversal of, this commitment to transformative, grassroots social change. The signs were there, in the Lula administration's contradictory commitments to both eradicate hunger *and* to respect the macroeconomic constraints imposed by the IMF. Symbolically, Lula's rousing appearance at the 2003 World Social Forum was delivered on his way to the Davos meeting—a sign of the compromises that were to come. The participatory ethos of Porto Alegre would not be federalized, although several local PT leaders were tapped for high-profile positions in the national government. So began to open what Iain Bruce characterizes as a "huge gulf [between] the PT's practice in Porto Alegre—its ability to combine pragmatic flexibility with radical innovation and creativity—and the troubling failure of nerve and vision that marked the PT's federal administration."[19] Corruption scandals, too, would later follow.

Even before Lula's election, though, some of the most astute, local observers of the PB process had been arguing that the project was showing signs of falling prey to a series of powerful, countervailing pressures associated with the dominant modalities of neoliberal rule, including long-term fiscal constraint, malign neglect by way of devolution, the instrumentalization of community action, the outsourcing of social policy, and the trend towards competitive self-management. Sérgio Baierle, for example, who had celebrated the achievements of PB in the 1990s—as a veritable "explosion" of progressive potential, associated with the "emergence of a new ethical-political principle"—had begun to sense, on the eve of Lula's election, that a "thermidorian" moment of bourgeois reaction and intensifying internal contradiction was about to engulf the Porto Alegre experiment.[20] The unbroken run of a decade and a half of PT administrations in Porto Alegre was by this time in its final term, as the *petistas* were to suffer a symbolic, home-territory defeat in the 2004 elections, after which the city was to be managed by markedly more centrist coalitions, together with conservative elements.

The new, post-PT administrations in Porto Alegre have continued to utilize—indeed to promote internationally—a defanged version of PB, which ironically has become more reminiscent of the diluted model of good-governance participation advocated by the World Bank, where it is coolly observed that the "open, informal, deliberative design [of PB] pioneered by Porto Alegre seems to be out of fashion."[21] In its symbolic birthplace, then, participatory budgeting has apparently become a pale imitation— some would say even parody—of itself.

The purpose of this chapter is to begin to probe the question of the extralocal salience of PB by exploring the ambiguities and tensions in its "originalist" form—to examine what Bruce refers to as the "contradiction at the heart of Porto Alegre's participatory budget," its perplexing mix of radical potential and reformist functionality:

> How can it be that the most radical experiment in direct democracy for decades—an experiment consciously inspired by the Paris Commune and the early Russian soviets, the sharpest challenge yet to prevailing identifications of democracy with the institutions of parliamentary representation—has developed, peacefully, within the constitutional framework of a dependent capitalist country like Brazil? . . . How has the PB become a reference point for both the radical left and the new right within Brazil's governing Workers' Party? How can a site of devotion for the left in the global justice movement . . . also be an object of praise for the United Nations' Habitat and even the World Bank? . . . PB appears to sit at the intersection of these different strands. In its radical, Porto Alegre variant, it may have something to say to both the libertarian and the orthodox traditions about the problem of the state and how a credible alternative can be established. . . . But it is also clear [that] the PB runs a constant risk of being coopted by the neoliberal variant of participatory democracy.[22]

And in terms of the specific problematic of policy mobility, it might be added that, in addition to the PB's apparent political promiscuity, it also represents an intriguing combination of an organically embedded policy innovation, the product of distinctive and coevolving local conditions, that has nevertheless displayed a remarkable capacity to move and mutate. What began life, in fact, as an open-ended, adaptive experiment, for which virtually nothing was fixed and everything was negotiable, has somehow spawned a mobile policy fix or template, often imposed from outside and above in the service of technocratic, managerial interests. PB consequently has functioned as both a radical catalyst and a rationalist cipher. Can it continue to serve these two very different ends?

## A Model Is Born

For all its subsequent stylization, PB never took the form of an immaculate blueprint. Its origins were in some ways rather inauspicious, reflecting the fraught conjuncture of Brazilian politics in the late 1980s. The PT had been the surprise victor in a number of municipal elections across Brazil in 1988, the year that the country's new constitution began to decentralize power to subnational jurisdictions. In Porto Alegre, the less than entirely unified PT inherited, under the leadership of Olívio Dutra, a municipal administration in crisis. The previous administration—which was nominally socialist, but with strong populist tendencies—had effectively sabotaged the incoming popular administration. Having suppressed public-sector pay throughout its term of office, the exiting administration voted 110 percent salary increases to municipal workers after losing the election, deliberately saddling the incoming PT council with a massively overcommitted budget and unserviced debts. With 98 percent of the operating budget absorbed by the wage bill, and loan payments immediately due, the new administration entered city hall in the throes of governance crisis.[23] These profound challenges inflamed a series of unresolved issues across the PT-led coalition, which was still debating, inter alia, if and how to govern in the sectional interests of the working class; whether to adopt a confrontational or conciliatory posture with respect to business, the bourgeois classes, and the corporatist-bureaucratic state; and how to engage the vibrant (but uneven) network of community and neighborhood associations across the city. The PT had campaigned on a platform of participatory engagement, including a commitment to empower "popular councils," but as Benjamin Goldfrank has explained in his definitive account of this period, in the election's wake it remained unclear whether this would represent, in practice, a commitment to more active consultation, to a new modality of "co-government," or to a radically decentralized vision of "all power to the soviets."[24]

The eventual (early) form of PB in Porto Alegre was forged through a series of compromises around these questions, coupled with concerted pressure from local social movements, through the first two years of the revenue-starved PT administration. Whether or not Porto Alegre deserves the status of the pioneer of PB remains subject to some debate. There certainly were previous experiences to draw upon, rooted in extant practice and earlier forms of participatory decision-making, but these were to be assembled into an especially compelling form in Porto Alegre. For his part, Bruce contends that there was "no prior experience anywhere in Brazil of anything resembling the participatory budget that began to emerge in Porto Alegre in 1989 and 1990," beyond the historical demonstration effect of the Russian Soviets and the Paris Commune found in various strands of Brazilian Marxism.[25] Goldfrank, on the other hand, documents a series of participatory and public budgeting initiatives developed by the Brazilian Democratic Movement in the late 1970s and early 1980s (in Lages, Boa Esperança, and Pelotas), which were apparently known to PT activists.[26] These community-based efforts, according to Gianpaolo Baiocchi and colleagues, "comprised a mix of practices: contestatory claims-making, collective self-improvement and mutual assistance, and consciousness-raising,"[27] practices that would become hallmarks of Porto Alegre's early experiment, consonant as they are with PB's initial radicalizing spirit. Perhaps more pertinently for the future design of PB policy, these initiatives also were known to Porto Alegre's Union of Neighborhood Associations (UAMPA), which had been citing them as precedents in its submissions to the City prior to the adoption of PB.[28] (Policy) success, to coin a phrase, has many fathers.

Notwithstanding such paternity claims, lodged in terms of (genetic) specificities in policy design, the broader and arguably more significant point is that these are all manifestations of the far-reaching reconstruction of left thinking and praxis in Latin America that had occurred post-1968.[29] This bore distinctly postauthoritarian as well as urban-solidaristic currents, in its embrace of, inter alia, radically open-ended democratization and demands for the recognition of new social subjects; direct participation and the construction of new rights of citizenship; the necessity for frontal challenges to corruption, clientelism, and related forms of distorted state practice; the development of non-state publics, spaces of deliberation and dissent, and protest; the prioritization of territorial redistribution; and the imperative of responding to the urgent material and social needs of the urban poor. While Porto Alegre, and the surrounding region of Rio Grande do Sul, measure up better than most of Brazil in terms of basic indicators of social development, this relative condition cannot conceal what were scarring circumstances of entrenched inequality and endemic poverty. The city of Porto Alegre's slum-dwelling population had doubled in the 1980s, and today one quarter of the population still lives in "irregular settlements," *favelas,* or *villas,* as they are known locally; conditions in the labor market have deteriorated markedly since the 1980s, including increases in unemployment, (working) poverty, and informal employment; and social inequality and spatial segregation has continued to rise.[30] Porto Alegre, like other Brazilian cities, is fundamentally marked by socioeconomic polarization: as the majority of its growing population is channeled into poorly serviced slum districts, the number of which has more than quadrupled since 1965, all of the land available for development at the end of the 1990s was controlled by just fifteen wealthy families.[31]

This was the challenging but ultimately generative environment in which Porto Alegre's signature experiment in participatory budgeting first took shape and then gained traction. The municipality's fragile fiscal situation, in the early years, meant that direct engagement with local communities was pragmatically focused on relatively marginal adjustments to existing services, like garbage collection and public transportation. Concerned that this circumscribed scope for meaningful neighborhood investments might translate into accountability deficits and problems of legitimation, the PT administration willingly granted direct participation rights (one person, one vote) to an enlarged network of sixteen neighborhood-level districts (regiões), and as increased revenues began to flow (following local tax reforms and an increase in fiscal transfers from the federal government), so did meaningful investments in basic infrastructure and services. In the process, the "city for workers" orientation of the PT was progressively displaced by a "city for all" ethos, based on the principle of broad and meaningful participation.[32]

A virtuous cycle was duly established, connecting an increased flow of resources (especially to the poorest neighborhoods) to heightened participation at community forums (across classes, social, and ethnic groups, with disproportionately high representation of hitherto marginalized populations), and consolidating support across the PT-led governing coalition (which would win reelection in 1992 with PB as its "central axis"). A wealth of statistical and ethnographic data has since confirmed that the Porto Alegre PB was associated, first, with significant levels of citizen mobilization, especially among the poor, with aggregate turnout at meetings across the city rising into the tens of thousands annually; second, with a boom in the number of active community organizations and neighborhood associations, measurably energizing the civic sphere; third, with marked improvements in infrastructure provision (such as roads and sewers) and basic services (such as public transport and education); fourth, with a reduction in clientelistic behavior and corruption, by virtue of more transparent systems of priority setting and budget allocation; and fifth, with a high degree of progressive sociospatial redistribution, albeit from the low base of entrenched inequalities, as the poor communities mobilized through ongoing rounds of neighborhood-level decision-making have witnessed a reallocation of spending priorities in their favor.[33]

This is not to deny that there are real political and fiscal limits on the process of participatory budgeting, even in locations, like Porto Alegre, where it has come to exhibit its most developed form. As Sérgio Baierle, Boaventura de Sousa Santos, and others have argued, municipal authorities in Brazil are confronted by both fiscal and institutional capacity constraints, given that they account for only 14 percent of public expenditures within a massively overstretched state system; local initiatives can likewise do little to turn the adverse tides of macroeconomic and macropolitical change, as progressive oases in a sea of neoliberalization; and there are practical and political limits to the extent to which participatory methods have been able to engage with strategic and city-regional issues, with the *formation* of policies as opposed merely to their distributive *effects,* and with the construction of more fundamental political frames, parameters, and objectives.[34] Nevertheless, there are few who dissent from the view that, on balance, the Porto Alegre experiment with PB was associated with a remarkable degree of grassroots mobilization, with the articulation *and satisfaction* of citizen demands for services and investments, and with broadly redistributive outcomes that favored lower-income districts and populations.

These are the foundational principles, in turn, upon which the transformative potential of participatory processes is claimed, with their promise of radical—and in some cases even revolutionary—change. The fact that PB experiments have been constrained in some places, and co-opted in others, and the fact that there is now a large hinterland of benign and managerialist "distortions" of the Porto Alegre model, should not be taken as a negation of the progressive *potential* of this enabling political technology. At least this has been the line of argument favored by the most articulate advocates of the PB philosophy, inside and outside Brazil. One of the architects of the Porto Alegre experiment, the city's first PT mayor, Olívio Dutra, countered the accusation that the internationalization of PB had coincided with a dulling of its radical edge:

> [We] are fully conscious that this revolutionary process is situated in a context of heightened struggle between two distinct projects. The traditional elites know perfectly well that this practice gives real content to democracy, ending privileges, clientelism, and ultimately the power of capital over society. This is a political struggle with a clear class (or class bloc) content which will continue to develop for a long time. That is why if anyone claims, and some do, that participatory budgeting is just a more organized form for the poor to fight over the crumbs of capitalism, or at best, that it is a slight democratic improvement

totally unrelated to socialism, they would be completely mistaken. Besides deepening and radicalizing democracy, participatory budgeting also is constituted by a vigorous socialist impulse, if we conceive socialism as a process in which direct, participatory democracy is an essential element, because it facilitates critical consciousness and ties of solidarity among the exploited and oppressed, opening the way for the public appropriation of the State and the construction of a new society.[35]

Expressed in such terms, the radical appeal, not to say potential, of PB is therefore not difficult to appreciate. In Brazil, where PB was diffusing "laterally" across PT-controlled municipalities at a rapid rate during the 1990s,[36] the spirit of participation animated Lula's historic election campaign of 2002, but his ascent to national office also marked the beginning of the end of attempts to "upscale" PB beyond the realm of local governance. But even as the project was stalled and diluted in Brazil, it would yield pervasive demonstration effects for left-leaning administrations across Latin America,[37] and indeed considerably beyond. "At a time when neoliberal policies were all pervasive in the [Global] North," Hilary Wainwright has observed, "the 'participatory budgets' of Porto Alegre became emblematic of the possibility of democratizing—rather than privatizing—the state."[38] For the left, this was PB's promise.

## Modeling Politics

On the heels of the collapse of state socialism in the Soviet sphere, and the concomitant rise of neoliberal end-of-history hubris, the ascendancy of corporate globalization, and (for a while at least) the celebration of American-style "deregulated" capitalism, the search for practical inspiration and "real utopias" had assumed a historic urgency for a beleaguered left. There has been no shortage of skepticism, of course. As Gret and Sintomer noted, "History has taught us to be wary of radiant myths which are subsequently liable to disclose a far less radiant reality"; but even discounting the hype of "miracle solutions," their early 2000s conclusion was that the "city of Porto Alegre is today a real laboratory for democracy."[39] Buoyed by a long sequence of positive results—especially in terms of the breadth and depth of participation and social outcomes—the city's PB experiment was indeed closely scrutinized by left scholars and activists, down to the fine detail of the timing of meetings and the micropolitics of decision-making, with largely reaffirmative results.[40] (Truly critical interrogations, however, have been quite rare, suggesting a degree of self-editing may have been a feature of some of this work.) The findings from Porto Alegre have been resonant because they appeared to offer an innovative response to the long-standing and troubled division "between a technocratic vision of public administration and a spontaneist and naive conception of participation," and although the model was not going to be "mechanically reproducible," either in other locales or at higher scales of governance, it could clearly generate constructive lessons.[41]

Erik Olin Wright and his collaborators in the Real Utopias project have done much to distill the essence of Porto Alegre's "institutional design," as an "instance of participatory socialism," while at the same time acknowledging the impossibility of replication. Here, recognition of policy-transfer realpolitik is balanced with a deliberately cultivated optimism of the intellect:

> It is, of course, far from clear how widely this innovative experiment can be extended to other places, issues, contexts, or scales. But of course in 1989, when this process was started by the PT in Porto Alegre, virtually no one would have imagined it would work so effectively there either. The limits of possibility are not something about which we can have definitive knowledge before testing them. In any case, a wide range of other places are experimenting with various forms of participatory budgeting . . . and preliminary research suggests that in at least some of these cases the adaptations have been successful.[42]

A feature of the body of critical scholarship on Porto Alegre, even as it retains a fairly consistent strand of active advocacy, has been the avoidance of the kind of fetishism of institutional design that has typified more orthodox approaches to "policy transfer."[43] Participatory budgeting is duly analyzed not as a technical fix but as an open-ended political process. Goldfrank's comparative study of Porto Alegre, Montevideo, and Caracas, for example, led him to conclude that "the design features that ultimately aided the deepening of democracy in Porto Alegre—a high degree of participant decision-making power, a wide range of issues under debate, and an informal structure—were contingent upon a decentralized national state that afforded resources and responsibilities to the municipal government and a set of weakly institutionalized local opposition parties that failed to resist the participation program forcefully."[44] This is confirmed by Baierle's in situ assessment, which locates not only the progressive potential but also the incipient contradictions and limits of the Porto Alegre experiment in what amounts to a distinctive historical, geographical, and political conjuncture: trends such as the "professionalization" of popular leadership, the hoarding of strategic decision-making capacity within the municipal administration, and the downloading of policy delivery responsibilities to the neighborhoods were aggravating "a dramatic tension between community militancy and the 'public service' defined in terms of [a] third-sector commoditication of social rights."[45] Soon, these underlying pressures were to be associated with significant ruptures in the politics of participatory democracy, both locally and nationally.

Participatory budgeting had been explicitly named in early formulations of the PT's national election platform in 2001, but according to one of those involved in the negotiations, Roberto Gomes, the prospects of some kind of federalized PB receded along with a gradual "process of cutting off links with the grassroots" during the subsequent election campaign. Olívio Dutra, former mayor of Porto Alegre and longtime confidante of Lula, put it more bluntly: "The participatory budget was not accepted by the party at the national level."[46] Lip service was paid to the legacy of PB, during the campaign and in the immediate afterglow of the election, but there had been a break with the radical ethos, as espoused by one of the municipal champions of PB, the late Celso Daniel, that the PT's responsibility was "to share power with the movements from whence it came."[47] There were arguably some legitimate concerns—for example, regarding the practicalities of enabling meaningful participation at the national scale and the uneven geography of PB experimentation, which heavily favored the south of the country—but there seems to have been little concerted effort to address such questions. In some quarters, the achievements of the PT and local social movements in the municipal sphere were treated with patronizing indifference. So when Sérgio Baierle presented the case for PB to federal policymakers on behalf of the Porto Alegre NGO, Cidade, he was bluntly informed, "We already have participatory democracy, for we have a worker in the presidential office."[48]

The ironic coda to these events came less than three years later, when the Lula government nearly collapsed under a far-reaching corruption scandal.[49] While Lula himself survived this debacle, the moral and political legitimacy of the PT did not. Splintering and disillusionment across left constituencies and social movements predictably followed. By virtue of its potentially catalytic role in pulling into public view "the secrets of the state," in Chico de Oliveira's phrase, PB might have made a difference in this context, many argued. As Olívio Dutra explained,

The corruption scandal is linked to the failure to develop participatory democracy. The Lula government ... tried to combat corruption by [way of] the traditional tools of the state. The fight against corruption has to involve other processes like the participatory budget, which makes it possible for the public to control the state and promotes active citizenship. I am certain that the participatory budget, which is a radical instrument, is the best way to fight corruption and to guarantee active citizenship and public control of the state in all its dimensions. But that has yet to happen. We achieved a lot in the city of Porto Alegre and the state of Rio Grande do Sul but the pace has slackened. There is a lot we still have to do in these places and we have to start practically from zero in the rest of the country.[50]

The pace had certainly slackened in Porto Alegre and in the state of Rio Grande do Sul, where Dutra followed his period as mayor (1989–1993) with a term as the state's governor (1999–2003). The *petistas* were to be voted out of office in both the city and the state, in 2004 and 2003, respectively, with subsequently more conservative administrations reversing or significantly diluting the advance of participatory democracy. The bold experiment with a state-level PB process under Governor Dutra ultimately failed, in part due to its role in raising expectations that ultimately could not be accommodated and in part, as Goldfrank and Schneider have compellingly argued, because the PB process itself was transformed into an arena for explicitly partisan contestation. [51] There were practical problems too. "You have this problem of scale, it's just impossible for it to work," one local supporter of PB later reflected on this attempt to transpose neighborhood- and city-level practices of deliberation to the statewide arena, but "the other problem was money, because the state government had a serious fiscal crisis."[52] Duly tarnished, Rio Grande do Sul's PB machinery was downgraded, under the succeeding Rigotto administration, to little more than a consultative process.

The policy shift—involving a simultaneous dilution and distortion of the founding (local) principles of PB—may have been less abrupt and more incremental in Porto Alegre, although in some ways it has been cumulatively more profound. The centrist coalition that defeated the PT in 2004 and which would govern, under the Fogaça administration (2005–2010), with the slogan "Preserving achievements, constructing changes," reconstituted PB into a more business-friendly, Third-Way form, as *governança solidária local* (local solidary governance, or LSG). Fogaça had made a campaign pledge to retain

PB, acknowledging the extent to which its practices had become embedded in the city,[53] but his subsequent reforms would largely blunt its radical, even reforming, edge. Fogaça defeated the PT by running to the center and exploiting the very openness of the PB method. As one local observer explained,

> For a period of time, it looked like the PT was indestructible . . . nobody could beat the PT in elections. There was a strong polarization in the population, a radical polarization between a part of the population that liked the PT and the other part that hated the PT. But nobody could beat the PT because the majority still preferred the PT. Then Fogaça arrived with the proposal to take a middle way: "I'm not PT, but I'm not anti-PT either. . . . We don't need PT anymore, we can do the same and better." In the campaign, Fogaça was selling PB more than the PT itself! He [said he] would continue the same politics, and the [World] Social Forum too. Fogaça made a political promise to continue with PB, but today it's different. . . . Now, it's much weaker.[54]

As a senior official on the Fogaça administration put it, the goal had been to "oxygenate" the PB process, by engaging with other actors and interests. The organic link to the PT would also have to be broken. PB, the Fogaça official continued, had previously been "tied to the PT, owned by the PT," but that had to change, the mayor "argu[ing] that participatory budgeting is owned by the city, by the community, and is not tied to a particular party."[55]

Soon, it would become clear what "oxygenization" really meant. The circle of participation was enlarged to include a series of interests allegedly "excluded" from the *petista*-designed PB process, including local businesses, foundations, universities, and churches, as well as other branches of the state. Superficially more "inclusive," this also had the effect of degrading popular participation to the status of a sectional or stakeholder interest, while layering on a quasi-corporatist ethos. In practice, the participatory process would become dominated by governmental and "NGOized" interests; local businesses demonstrated little motivation to participate, while popular participation declined. As Daniel Chavez has pointedly observed, LSG might have been "praised by the World Bank and the EU but [it was] strongly criticised by local NGOs, other civil society organisations and by many of the most active participants in the participatory budget process itself."[56] Interpretations vary, but this neutralization of the promise and practice of PB in Porto Alegre seems to have been politically imposed, rather than an outcome of some internal process of exhaustion. The electorate, it seemed, had rejected the PT's increasingly complacent style of municipal governance, not the principle of participation per se: Cidade's Sergio Baierle tartly observed that "it wasn't the participatory budgeting process nor the World Social Forum who were defeated in 2004, but the government led by the PT."[57] Not only had the PT been in control of municipal government since 1989, Lula's federal administration was also lagging in the polls. PB had risen with the PT; now it seemed to be falling with it too.

Fogaça's Secretary of Political Coordination and Local Governance, César Busatto, who had previously worked as a political consultant for the state's leading business association and as an architect of public-sector downsizing and privatization schemes for the conservative state government of Antônio Britto (1995–1998), explained his administration's communitarian reconstruction of PB this way:

> Local [Solidarity] Governance is an executive forum, not a deliberative one; it is a [form of] network coordination that seeks to reach co-responsibility pacts. In this venue there is no dispute, no voting and no delegates. . . . [This is a] model of co-responsibility in favor of social inclusion. The central idea is to establish in Porto Alegre an enduring partnership among the government, the private businesses and the third sector that seeks to solve the problems of the city.[58]

Busatto also actively encouraged PB participants to seek out charitable donations, rather than relying on government investments, suggesting that they "make the rich people cry . . . so that they open their pocketbooks and put some of their money in this neighborhood."[59]

Under the LSG regime, some of the tropes of participatory democracy were retained, but their substantive meaning and political intent was all but inverted. The Fogaça administration (somewhat obliquely) acknowledged the previous two decades of experience in participatory budgeting, along with its status as an "international reference," but chose to emphasize the manner in which its newly created structures of local solidarity governance are effectively superimposed on the inherited routines of the Orçamento Participativo, establishing an ethos of partnership,

> a new way for everyone to commit their share of contribution for the development of the city. . . . [In] this vision [, just] as important as demanding solutions

is to learn how to suggest development alternatives. Likewise, "doing" becomes as valuable as "demanding" when the time comes to search for paths to improve the quality of life and social conditions.[60]

Along with the shift from agitational *demanding* to conformist *doing,* LSG also drew on the obfuscatory language of cross-sectoral partnership and social-capital building borrowed from international development practice. And its overhauled model of participation-through-governance was bolstered, at least symbolically, by a cooperative agreement struck with UNESCO in 2005—which was taken in some quarters to imply the joint governance of the participatory process itself. The impenetrable verbiage of this agreement, however, which blended multilateral governance discourse with a local political ethos that seemed deliberately opaque, would never win praise for its transparency. On the contrary, the LSG was presented in terms reminiscent of Orwellian doublespeak, as a "multidisciplinary network that organizes territorially in order to promote havens of common living experiences capable of potentializing the culture of solidarity and cooperation between government and local society [with the objective of stimulating] partnerships based on principles of participation, autonomy, transversality and co-responsibility . . . deepening the commitment to governance structures with local communities in an environment of dialogue and plurality, establishing relations ever more horizontal."[61]

An international assessment of the Fogaça administration's model of local solidarity governance concluded, rather skeptically, that it was associated with no more than "scarce results."[62] As Leubolt, Novy, and Becker saw (through) it, the LSG makeover of PB was intended to maintain "the *appearance* of participatory governance," while effectively reversing the policy, based on redistributive democratization, of the preceding PT administrations.[63] In the words of a well-placed local activist, the PB process under Fogaça had been reduced to "a parody" of its original, pioneering form, or as Daniel Chavez would sarcastically characterize it, "participation lite."[64] The Fogaça administration had cynically stepped up its marketing efforts around the *remodeled* Porto Alegre model, particularly among international audiences, while disingenuously facilitating the erosion of participatory channels and structures on the ground. One manifestation of this de facto policy shift, according to Cidade, is that there was "a remarkable decline in the attendance [at] PB plenaries by government officials [following the introduction of LSG], which means less technical assistance and less accountability," while the administration's budget proposals were to be decried as nothing short of an "exercise in fiction."[65] Some neighborhood PB groups remained active, but many lost their momentum, while others degenerated into unproductive standoffs with municipal officials. Momentum and energy dissipated, as one longtime advocate explained, as "the rate of renewal inside the participatory budgeting process [declined]. . . . So there are very few newcomers to the process, in terms of leaders, delegates, and councilors."[66] There were also signs that the generally virtuous cycle, established during the 1990s, between concomitant increases in public investment and popular participation had been degraded into a vicious cycle of disinvestment, demobilization, and distrust. This is the "thermadorian moment" that Baierle had predicted midway through what was to be the last of the post-1989 sequence of PT administrations. Novy and Leubolt came to a similarly sober, if not somber, conclusion: in so far as it can be understood as a counterhegemonic strategy, of continuously deepening, radical state/society transformation, the Porto Alegre model—in situ at least—must be considered a "failure."[67]

## Porto Alegre Redux

If the failures of the PT at the national and local scales in Brazil seem to have largely incapacitated PB as a transformative project, its trajectory as a globalizing urban-governance fix has followed a radically different course. In the realm of the multilateral banks, international policy brokers, and orthodox policy networks, participatory budgeting has been folded into an evolving elite consensus around "good governance," where it resonates with established emphases on decentralized management, extra-state institutional building, transparency, inclusive governance, and partnership-based delivery. This reflects a critique, such as the one articulated by Frannie de Leautier, vice president of the World Bank Institute, in the Bank's primer on PB strategies, that "[m]any developing countries . . . suffer from unsatisfactory and often dysfunctional governance systems that include rent seeking and malfeasance, inappropriate allocation of resources, insufficient revenue systems, and weak delivery of vital public services."[68] PB, in this context, is seen as an antidote to state failure. Variants of PB have been mobilized in the service of the attendant policy agenda because, as the lead economist for public sector governance, Anwar Shah, goes on to explain, they offer citizens at large an opportunity to learn about government operations and to deliberate, debate, and influence the allocation of public resources. It is a tool for educating, engaging, and empowering citizens and strengthening demand for good governance. The enhanced transparency and accountability that participatory budgeting creates can help reduce government inefficiency and curb clientelism, patronage, and corruption. . . . Participatory budgeting also strengthens inclusive governance by giving marginalized and excluded groups the opportunity to have their voices heard and to influence public decision making vital to their interests. Done right, it has the potential to make governments more responsive to citizens' needs and preferences and more accountable to them for performance in resource allocation and service delivery. In doing so, participatory budgeting can improve government performance and enhance the quality of democratic participation.[69]

Participatory approaches to local governance, Shah recognizes, can in some cases simply mask power inequalities and bureaucratic inefficiencies, but in the right circumstances they can be molded so as to "yield outcomes desired by the median voter."[70]

The language of median voting, of course, had hardly been borrowed from Porto Alegre. While the PB process had indeed facilitated a degree of cross-class consensus formation around certain local development objectives, its most significant *political* achievements were more often measured in terms of the mobilization of the poor, the marginalized, and the nonorganized.[71] In the world of the multilateral lending agencies, however, these developments were being interpreted as a "quiet revolution" in local governance and "public choice making," in the words of the head of the World Bank's urban program, Tim Campbell.[72] Starting in the 1990s, a wave of governmental decentralization, especially across Latin America, had progressively melded with the shifting agenda of the multilateral agencies, whose "second-generation" reform efforts were beginning to focus on institutional transformation, innovations in governance, and localized delivery.[73] Campbell's explanation of these developments is that

scores of mayors invented or borrowed ideas in order to implement new and more effective ways to mobilize local finance, to foster institutional change, and to mobilize popular participation in local public decision making. . . . The most striking of these innovations is the reconstruction of a "contract of governance" between elected officials and voter-taxpayers. . . . The essence of this governance innovation was fiscal decision making through participatory democracy at the local level. . . . For nearly ten years, central governments were coaxed and wheedled by the International Monetary Fund (IMF) and the World Bank to reform the public sector in order to restore growth. These efforts met with mixed success [, but] the next stage of reforms in the region was shifted to the local level, where new models of governance were being invented.[74]

Campbell readily acknowledges that the multilateral agencies, and the accompanying network of technical-assistance organizations, "followed rather than led" this process of transformative decentralization, not least because most are formally barred from any involvement in explicitly political or partisan activities. Fortuitously, however, local governments across the region were "invent[ing] through trial and error new ways of doing political business," driving the reform agenda and, in the process, "creating new pages in the manuals of prevailing wisdom in agencies like the World Bank."[75]

Such appropriations of the PB model are regarded as relatively benign instances of policy mainstreaming by some in Porto Alegre, indeed a positive spur to the city's "self-esteem" by others.[76] There are many on the left, however, who discern a more calculating rationale on the part of the multilateral agencies, particularly the World Bank, with which post-*petista* municipal governments in the city are seen to have implicitly or explicitly connived. For the World Bank, one local observer remarked, PB "is a way to control [social] demands, without delegitimating the government. It's a very dangerous mechanism if you want to [use it for the purposes of] control."[77] Less conspiratorially, the World Bank also has strategic interests in the propagation of multiparty "stakeholder" models of local governance, which dilute local power blocs and dissipate disruptive forces. (This echoes Fogaça administration's reform of the PB system as a means of "oxygenating" local governance, in contrast to the original PT vision of transformative democratization.) Some mutations of PB can be "functional" in this regard, too, acting as technologies of containment.

By the mid-1990s, the Porto Alegre "model" was beginning to circulate both as a best-practice technique and as an urban innovation ripe for emulation. The World Bank's innovations program, launched in 1995, identified

Porto Alegre as a "change making" location, by virtue of its pioneering role in the construction of participatory practice, later selecting the Brazilian city as one of eleven sites from the Bank's Latin American portfolio deserving of intensive (case) study.[78] This would be among the first of many efforts to capture and systematize the essence of the Porto Alegre experiment. Even though the Bank's outsourced study of Porto Alegre emphasized a series of impediments to technocratic diffusion—likely to "limit the opportunities for replication"—the international program on subnational innovation would eventually reach the conclusion that, for all the idiosyncrasies of the cases in question, "visionary local leadership" and risk taking were decisive factors, and that "Latin America's experience can be helpful to leaders in other parts of the world."[79] It was local policy entrepreneurs, of one kind or another, who had led the way in

> inventing successes and best practices of government that are "closer to the people." Numerous examples throughout Latin America indicate—often despite macroeconomic instability, high inflation, and strong top-down regulation— that subnational actors have repeatedly achieved what their central counter- parts preached: sound policymaking, better administration, better services, more participation, and sustained economic development.[80]

Already, by the mid-1990s, PB was beginning to appeal to multiple constitu- encies, symbolizing everything from an administrative technique to a source of political inspiration. Even within the World Bank, it was being simultane- ously advanced as a corruption-resistant guarantor of transparency by audi- tors and accountants, as a model of good local governance impervious even to environments of macroeconomic turbulence, and (by advocates of social engagement) as a step beyond the "protest-based culture of the 80s . . . par- ticipatory budget exercises hav[ing] fostered a more 'civil' and less disrup- tive form of conflict resolution through dialogue and negotiations."[81]

If World Bank researchers and policy advocates were ideologically disin- clined to embrace the organically political face of the Porto Alegre experi- ment, it was precisely the open-ended and transformative *social* potential of PB that was alternately emphasized in left treatments, as a radically *Southern* modality of political practice, as a pathbreaking innovation in empowered participatory governance, and as an emergent form of "technodemocracy."[82] Meanwhile, somewhere in between, Porto Alegre was also being celebrated by multilateral NGOs, and in the various orbits of the UN-Habitat program, as a tool of social participation. This mainstreaming of participatory budgeting would have far-reaching consequences. It was the UN's Istanbul conference, Habitat II in 1996, that truly propelled Porto Alegre into the international spotlight. One of eighteen models of "innovative local government" selected by the centrist Cardoso administration for the Brazilian exposition at the conference, along with seven other exemplary cases of *petista* governance, prompted the PT to design a self-congratulatory poster, pointing out that "the party administers less than 1% of our cities, but contributes 44% of the projects that officially represent Brazil."[83] These, though, were only the first signs of PB's potency as mobile policy model. As Gianpaolo Baiocchi would later reflect, ultimately, "Porto Alegre's significance may lie in its impact on other places."[84] It is to this question that we now turn.

# 7

## Democracy on the Move

The Shanghai World Expo of 2010 was dedicated to the theme "Better city, better life"—its vision being that of "Cities of Harmony," where the problems of a rapidly urbanizing world would meet their match in the form of an unprecedented wave of urban innovation. A centerpiece of the event—touted as the largest and most expensive in history—was an Urban Best Practices Area, where about fifty cities from around the world were invited to showcase their achievements in building a better, more sustainable, and more livable city. Here, Porto Alegre, which had earlier rebranded its well-known PB model as Local Solidary Governance in a joint venture with UNESCO, found itself in the company of decidedly big-city players like Cairo, London, Milan, Chicago, Moscow, Taipei, and Montreal. What had begun as a grassroots movement for organic democratization had apparently completed its transformation into what UNESCO had taken to calling a "world best practice."[1]

The phonebook-sized *Shanghai Manual* that accompanied the proceedings was addressed to "mayors, urban planners and decision-makers of cities around the world," presented as a compendium of "innovative ideas . . . based entirely on practical solutions." Here, the Porto Alegre model was lauded less for its energizing effects on local democracy (and certainly not for its radically disruptive potential) than for its success in "improving urban management." The Porto Alegre model's "positive impacts on city management" were held to include

> greater transparency, greater rationality in administrative procedures, strict control of finance, constant public monitoring of governmental performance,

and an established routine of efficient allocation of public resources. . . . Specific political results included: increased approval ratings, decrease in nepotism and unethical practices, and increase in democratic practices (including among low-income groups). There was also a positive effect on municipal government of increased functional efficiency, improved staff morale, improved monitoring resulting in less waste and delays, reduced costs of public works, and greater transparency with respect to taxes paid and services rendered.[2]

Perhaps the Brazilians had witnessed an "increase in democratic practices," as a "result" of these managerial innovations, but this was a far cry from the early image of PB as a catalyst for political transformation. Although, perhaps it was still possible for PB to be a carrier of diverse, even contradictory, political projects—a managerial best practice for some, a site of radicalization for others? The kaleidoscopic quality of the Porto Alegre model—both at home and abroad—found an appropriately ambiguous reflection in the city's pavilion in the Urban Best Practices Area in Shanghai, the glass-walled, five-section design of which was reckoned to look "like a big crystal maze," within which the city's mayoral delegation sought to make the most of its elaborately constructed "communication platform."[3] Here, visitors were invited to learn the benefits of participatory politics by way of an interactive games installation.

As the PB model has globalized, "Porto Alegre" has become properly polysemic. Invocations of the Brazilian city have acquired a ritual quality in the sprawling discourses of participatory budgeting; they acknowledge, and defer to, a place of origination, if not a site of deliberate model building. While it is commonplace to see PB tagged as a Porto Alegre "invention," more careful observers recognize that this municipal innovation was created, not by technocratic fiat, but across the indeterminate terrain of political contestation. "Once upon a time in Porto Alegre" is the tongue-in-cheek way that Yves Sintomer and colleagues recount the tale, stressing that PB was, in reality, "the outcome of a conjunction of top-down and bottom-up processes. . . . It is important to emphasise that the 'participatory budgeting' mechanism was a pragmatic invention, and not the application of an intellectual or political design."[4] If anything, however, this means that the global diffusion of PB—possibly to more than 2,500 sites around the world today, spanning every continent and reaching just about every social and political system—was even more remarkable (see Figure 9). The fact that there are multiple translations, in scores of countries, not only of PB terminology but of actually existing participatory budgeting *practices,* has led the authors of a recent global assessment of this "success story" to observe that

> this phenomenon is astonishing, because whereas technological innovations such as mobile phones, MP3 players and the Internet spread around the world extremely quickly without any problem, special techniques for dialogue and decision-making normally require more time. This development is also unique because participatory budgeting is a procedure invented in countries of the Global South.[5]

Undeniably, what was achieved in Porto Alegre represented a "real institutional innovation,"[6] but in order to travel so far so fast, this also had to be a political technology that resonated positively across diverse contexts. In this respect, the PB model would eventually find the wind at its back. In retrospect, there was self-evident appeal in a model that stood for principled governance and citizen involvement, especially one originating from a country that was itself clearly making large strides in democratic renewal, social progress, *and* economic growth. The feel-good appeal of this "lesson from the South" transformed PB into the political equivalent of motherhood and apple pie.

An aura duly formed around the Porto Alegre experiment that enveloped even distant relatives of the original model in a soft-focus haze. While arguably still aiding the noble cause of democratic innovation, some have argued that this has deflected attention away from the need for *continual* political and institutional reconstruction in what remains the conflict-riven and often zero- or negative-sum arena of municipal politics and financing, while unhelpfully inflating expectations that PB itself, as a technical fix, might be the silver-bullet solution.[7] One of the closest observers of the Porto Alegre model, in situ and abroad, complained of what he saw as a "romantic vision" of the Brazilian experience of PB in Europe: "We have a problem because the Porto Alegre model has become some sort of myth, in Brazil, but in the world also, [which creates] difficulties in solving the problems of the model. . . . There is some disillusionment now in Brazil. The myth is losing its appeal."[8] But even if the model was losing some of its sheen at home, this had apparently not impeded the propagation of its many derivatives in various export markets. Some notably entrepreneurial careers had been forged along the way, as this respondent went on to somewhat wistfully reflect:

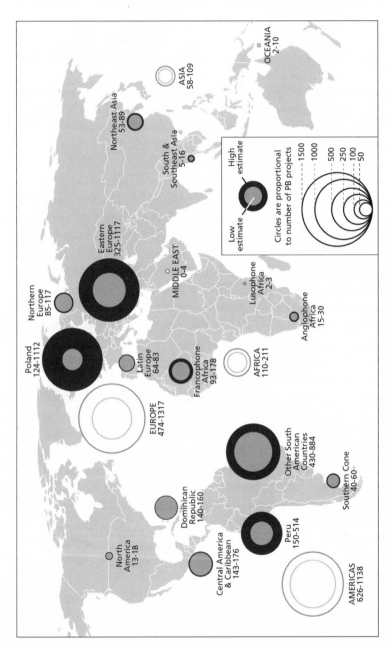

Figure 9. Globalizing Participatory Budgeting. Source: Derived from Sintomer et al. 2013.

It's very interesting, the movement of people from the original [PB] experiments, because there is a lot of people from the radical left who now work for the World Bank, the United Nations. There is a career in this for these people, people who know how to implement this participatory democracy. . . . There's a lot of guys from Europe, from the NGOs, who work just applying participatory budgeting around the world. They are *selling* this experiment![9]

Such sentiments are in many ways understandable, as the energy (and in some cases even the belief) of hometown advocates of the Porto Alegre model has been sapped, as the model itself has become instrumentalized, and as local political relations have soured. The attitude of post-*petista* administrations in Porto Alegre toward PB seems hollow to some—especially to those on the left—and strategic and calculating to others, while at the same time the international hawking of the model qua model has continued almost unabated. It is notable, however, that it is "pasteurized" versions of PB—the production and propagation of which also has a Porto Alegre component[10]— that have been traveling farthest and fastest in recent years. These days, stylized renderings of the PB model tend to be delivered by technocratic advocates and policy entrepreneurs, rather than by political champions or grassroots networkers.

For many observers, the transformative promise of the original model has not only faded, the model itself has been actively degraded and politically (mis)appropriated, in some cases to the point of parody. And the local social contract that had been won in Porto Alegre through the medium of PB has no meaningful parallel in the majority of these "replication" efforts. There may, however, be certain characteristic patterns of *adaption*, reflecting contextual circumstances and the balance of local forces. The "uses" of PB sometimes say more about the user than the technique. In the words of one seasoned PB practitioner, "It all depends on *who* is doing the adaptation [because, ultimately, PB] can mean anything to anybody. The Chinese are interested because they think participatory budgeting is a co-governing model that can be less threatening to their administrations. If you had said that to the [Brazilian] Workers' Party in 1989, they'd have had a problem!"[11] Similarly, as one of those present at the initiation of the Porto Alegre experiment reflected,

As a strategy, [PB] was a tool for democratizing the state, after twenty-one years of dictatorship. The replication internationally is much more about transforming it into a social-assistance tool for how to deal with strong demand from the poor with very little resources. . . . It's interactive, but like a game on the internet, the options are closed. So in China they are now doing participatory budgeting! . . . The [Communist] Party selects some leaders from the community . . . and then they decide on three options for investment—a park for kids, a center for old people, and some other project. Then they organize a voting day, where people are invited to vote for the projects. . . . *There is no real deal.* The good thing [in Porto Alegre], at the beginning, there was a deal. . . . "We will increase taxes, you use the taxes to address poverty issues. OK, this is the deal." In most of these [international] experiences, there is no deal. It's more like a favor.[12]

Like the interactive games in the Porto Alegre pavilion at Expo 2010, many of these simulations seem to offer no more than the appearance of true participation. There are many translations, as it turns out, of the phrase *orçamento participativo.* What for Spanish speakers is *presupuesto participativo,* becomes *Bürgerhaushalt* in Germany, while the Chinese have their very own *canyushi yusuan* (or "participation-style budgeting"). Much is lost, but some things are also gained, in these and other translations.

Translation is the concern of this chapter, which begins with the "mainstreaming" of PB, primarily through the UN-Habitat network, before turning to some of the distinctive ways in which the model has traveled through the networks of the left, like the World Social Forum, and those of the more conservative and managerialist multilateral development agencies, notably the World Bank. We then draw some contrasts with the course of PB politics in Europe and North America, before concluding with a commentary about the role of power in this far-reaching but deeply polyvalent form of policy "diffusion."

## Template Democracy?

The moment when participatory budgeting became a transnational model can be dated to the UN-Habitat II conference, known as the "city summit," which took place in Istanbul in June 1996. It was at this conference that PB acquired its officially sanctioned "best practice" status for the first time. The Istanbul conference launched the Habitat Agenda, a commitment to action largely animated by the principles of participation and social inclusion. Its official declaration stated,

We adopt . . . the principles of partnership and participation as the most democratic and effective approach for the realization of our commitments. Recognizing local authorities as our closest partners . . . we must . . . promote decentralization through democratic local authorities and work to strengthen their financial and institutional capacities in accordance with the conditions of countries, while ensuring their transparency, accountability and responsiveness to the needs of people. . . . [W]e must facilitate capacity-building and promote the transfer of appropriate technology and know-how.[13]

In Istanbul, one of the winners of the Tokyo Award for Excellence in Improving the Living Environment was Yves Cabannes, who had been working in Brazil for a French NGO, the Groupe de recherche et d'échanges technologiques (GRET), as coordinator of their Latin American urban program. Cabannes, who had worked closely with multilateral development agencies, transnational NGOs, local governments, and grassroots organizations, including on human-settlements projects in dozens of counties, would soon be tapped to run the UN's Urban Management Programme (UN-UMP), with responsibility for Latin America and the Caribbean. Here, he drew upon his "broad experience with urban social movements,"[14] with which he would retain—rather unusually in these circumstances—deep connections. Cabannes would become an effective champion of participatory initiatives in the spirit of Porto Alegre, in a context in which "[s]upport for PB [was established] as one of the [UN-UMP] programme's highest priority tasks."[15]

Steps taken to facilitate international learning and exchange in the PB field under the aegis of the UN-UMP included the establishment of a digital library, as a clearinghouse for the burgeoning "grey literature" on participatory practices; the codification and circulation of a "set of tools" for policymakers concerned with those practical and technical instruments, policy routines, and laws and regulations deemed useful in the implementation of PB; and the creation of a directory of "resource people," featuring the preeminent organic intellectuals of the PB movement, academic advocates, peripatetic experts, and "approved" (and therefore trusted) consultants, as well as contacts at the administrative and political levels in a number of cities that had pioneered the latest wave of participatory approaches. These efforts were accompanied by a weighty "conceptual framework" paper, which sought not only to articulate but to deepen the intellectual and political rationale for

PB programming,[16] and a handbook in the UN-Habitat Urban Governance Toolkit series that rather laboriously answered "72 frequently asked questions about participatory budgeting."[17] Anna Kajumulo Tibaijuka, the Executive Director of the UN-Habitat program, explained in the foreword to this widely circulated manual that her organization had embraced PB as a "positive process," a catalyst both for progressive urban governance and local democratization:

> Participatory Budgeting is emerging as an innovative urban management practice with excellent potential to promote principles of good urban governance. Indeed, participatory budgeting can yield many benefits to local government and civil society alike. It can improve transparency in municipal expenditure and stimulate citizens' involvement in decision making over public resources. It can help in boosting city revenues. It can redirect municipal investment towards basic infrastructure for poorer neighbourhoods. It can strengthen social networks and help to mediate differences between elected leaders and civil society groups. By broadening and deepening citizen participation in the allocation of public resources, Participatory Budgeting appears as a positive process for the construction of inclusive cities, where those who are traditionally marginalised are breaking out of the cycle of exclusion. By contributing to principles of good urban governance, Participatory Budgeting is proving to be an important tool in the democratisation of cities. An increasing number of cities are adopting it, with many local variations.[18]

On the face of it, this might be read as an(other) example of technocratic stylization, following the well-worn path of translating a complex, contextually dependent, and multidimensional institutional innovation into an anodyne and conveniently portable "best practice." Organizations like UN-Habitat are hardly immune from these practices. And there is certainly more than a suggestion of the catch-all solution in Tibaijuka's promotion of participatory budgeting. But in the case of the UN-UMP program there were clear indications of a more reflexive form of realpolitik, which resisted best-practice reductionism while seeking to learn, constructively and openly, across an irreducibly variegated family of local cases, projects, and experiments.

If UN-Habitat's adoption of PB as a signature initiative, post-Istanbul, represents a clear instance of transnational mainstreaming of what began life as an organic and open-ended political project, it also represents an instructive instance of a distinctively left-inflected form of mainstreaming. For his part, Cabannes remained explicit about the fact that PB had merely "allowed a first step to be taken in the social control of municipal resources," an intrinsically political process that should not be, indeed *could* not be, technocratically canned, preserved, and marketed for consumption else-where; each PB project had to be understood, he insisted, as a "part of a culture of participation and relationships between local government and society [requiring] a mobilized citizenry as a *precondition for success.* To a certain extent, this feature protects against technocrats, international agen-cies and some NGOs that see PB as a recipe for 'implanting' participation and transparency."[19] The UN-UMP self-consciously wrestled with the dilem-mas inherent in promulgating the mainstream practice of model building, in which a stylized rendering of PB would be made conveniently availa-ble for international circulation and emulation, by steadfastly refusing to depoliticize or degrade the exuberant variety of actually existing PB experi-ences. This principled stand against the ever-present threat of dilution into an analgesic derivative, "PB lite," necessarily came at the price of presenta-tional parsimony for the UN-UMP, but this was evidently taken to be a price worth paying. So the sometimes-tangled narratives of pioneering cities were not to be picked over, or cherry-picked, for decontextualized lessons, but were to be read in conjunction with the executive-summary version of PB for beginners. The UN-UMP's fact sheets on more than a dozen urban expe-riences of PB were furnished in order to illustrate the "variety of approaches. They invite the user to drop the 'model' approach and to consider the range of possibilities and their applicability to local conditions."[20]

On this presentation, the attendant image of PB was not one of a design-determined institutional fix, but rather that of a "space of positive tension,"[21] between the demands of social movements and the goals of progressive urban governance, and between the multiple rationales and rubrics of par-ticipatory budgeting: to improve municipal efficiency and accountability; to "invert priorities" in favor of the poor, the marginalized, and the histori-cally underserved; and to deepen local democracy. There remained an ide-alistic current here. Yet this was not a technocratic idealism but rather a progressively politicized form of "Real Utopia,"[22] constructed through prac-tice. Not all of this practice, it need hardly be said, was politically heroic or administratively beyond reproach. A willingness to acknowledge this, albeit rather unevenly, was a hallmark of the UN-UMP's wide-ranging efforts in the PB field, which in addition to the usual repertoire of information-sharing events, networking initiatives, and actual (as opposed to selectively best) practice manuals, sought to build bridges between multilateral development agencies (including the World Bank, at least for a time), branches of the UN, major donor organizations and cooperation programs (mostly in Europe), and some of the "most progressive Latin American local governments."[23] The UN-UMP was prepared to acknowledge that the real world of participatory budgeting practices spanned the full "range from symbolic gestures with little impact, to structural changes in cities' governance systems and measurable improvements in the quality of life of their citizens," demurring from advocating "the 'best' kind of Participatory Budget."[24] At the same time, attempting to make sense of this scattered and uneven practice, in a context of "remarkably" weak systems for information gathering and monitoring at the municipal level,[25] involved some degree of standardization, categorization, and templating—though even this was pursued in such a way as to facilitate not only the classification of PB practice, but its *deepening* toward more "maximal" forms (see Figure 10).

Especially important among these newly formed transnational networks was URB-AL, the EU's program for regional aid and municipal cooperation with Latin America, which had been established in 1995. Porto Alegre was a leading member of what would become  the URB-AL Network 9 on Local Finance and Participatory Budgeting, which eventually expanded to include 282 local and regional governments across Latin America and 128 partners in Europe.[26] There was a significant degree of overlap between the prime movers of Network 9 and the UN-UMP's Latin American operation (known as PGU-ALC), most of the accompanying "base document" having been drafted by Yves Cabannes in close association with municipal officials and NGO leaders in Porto Alegre.[27] The activities of URB-AL's Network 9 extended to quite routine forms of information sharing, ritualistic exchange, and rudimentary networking, but at its best the network productively reversed the traditionally one-way flows of expertise, influence, and model following, which conventionally ran *with* regional development assistance, out of Europe and into Latin America. Instead, URB-AL became a vehicle for learning *from* Latin America, conferring on some of the region's leading municipalities the status not only of "models," with the imprimatur of the UN and the EU, but the respect of peers on the old continent. It was recognized that the testing of PB models in Europe had produced "mixed results,"[28] and at their most

| Dimensions | Variables | Minimal arrangement | Intermediate arrangement | Maximum arrangement |
|---|---|---|---|---|
| I. Participatory (Citizens) | 1. Instance of final budget approval | Executive (partial consultation) | Council (consultative) | The population (deliberation and legislative approval) |
| | 2. Forms of participation | Community-based representative democracy | Community-based representative democracy open to different types of associations | Direct democracy, universal participation |
| | 3. What body makes budgetary priority decisions? | None | Existing social or political structure, government and citizens (mixed) | Specific commissions with elected council members and a citizen majority |
| | 4. Community participation or citizen participation | Neighborhood level | City-wide level, through thematic contributions | Neighborhood, regional, and city-wide level |
| | 5. Degree of participation of the excluded | Thematic and neighborhood plenaries | Neighborhoods, themes (including civic issues) | Neighborhood + thematic + actor-based, preference for excluded groups (congress) |
| | 6. Oversight and control of execution | Executive | Nonspecific commissions (PB Councils, associations) | Specific commissions (Cofis, Comforça, etc.) |
| I. Participatory (Local Government) | 7. Degree of information sharing and dissemination | Secret, unpublished | Limited dissemination, web, official bulletin, informing delegates | Wide dissemination, including house-to-house distribution |

Figure 10. Dimensions of Participatory Budgeting. Source: Yves Cabannes.

| Dimensions | Variables | Minimal arrangement | Intermediate arrangement | Maximum arrangement |
|---|---|---|---|---|
| | 8. Degree of completion of approved projects (within two years) | Less than 20% | 20% to 80% | Over 80% |
| | 9. Role of legislative branch | Opposition | Passive, non-participation | Active involvement |
| II. Financial and Fiscal | 10. Amount of debated resources | Less than 2% of capital budget | From 2% to 100% of capital budget | 100% of capital and operating budgets |
| | 11. Municipal budget allocation for functioning of PB | Municipal department/team covers cost | Personnel and their activities (e.g., travel) | Personnel, activities, dissemination, training |
| | 12. Discussion of taxation policies | None | Deliberation on tax policies | Deliberation on loans and subsidies |
| III. Normative / Legal | 13. Degree of institutionalization | Informal process | Only institutionalized or only self-regulated annually | Formalized (some parts regulated) with annual self-regulation (evolutionary) |
| | 14. Instrumental or participatory logic | Improvement in financial management | Ties with participatory practices (councils, roundtables) | Part of the culture of participation, participation as right (e.g., San Salvador) |
| | 15. Relationship with planning instruments | Only PB (no long-term plan exists) | Coexistence of PB and city plans, without direct relationship | Clear relationship and interaction between PB and planning in one system (e.g., a congress) |

| IV. Physical / Territorial | 16. Degree of intra-municipal decentralization | Follows administrative regions | Goes beyond administrative regions | Decentralization to all communities and neighborhoods |
| --- | --- | --- | --- | --- |
| | 17. Degree of inclusion of rural areas | PB in either urban area or rural area | The entire municipal territory | Entire municipality with specific measures for rural areas (preferences) |
| | 18. Degree of investment | Reinforces the formal city | Recognizes both formal and informal city, without preferences | Priority investment in most needy areas (peripheral, central, rural) |

Figure 10. (*Continued*)

effective these transnational networks learned candidly from these uneven outcomes, even if for external consumption this was concealed beneath a promotional veneer.

## Pink Tide

For a while, in the early 2000s, "learning from Porto Alegre" was the thing to do, particularly, it seemed, for left-leaning local and regional governments in Europe for which the Southern city had become something of a "beacon."[29] The PB model's center-left appeal had been augmented by positive endorsements from most of the major development agencies and from the various organizations of the UN. Perhaps more surprisingly, this mainstream acceptability seemed to be doing little to erode enthusiasm for PB in more radical left circles. As Gianpaolo Baiocchi remarked at the time, "It appears that Porto Alegre, participatory budgeting and what it stands for have become a cause célèbre among progressives, as a vision of grassroots democracy and empowerment irrevocably opposed to the vision of neoliberal technocracy promoted by agencies like the World Bank and the IMF."[30]

Indeed, when activists from France, Brazil, and elsewhere gathered in Paris in 2000 to formulate a plan for an "anti-Davos," a global focal point for the advocacy of alternatives to neoliberal hegemony, Porto Alegre was nominated as the "ideal home" for what became the World Social Forum (WSF).[31] Remembered for combining almost equal measures of carnival, chaos, and commitment to a still only weakly articulated cause, the inaugural gathering of the WSF in Porto Alegre may have been united in its opposition to corporate rule and neoliberal-style "McGovernment," as advocated by the deregulators of Davos, but it did not hew to any single line, either in principle or in practice. The charter of principles later issued by the organizing committee of the first meeting sought to codify working guidelines for what was intended to be a nonhierarchical "movement of ideas," based on "respect for human rights, the practices of real democracy, participatory democracy, peaceful relations, in equality and solidarity, among people, ethnicities, genders and peoples." The declaration read:

> The World Social Forum is a plural, diversified, non-confessional, non-governmental and non-party context that, in a decentralized fashion, interrelates organizations and movements engaged in concrete action at levels from the local to the international in order to build another world.[32]

These commitments to decentralized, participatory democracy resonated strongly with the spirit of Porto Alegre in general and mechanisms like PB in particular. While almost reflexively critical of universalizing maneuvers or uniform methods, many of those in the WSF's movement of movements were able to embrace the Porto Alegre model. Eric Toussaint and Arnoud Zacharie of the Committee for the Annulment of Third World Debt declared that the "participatory budget as practiced in Porto Alegre ... should be adopted on a worldwide scale and inspire original policies of radical democracy," while Michael Hardt and Antonio Negri also advocated this "common process [whereby] connections are transformed into discussions and the network becomes a list of demands and projects."[33]

The Porto Alegre model, in this respect, stood as both an inspiration and a challenge—where the challenge referred to that of scaling up, or networking out, from such progressive experiments, when these were (fully) understood to be politically fashioned and contextually embedded. As Fisher and Ponniah synthesized the conversation at the WSF, "All policies and practices should be characterized, as in the case of the Porto Alegre budget process, by a radical and participatory democracy that runs through the local but goes even further than the Brazilian experiment, by extending into the national and the global."[34] As an instantiation of what has been called "maximal democracy," PB seemed to crystalize many of the goals and aspirations of the WSF, which for some it would come to symbolize. "A wonderful example of the pluralism that the WSF stands for," one commentator reflected, "the city of Porto Alegre was able to advance a new kind of maxD governance based on citizen participation, redistribution of wealth, and ... competent [municipal] administration."[35]

In keeping with this crystalline quality, however, visions of PB could also be refracted according to different (political) perspectives. For all its pluralist, "dispersive" character, the WSF was also a space in which debates and differences between what Michael Hardt portrayed as an "anti-globalization" position, focused on the democratic recapture of the nation-state as a bulwark against neoliberal globalism, and a "non-sovereign alternative globalization" position, heterogeneously anticapitalist, more horizontalist in outlook, and distrustful of the state.[36] Both of these progressive tendencies were drawn to PB, albeit for rather different reasons. Those intent on reclaiming, repurposing, or reforming the state saw PB as a symbol of progressive governance, available for scaling up—a trajectory personified by Olívio Dutra's ascent from mayor of Porto Alegre to governor of Rio Grande do Sul and then to the federal Minister for Cities.[37] Those favoring more autonomous, horizontalist forms of engagement, propelled by social movements and less concerned with (or constrained by) the state, on the other hand, could read PB as an invitation to a new mode of "transversal" politics, constructed through nonhierarchical "local-local interactions."[38] What for the first group might be a problem of *transmission*, of recalibrating the technology of PB for use in higher tiers of government, would for the latter be seen as a dilemma of *translation*, of learning reflexively across different political cultures.[39]

There was, according to many accounts, some friction between the more hierarchical and more horizontalist factions at the first WSF gathering in Porto Alegre, not least because the PT—in the form of the administrations of the City of Porto Alegre and the state of Rio Grande do Sul—was effectively the host of the event. Naomi Klein, for one, was taken by "the living alternative of Porto Alegre itself," where "democracy isn't a polite matter of casting ballots; it's a contact sport, carried out in sprawling town hall meetings," and where PB had enabled the growth of a citizen-powered "shadow city council." As Klein saw it,

> In Porto Alegre, the most convincing responses to the international failure of representative democracy seemed to be this radical form of local participatory democracy, in the cities and towns where the abstractions of global rule become day-to-day issues of homelessness, water contamination, exploding prisons and cash-starved schools. Of course, this has to take place within a context of national and international standards and resources. But what seemed to be emerging organically out of the World Social Forum (despite the best efforts of some of the organizers) was not a movement for a single global government but a vision for an increasingly connected international network of very local initiatives each built on direct democracy.[40]

Formative experiences of PB had indeed been "very local," holding city governments to account at the neighborhood scale. Less local versions of this kind of political practice would invariably (and perhaps necessarily) entail more formal and/or less direct forms of democracy, for example through referenda or by somehow "aggregating" interests via representative organizations, movements, or parties. Whether such reformulations really reflect the spirit of Porto Alegre is certainly a contestable issue. For Naomi Klein,

"The real lesson from Porto Alegre is that democracy and accountability need to be worked out first on more manageable scales—within local communities and coalitions and inside individual organizations."[41]

All manner of lessons from Porto Alegre continued variously to radiate, spiral, and pulse out of the WSF gatherings, even as they were subsequently convened in other locations. A banner at the opening ceremony of the first WSF had demanded "global participatory budget planning," while leaflets distributed to participants by the municipality of Porto Alegre, where "participation speaks louder," promoted the city's experiment with PB as a "role model for the whole world."[42] The social forums themselves have certainly made much of the symbolism of participatory democracy, even if they have been less than entirely successful in realizing this in their own practice.[43] These left channels of the PB dissemination process have their reformist as well as more radical currents. A network of left-leaning local authorities and aligned social movements, the Foro de Autoridades Locales por la Inclusión Social y Democraticia Participativa, or Red FAL, was formed at the first World Social Forum, with a remit to spread participatory practice in conjunction with explicit opposition to neoliberal globalism.[44] Red FAL's membership overlaps substantially with more active elements within URB-AL and UN-UMP.[45] More broadly, the WSF "has been very important for horizontal exchange among political and NGO activists—in Latin America but also far beyond it."[46]

As a concrete initiative that advances so many facets of the WSF program—democratizing state budgets, building capacities for self-governance, alleviating socioeconomic inequality, organizing the unorganized, and promoting the case for autonomy, accountability, and self-development across other spheres[47]—it is perhaps to be expected that PB should enjoy wide currency in such circles. It may be more surprising, though, that the allure of PB has not faded more completely, even after the left lost control of Porto Alegre itself; indeed, the conclusion of a 2010 assessment was that "PB is still part of the World Social Forum Agenda."[48] However, the decade following the inaugural WSF gathering in Porto Alegre in 2001 revealed that, even as the symbolic reach of PB was being extended, as a flag bearer for a new kind of left-leaning grassroots internationalism, its real political traction was beginning to wane—at least in comparison to the Latin American wave of the 1990s. Across PB's "home" region, a succession of left leaders ascended to national office, drawing attention and political-class talent with them, and diverting considerable energy from local issues; the radical fervor of the early WSF meetings was tempered, according to some, because the arena had become increasingly "NGOized," and to others, because what had become known as the global justice movement seemed to be struggling to push its self-driven project to the next level, whatever that might be.[49]

Some of those most closely associated with the PB model had long been warning, in fact, that what had been a meaningful and consequential political innovation in the newly democratizing Brazil of the 1990s should not be mistaken for a twenty-first-century cure-all. This was certainly the more sober and realistic tenor of the discussion in the URB-AL and Red FAL networks. As Cidade's Sergio Baierle argued, in a document produced for URB-AL, the PB process was an outcome of a negotiated partnership between a popular administration and social movements in Porto Alegre, one that had been successful in "extending the rope of liberal citizen[ship]," but these strategic gains had been secured in the context of a tense and contradictory "social 'force field,'" effectively superimposing

> popular sovereignty on the principle of technocratic rationality and on patri-monialist management. The finances were recovered, the richest started to pay more in municipal taxes, priorities were inverted, investments were chan-nelled to the poorest areas in the city, and the public sector was open to the citizens' direct participation. . . . However, Porto Alegre is not an island in the desert of neoliberal policies. It is impossible not to suffer the consequences of national macro policies. However hard one has been seeking to counteract the logic of deconstitution of the public sector by implementing anti-cyclical policies, by taking advantage of the surplus of resources provided by the small decentralisation entailed by the Constitution promulgated in 1988 and by the improvement of locally obtained revenues, municipalities still control but a small part of the national public budget.[50]

In the wake of the WSF, Zander Navarro likewise argued that Porto Alegre had acquired "the image of a city able to stand as an inexpugnable fortress amidst the neoliberal sea," somehow immune from the pressures of market-driven restructuring.[51] For Baierle, these pressures were seen to be practi-cally inescapable, being duly revealed in a "dual state" form, as federal gov-ernments pursued macroeconomic policies according to a predominantly neoliberal logic, while local states struggled to deliver social-compensatory policies under conditions of constrained fiscal capacity. One of the principal animateurs of the URB-AL discussions, Yves Cabannes, shared this visceral sense of the "negative effects" of continuing neoliberalization, positioning PB as something of an intermediate achievement, "occupying the fragile space that exists between a freedom that is conquered by the movements and a right that is granted from the public sector."[52]

This kind of recognition of the political-economic force field that was, of necessity, the "operating environment" of early PB experiments was not, however, a premonition of their imminent demise. Quite the opposite, in fact. In the context of intensifying dual-state pressures, an *increased* reliance on PB-style measures could be anticipated—albeit in a relatively shallow form— as a means of legitimating the rationing of public investment, while managing the political consequences of what in Third-Way parlance were being described as "hard" *but necessary* "choices." Cabannes may have been one of the first to see this trajectory (toward the proliferation of *PB lite* strategies), under what seemed likely to remain straitened political and fiscal conditions. Writing for URB-AL, one of his conclusions was that "after participatory budgets cease to be 'trendy' as they currently are, one can legitimately think that the number of cities that will adopt and adapt them will keep growing exponentially."[53] However, within just a few months of this statement, and coinciding with the publication of the UN-Habitat's widely used "frequently asked questions" manual,[54] the PGU in its Latin American form was no more. There had been a strategic decision to fold the programs and mission of the UN-UMP into the Cities Alliance, in partnership with the World Bank, and to terminate, wind down, or refocus the UN's remaining commitments in the urban-development field.

This would be a prelude to the political dilution of the PB project within multilateral circles. Benjamin Goldfrank likewise identifies 2003 as the tipping point, as the spirit of Porto Alegre really began to dissipate, just as the World Bank assumed the mantle as the principal proponent of a new and diluted model.[55] The UN-UMP had been a key space for the "legitimization, dissemination, and experimentation" of a radical, PT-style of participatory budgeting within the framework of the United Nations, but this left-leaning project had "generated lots of political tensions" within the organization, one of those most closely involved recalled,[56] having had to rely on bilateral sources of funding from northern European donors. The transition from the UN-UMP to the Cities Alliance brought this to an end. Formed in 1999 by the World Bank, UN-Habitat, and a number of national governments, donor agencies, and multilateral associations, the Cities Alliance is a "global partnership for urban poverty reduction and the promotion of the role of cities in sustainable development," with a particular focus on slum upgrading. The momentum established around active and developmental experimentation by way of PB strategies under the UN-UMP umbrella, especially its Latin American operations through the PGU, rapidly dissipated following the absorption of these activities, nominally, into the Cities Alliance. The radicalizing current had been suppressed; under the Cities Alliance, this "dynamic died out," one of the key players recounted, and it has not since been recovered.[57] As Sintomer et al. diplomatically put it, the "Cities Alliance, dominated by the World Bank[, is] a programme in which the degree of real innovation is variable."[58]

## Taking Accountability to the Bank

The Cities Alliance internalized what Vinit Mukhija has called an "embedded contradiction," between a World Bank agenda concerned principally with urban competitiveness and a UN remit that would become instrumentally focused on the issue of slum upgrading.[59] The Cities Alliance has not prioritized PB, and its main significance in this latter regard may have been to have sapped the forward momentum of the UN's previous efforts on this front. This had been maintained, for a while, under the remit of URB-AL, but the emphasis on active and creative innovation was never regained. Meanwhile, the World Bank would soon be developing its own interests in PB, opening a path to a more constrained and instrumentalist form of "mainstreaming."

The World Bank's scrutiny of PB and the Porto Alegre model intensified around 2000–2001, a period dominated by controversies over the production and heavy-handed editing of the Bank's signature policy statement, the World Development Report (WDR), on the theme of attacking poverty. This had exposed, in unusually raw and public form, tensions been the goals of "sound" macroeconomic management, on the one hand, and "pro-poor" policy, on the other, as well as between financial and civil-society interests within the Bank.[60] A self-described "outgrowth" of the troubled 2000–2001 WDR process was a sourcebook on *Empowerment and Poverty Reduction*, which sought to articulate the "World Bank's approach to empowerment for economic growth and poverty reduction," connecting this newfound orientation to concrete measures and strategies.[61] The sourcebook also represented an attempt to reconcile the goals of promarket economic policies with an attenuated vision of pro-poor empowerment. It sought to leverage what was described as the Bank's "comparative advantage," economically summarized in the document as "obviously, not to work at the community level but to advise governments based on analytical and evaluative work, to facilitate links to financial investment, and to enable others directly or indirectly to work on the empowerment agenda."[62] A lengthy section of the sourcebook on "tools and practices"—in effect, *approved* tools and *favored* practices—described twenty extant initiatives deemed to be compatible with the Bank's empowerment agenda. Participatory budgeting was number six on this list. Illustrated with short case studies of PB in Porto Alegre, Ireland's deployment of social-partnership agreements, and the women's budget initiative in South Africa, the sourcebook (re)defined participatory budgeting as

> a process in which a wide range of stakeholders debate, analyze, prioritize, and monitor decisions about public expenditures and investments. Stakeholders can include the general public, poor and vulnerable groups including women, organized civil society, the private sector, representative assemblies or parliaments, and donors. . . . Increased participation in budgeting can lead to the formulation of and investment in pro-poor policies, greater societal consensus, and support for difficult policy reforms. Experiences with participatory budgeting have shown positive links between participation, sound macroeconomic policies, and more effective government.[63]

Here, the circle of participation is widened to include business and donor agencies in ways that echo the post-PT, "pasteurized" model of PB in Porto Alegre, while the compatibility with "sound" macroeconomic policymaking is privileged. This appropriation of the PB method exemplified what has been termed the "primacy of process" at the World Bank,[64] as well as the organization's formidable powers of incorporation and cooptation. More sobering, perhaps, for left advocates of PB, the World Bank's embrace of the technique, if not its motivating purpose, underscored the ready *availability* of the model for much-less-than-radical political ends. This accounts for the unease that is typically registered in left discussions of the multilateral mainstreaming of PB.[65] On the one hand, this effectively recognizes, validates, and legitimates the process, on the other, it speaks to its potential or actual degradation. Commenting on the advocacy of PB among some of these "bastions of neoliberalism," Gret and Sintomer conclude their discussion of the Porto Alegre experiment this way: "Today, the World Bank is not satisfied with merely helping Porto Alegre to obtain low-interest loans; it distributes brochures extolling the city's participatory budget in other countries in the Third World. Whatever the ulterior motives behind this publicity, it is a revealing symptom."[66]

The World Bank's advocacy of PB is a revealing symptom indeed, even if its motives have since become less than ulterior. To some extent, the salience of PB is a manifestation of the efforts of relatively progressive elements within the Bank itself, while more cynical observers are prone to dismiss talk of participation and empowerment among the agencies of the (post) Washington Consensus as mere window dressing. Perhaps more pertinently, however, it is also revealing that such an appropriation-cum-retasking of PB is quite compatible with the World Bank's stated commitments to fiscal restraint (and strict scrutiny of public spending), to stakeholder governance (extending to the private sector and multilateral donor agencies, thereby constraining or outflanking state and community interests), to decentralized delivery (in the context of external surveillance, also constraining state interests), and to neoliberal economic policies (with an emphasis on deregulation in labor and other markets, together with a preference for narrowly targeted and conditional social policies). The virtues of participatory governance, from the World Bank's perspective, are duly summarized as follows:

> Participatory Budgeting (PB) is an innovative mechanism which aims to involve citizens in the decision-making process of public budgeting. By creating a channel for citizens to give voice to their priorities, PB can be instrumental in making the allocation of public resources more inclusive and equitable. By promoting public access to revenue and expenditure information, *PB effectively increases transparency in fiscal policy and public expenditure management, reducing scope for clientelistic practices, elite capture, and corruption,* thereby enhancing the government's credibility and the citizens' trust. PB can also *improve service delivery by linking needs identification, investment planning, tax systems and project management.* Thus, PB goes beyond a simple participatory exercise to being an integrated methodology for promoting social learning, active citizenship and social accountability, opening new ways of direct participation which complements traditional forms of representative governance.[67]

Inevitably perhaps, Porto Alegre served as one of the (critical) cases for the World Bank in formulating its approach to participatory budgeting. The Participation Thematic Group of the World Bank's Social Development Department was developing an analysis of the Porto Alegre experiment by 2001, shortly after the controversial release of the *Attacking Poverty* edition of the WDR.[68] This largely followed the format of countless other summaries of this Brazilian model, describing the origins of the policy, detailing the administrative and consultative processes involved, and summarizing the proximate "results," both locally and in terms of the model's emulative potency. "Overall," the World Bank's case study concludes, "from a protest-based culture of the 1980s, these participatory budget exercises have fostered a more 'civil' and less disruptive form of conflict resolution through dialogue and negotiations."[69]

The latter's more benign variant of the PB philosophy has duly spread across the World Bank's operations. The always-expanding list of PB projects supported by the Bank reaches Albania, Bangladesh, Bosnia, the Dominican Republic, Ecuador, the Gambia, Honduras, Indonesia, the Kyrgyz Republic, Madagascar, Mozambique, Peru, the Philippines, Uganda, Uruguay, and beyond.[70] As one senior official explained, "We strongly support it [participatory budgeting]. We not only support it through our lending, through our educational programs . . . it's part of our social accountability [process]. We have a sustainable-development network which also supports it. We have lending operations which support it, often requiring that there should be a participatory process. . . . People are convinced that this is the way to go."[71] In this respect, PB truly has become "mainstream."

The practice of participatory budgeting was folded into the World Bank's evolving concept of "social accountability" (SA), which would be defined as "an approach to building accountability that relies on civic engagement, i.e. in which it is ordinary citizens and/or civil society organizations who participate directly or indirectly in exacting accountability."[72] While there were those, inside as well as outside the Bank, pressing for a more open-ended and "horizontal" conception of PB, as a means of facilitating progressive partnerships for development, the accent was more often placed on tempering and disciplining (local) government: *exacting* accountability was seen as necessary in order to combat the "three-headed monster" of the state—corruption, clientelism, and capture.[73] Holding government accountable, enforcing transparency, and giving voice to sanctioned stakeholders would characterize this relatively shallow and calculating approach to participation, "most experiences with participatory processes in the context of Bank lending hav[ing] taken place at the micro or project level."[74]

At the same time, the Bank was being urged in some quarters to embrace a more expansive vision of participation. In a paper commissioned by the World Bank, John Ackerman of FLACSO-Mexico argued that "transparency is key, but not enough on its own. Opening up the dark chambers of the state to the eyes of the public is a major move forward, but it is only a first step."[75] The Bank had recognized that social-accountability measures could play a key role alongside its favored drivers of public-sector reform, alongside fiscal discipline, privatization, and the purposeful mobilization of competitive pressures, achieved through various forms of decentralization. An advocate for what he called the "participative school" of New Public Management (as distinct from the dominant "market school"), Ackerman maintained that "[m]arketization is not the only way to tap into the energy of society," participatory measures being one way to "invite society into the state," rather than decomposing the state into society.[76] Subsequently, he would argue:

> Although devolution and decentralization are important because they bring government closer to the people, if carried out blindly they tend to reinforce inequalities both within the newly "autonomous" local units as well as between them. Local power holders are allowed to run free, and underprivileged localities are abandoned to their own devices. Decentralization is only productive if it is accompanied by pro-active efforts to involve citizens and stimulate pro-accountability processes. Fortunately, at the local level it is usually easier to stimulate community participation. In addition, change at this level can often appear less threatening to national powerbrokers, thereby reducing resistance to citizen participation by the regime in power.[77]

The full potential of participatory engagement, in these terms, does not arise spontaneously, however. Here, it is seen to take the conscientious efforts of "pro-accountability entrepreneurs . . . to design mechanisms that both help translate this potentiality into action and privilege social actors that work for the public interest," Ackerman maintained, with the added twist that "context is absolutely crucial. There is no single 'silver bullet' or special recipe for creating successful social accountability initiatives."[78] Communities could not, according to this account, be left to their own devices—since in such a situation the ministrations of pro-accountability entrepreneurs would be unnecessary. Yet outcomes would nevertheless remain perplexingly uncertain and context dependent.

A further dilemma for World Bank reformers, it follows, is capitalizing on local innovations and best practices through replication and "scaling up." Having decentralized, devolved, and decomposed the state, as it were, in its own image, the Bank then faces the challenge of consolidating and aggregating these new forms of governance without reawakening the three-headed monster. "The difficulty in the area of decentralization and community driven development is the issue of 'scaling up' [, involving] the linking together of local initiatives into a national social accountability strategy or, what seems to be even more difficult, the use of similar mechanisms at the national scale," Ackerman acknowledges. "The forces working against social accountability are often much more powerful at the national than at the local level [, although] this may not be reason enough to give up the struggle and abdicate the national arena."[79] Far from giving up, however, the Bank has been keen to promote SA measures across much of its wide portfolio of activities.

The strategy for operationalizing an approach to SA compatible with the Bank's remit was the focus of a learning module later developed around Ackerman's conceptual paper, with additional financial support, in this instance, from the governments of Canada, Finland, and Norway. Assembled by Social Impact Inc., the learning module sought to ground the SA approach in (evolving) World Bank practice, to distil its basic (design) principles, to identify diagnostic indicators for country-wide and program-level assessments of the role of SA measures, and to enable the training of trainers in SA techniques. This instrumentalization of the SA approach was rationalized in terms faithful to the 2004 WDR, *Making Services Work for Poor People*, which had concluded that "service provision falls short because of weak incentives for performance, corruption, imperfect, or nonexistent monitoring, and administrative logjams."[80] Emphasis was duly placed on rationalizing and refining existing programs and delivery systems, enhancing service delivery through democratic efficiency and transparency, as opposed to a more open-ended and transformative understanding of SA.

Social Impact's instruction manual operationalizes an approach to participatory budgeting that is effectively brokered by trained experts, and therefore imported from the outside. Would-be trainers are walked through a series of PowerPoint slides, summarizing the Bank's approach to SA in bullet-point form, clarifying its rationale in "hold[ing] public authorities accountable," and providing sidebar tips to trainers: "Tell the group: 'Now that you have a sense of what SA is, you can probably imagine that it brings with it many potential risks.'" Key among these, anticipated in the next slide, are that governments might lack "the capacity or financial means to sustain improvements in services," and that local initiatives in particular might be subjected to "elite capture."[81] (While steps might be taken to guard against elite capture, fiscal and institutional constraints are effectively pregiven "facts of life"; SA measures are to be implemented in the context of these constraints, not in the service of questioning the constraints themselves.) So prepared, the trainers were instructed to organize breakout groups in which rudimentary SA strategies would be developed by program participants, with the aid of prepared handouts, in the space of forty-five minutes. This would begin with some diagnostic analysis, to determine whether "SA approaches are really feasible in a given setting, and if they are, which ones might have the highest potential for success." The groups were advised in the handout:

> Designing an effective social accountability (SA) strategy grounded in the experiences and realities of a particular country is not easy. This task requires a good eye for windows of opportunity and a highly developed sensitivity to the country's history, culture, and politics. Although no single recipe can be applied in all cases, experience shows that the most successful cases of designing and adapting social accountability systems follow a basic pattern.[82]

Encouraged to mix and match, crib and customize a "first-cut" SA strategy, the groups were to be summarily marched through a three-step method on the way to a flipchart summary and plenary presentation: first, "conduct a brief SA diagnostic of the district or municipality you have selected"; then, "identify a few candidate SA approaches or mechanisms that might be a good fit"; and finally, "quickly review some of the main characteristics of the candidate SA approaches to see how they fit with your diagnostic. . . . Select the best SA approach." This brusquely retrofitted approach should be attentive to "preexisting SA demands and practices in country," but it should also "[d]raw on good practices and lessons that have been discussed during this workshop."[83] This might resemble one of the "classic" models—borrowing from eight thumbnail cases summarized in the accompanying materials—or it might cherry-pick from these, constructing new hybrids. The latter approach was illustrated, indeed encouraged, in the learning module through the example of the "participatory public expenditure management cycle," which combined a Porto Alegre approach to budget formulation with budget review and analysis techniques inspired by best-practice experiences from Gujarat, India, a state-of-the-art expenditure tracking system from Uganda, and performance monitoring by way of citizen scorecards as perfected in the Philippines.

Similar attempts to build operational approaches to SA, customized to local conditions, were soon proliferating globally. The World Bank Institute's ANSA program (Affiliated Networks for Social Accountability), for example, was established in 2006 in order to build capacity among civil-society organizations in the monitoring of government performance and in making the case for enhanced transparency and accountability.[84] By 2010, ANSA was working in Africa, East Asia and the Pacific, South Asia, and across the Middle East, having formulated a "core learning program" on SA in collaboration with the World Bank Institute. Launched as an e-learning platform, this would later expand into a sprawling complex of ten-day workshops, video conferences, seminars, distance-learning modules, and other "learning events." Under this rubric, the SA approach was distilled into three elements, or core courses—on social-accountability theory, governance frameworks, and communication strategies—all based on the four basic "SA tools," of budget analysis, PB, expenditure tracking, and performance monitoring.

In parallel with these efforts, the World Bank has also been working to sift and systematize the narrative of PB, to refine the core features of the model, and to make the resulting policy product accessible to new audiences. The Bank's own version of a PB manual, *Participatory Budgeting*,[85] characteristically aspires to definitive status, articulating a generic version of the model available for global circulation. The book combines regional surveys with detailed country cases, a "primer" on effective participation, and a potted history of PB diffusion, predicated on the "assumption . . . that the tools and institutional means developed to date are, in small or large part, transferable to other locales."[86] The tone, however, is restrained and utilitarian rather than celebratory, the Bank having tried to insulate its analysis of PB from the genre of advocacy writing typical of the field. As one of those involved in commissioning the book for the Bank protested,

> Forget about Porto Alegre! . . . One problem is that . . . anything that is written
> about participatory budgeting is by NGOs or advocacy groups or academic

consultants who are advocates for participatory budgeting. We wanted . . . a more detached, more objective look, but we could not find a single consultant who would provide this. They were all advocates. . . . [The problem is] there is no independent evaluation, by people who are not engaged in this process.[87]

The correspondingly sober conclusions included the observations that (1) in Latin America, the "open, informal deliberative design pioneered by Porto Alegre seems to be out of fashion [, having been displaced by] more regulated, formal, consultative designs" focused on preexisting civil-society organizations; (2) in Central and Eastern Europe, participation "remains weak" by virtue of mistrust of the state, limited capacity in local government, and the fact that "[w]ith few expectations, development agencies or international NGOs were the initiators of participatory budgeting mechanisms in this region," so few were homegrown, and; (3) in North Africa and the Middle East, while PB experiments were hardly rare, "many of the factors that facilitate citizen initiatives are absent [, including] openness and democratic depth."[88]

To be sure, true believers in PB can be found in the World Bank, and in many of the organization's wider circles, especially among those tasked with the development of civic participation and social accountability remits.[89] But those involved in the lending operations, the professional economists, and some of the more world-weary are typically much more reserved, more inclined to constrained, instrumentalist applications, more temperate, and, in some cases, more cynical. One such account, from a Bank insider, called attention to a defensive, self-legitimating logic in the organization's fulsome embrace of PB: "The urgency has come about because of the increasing criticism of the World Bank, and the international development agencies— that their projects do not relate to what people want. The governments are using the [World Bank's] money and building white elephants. It's a response to those criticisms."[90] An observer from a neighboring institution inside the Washington, D.C., beltway commented that while the Bank had become a "big driver" of budget-transparency measures, much of this was a result of anticorruption concerns, where for some an adapted version of PB had become "the new golden bullet."[91]

Another insider at the Bank struck a different kind of skeptical tone, explaining that there was an irreproachable, apple-pie-like quality to participatory methods like PB, which often concealed a hollowness in execution and in some cases even the true intent:

What happens in most places is that participatory budgeting exists only in name. It's basically donor driven. The World Bank comes up with part of the money, [other agencies provide] part of the money, all the donors. For them it's a motherhood-and-apple-pie issue. . . . Everybody is putting a lot of money into it, and they are helping to create these processes of consultation. But in the end, in most places it's yielding *nothing*. [However], one cannot criticize this tool. After all, it's desirable that citizens are consulted. And it's desirable that citizens know what value for money they are getting for the taxes they pay. But the question is whether the actors who are involved are seriously engaged in this effort.[92]

While PB-style measures were being appended to World Bank initiatives and programs across scores of countries, it was not only local critics who complained that this was a shallow form of routinized replication, tantamount in some cases to going through the procedural motions. Some in the Bank conceded this too. Asked to define the locus of innovation, this inside observer could honestly claim little for the Bank's own efforts: "Porto Alegre everybody points to," he acknowledged. "I'm not sure there are any distinguishing features . . . in the World Bank's [approach]."[93] Meanwhile, the more procedural, "pasteurized" variant of the model travels far and wide, enveloped in virtuous circles and positive-sum feedback loops. Maybe this was PB "only in name," but the name did seem to serve legitimation purposes.

In contrast, fiscal realists at the Bank recognized that PB often exerts no more than a modest, marginal influence on the budgetary process, either in terms of its distribution or its overall scope. The "focus groups" associated with donor-driven, PB-lite models may have provided a check on outright corruption and waste, but made relatively little constructive difference to eventual outcomes. As a senior official at the World Bank explained,

There is very little budgetary flexibility. Typically, if you look at municipal budgets, only 15–20 percent is capital spending and the rest is spending on salaries and operating expenditures. On the operational side, local governments have very little flexibility. A lot of them are basically job-creation agencies. There is over-employment, but politically it's impossible to fire [local government employees]. So what participatory budgeting can affect is [only] a small portion of the budget. [Furthermore], these focus-group meetings [are often subject to] interest-group capture. So what was intended to be a voice of the common people, or [a medium for] median-voter choices, is no longer followed.... Donors are happy [, though,] because there has been a huge number of town hall meetings, and budget issues were discussed, and officials came and went. The donor can demonstrate to their own stakeholders ... that they are doing something very useful. But I'm not sure that the objectives are being achieved.[94]

PB may, as this respondent put it, have "spread like wildfire ... now, participatory budgeting is everywhere, in some form," but perhaps more than the policy's intrinsic efficacy, this rapid diffusion reflected what economists at the Bank like to call a political-economy calculus, that "politicians and the donors [share] the same incentive, to *demonstrate* that what they are doing is in the broader interest of the public."[95]

## Atlantic Crossings

The extensive global reach of PB, and PB-like practices, far exceeds even the long arms of the World Bank, however. The technique retains a certain allure in many left circles, especially in those locations were it still has some novelty value. The practice has also been associated with a substantial degree of mainstreaming across reformist administrations some distance from both the source region of Latin America and from the recipients of multilateral aid in developing countries. A number of transnational policy networks have been established to facilitate the movement of participatory budgeting, along with other municipal government reforms, establishing new "horizontal" linkages between cities and across continents. The mission of networks such as the International Observatory on Participatory Democracy (IOPD) and United Cities and Local Governments (UCLG) is to promote decentralized government and to further the development and dissemination of municipal government innovations. The UCLG comprises one thousand local governments in ninety-five countries along with more than one hundred Local Government Associations, while IOPD has five hundred government and NGO members. These networks function as broad-based spaces of policy learning and exchange, and they have been instrumental in the extensive global diffusion of PB-like policies that has occurred over the past two decades.[96]

In 2007, the World Bank partnered with the OECD to undertake a "stock-taking exercise" of SA measures in twenty-seven of the affluent nations of the OECD zone. Some forty "templates" of SA activity were subsequently identified, many of them involving variants of PB, in Belgium, Australia, Spain, Canada, South Korea, the European Union, and elsewhere. Ostensibly taking stock, the authors of the OECD–World Bank Institute report were perhaps rather easily impressed by the "wealth of innovative practices," given that hardly any had been subject to rigorous evaluation, while many of the self-reported "innovations" looked rather derivative. Nonetheless, all could bask in the warm glow of democratic renewal:

> Democracies, both old and new, have much to learn from one another. As [this] cross-regional SA stocktaking exercise illustrates, innovative practice in strengthening government accountability and engagement is by no means the exclusive preserve of OECD countries. The emergence and spread of participatory budgeting is itself instructive in this regard. This methodology was originally developed in Porto Alegre, Brazil, and has since been taken up by a growing number of cities across Europe. Countries that have traditionally been propagators of democratic values and practices now find inspiration from younger democracies. This exchange of experience, and the increasingly widespread experimentation with innovative tools for accountability, bodes well for the future of government openness.[97]

Whether or not these high-minded conclusions are truly warranted, the rapid diffusion of PB-like initiatives has been remarkable, especially across Europe. Sintomer and colleagues report that while these could have been counted on the fingers of one hand in the late 1990s, by the end of the following decade they were numbering around 250 and covering a combined population of more than eight million.[98]

On this evidence, it is clear that *something* is being transferred across the Atlantic, and from the Global South to the Global North, but what actually survives the journey, if not some decanted spirit of Porto Alegre? Elsewhere, Sintomer et al. candidly note that "the political dimension is far less present in Europe than in Porto Alegre," and yet that "very peculiar" Brazilian context could nevertheless be credited with the generation of "a procedural model . . . that, year after year, has been considered as a source of inspiration by other cities."[99] Through detailed comparative analysis, Sintomer and colleagues' extensive studies have gone on to demonstrate that, in the course of its travels, PB had gone from being one model to many.[100] While some European experiences, such as those of Seville and Cordoba in

Spain, can be considered to be adaptations of the Porto Alegre model, from a wider perspective there has been a proliferation of parallel models, as opposed to submodels. These can be divided into three broad strands, or post–Porto Alegre trajectories:

- *Porto Alegre adapted for Europe meets organized interests* refers to a process of deliberative and open local democracy found in parts of the Iberian peninsula, sometimes visibly influenced by the left currents of the alt-globalization movement, sometimes involving unmediated citizen engagement, in others operating through "secondary organizations" like labor unions or NGOs;
- *Local community funds meets the public/private negotiating table* is a combination of models from the UK and Eastern Europe that share the characteristic of being at arm's length from local government, since the funds or projects in question derive from other public or private sources, dispersed locally through participatory means and often engaging disadvantaged populations in particular; and
- *Proximity participation meets consultation,* more typical of France and Germany, involves various forms of local consultation short of citizen-led priority setting, sometimes portrayed as "selective listening," where the echo of Porto Alegre is quite faint and the influence of New Public Management rationales tends to be stronger.[101]

Plotting the strategies of various European cities in terms of these three approaches, each with their own submodels, allowed Sintomer and his colleagues to visualize a diverse universe of PB-style policy development, and quite possibly one marked by increasing divergence (see Figure 11).

A practitioner with extensive policymaking experience in numerous countries summarized the situation in this way:

> There are a number of Latin American countries that have tried adapting different models, but [their] influence waned as [they] started crossing the Atlantic. . . . In the European experience, the central commitment around citizen participation that drove Porto Alegre seems to get diluted as it gets adapted.[102]

In some cases, suggestions of waning influence or diluted potency would prove to be dramatic understatements. In the UK, for example, the combination of a particularly severe financial crisis, a shift in national government

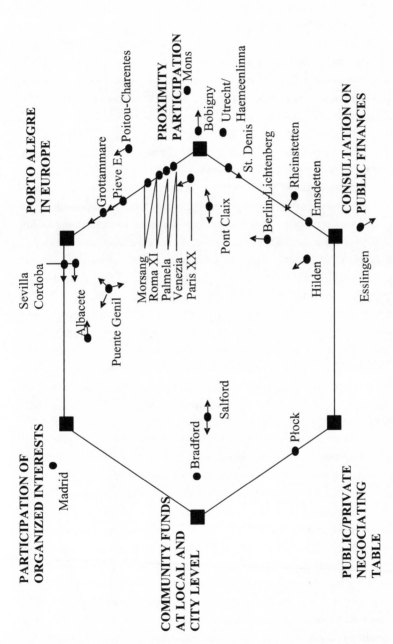

Figure 11. Proliferating PB Experiments in Europe. Source: Sintomer et al. 2008.

to the right, and the adoption of an especially dogmatic form of devolved austerity politics[103] reversed what had been a growing momentum for the institutionalization of PB. In the final years of the Labour Government (1997–2010), PB had been championed by Hazel Blears, Secretary of State for Communities and Local Government,[104] as well as being pushed by grassroots organizations and advocacy groups like Church Action on Poverty. The Labour government established a PB Unit in 2006, with the plan to have PB initiatives operating in every local authority area in England by 2012, but this was abruptly halted with Labour's general election defeat. While the incoming Coalition government espoused an agenda for radical localism under its flagship "Big Society" initiative, there was no place for PB in what amounted to an unprecedented program of public-sector downsizing and local outsourcing. Lacking the oxygen of government support, or indeed a meaningful flow of new projects at the local scale, the British PB wave seems to have stalled. The chief executive of the National Association for Voluntary and Community Action, Kevin Curley, while a supporter of participatory approaches in principle, conceded that the achievements of PB in the UK had been "frankly marginal. Giving local councilors and groups small amounts to spend on traffic calming, improving play areas and smartening up community buildings barely touches the big problems local people face."[105]

The experience of PB in Germany has been less volatile but in some ways no more encouraging. More than one hundred local authorities across the country have adopted PB approaches in recent years. Implemented with a high degree of technical proficiency, there seems to have been an expectation in some quarters that effective administration will somehow secure meaningful and effective outcomes.[106] However, this functionalist faith has not been repaid in practice. Introduced in the context of fiscal stress (albeit in a far less crisis-driven fashion than in the UK), German PB experiments have tended to follow one of two trajectories. The relatively conservative Emsdetten approach sought to modernize and rationalize municipal administration according to the principles of New Public Management, effectively engaging citizens in budget-balancing exercises. As Carsten Herzberg has concluded, in a perceptive survey of the German experience, the goal of such efforts was "not to assess public services but to generate proposals to re-balance the budget [, which] can take the form of staff cuts, reduced public expenditure, decreased optional spending (culture, sport, leisure activities, etc.) or tax increases."[107] While in a few notable instances local tax increases have been proposed and sustained, it has been more common for this style of managerialist PB to be deployed in the apportionment of budget cuts and service reductions. Herzberg's sober conclusion is that "German participatory budgets have had [only] a few social effects."[108] A second, more explicitly political model, however, did initially create rather more excitement, if not necessarily any deeper impact. Advertising direct links to Porto Alegre, both institutionally and philosophically,[109] the Berlin model enjoyed "avant-garde" status in Germany for a while, Herzberg observed, but this stronger political commitment to participation proved to be no match for an increasingly adverse fiscal climate. His candid assessment is that the overall impact of PB experiments in Germany has been "slightly more than symbolic."

> [T]he approach used in Emsdetten has become a fad. The overriding aim of new PB processes . . . is to discuss solutions to financial problems. The people are invited to make proposals to economize a predetermined amount of money. . . . Furthermore, participation seems to become even more symbolic than before. . . . The German case shows that procedures of democratic innovation are not necessarily linked to perceptible policy improvements. Although they were often technically well organized, PB has not led to remarkable results. . . . In Germany, PB was supported by all kinds of parties, without any deeper vision at its foundation.[110]

The administrative execution of participatory budgeting in Germany may have been impressive, but the effects have been far less than transformative. Herzberg believes that the political class ultimately had no intention of transferring real power to local citizens through the PB process. The mechanism seems to have been used more as a tool of political management.

More prosaically, there was an almost ritual aspect to the way in which PB was deployed in some European cities. Participatory techniques are used to inform the determination of neighborhood spending priorities in some Dutch cities, for example, even though many of these comparatively affluent neighborhoods are characterized by a relative absence of pressing social needs. A social-sector consultant engaged as a facilitator, to assist some of these neighborhoods in determining workable and fundable projects, drew a sharp contrast between the levels of social need and indeed urgency in what were essentially middle-class parts of the city and the role that PB had played in the Brazilian *favelas*: "I work in [a Dutch city], where one of my projects is to encourage ideas, because there is so much money but there is too [few] ideas. . . . In Holland, there is more money than ideas! In Brazil, it's the other way around!"[111]

This was one reason for the shortage of local political energy around some PB experiments in Europe. Others felt that the Brazilian experience was being oversold by some peripatetic advocates, or that PB felt like a passing political fad. As a Dutch policy advisor reflected, "I first heard about participatory budgeting in 2001, and of course we looked at Porto Alegre. . . . And at the same time we met some people from Japan [who were also engaged in participatory experiments]. There is a literal translation from a Dutch saying, that the coin falls at the same time in those [different] places— the same idea emerged in those different places. Of course you learn from one another . . . but when we first learned from them [the Brazilians], we did not have the [impression] that they were miles ahead."[112] These sentiments were echoed by a Berlin-based activist and PB advocate, who recalled the "phase when *everyone* wanted to hear about PB"; after the initial excitement, however, many of the local politicians proved to be "very cautious," eventually reducing PB to little more than "an administrative approach."[113] Here, as in other European cities, PB had generated some early enthusiasm, but its influence had quickly "faded."

Few would claim that the participatory spirit was fading in Spain. The *indignados* movement has brought millions onto the streets in protests against unemployment, welfare-state cutbacks, austerity policies, and the political establishment as a whole. The participatory ethos of the *indignados* movement has been likened to an organic form of deliberative democracy, animated by a rejection of business-as-usual party politics. The movement's "central demand," Baiocchi and Ganuza have written, is "for a direct, deliberative democracy in which citizens debate issues and seek solutions in the absence of representatives."[114] But if a participatory spirit runs through parts of this broad and somewhat spontaneous movement, its scale and scope also calls into question the rather circumscribed achievements of earlier PB experiments in Spain. Prior to the *indignados* uprisings, the origins of which can be traced to simultaneous protests in fifty-eight Spanish cities on May 15, 2011, there were approximately fifty PB initiatives operating at the local level across the country. Seville's PB experiment is widely regarded as one of the "most ambitious" in Europe, although even here the participatory component was confined to less than 2 percent of the municipal budget.[115] This experiment had been an initiative of the municipality's Socialist and United Left coalition government. Launched in 2004, it had allocated at least half of the (rather modest) budget for local districts according to participatory principles, which local residents redirected toward community swimming pools, sports facilities, and an expanded cycle-lane network, among other projects.[116] These initiatives proved to be popular, but they did little to sustain support for the Socialist Party, which was removed from national office in 2011, also suffering precipitous losses in local and regional elections, when the popular vote shifted to the right. The *indignados* movement, scornful of electoral politics, had encouraged its supporters to abstain, spoil their ballots, or vote for a minority party. The future of many of Spain's participatory experiments is now uncertain, since they largely were opposed by conservative politicians. Some in the *indignados* movement, however, seem to be looking back to a different kind of future with PB: according to activist Kike Tudela, "It's a debate we have to have within the movement, but perhaps we can create new political forms from below. We are interested in Latin American models."[117]

## Democratizing Democracy?

Interest has also been displayed in these models—in practical and political as well as theoretical terms—in North America, one of the more recent beachheads in the globalizing, experimental field that has formed around participatory budgeting. These efforts have been variously supported, orchestrated, and coordinated by a fast-growing nonprofit organization, the PB Project, the origins of which can be traced to a meeting of a small group of Canadian and US-based activists at the 2005 World Social Forum in Porto Alegre. A North American toehold for PB had been established in 2002, when Toronto Community Housing formally adopted a participatory process that would engage local residents in the determination of capital expenditures, safety projects, and various initiatives for young people.[118] The next milestone came in 2009, when Chicago alderman Joe Moore became the first elected official in the United States to adopt PB, enabling residents of the city's forty-ninth ward to have a say in the annual allocation of $1 million in discretionary funds. Similar initiatives were soon to be pursued, notably, in a multidistrict effort in New York City, where the slogan is *"real money, real projects, real power,"*[119] in a citywide process in Vallejo, California, in the wake of the declaration of a municipal bankruptcy,[120] and in some additional wards in Chicago. In parallel, the PB Project stepped up its programming efforts through networking, fundraising, and advocacy; technical assistance, research, and evaluation; and a series of well-attended conferences. These combined efforts were to receive high-profile endorsement when two PB forerunners, New York City council member Brad Lander and Chicago alderman Joe Moore, were nominated by the White House in the select company of fifteen of the country's leading "Champions of change" in the cause of open government. Moore's White House citation recognized the alderman

> as a pioneer for political reform, governmental transparency and democratic governance, [and] the first elected official to bring "participatory budgeting" to the United States. Each year, Moore turns over $1 million of his discretionary capital budget to a process of democratic deliberation and decision-making in which his constituents decide through direct vote how to allocate his budget. Moore's participatory budgeting model has since been adopted by four of his Chicago City Council colleagues, as well as city council members in New York City, San Francisco, and Vallejo, California.[121]

In a case of what the *Chicago Tribune* aptly described as "only-in-Chicago political timing," the announcement of the White House award occurred on the same day that Moore was reported to be under investigation by the FBI and the City of Chicago's Legislative Inspector General for violations of ethics rules concerning staff in his north-side office.[122] Moore denied the allegations, but the White House decided place the award on hold, pending the outcome of the investigation.

Alderman Moore's perhaps temporary difficulties seem to be the exception rather than the rule, however, for PB politics in the United States, which has been one of the last countries in the hemisphere to catch the participatory bug. For the most part, pioneering deployments of PB here tend to be associated with independently minded, reforming politicians, of various stripes, and genuinely grassroots mobilizations, often in mixed- or low-income communities with significant minority populations. This is mostly Democratic Party territory, although the New York City PB initiative also involves a maverick young Republican, council member Eric Ulrich of Queens. There has been considerable energy around these initiatives, in part by virtue of their first-mover novelty, in part because many of the districts in question have been underserved, both in terms of services and in terms of political attention, and in part courtesy of the "multiplier" effect of the PB Project, which has both promoted and supported these local efforts. The cumulative weight of this labor-intensive organizing drive, it must be said, vastly exceeds the still-modest sums of public funds that have, so far, been channeled through participatory structures in the United States. In fact, it has been observed that, here, the funding capacity of PB is the "worst in the world," given the tiny fraction of (usually discretionary, district-level) budgets that has been opened up to the participatory process.[123] Those who have joined the process, needless to say, are acutely aware of the discrepancy between neighborhood needs and the flow of funds that has thus far been made available through participatory measures, but district-level PB initiatives are generally seen as a welcome step in the right direction. Two community activists from New York City explained the rationale, from the perspective of what are inevitably overstretched and underresourced local organizations:

We're amazed that over a thousand people participated in each of the four districts, and we consider that a success because that's a thousand more people in each district making a decision than ever made that decision before. But it's not enough. We recognize that it's going to take time to reshape things . . . and it's going to be a slow building process, but the potential is really incredible.[124]

Why is it important? It is not important because it is a million dollars. A million dollars is *nothing!* Let's keep it real. Let's recognize that. What this is doing, the reason it is shifting the debate, is because it is changing the narrative. It is breaking down the class divide. It is breaking down economic divides. It is breaking down the age divide. It is breaking down racism. Because you are fighting for people to be together at the table who have never, *ever,* spoken with each other. . . . The money is nothing. The fact that you have brought people together who have never spoken to each other . . . to come together to say, "This is what I need, this is what I am going through, and I'm human just like you," makes people start to think differently, start to think critically, and start to come together *as a people,* no longer living along those divides.[125]

Those who have mobilized around PB in the United States are those who respect its *process* of inclusivity and engagement. In the words of New York City council member Melissa Mark-Viverito, "You are bringing into the fold people who historically have been excluded from decision-making."[126] But almost none are content with this as an end in itself. Overwhelmingly, PB is seen to be a transitional moment, on a path to deeper and wider change. Activists in New York, for example, recognize that "one of the biggest challenges we have [here] is that we piloted a project at such a micro level in the communities that it's not yet touching the citywide budget. . . . That bigger budget is really what is the critical part. So figuring out how to make that leap and whether this [PB] will make that leap harder is one challenge that I spend a lot of time thinking about."[127] In both New York and Chicago, PB began at the district level and it remains at that level, gradually enrolling small numbers of elected members "laterally," but making little or no progress "vertically," into centrally held budgets, mayoral initiatives, or cross-city programs.

It remains, in other words, a tenuous achievement, viewed by some skeptics as symbolic politics and even by many supporters as a something of a time-limited experiment. There are continuing debates, in fact, over whether PB represents a meaningful step toward deeper political change in the United States or a distraction, perhaps even a sideshow. As the leader of a national social advocacy organization explained of her organization's somewhat-conditional support for PB:

> In New York, half of the things people put up as ideas [for PB projects] are things the city is responsible for doing anyway. That is not to devalue the process. . . . There is real value in the process, but the process alone . . . won't produce systemic change. It just hands over responsibility [from] government to the citizenry. And if it is couched in the same batch of values and the same kind process—no questioning or examination of how budget priorities move or where revenue is coming from—then you have just made city council members' jobs easier."[128]

As a colleague commented, "If this is *just* a process, [one] that we're being granted by politicians, as soon as the party lines change or people's politics move, we can see it washed away. There has to be a connection to the politics. . . . I think that PB can be a really small part of that, it can be a great entrance point, but [not] if it's divorced from the politics. . . . It's something that is the right of the people to do, not granted by elected officials."[129]

The strategic response, notably on the part of the Right to the City Alliance and its members, has been to anchor the participatory process within strong and well-organized community organizations, rather than allow PB to be operated at the discretion of elected officials. Thus far, however, experiments with participatory budgeting in the United States have tended to work as extensions or elaborations of the formal sphere of municipal politics, initiated by individual elected officials; community organizations have often been vital partners in this process, but few (if any) could credibly claim to be driving it. Here, it is local politicians who are making the rules, and establishing (acceptable) terms for participatory engagement, rather than residents themselves. This speaks, fundamentally, to the issue of the role of PB in social transformation, to its founding principles, and to what is variously invoked, (re)constructed, or romanticized as the spirit of Porto Alegre. Detached from transformative politics, PB can become a mere device political management; embedded in those politics, it continues to offer the promise, at least, of much more. The adoption of PB systems has been, by international standards, remarkably timid in the United States. It is notable, however, that wherever it goes, the process (still) tends to raise—even if, alone, it cannot fully resolve—fundamental questions of social justice and political rights. As an activist from the Right to the City Alliance put it, "We view participatory budgeting as a tool toward a larger goal, toward a specific end . . . the complete transformation of the society we live in. Not a kinder and gentler one nor more manageable one . . . but a true transformation. . . . If PB is moving in a space where the dominant hegemony is accepted, and it is just being used to make things more manageable, and then PB is just a tool to further that hegemony."[130]

# 8

## Reflections

### Headwinds, Hollowing Out

Participatory budgeting is a striking example of a conspicuously fast-moving policy, one that through its transnational movement might, at first blush, appear capable of transcending the local context to deliver substantially similar results in different places. That PB, in its polyvalent forms, has been implemented across six continents and by governments of widely varying political stripes speaks to the ways in which the model has been adapted to a (sometimes surprising) range of politico-institutional settings. The construction of PB as a "global best practice," both by the left and by the right, albeit in different ways, is an indication of the ease with which some policy models can be appropriated by actors and organizations with diverse motivations and goals. In this case, a policy that announced itself to the world as a radical form of direct democracy, one that was championed by social movements because of its redistributive aims and disruptive potential, has proved to be vulnerable to cooptation and reinvention, not least by some of the very forces it was designed to counteract.

In some respects, the adaptability or plasticity of a policy like PB can be considered to be an asset, since this permits refinement and customization, while the ability to disembed the policy from its home context facilitates transferability. There was a particular configuration of characteristics that, in retrospect, primed the Porto Alegre experiment for accelerated mobility. The participatory budgeting field has had the benefit of an inspiring invention narrative, as a pro-poor policy of social engagement forged in the context of Brazil's transition to democracy, a founding narrative that has been raised to mythical status in some circles. This meant that the policy traveled, not only with a positive story, but with a galvanizing *spirit*. No less importantly, however, PB was associated with a cluster of material (and, on the face of it, replicable) practices, from indicative schedules for neighborhood assemblies to refined rules of deliberation and voting, all of which endowed the model with a concrete, tangible form. If the spirit of Porto Alegre provided the ideological fuel, these instituted practices enabled its practical traction.

These "internal" (or design) characteristics of the PB model have also interacted, for the most part fortuitously, with a set of conjunctural conditions that have had lasting consequences for what has become a transnationalized field of participatory budgeting. First of all, participatory budgeting was a product of a very particular Brazilian conjuncture, the nexus of social-movement organizing in Porto Alegre and the reciprocal efforts on the part of the PT to build a governing coalition in the city. The direction of causality here is vital. Participatory budgeting was an *organic* product of this conjuncture; it did not produce the conjuncture. Radical politics produced PB, not the other way around.[1] In this respect, PB was a profoundly endogenous creation, deeply embedded in a unique (and essentially nonreplicable) political context. Some of the attendant lessons may have been easily transportable to other PT-held cities in the early 1990s, but needless to say their resonance with circumstances in, say, contemporary Chicago, or to many other "borrowing" locations, is considerably more limited. Secondly, PB's path to transnational influence was facilitated by a no-less-particular global conjucture, decisively shaped by the post–Washington Consensus embrace of decentralized governance, inclusive development, financial accountability, and (a more restrictive vision of) pro-poor policymaking. PB was not made for this conjuncture, either, but there was a certain logic to the adoption of the policy—in its adaptive, depoliticized, and more *synthetic* form—by a wide range of local, national, and transnational actors. "Portable PB," in its more politically conformist manifestations, would display a remarkably propitious "fit" with these environmental conditions.

Disembedded from the first of these conjunctural contexts, its local-organic moment in the policy's Brazilian birthplace, PB duly became something of a creature of the second, its global-synthetic moment, which witnessed the transnational embrace of decentralized governance under neoliberal hegemony. If PB possesses progressive political integrity, this stems from the politics with which it is infused; experience has shown that it is not an essential or intrinsic feature of the administrative technology itself. For the past three decades at least, progressive political projects like PB have been pushed into the stiff headwinds of neoliberalism, understood as a complex of counter-vailing, and hegemonic, ideological forces. But experience has shown that in its diffuse, synthesized, and compromised forms, PB can be almost completely hollowed out by these forces—leaving a shell of participatory maneuvers largely devoid of disruptive political capacity. This speaks to the polysemic, heterogeneous quality of participatory budgeting as a mobile discourse and as a bundle of adaptive practices, which can provide a space for imagining radical programs of political transformation in some locations, but serve as a fig leaf for World Bank restructuring projects in others. It also speaks to the rather confounding fashion in which PB has been able to circulate, simultaneously, through various left channels while being coopted into not only mainstream, but outright neoliberal, circuits.

Fast policies, like PB, it must be emphasized, are not free-floating or self-propelling technologies that move through frictionless space before touch-ing down. They are the objects of active advocacy and persuasion. They encounter resistance—ideologically, institutionally, and operationally—but they also often remake the terrains over which they travel. This coda to part 3 reflects on the case of PB in Porto Alegre and beyond, exploring three aspects of this particular experience of accelerated policy mobility—motives, media, and mitigation. We reflect on some of the ways in which policy models travel through different channels, as ideological and practical constructs, as well as the means by which policies like PB are disembedded from particular places, only to be reembedded in transnational networks of different kinds.

## Motives

It has been argued that Latin America served as a "laboratory of neoliberal-ism"; Emir Sader writes, "Here it was born, here it spread and here it took its most radical forms."[2] But Latin America was also the region where a wide range of anti- and post-neoliberal experiments was founded, with goals that included deepening democracy, reclaiming the state, reanimating channels of social redistribution, and redirecting public-sector investment in the inter-ests of the poor.[3] Participatory budgeting was conceived in Porto Alegre in the midst of the long neoliberal ascendency in Latin America, in part to redress historic inequalities within the city itself and in part as a response to the hegemony of Washington Consensus policymaking throughout the wider region. PB, in short, was among those social policies enacted by left governments "that espouse a different logic" from the policy prescriptions of the neoliberalized mainstream.[4]

Ernesto Ganuza and Gianpaolo Baiocchi have identified two phases of PB diffusion-cum-mutation, mapping closely onto the organic and synthetic moments discussed above. "In the first phase, PB emerged out of the cauldron of leftist experimentalism in Brazil in the early 1990s, as a particularly successful instrument of inclusive local governance, one that seemed to render compatible social justice, good governance, and electoral fortunes for the left."[5] During this phase, the PT and other leftist advocates were promoting PB with an eye toward progressive replication, first in PT-governed municipalities across Brazil, then throughout Latin America by building on bilateral relationships between newly elected left governments in the region, and ultimately around the world, increasingly with the assistance of international aid agencies. Seeking to live up to the hubristic slogan adopted by the municipal administration in Porto Alegre, "Orçamento Participativo—Bom para todo mundo" (which can be translated as "Participatory Budgeting—Good for the Whole World"),[6] the Workers' Party positioned PB as the symbolic and practical centerpiece of a program of sweeping municipal reforms, finding a receptive audience both domestically and abroad. During this "organic" phase, PB was able to travel, for the most part, with its core principles and political integrity intact: renewing democratic participation through the creation of formalized spaces for public debate and dissent; giving the poor and disenfranchised a direct voice in municipal affairs; fortifying an interventionist local state so as to better meet the needs of residents living in areas previously starved of services and investment; and affecting a redistribution of municipal resources in favor of poor and working-class districts. The initial diffusion of PB by proponents on the Brazilian left was, as one social activist deeply engaged with the project at the time characterized it, "a tree-like expansion, from the same trunk."[7] Traveling during this period as a still-integrated model and retaining, as it did, its ideological, technical, and sociopolitical components, PB became a concrete policy expression of the antiglobalization mantra "Another world is possible." This was a time when social activism melded with policy innovation in a mutually reinforcing fashion. As this activist, central to the Brazilian project, recalled of the first and most important "strand" in what would become the globalizing phenomenon of participatory budgeting,

The original, from Porto Alegre, is [based on] power to the people. [Here,] PB is the launching field for societal transformation, where people might have more power, [where there is] devolution of power and real decision-making [capacity]. . . . It's the old idea originally from Porto Alegre of inverting priorities—social, territorial, political. . . . To me, one of the indicators is . . . when a policy changes rights, or transforms rights . . . *that* is an indicator that a policy has deepened democracy. . . . What has to be kept is the capacity of the people to adapt and change the rules.[8]

This was not a matter of selectively *granting* rights of consultation, or moving resources around within existing state structures. Rather, it was an approach predicated on a principle of shared power, which in its Porto Alegre form was a joint achievement of the social movements and the PT's popular government. It aspired to remake the field of social rights, to change the rules of the game. From this perspective, faux PB initiatives—in which the rules and parameters are pregiven and nonnegotiable—represent nothing less than a travesty of the original concept.

In the second phase, beginning in the late 1990s, a politically denuded version of PB achieved international acclaim, traveling as a *technique of good government,* often in piecemeal fashion or as an overly simplified template for citizen consultation, devoid of any broader radical agenda to transform state–society relations from below, or even to fundamentally alter resource distributions. This mainstreaming process resulted in PB becoming instrumentalized through the selective appropriation of depoliticized technologies and routines. Having been disassembled from the original model, these technologies could then be reengineered and recombined in different ways to render PB compatible with a wide range of political systems, institutional arrangements, and development projects. Actually existing forms of PB diversified liberally, if not promiscuously, around the various visions of the model, first as a political ideal and then as a "best practice," promoted from Porto Alegre (the World Social Forum) to Istanbul (the UN-Habitat II) to Shanghai (the World Expo) and beyond. Increasingly, the participatory model traveled as little more than an inspiration or even just a label, a symbol of a municipal government's openness to the inputs of citizens and stakeholders. In its most denuded form, PB has been nothing more than a ruse, an institutional (mis)indication that government is prepared to devolve decision-making authority to local residents, while decisive issues regarding overall budgetary priorities, aggregate spending limits, and most importantly, the prevailing rules of the game itself, are (pre)determined "on high," and sequestered from public deliberation.

This second phase of diffusion/mutation witnessed the ascendency of PB as a global best-practice model trumpeted by multilateral agencies—initially by the UN and the EU, and later by the World Bank. The Bank has since emerged as the most important propagator of synthesized PB approaches, both in terms of the broad dissemination of technical expertise and through the provision of funding to support local PB experiments. In the course of the (somewhat improbable) process by which the World Bank has superseded the Brazilian Workers' Party as "the most active promoter of PB," Goldfrank comments, "participatory budgeting [has] gone from a local innovation in democratic practice by avowedly socialist parties to [an] international aid project," indeed a "global script."[9] It has been estimated that, in the period since 2002, the Bank has issued loans and grants well in excess of $280 million to support PB efforts in Africa, Asia, Eastern Europe, and South America.[10] Multilateral development agencies have been drawn to PB for several reasons, including, inter alia, the increasing importance of participation and multiple-stakeholder engagement in development projects; the perceived role of "good governance" in securing the conditions for economic growth; the need to create functioning governance institutions in places undergoing democratic renewal; the desire to educate citizens about government financing and administration; the need to counter (or at least obfuscate) the legitimacy deficits of externally designed, donor-supported development projects; and the imperative of combating clientalism and corruption, while promoting (and being seen to promote) budgetary transparency.[11]

Some, but certainly not all, of these aims were shared by PB's earlier proponents on the left. But, as Ganuza and Baiocchi astutely observe, the transformation of PB into an anointed best-practice model was predicated on a debilitating simplification: "PB was defined as a sequence of meetings premised on universal participation and a fair and transparent decision-making. *Ideas about state reforms as necessary conditions for establishing PB all but disappeared, and the close connection between participation and administration was severed.*"[12] This degradation of the model fundamentally altered the future travels—and perhaps potential—of participatory budgeting. As the model was simplified and essentialized, a certain ease of movement was facilitated, but, for all intents and purposes, the possibility that PB might truly transform municipal policy agendas was seriously compromised. For PB to really work, in its original terms, it had to be a step in a cumulative process of radical political change. In contrast, its faux versions became ends in themselves.

At a deeper level, the struggle over PB as a governance model reveals tensions between competing ideological notions of participatory democracy. Whereas the left sees PB as a vehicle for transforming the state, while augmenting the capacities of popular movements, the right envisions a more limited, consultative approach consistent with the drive to reduce the scope of the state through the mechanisms of accountability, austerity, and restraint. One is about radical empowerment; the other is about customer satisfaction. Whereas the left sees PB as means for deepening and radicalizing democratic processes, the right worries that such insurgent experiments in direct democracy might destabilize the established order. As one World Bank official paradoxically insisted, "[PB] also undermines, in some ways, the democratic process. . . . You *elect* local councils, [but] the local council's role ·is significantly reduced through [the PB] process."[13] Whereas the left conceived PB as an evolving set of institutional arrangements and accompanying procedures, always subject to modifications by participating publics, the right attempts to formalize public deliberation and to harness dissent through state-directed bureaucratic structures. And whereas the left sees PB as a way to bolster an activist state, intervening in the interests of the poor and disenfranchised, the right focuses on techniques to exert greater fiscal discipline over government affairs and to advocate for more minimalist, less interventionist modes of governance. As one PB advocate succinctly put it, the right's version of PB "basically . . . improves governance in the most neoliberal [sense of the word]. It reinforces and modernizes neoliberalism."[14]

## Media

The mobility of PB as a template, or recipe for radical reform, has been propelled, all along, by ideologically invested actors who have sought to advance their preferred version of the model through policy networks. And each of these networks has exerted a distinctive influence on the reproduction of PB as a transnational policy project. Some of these networks, notably those connected with World Bank programs, and to a lesser extent the UN-UMP and URB-AL, have been quite formalized, relatively enduring, and well resourced. Some are state directed and supported, as in Peru or, for a while,

the United Kingdom; there are those that have emerged as "lateral" partnerships or mutual support networks, like Red FAL; others are almost entirely
creatures of donor organizations; while still others are animated by advocacy NGOs, like the PB Project in North America. Across all of these cases,
though, policy actors are working through formal and informal networks
in order to identify elements of policy "success" as a lever for change in other
sites and locations. For all the talk of evidence-based learning that permeates
contemporary policy development, the attendant processes of interpretation
and identification are ideologically laden; they are structured by relations
of power and authority. In this context, the power to identify, anoint, and
circulate "local" success stories—in order not just to lever reform elsewhere
but to preemptively pattern the conversation around the change-repertoire
itself—has assumed increased significance.

In a world of globalizing policies, networks have become the principal
media through which policies travel. Networks themselves, of course, are not
new. "But what *is* new about our age," David Singh Grewal has argued, "is
the accelerated emergence of, and linkages among, these global networks . . .
[leading to] certain versions of local practices, routines, and symbols . . . being
catapulted onto a global stage."[15] It is important to remember that, notwithstanding the social futurology that often accompanies discussions of
"network space," this is far from a politically leveled world in which policies
pass freely through open-source circuits. It may be more appropriate, in fact,
to think of policy networks as something more akin to sinews, sinews that
are charged with varying degrees of energy and which are attached to different degrees (and forms) of policymaking "muscle."

This is not to say that nothing has changed, of course. A muscle-and-sinew
regime works differently from a top-down diffusion system, as the realization of power and influence through networks is often a nonlinear and idiosyncratic process. The PB story is very much a story of networking, indeed
of competing networks. But even if the broad trajectory has been toward
the synthetic degradation of the original model, there have also been more
orthogonal developments. The PB world has been characterized by the proliferation of distinctive channels of policy mobility, but many of these channels that initially were separate and distinct later began to intersect, tangle,
and hybridize. In the first, organic phase, early champions of the policy
developed a left channel to promote PB among politically and ideologically
aligned governments within and outside Brazil. Events like the World Social

Forum contributed to the policy's visibility while also endowing the Porto
Alegre model with the imprimatur of the antiglobalization movement. Various Latin America governments, along with some in Spain and Italy, closely
followed the Porto Alegre model,[16] deferring to the original policy construct
with only minor modifications, while this approach also inspired representatives of countless NGOs throughout the world to pursue participatory
approaches to reclaiming and retasking the state, with varying degrees of
success. Policy mobility during this phase was facilitated by techno-*political*
networks, which sought to transport the animating spirit of PB along with
its practical procedures. This kind of organic networking occurred through
a no-more-than-loosely orchestrated form of radical contagion at the WSF
meetings, but would later display a more concerted and systematic (if perhaps muted) form under the UN-UMP and Red FAL.

In the synthetic phase, two initially independent developments occurred.
First, a neoliberal channel was formed by multilateral organizations, including USAID and the World Bank, along with more conservative elements
within the United Nations family of organizations and the EU, to construct
and disseminate PB as a best-practice model of municipal governance, a move
that "was premised on the decoupling of Participatory Budgeting from a
broader set of institutional reforms of which it had been a part in the 1990s."[17]
These organizations incubated and resourced an array of synthetic diffusion
networks reaching into Africa, Asia, and Europe, as well as (to a lesser extent)
North and South America. These are the channels through which PB *lite*
has been propelled, as a consultative and monitoring device, and more in
the service of legitimating (planned) interventions than ceding control over
financing and prioritization. Here, PB starts to look more like PR. As a World
Bank official explained, one reason why PB had become a "very strong movement, spread[ing] like wildfire" is that

> both the politicians and the donors [have] the same incentive, to *demonstrate*
> that what they are doing is in the broader interest of the public. And something
> that can show [that] is very valuable to politicians.[18]

In parallel with these developments, the left channel—having never been
especially well resourced, of course—was increasingly sapped of its first-
generation energy and creativity. Increasingly, these activities were diluted
into centrist forms of policy advocacy. Some veterans of earlier left-advocacy

efforts migrated to these more reformist networks, or retooled themselves as peripatetic policy entrepreneurs. A "soft center" of PB advocacy was duly formed, cross-fertilizing with World Bank networks in some cases. Consolidating this centrist, "consensual" model of PB are groups like IOPD and UCLG that have been dedicated to promoting PB and other participatory practices internationally. In a similar fashion to many of the other networks, these provide technical assistance, bestow awards for "best practices," and construct legitimizing narratives around approved forms of participatory democracy. There is a tendency here to indulge (quite literally) in selective readings of the successes of participatory budgeting, sidestepping thorny issues regarding the types of broader institutional change upon which PB's positive impacts have been predicated, and succumbing to a technocratic fascination with specific programmatic components, a preoccupation that borders on design fetishism.

These proliferating policy networks are themselves complex social institutions that do far more than simply transmit policy advice; they are actively engaged in reconstituting, narrating, and legitimizing what are deemed to be the "essential" elements of policy models. In this sense, globalizing policies are recursively and socially embedded within networks—which become the arenas, and indeed the media, for policy development and mobility. Networks also possess distinctive forms of power, which in turn often grows in proportion to their membership characteristics, their size, and their reach.[19] For this reason, consideration of sinewy policy networks must always be attentive to the flexing of political muscles. Well-resourced and powerful members of transnational networks, such as national governments and multilateral organizations, tend to have greater influence over policy agendas than do more marginal members. But just as importantly, as membership in a given network increases, the "social momentum" from this growth produces important feedback effects that alter the relative power of all actors in the field.[20] The mainstream efficacy of PB, in this context, stems from its capacity to achieve results across a diverse array of sites, this message of extralocal and cross-local salience being communicated and validated through networks. Delocalizing and relocalizing policy models is therefore a distinctive capacity of always-flexing networks. The atrophying capacities of PB's left channel is a case in point. The PT's electoral defeats during the mid-2000s sapped the policy development process of its experimental energy, detaching the model from its most potent sites of leftist innovation, adaptation, and even authenticity. The neoliberal channel, on the other hand, extended its sprawling reach, supplying new sites with its own version of pasteurized PB.

## Mitigation

PB projects are very much a *local* technology of participatory governance. More than this, because participatory democracy "implies decentralization," in order to connect meaningfully with citizens, its principles and practices favor what Patsias and colleagues have called "the local of the local," or "infra-local," neighborhood-scale approaches.[21] This localist orientation was fatefully to coincide, historically, with the multilateral banks' parallel embrace of decentralized stakeholder-governance models, under the guise of which PB was appropriated as a convenient means of providing legitimatory cover without ceding significant power, and which amounted in some cases to the political capture (or annexation) of the local scale. It also resonated with the widespread embrace of localism across many currents of left thinking, from Third-Wayers to *horizontalistas*. Now, the upside of left localism is that this can be an effective scale for mobilization and for the development of grassroots, organically embedded projects. There is a potential downside, however, especially if localist projects are disconnected from supportive structures at higher spatial scales and from redistributive financing channels, because in the context of isolated initiatives, local actors must often accept the role of rule takers rather than rule makers. Prioritizing the local scale can therefore be a sign, in some circumstances, of weakness rather than strength. It is notable, for example, that the recent mobilizations around PB in the United States, for all the energy and inventiveness they have tapped, have been confined to the district-level, if not the political margins. The challenges of "scaling up" in this context are underlined by the fact that radical and creative left policymaking is almost completely absent from the wider municipal, state, and federal levels in the United States.[22] Bluntly put, there are no beachheads of left control at these higher scales, and therefore very little with which infralocal PB experiments can connect.

For some on the left, this reflects an intrinsic weakness, or limitation, of PB as a medium for progressive reform. "PB is a resolutely localist project," Greg Sharzer has complained, which "accepts the existing distribution of budget funds."[23] A defining feature of synthetic, as opposed to organic PB, is this deference to the extant distribution of funds as an essential fact of life, limiting participatory procedures to the prioritization of local projects within fixed (or even shrinking) parameters. If "[t]he budget," as Joseph Schumpeter once wrote, "is the skeleton of the state stripped of all misleading ideologies,"[24] then the relegation of PB to the infralocal redistribution of relatively modest, discretionary budgets exposes the truth of what in some cases has been reduced to a cynically staged form of street theater.

There is a cruel irony in the way that some forms of PB have been folded into the very neoliberal hegemony that the original model was designed to contest. What began as a left success story seems consequently to have morphed into yet another dispiriting tale of conservative annexation. But it is important to recognize that just as the successes of the Porto Alegre experiment were never narrowly attributable to matters of institutional design, the waning political traction of synthesized forms of PB has a more complex explanation too; it has not simply been a "design failure." The ideological headwinds with which the original PB experiment was forced to contend were exceptionally strong; they were strong enough, in fact, to stall its forward (progressive) movement, and some would say to blow the experiment itself off course. As Boaventura de Sousa Santos has observed,

> [P]opular initiatives like PB are placed in a cruel dilemma: they either fail in a concrete situation and are declared to be bound to fail and therefore dismissed as foolish utopias of participation, or they succeed in a concrete situation and are turned into a general recipe for participatory institutionality, to be adopted by the World Bank . . . [after which they are duly] ground up, pasteurized, and converted into new items of conditionality for the concession of subsidies or loans."[25]

Radical impulses and aspirations have been gradually leached out of PB in the course of its mutation into a globalizing best-practices model. The reductionist deconstruction and instrumentalist reassembly of PB undermined the *political* premises and principles that had earlier secured impressive impacts in Porto Alegre. These impacts were obtained, though, in a context marked by political urgency as well as by the legacy of unmet social needs. The social content of PB deliberations is, not surprisingly, very different in the middle-class neighborhoods of European cities, where votes might be cast on priorities for playground furniture, rather than on a much more difficult (and divisive) choice between paved streets and a daycare center. Hence the ironic observation of the Dutch activist that we interviewed who said that while the Brazilians might have had more ideas than they did re-sources, some of the PB projects he worked on seemed to have more money than ideas.

Whether the animating forces associated with PB's organic moment, in the democratizing Brazil of the early 1990s, can be rekindled remains to be seen, but the model's protracted hollowing out, and the increasingly faint flickers of truly radical promise that have marked its synthetic diffusion phase, suggest that some kind of political sea change will be required for the spirit of Porto Alegre to be resuscitated ex situ. For the left to reclaim "own-ership" of PB, the model will have to be regrounded in political praxis. This has been an aspiration of the Right to the City Alliance in the United States, for example, though most in this network have taken the view that while PB might yet prove to be a means to more radically transformative ends, it certainly cannot be an end in itself. There may, however, be new openings for PB-like strategies in historic moments of democratization. Some positive reports have been received, for example, from rural China.[26] Perhaps there is scope, still, for participatory budgeting to spring a few surprises.

# Conclusion

## Exploring (Fast) Policy Worlds

This book has been an exploration of two policy fields, both of which can trace some of their deepest roots to Latin America but which would eventually reach to every continent, in some form or another. Given that both policies—conditional cash transfers and participatory budgeting—became recognized and codified only in the 1990s, their rapid, long-distance diffusion to scores of jurisdictions in the space of less than a decade is testament to a certain speed of movement. The concept of fast policy that we have been seeking to operationalize and problematize here, however, cannot be reduced to a measure of mere velocity. Rather, it refers to a policymaking *condition* characterized by the intensified and instantaneous connectivity of sites, channels, arenas, and nodes of policy development, evolution, and reproduction. Fast policy cannot be reduced to some measurement of the elapsed time between the occurrence of a policy invention at site A and its emulation at site B. For a start, many tales of endogenous policy innovation are hubristically exaggerated, deliberately mistold, or mythologized after the fact, so "invention" is not such a clear-cut or unilateral phenomenon in the first place. Furthermore, fast-policy fields comprise much more than a zone of bilateral transactions; they are made up of dense networks of hierarchical and lateral relations, and multiple nodes of translation and reinvention. In order to earn the status (and influence) of a "model," global policy models invariably command an extensive audience, many of whom will be actively engaged in the work of complex adaptation rather than simple mimicry, while these circuits of extralocal influence and multipolar mutation will also themselves be characterized by different degrees of resourcing, different forms of advocacy, different geometries of power, and so on. Once again, this is why fast policy refers less to a quantifiable state, more to a social condition.

This tangle of fast-policy conditions entails, inter alia, increased reflexivity and porosity of policymaking locales; the transnationalization and cosmopolitanization of policy discourses and communities; an exaggerated deference to global best practices and models, along with the pragmatic embrace of "ideas that work"; the foreshortening of research and development phases and the preemption of local deliberation and endogenous policy development; the expansion and elaboration of the "soft infrastructure" of global policy development; the ascendency of a transnational regime of systematic "experimentality" in policy formation, including new systems for the manufacture of "demonstration effects," validated by pragmatic practice and/or by evaluation science; and perhaps above all, the deepening "relationality" in policymaking processes and practices between often-distant sites. Below we elaborate on some of the characteristics of the fast-policy condition.

- **Increased reflexivity and porosity of policymaking locales.** Policymaking occurs not in isolation but in a knowingly comparative context, relative to recognized models and alternatives, and to a partly shared consciousness regarding leading "fronts" of reform.
- **Transnationalization of policy discourses, debates, and dialogues.** Increased cross-border interconnectedness and mutual referencing in policymaking talk and action; continuous work of "message management" on the part of multilateral agencies.
- **Cosmopolitanization of policy actors and action.** A globally connected social complex of policy advocates; gurus and champions; norm, message, and practice entrepreneurs; evaluation experts engaged in the promotion of portable policy paradigms, documented success stories, and silver-bullet fixes.
- **Deference to global best practices and models.** As objects of policymaking desire and emulation, technocratically stylized models, often pushed by powerful agencies and interests, codify and condense preferred strategies; models are proxies for and carriers of policy rationalities.
- **Foreshortening of research and development phases.** Enabled by the rise of global models and the increased availability/visibility of information and advice on policy innovations and experiments in extralocal locations; compressed R&D is a consequence and cause of compressed turnover time in policy designs.

- **Performance of pragmatism, embracing "ideas that work."** Deference to actually existing, working models as an indirect means for adaptively reproducing the extant policy order, since the production of models itself occurs within a narrow ideological bandwidth.
- **Expansion of the "soft infrastructure" of global policy development.** The social and institutional "scaffolding" for policy mobility; growth and augmentation of circulatory systems, comprising expert conferences, resource banks, (virtual and physical) learning networks, case-study manuals, and web-based materials, populated by intermediaries, advocates, and experts.
- **Manufacture of "demonstration effects."** Successful policy models are made rather than found; cultivating and circulating best-practice lessons becomes a new industry in its own right, dominated by multilateral agencies and globalizing policy networks.
- **Ascendency of systematic "experimentality" in policy formation.** Experimental churning within narrow (financial, institutional, ideological) parameters as a means of engendering continuing adaptation and development, in the context of repeated policy failure under neoliberal hegemony; managed through expert networks and the work of evaluation science.
- **Deepening "relationality" in policymaking processes.** New, mutually responsive connections are forged across dispersed policymaking sites, as the frontiers and hinterlands of policy innovation shift, and as the makers and followers of models interact, yielding new hybrids.

The intensification of fast-policy conditions means that individual policies and programs, even if they are not close relatives or chips off the same block, are *relativized*. They exist with and in relation to one another, in dense networks of mutual citation, some at the experimental fringe, others in the broad mainstream of "normal-science" policy development. They are also situated, implicitly or explicitly, in relation to evolving policy frames, models, technologies, narratives, and communities of practice, as well as to larger "frontal" programs of socioinstitutional transformation. Even as they are hybridized or customized in locally specific ways, fast policies nevertheless exhibit a "glocal" identity, as a fusion of the here and there, the near and far. Instances of participatory budgeting and conditional cash transfers, then, are understood as localizations. They are understood to have a relevant "outside," to belong to a larger community or family, and to occupy a particular position in relation to this outside. They also are specifically localized in relation to cross-jurisdictional patterns (or fronts) of change. And this means that the transnational fields that these policies occupy represent more than some inert background; they possess constitutive significance. Understanding fast policies consequently means locating these phenomena on the moving landscapes and in social worlds of which they are an integral part, which are crosscut by sinewy networks, structured by powerful institutions, traversed by mobile models, and populated by cosmopolitan actors.

The distended case-study method that was improvised in the project that lies behind this book was developed as a means of exploring the two policy fields, CCTs and PB, led us into some of the networks, arenas, and sites that have been proliferating around these globalizing communities of expertise and practice. We also traveled to some of the more notable (and storied) locations as we developed a better sense of morphology of the two policy landscapes, as well as some of the lesser-known sites. None of this could be exhaustive, of course, but at a minimum it was necessary to crisscross these fields in order to document some of the diversity that we expected, and did indeed encounter, among networks and sites, and to venture both near to and far from the various centers of power and persuasion. The reflections chapters that closed the three parts of the book were intended to draw out some of the analytical implications of the two case studies, which to a considerable degree are specific to the two policy fields, in a constitutive rather than merely contingent manner. Concrete, policy-level conditions make a real difference, in other words. However, implicit in this, and in our comparative research design, was an aspiration, ultimately, to think about fast policy not only within but across the cases, or at least not to presume a singular form of movement or evolution. What we were learning about the two cases, and about fast-policy development more generally, was inescapably informed by the fact that we were exploring them simultaneously. In this closing chapter we address this question of cross-policy comparison, explicitly reflecting on parallels and contrasts between the two cases, and on what this might mean for the emergent concept of fast policy. The dimensions that we address here, which should be read in conjunction with the commentary in the preceding reflections chapters, are those of mimesis, mutability, and modeling.

## Mimesis

They say that imitation is the highest form of flattery, but it is sometimes a form of flattery meant to deceive. And some would claim that deception is not too strong a word to apply to those hollowed-out versions of participatory budgeting that invoke the promise and allure of meaningful citizen participation, if not control, while in reality retaining a tight grip on the purse strings and indeed the very rules of the participatory game. The fact that early PB experiments achieved a measure of bipartisan credibility fortified their reputation as an appealing policy "brand," establishing a form of democratic legitimacy from which downstream experiments would seek to borrow. Ironically, this kept the much-celebrated "spirit of Porto Alegre" alive, even after this pioneering innovation had been robbed of its forward momentum in situ. Even more ironically, post-PT administrations in Porto Alegre have attempted to shore up the flagging model by trading on its international reputation, one forged during a phase of radical experimentation, the animating spirit of which has since largely dissipated.

Few at the World Bank, it must be said, were ever seduced by the mythology of Porto Alegre, and neither were they remotely inclined to replicate the Brazilian Workers' Party's vision of radical democracy. Their more instrumentalist calculus was that a depoliticized variant of the same bundle of participatory routines might serve the Bank's own ends: widening the constituency of stakeholder support for investment projects, fostering at least the impression of local buy-in, and perhaps providing some measure of inoculation from the charge of unilaterally imposing "Washington solutions." PB was duly drawn into the orbit of the multilateral agencies, the modus operandi of which increasingly defers—at least symbolically—to the sanctity of local knowledge and public participation, while at the same time tweaking preferred models and styling "best practices" based on technocratic designs or bullet-point lists of good-governance procedures. This said, local democracy—even faux local democracy—is a sufficiently messy and unruly practice that even stylized and defanged versions of PB retain their contextual idiosyncrasies.[1] There is always the possibility that they might open the Pandora's Box of real citizens' involvement and deep democratization. This is the somewhat-utopian hope onto which progressive advocates of PB cling, while at the same time being acutely aware of the degradation of the policy that has taken place in the hands of established powers.

On the face of it, the situation is rather different with CCTs, perhaps because the barriers to entry are so much higher for what are extremely costly and sometimes cumbersome interventions, and because (partly as a result) the multilateral agencies have a much more overbearing presence—

not just as financiers, but as the arbiters of expertise and the gatekeepers of technocratic knowledge. The costs of failure, in nationally delivered cash-transfer experiments, can be prohibitively high in both financial and political terms. This alone tends to create a degree of dependency on expert knowledge and past programming experience, helping to explain the "crowding" of new programs around currently favored and externally validated designs. In DiMaggio and Powell's terms,[2] this is a combination of mimetic and normative isomorphism: uncertainty produces clustering around approved models, the terms and terminology of which becomes recursively normative. It is no accident, then, that a quasi-scientific, experimental ethos enveloped the experimental field of CCTs from the very start, courtesy of Santiago Levy's decisive actions, with more than a little help from his friends in Washington, D.C., in a moment of unprecedented openness in the Mexican social-policy conjuncture. External validation, in the form of a Cadillac-standard evaluation framework, was judged at the time to be necessary for securing the PROGRESA/Oportunidades experiment, while the favorability of the RCT results that followed not only ensured the program's domestic longevity but also hailed an extranational *audience* for the model.

RCTs have proved to be a transformative new technology of evaluation, operating as as a fast-policy accelerant. The massive cost of randomized trials itself raises extraordinarily high barriers to entry into this branch of the evaluation market, which systematically favors big players like the World Bank. The attendant power to control program design and, as a result, the program characteristics that are deemed worthy of experimentation and measurement, facilitates new forms of message management—effectively "at source"—by these multilateral agencies, who also get to seed and steer the evaluative field, by virtue of their large-scale investments in program research, and therefore the flow of policy knowledge. This amounts to a (new) form of technocratic closure, which has had an observable impact on the deepest currents of CCT policymaking, contributing to a pattern of managed, incremental development within a strictly codified and controlled policy frame. None of this is any assurance to World Bank economists, needless to say, who continue to fret about the institutional variability of CCTs in their actually existing forms, and the design compromises that this necessarily implies.[3]

So even though the regime of experimentality has been pushed much closer to the scientific ideal of closed-system testing in the case of CCTs than with the more unruly practices of PB, complete closure remains out of reach. In fact, the very strength of the preoccupation, among the Washington Consensus agencies, with the conditionality of cash transfers has paradoxically left open many questions about the viability of *un*conditional cash transfers. The relatively small band of UCT advocates, even with the assistance of progressive donor organizations, has been unable to even remotely match the evaluation-evidence firepower of the CCT-RCT complex. But the flickering flame of UCT programming has been kept alive with some comparatively sparse evaluation data from Namibia, for example, along with accumulating evidence from a range of less-conditional programs and the support of progressive factions within the ILO, the UN, the multinational NGOs, and the academic community. In a quite different fashion from Porto Alegre's role as a still-unmatched truth spot for PB, Brazil has exerted a distinctive demonstration effect in the CCT field too. But in the case of Bolsa Família, it was a marked *failure* to replicate that initiated a prosaic but consequential mutation of the CCT model.

## Mutability

When President Lula authorized an agreement with the World Bank to consolidate various Brazilian proto-CCT programs into what would become Bolsa Família, with technical assistance and supplemental financing from the Washington-based agency, he did so knowing that the Bank's seal of approval for this form of new-age cash transfer would help to protect this centerpiece of the zero-hunger initiative from right-wing attacks. The strategy was largely successful, as broad social support for the program was quickly secured, even if the skeptics were never to be fully convinced that Bolsa Família was, in practice, a *truly* conditional program. This proved to be more, however, than a pale imitation of the Opportunidades model—the inspiration for so many CCT experiments in Latin America and beyond. Not only would Bolsa Família soon achieve the distinction of being the largest CCT program in the world, its "loose" attitude toward enforcing conditions and penalties, coupled with a pragmatic approach to extending social rights on an incremental basis along with a gradual improvement in health and education services, broadened the appeal of attenuated CCT models. Second-generation adaptations of the CCT approach in this Brazilian style would resonate with countries with the growing interest in more "developmental" social policies, as well as among some of those with more uneven (or limited) capacities for comprehensive

*[handwritten annotations: "why 'Bolsa Familia' worked" and "focus on social advancement"]*

service delivery. So emerged a more progressive permutation of the CCT model, less focused on the human-capital and conditionality-monitoring approach pursued in Mexico, and more concerned with the mutually reinforcing development of social rights, social capacities, and social services. This departure from the authorized CCT model, which had been constructed as a joint venture between the World Bank/IDB and Mexico, was an unscripted departure from the Washington Consensus plot line; it would stretch, and threaten to violate, the boundaries of the mode of social-policy "monocropping" that remains the preferred practice there.

There are many in Brazil who continue to claim paternity rights over CCTs, many of whom also derive some pleasure from denigrating the Mexican model as a technocratic mutation. In truth, all such policy trajectories typically tend to have multiple points of departure, rather than a single source, though those origin stories that subsequently stabilize tend to do so for a reason—and with consequences. The story of PROGRESA/Oportunidades, in this respect, can be seen as a parable of these fast-policy times, since from the moment of carefully planned conception this was preordained to be designed and manufactured *as a model,* and it would subsequently also be distributed as such. (One might observe that the birth of PB in Porto Alegre appeared to be a more "natural" occurrence in the sense that its formation was characterized by a significant degree of social spontaneity, political negotiation, and organic evolution, whereas the immaculate conception of PROGRESA was the result of meticulous, technocratic planning and projection.) The Mexican CCT model arrived, then, as an orthodoxy-in-waiting, having been built as a paradigm-positive experiment. And it would exert a strong, prefigurative influence on the subsequent course of policy development.

Designed for hegemonic consistency, this multilaterally anointed version of the CCT model would subsequently shape a hegemonic front of reforms, not all necessarily in the precise image of PROGRESA/Oportunidades, but invariably defined in relation to this benchmark program. But if the Mexican experiment established the initial frame—against which all manner of corruptions, compromises, or contending projects might be imagined or enacted—the complexities, contingencies, and outright contradictions of the policy-making world were always going to exceed and destabilize that frame. More than this, in fact, the overall arc of CCT programming seems, if anything, to have trended *away* from the singularly technocratic, Mexican model, though not toward a polar or even singular alternative, but instead in the direction of constrained proliferation. This resembles an arc from premature ortho-doxy to skewed heterodoxy, as second- and third-generation experiments in Brazil, southern Africa, Indonesia, and elsewhere have stretched the evolv-ing, experimental matrix of cash-transfer programming. True, the grip of the orthodox policy paradigm remains strong in the CCT field, as a kind of induced central tendency, not least by virtue of the multilateral banks' overwhelming control over the channels both of funding and expertise, but this grip is *never* complete. And not only paradigm-bending but paradigm-challenging practices have continued to proliferate "in the wild."

In marked contrast, if an arc can be detected in the global pattern of PB ex-perimentation, this would seem to be almost the reverse—as an early empha-sis on locally grounded heterodoxy, in the organic phase of PB development, has been gradually diluted and degraded into a much more orthodox tem-plate, a receipt for benign local governance under a climate of low-intensity consent. Lacking the prodigious capacities of the Washington Consensus agencies (as measured by financial resources, expert infrastructures, and control of dissemination channels, for example), the various organizations and networks that together constituted PB's left channel were, in the final analysis, unable to sustain an organic dissemination effort, which at its best had been marked by an insurgent style of political integrity and by the em-brace of radically open, democratic innovation. Instead, this would become a (more familiar) story of technocratic capture and instrumentalization, as PB was progressively absorbed into the policymaking mainstream. There are multiple currents, however, even here, since "within the World Bank one can find both kinds of advocates," Goldfrank points out, "those who believe in PB's democratizing potential and those who use the language as a kind of Trojan horse for their own marketizing agenda."[4] The latter agenda, however, has been the dominant one, inside as well as outside the Bank, as diluted variants of participatory budgeting far outnumber the remaining pockets of radicalism. The synthesized, "pasteurized," and off-the-shelf version of PB has been made widely available, but it conspicuously lacked the political punch of the original.

None of this, however, was inevitable. Even in a context of neoliberal hege-mony, which establishes a selection bias in favor of market-complementing, paradigm-affirming interventions, not all policy experiments are born equal. In fact, that the arc of CCT policy development showed some evidence of trending *away* from World Bank orthodoxy, or at the very least proliferating beyond the tight cluster of favored approaches, suggests there are limits to hierarchical or nodal control—even for the most powerful "establishment" players. By the same token, the pasteurization of PB was neither preordained nor irreversible. True, the serried forces of neoliberal constraint and capture pose a continuing threat to policy initiatives that seek to contest the established order, or to otherwise buck market logics. But these forces are neither omnipresent nor are they omnipotent. And more positively, the fact that policies not only mutate through their travels but mutate in norm-bending ways suggests that fast policies do not necessarily move as unilaterally controlled vectors, along singular trajectories, but can instead diverge, splinter, or rebound in various ways.

Furthermore, the two cases examined here suggest that there may be factors both intrinsic and extrinsic to the policies themselves that influence these sometimes path-altering journeys. On the one hand, with regard to intrinsic factors, policies that display a high degree of modular integrity, in that a particular bundle of program components is deemed (or demonstrated to be) necessary to secure favored outcomes, might be less prone to unbundling or deconstruction en route than those policies that advertise their availability for improvised reconstruction, customization, or bricolage. If CCTs more closely resemble the former of these types, being sold as a package deal, and PB looks more like the latter, being promoted as a relatively open space for rebundling and experimentation, then one might expect the relative grip of the original model to be stronger in technocratically framed and marketed programs like CCTs than with grassroots experiments like PB. The World Bank has been unable to build a replicating machine, but when it seeks to sustain its policy endorsements with evidence from randomized control trials, elaborate technical assistance programs, and best-practice marketing, some favored models—like CCTs—have been relatively successful at holding the policymaking center of gravity.

*Relatively* successful, that is, because even in the CCT case there have been provocative countercurrents. Where these have been strongest, the countercurrent may reflect intrinsic frailties or flaws in the original model. Conditionalities, for example, may or may not be strictly necessary, opening the door to (authorized or unauthorized) experiments with less-conditional programming methods. But extrinsic conditions are arguably no less significant. The availability of sponsoring agencies, like the network of NGOs and development institutions that combined to initiate Namibia's BIG experiment, can be a decisive factor, as can the availability of "sponsorship" from more centrist international organizations like the ILO or parts of the UN system, or by robust advocacy networks. Social, economic, and political circumstances can also disrupt established diffusion trajectories, as in the case of the global financial crisis of 2008–2009 or the periodic food-supply crises that ravage countries in the Global South, which can shift the terrain in favor of alternative approaches. Moving the needle on CCT policymaking, however, is an expensive and time-consuming business; absent this, there will be a strong tendency for it to roll along the preferred pathways.

In contrast, PB experiments seem to be more acclimatized to conditions of political "opening," for instance in the context of historical moments of democratization, or perhaps with the arrival of a reforming administration or major investment program; their allure seems to fade in more "normal" times. The transnational impetus of various PB projects also seems to be positively correlated with extrinsic circumstances like the degree (and form) of support of the intermediation infrastructure. The suturing of progressive elements within the UN network to the most promising of the Latin American PB experiments enabled, for a time, constructive forms of learning across sites and contexts in a manner superior to conventional styles of best-practice reductionism. As these progressive learning networks faltered, however, the transnational field was soon to be dominated by, on the one hand, instrumentalist appropriations of the PB method by the likes of the World Bank, and on the other, by more sparsely resourced advocacy networks.

Finally, it must be emphasized that mutation, even if to some degree it is inevitable, is rarely a haphazard or spontaneous process. The work of paradigm building and maintenance involves many hands and substantial resources; significant social, institutional, and political capacities are necessary to sustain (or indeed to alter) established courses of policy development. The allure of policy innovations tends to fade quite quickly, however—another manifestation, surely, of the fast-policy condition—so the work of maintaining transnational "fronts" of policy development is one of constant renewal. In this respect, the "translation" of policies is a continuous process; they must be constantly reworked to meet new challenges and to fit different circumstances. And this is also a social process, needless to say, even in policy fields dominated by technocratic impulses and highly stylized models. Mobile models too have their makers.

## Modeling

All models have their makers, then, but the generative capacities and down-stream consequences of models invariably exceed and outrun those of their architects. While policy models can never remake the world in their own perfect image, as if by some automated process, they nevertheless possess the potential for shaping, structuring, and skewing fields of experimentation and intervention over long distances. Global policy models, in particular, cast very long shadows, shaping (if rarely dictating) the terms of far-off policy conversations. They establish technical and terminological frames around which solutions are sought, and against which alternatives are often dialogic-ally formulated. The act of commanding attention is central to the very definition of *model,* of course. This is what models do.

The remarkable rise of CCTs to the status of a "new norm," validated and promoted by the international development community,[5] can be seen as a quintessential expression of "model power."[6] This model—in the shape of the much-lauded Mexican prototype—was the outcome of intentional design, a design process in which a selective cluster of social-scientific claims and assertions not only melded with political calculations but, in some instances, overrode or actively facilitated them. As insider accounts have revealed, a stra-tegic goal of the group of expert-advocates that formed around PROGRESA was to focus "discussions as much as possible on objective and technical elements," where necessary calling upon "well-known national and interna-tional experts" to bolster the case for controversial aspects of the plan as a means of technocratically settling matters "where there [were] differences of opinion."[7] The incorporation of a randomized-trial evaluation, not ex post facto but as an integral component of the program itself, proved to be crucial in securing these goals—first in Mexico and then beyond.

What Anthony Hall has characterized as the "onward march" of CCT programs globally has been fueled by expensively marshaled evaluation evi-dence and guided by expert networks.[8] These pseudoscientific trappings speak not just to an attempt to purify the process of policy modeling, but to a far-reaching depoliticization of what is in effect a long-distance proxy for (or condensate of) World Bank policy advice. This evokes another underlying meaning of "modeling," which involves not only the construction but the *pro-jection* of an allegedly coherent, relatively self-contained rationality, scheme, or design. The model itself, of course, is a representation—in the sense of an architect's vision or a designer's blueprint—but as such it expresses a desire for replication or *reconstruction*, typically at another location. Models thereby lay a claim to ex situ and cross-contextual functionality; they contain a set of constituent relations or elements that together ostensibly comprise a functioning system. The modeler's conceit is that the attendant logic is an internal one, that it is *designed in,* and that if these designs can be replicated, so can their effects. Policy models invoke coherent, functional designs, designs that are readily codified and systematized; but rather than pure abstractions, they tend to be most effective when they are founded on some proof of concept in an original form or location.

If this combination of theory and practice, suturing a scientifically codified concept to a concrete authentication of that concept, proved to be a remarkably potent and propitious one in the case of CCTs, the same cannot be said for participatory budgeting. In as far as Porto Alegre represented a model, it was one built from the ground up and very much out of socially improvised and political practice. This was never a design-driven initiative, and the extent to which the integrity of the model was ever vested in an institutional design, as opposed to a continuing political process, has always been a rather controversial question. In fact, there could hardly be a sharper contrast between the CCT model's implicit promise of a well-articulated *and prefabricated* policymaking "answer," presented at the time of the birth of the experiment itself, and the spirit of open-ended questioning that has accompanied the rollout of PBs—recall that the UN's widely circulated manual on participatory budgeting traveled under the relatively unassuming title *72 Frequently Asked Questions about Participatory Budgeting.*[9] Undeniably, there were aspirations to projection and promotion, too, in the learning networks that the UN and other agencies sought to construct around PBs, but these invoked Porto Alegre more as inspirational experiment than as immaculate design. The tightness of the connection between the in situ logic of the policy model and its claim to ex situ salience was therefore much stronger in the case of CCTs than PB. The supply-side conditions for the production of these two models, then, were rather different: CCTs were conceived and launched as models, the template and the prototype being simultaneously manufactured, and while the improvised product that was PB would eventually also travel in a highly stylized, essentialized form, this institutional design was reverse engineered rather than planned.

A characteristic that the two policies share, and a necessary feature of all such received and lauded policy models, is that they have each acquired a global audience. As objects of imitation, models must possess hinterlands of influence. More than fields of passive reception, these are spaces of active co-constitution, because these audiences are continuously engaged in translating and rewriting the original script. It is in this sense that models are fundamentally *relational* constructions, because the path to recognition implies not only the designation of a space of projection and the enrollment of an (approving, aspirational) audience, but the cross-referential enactment of versions of that model. Successive generations of policy models both appeal to a recognized lineage, while staking a claim to adaptive significance. Fast-policy development is enabled by these shorthand connections, in that original models—based on imported designs—are often made readily available for adaptation, leading to the formation of mutually referential, experimental fields. Augmentation may be the path of least resistance, but more disruptive adaptations may occur too.

In the case of CCTs, there has been a series of World Bank–approved augmentations of the original model, incorporating case-management systems or time limits in the manner of Chile Solidario and other such second-generation approaches. But places like Brazil have been important sites (often elsewhere) for more wayward adaptation, which in turn have begun to open the space for experimentation with less conditional or even unconditional approaches. Even if these represent a somewhat countercultural presence in a field still largely dominated by orthodox forms of affirmative, paradigm-positive experimentation under the pastoral influence of the World Bank, their very existence is testimony to the heterogeneous and evolving nature of global policy fields. Participatory budgeting, of course, was born as a counter-cultural experiment, running against rather than with the hegemonic grain. Progressive advocates of PB have long insisted that these are practices that must be cultivated locally; they cannot be imposed from above or from outside. "Template" versions of PB are typically disparaged on the left as mere corruptions or ruling-class ruses. As a PB activist from the United Kingdom put it, "If it feels like *we* decided, it's PB. If *they* decided, it's not."[10] The sober reality, however, is that such genuinely organic forms of PB have been exceedingly rare achievements; they are, by definition, slow to build and their accomplishments are difficult to replicate. In contrast, the depoliticized and technocratic form of PB favored by the World Bank has displayed a diffusion pattern that has been fast, broad, and shallow.

"PB must be cultivated locally"

The speed and reach of less disruptive models, like heavily bankrolled CCT programs or boiled-down versions of PB lite, must not be tagged too narrowly to the internal characteristics or capacities of these models. They are traveling, after all, across neoliberalized terrains, the imperatives, constraints, and strategic orientations of which are reciprocally reinforced by the models themselves. While it would be a drastic oversimplification to claim that fast-policy regimes are no more than a functionally induced support system for neoliberalism, the fact that they have emerged, historically speaking, more or less in tandem with ongoing processes of neoliberalization has been profoundly consequential. We have emphasized here that the regimes of experimentality that have been propagated by the Washington Consensus agencies and their allies over the past two decades can be seen as an institutionalized coping mechanism, as a means of managing the serial policy failures associated with particular neoliberal policy initiatives. Experimental churning, in this sense, can be seen as a characteristic of the contradictory reproduction of neoliberalism itself.

But what of anti-neoliberal experiments? Disruptive policy technologies, like developmental UCT programs or radicalizing experiments in PB, have made some headway. Their very existence attests to the fact that policy change, even under conditions of entrenched neoliberal hegemony, is a heterogeneous, more-than-neoliberal process. But the playing field is not a level one. Alternative policy projects have to be pushed up hill in these circumstances; they must always contend with the multifaceted countervailing force that is the nexus of hegemonic interests. Superior "alternative" designs are no doubt necessary but they are certainly far from sufficient in this context. If there is a lesson to be borrowed from the World Bank's adopted role as a model-peddler it is surely that effective strategies for extralocal distribution and dissemination are at least as important as innovations in design. There may be some limited consolation, for progressive policy advocates, in the fact that the imitative influence of orthodox global policy models is always a less-than-total, less-than-complete process, and that policy mutations are continuous and far from entirely controllable.

But happenstance mutations and little victories, on their own, will never be enough to disrupt the hegemonic pattern itself, or to challenge the authority of the most fortified power centers. The task of driving policy processes in the direction of more just and more sustainable strategies demands radically new approaches. Loosely coordinated forms of horizontal networking, long favored by some sections of the left, have manifestly not been delivering on a generalized basis, even as they seek to make the most of local successes, especially in a context in which centers of hierarchical coordination and persuasion have been increasingly monopolized by conservative forces. If fast policy is to become an effective tool for the left, as it has been for the right, then a very different kind of social and technical infrastructure will be required, one that sustains rather than saps *cumulative* forms of progressive experimentation and which prioritizes alternative methods for marrying radical designs to redistributive and emancipatory strategies. There may be lessons, both strategic and tactical, to be drawn from the short but dynamic history of fast-policy development, but in a deeper sense these really are questions for the future.

# Notes

## Introduction

1. For further discussion of these and similar examples, see Roy 2010; Peck 2012c; Matin et al. 2002; Kong et al. 2006; Prince 2012.

2. See Simmons et al. 2008a.

3. Kingfisher 2013, 11.

4. For signature contributions, see Walker 1969; Dolowitz and Marsh 2000. For a recent reconsideration of this line of research in political science, see Benson and Jordan 2011, 2012, and the further discussion in chapter 1.

5. See Robertson 1991; Wedel et al. 2005; Hall 1993.

6. See especially Wedel et al. 2005; Djelic and Sahlin-Andersson 2006; Simmons et al. 2008a; Shore et al. 2011; Kingfisher 2013. On critical policy studies more generally, see Fischer 2003; Fischer et al. 2009;Yanow 2007; Jessop 2009; Czarniawska 2010.

7. For discussion and examples, see Peck and Theodore 2010; Roy 2010; McCann 2011; McCann and Ward 2011; McFarlane 2011.

8. For further discussion of the meaning of policy models, see Peck and Theodore 2015; see also Roy and Ong 2011; McCann and Ward 2011.

9. See Lendvai and Stubbs 2007.

10. See Latour 1987; Morgan 2008.

11. Wedel et al. 2005, 39; see also Ferguson and Gupta 2002.

12. See, for example, Peck 2012c; McCann 2011.

13. See especially Fischer 2003; Simmons et al. 2008a; Shore et al. 2011; Kingfisher 2013.

14. For an extended discussion, see Burawoy 2009. See also Evens 2006; Marcus 1998.

15. See Lendvai and Stubbs 2007.

16. Mosse 2004, 646.

## 1. Geographies of Policy

1. Gress 1996; Stubbs 2005; Garrett et al. 2008.
2. See also Peck and Theodore 2010; Peck 2011b.
3. Jessop 2008, 193.
4. Ibid., 194.
5. Among many contributions on these themes, see Dezalay and Garth 2002; Ferguson and Gupta 2002; Peck 2002b; Brenner 2004; Goldman 2005; Levi-Faur 2005; Ong 2006; Jessop 2007; Leitner and Miller 2007; Peet 2008; Larner 2009; McCann 2010; McFarlane 2011. See also Prince 2010; González 2011.
6. Mörth 1998.
7. Dolowitz and Marsh 2000; Kingfisher 2013.
8. Simmons et al. 2008.
9. See Fischer et al. 2009; Peck and Theodore 2010; Shore et al. 2011.
10. See Walker 1969; Dye 1990.
11. Dye 1990, 15; see also Teibout 1956; Friedman 1962.
12. Walker 1969, 890.
13. Simon 1957; Hagerstrand 1967.
14. Walker 1969, 898.
15. Strang and Meyer 1993, 503.
16. McVoy 1940; Walker 1969.
17. See Brock 1984; McDonagh 1992; Carpenter 2001.
18. Levi-Faur 2005; Weyland 2006; Simmons et al. 2008.
19. Walker 1969, 881, 885.
20. See, classically, Goodman 1979; Eisinger 1988. See also Gray 1994; Gray and Lowery 1990; R. L. Hanson 1993.
21. Eyestone 1977, 446.
22. See Harvey 1989; Peck 2002a.
23. Rose 1991, 5.
24. Ibid., 20.
25. Ibid.
26. Ibid., 7.
27. cf. Hall 1993.
28. Rose 1991, 7.
29. Ibid., 9.
30. Wolman 1992, 29.
31. Ibid., 32–33.
32. Ibid., 37.
33. See Robertson 1991, 55.
34. Wolman 1992, 41.
35. Peck 1995.
36. Robertson 1991, 64.
37. Ibid., 70, 75; see also Peck 2002a.
38. Wolman 1992.

39. Ibid., 42.

40. Dolowitz and Marsh 1996.

41. Kingdon 1995, 131.

42. Dolowitz and Marsh 1996, 344.

43. Dolowitz and Marsh 2000, 21.

44. Cf. Stubbs 2005.

45. See Evans and Davies 1999; Bulmer and Padgett 2004.

46. Radaelli 2000, 38.

47. See Mörth 1998; Jacoby 2002.

48. Dolowitz and Marsh 2000, 5.

49. Dolowitz and Marsh 1996, 357.

50. Dye 1990.

51. Offe 1996, 212.

52. Offe 1996, 1997.

53. Peck 2010.

54. Offe 1996, 213.

55. Strang and Meyer 1993, 500.

56. Offe 1996, 214–15.

57. Cf. Dolowitz and Marsh 1996.

58. See Porter and Craig 2004; Peck 2011.

59. See the discussion in Brenner et al. 2010 and Peck 2013a.

60. See Hall 1993. Note that only in the business-as-usual world of first-order policy changes is there much resemblance to the diffusionist universe of satisficing behavior, incremental change, and routinized decision-making.

61. Bockman and Eyal 2002, 313.

62. Hall 1993, 279.

63. Blyth 2008.

64. Hall 1993, 280.

65. For discussion, see Peck 2013a.

66. Garrett et al. 2008.

67. Simmons et al. 2008, 34.

68. Ibid., 32.

69. See Haveman 1993.

70. See Haas 1992.

71. Rose 1993.

72. Meyer et al. 1997; cf. Guillen 2001.

73. See Knorr-Cetina 1999; Kogut and Macpherson 2008.

74. Simmons et al. 2008, 31.

75. Hall 1993.

76. Garrett et al. 2008; Peck and Theodore 2010c. See the further discussion in chapter 3.

77. Simmons et al., 2008, 17.

78. Harvey 1989.

79. Robertson 1991; Rodrik 1997.

80. Simmons et al. 2008, 10–11.

81. Gill 2002.

82. Gilardi 2005; cf. Brenner et al. 2010.

83. Garrett et al. 2008, 359.

84. DiMaggio and Powell 1983, 1991; Radaelli 2000.

85. DiMaggio and Powell 1983, 153.

86. See Babb 2001; Dezalay and Garth 2002; Goldman 2005; Larner 2009.

87. Kogut and Macpherson 2008, 136.

88. Ibid., 107.

89. Bockman and Eyal 2002, 315.

90. See Wayland 2006; Kogut and Macpherson 2008.

91. See Desai 1994; Feigenbaum et al. 1998; Prasad 2005; Mansfield 2008.

92. Cf. Dolowitz and Marsh 2000.

93. Consider, for example, the contrasting but highly effective approaches adopted by Peter Hall (1993) and Catherine Kingfisher (2013).

## 2. Reflections

1. For some of our own contributions to this literature, and its methodological implications, see Peck and Theodore 2001, 2010b; Theodore and Peck 2001, 2012; Peck 2000, 2001a, 2003a, 2012b, 2013a.

2. See Brenner and Theodore 2002a; Brenner et al. 2010; Peck 2010; Peck and Theodore 2012; Peck, Theodore, and Brenner 2013.

3. Castaneda 1992.

4. See especially Ferguson 2010; cf. Lavinas 2013.

5. See E. O. Wright 2010.

6. See Hart 2004.

7. S. Wright 2011, 27, emphasis in original. See also Peck 2013a.

8. On the Manchester School, see Evens and Handelman 2006. For Berkeley contributions, see Burawoy 2009 and Burawoy et al. 2000.

9. See discussions in Thiem and Robertson 2010; Hughes and Cormode 1998; Cochrane and Ward 2012. See also Freidberg 2001.

10. Wedel et al. 2005, 41.

11. See Dunn 2007; cf. Kuus 2013.

12. See Schoenberger 1991; Soss 2006; Kuus 2013.

13. This said, interview programs must always be contextualized through those means available, such as observations for example, site visits, conferences, meetings, in addition to regular forms of documentary "due diligence" and textual analysis.

14. Kuus 2013, 118.

15. Mosse 2004.

16. Burawoy 1998, 17–18.

17. Hart 2004, 96.

18. The term is from Bair and Werner 2011.

19. See the further discussion in Peck and Theodore 2010b.

20. Burawoy 2001, 148. See also McCann 2011; Peck 2012b; González 2011.

21. Pollitt et al. 1990, 174–75; see also Wedel et al. 2005.

22. For a classic discussion of these issues, from a Manchester School perspective, see Mitchell 2006.

23. Burawoy 2001, 2009.

24. Peck and Theodore 2010a.

25. Brenner et al. 2010.

26. For further discussion, along with an empirical application, see Theodore and Peck 2012.

27. Burawoy 2009.

28. Tsing 2004.

29. Pollitt et al. 1990; Mosse 2004.

30. See the constructively skeptical discussion in Eliasoph and Lichterman 1999.

31. See Peck 2005, 2011a.

32. See the discussion in Venesson 2008.

33. See Peck 2001b, 2002b. See also Schram and Soss 2001; Schram 2000.

34. See, for example, Theodore and Peck 1999, 2001; Peck 1999a, b; Theodore 2007.

35. These first took shape in Jessop and Peck 1999. For a subsequent discussion, see Peck and Theodore 2001; Jessop 2008.

36. See Jessop 2002, 2010; Peck and Jones 1995; Peck and Tickell 1994.

37. Handelman 2006, 113, 94. On the social and political context of the Manchester School, see Mills 2006.

## 3. New Ideas for New York City

1. See O'Connor 2008; Peck 2010, chapter 4.

2. See Krinsky 2008; Peck 2001b.

3. Former member number 3, Commission for Economic Opportunity, interviewed by Jamie Peck and Nik Theodore, December 2008.

4. CEO 2006, 12.

5. Quoted in City of New York, press release PR-093–07, March 29, 2007.

6. Quoted in E. J. Dionne, "Bloomberg's Brave Bet on Innovation," *Washington Post*, December 22, 2006.

7. Of the $50 million initial rollout costs, $10 million each was provided by the Rockefeller and Starr Foundations, $5 million came from George Soros's Open Society Institute, $2 million was donated by the finance group AIG, and undisclosed amounts came from the Robin Hood and Broad Foundations, and from Bloomberg himself. See City of New York, "Mayor Bloomberg and Major Philanthropic Foundations Unveil Size, Scope, and Schedule of *Opportunity NYC*, the Nation's First-Ever Conditional Cash Transfer Program," press release PR-093–07, March 29, 2007.

8. See J. Traub, "Pay for Good Behavior?" *New York Times Magazine*, October 8, 2006; Cramer 2007. On Bloomberg's political style, see J. Hailemann, "His American Dream," *New York Magazine*, December 11, 2006; Brash 2010.

9. Quoted in Brookings Institution 2007, 9.

10. "Mayor Bloomberg Tackles Poverty," *New York Times,* January 22, 2008.

11. Quoted in World Bank, "Successful Anti-Poverty Policies Are Now Applied in New York City: Rich Countries Learn from Experiences in the South," press release 2008/166/LAC, accessed at http://web.worldbank.org/WBSITE/EXTERNAL/NEWS /0,,contentMDK:21595624~pagePK:64257043~piPK:437376~theSitePK:4607,00 .html.

12. Ibid. Incorrectly, the World Bank stated that Opportunity NYC was the result of "extensive collaboration with a similar program in Mexico." The collaborative relationship did not begin until after Mayor Bloomberg announced the program.

13. Director, social-advocacy agency, New York City, interviewed by Jamie Peck and Nik Theodore, December 2008.

14. Antipoverty activist, New York City, interviewed by Jamie Peck and Nik Theodore, December 2008.

15. Senior executive, community organization, interviewed by Jamie Peck and Nik Theodore, December 2008.

16. As one of the delegates recalled, since "the Mayor's office . . . was going to make an investment in a pretty big thing from a different country, they wanted to 'look under the hood,' and appropriately so. It really exposed City government and big antipoverty agencies in the city, some of the chattering classes, and a number of other folks to these ideas. There is no substitute for hearing from sober, pragmatic officials. They are of the same stripe as city hall. They are people who have to run programs, and be accountable to politicians for programs. They were absolutely the best deliverers of [the message concerning] what's good and what's bad and what's not possible." Senior policy consultant, New York City, interviewed by Jamie Peck and Nik Theodore, December 2008.

17. M. Bloomberg, 2006 State of the City Address, accessed at www.gothamga zette.com/article/searchlight/20060126/203/1738, 5.

18. Quoted in City of New York, press release PR-437-06, December 18, 2006; see also D. Cardwell, "New Office Would Battle City Poverty," *New York Times,* December 19, 2006.

19. Michael Bloomberg, quoted in Brookings Institution 2007, 16.

20. J. Traub, "Pay for Good Behavior?" *New York Times Magazine,* October 8, 2006.

21. CEO 2006, 10.

22. CEO 2006, 7.

23. Under Mayor Giuliani, New York City played a prominent role in the workfare experiments of the 1990s, which were premised on the claim that the underlying problem to be solved was the postindustrial condition of "welfare dependency," rather than poverty per se. Work, or simulated work, was presented as the appropriate solution. The "job-ready" were promptly "diverted" into private-sector jobs; forty thousand others wore the orange vests that became the symbol of New York–style workfare, cleaning parks and subways in exchange for their benefits. See Piven 1999.

24. CEO 2006, 7.

25. "Mayor Bloomberg Announces Recommendations of the Mayor's Commission for Economic Opportunity," September 18, 2006, accessed at www.nyc.gov.

26. See Rawlings 2004; Rawlings and Rubio 2005; de la Brière and Rawlings 2006.

27. Rawlings and Rubio 2005, 33, 52.

28. Aber 2009, 58.

29. Quoted in City of New York, press release PR-123–07, April 24, 2007.

30. City of New York, press release PR-201-07, June 18, 2007.

31. Doug Muzzio, *City Talk,* CUNY TV, December 19, 2006, www.cuny.tv/series/citytalk.

32. "Giving me time-based, cash assistance at a certain moment for certain behaviors . . . has the assumption that I wouldn't do these things normally, which is belittling." Executive director, community organization, interviewed by Jamie Peck and Nik Theodore, December 2008.

33. "[O]nce payments are institutionalized, it will be difficult to dislodge the expectations that they will create." Mac Donald 2007, 19.

34. Former members numbers 3 and 2, Commission for Economic Opportunity, interviewed by Jamie Peck and Nik Theodore, December 2008.

35. Former member number 1, Commission for Economic Opportunity, interviewed by Jamie Peck and Nik Theodore, December 2008.

36. Senior program manager, Opportunity NYC, interviewed by Jamie Peck and Nik Theodore, December 2008.

37. Ibid.

38. See Peck 2001b.

39. Senior program manager, Opportunity NYC, interviewed by Jamie Peck and Nik Theodore, December 2008.

40. Program manager number 1, Opportunity NYC, interviewed by Jamie Peck and Nik Theodore, December 2008.

41. Program manager number 2, Opportunity NYC, interviewed by Jamie Peck and Nik Theodore, December 2008.

42. Senior program manager, Opportunity NYC, interviewed by Jamie Peck and Nik Theodore, December 2008.

43. Aber 2009, 57.

44. Riccio 2010.

45. Senior program manager number 1, World Bank, Washington, D.C., interviewed by Jamie Peck and Nik Theodore, May 2009.

46. Aber 2009, 62.

47. Former member number 1, Commission for Economic Opportunity, interviewed by Jamie Peck and Nik Theodore, December 2008.

48. The mayor's own political aspirations were also the subject of much speculation. As a World Bank official recalled, "I'd love to see Obama pick this thing up, I think it would be really cool. . . . We wondered maybe, with the Opportunity NYC, if

Bloomberg wasn't testing the water on, you know, if he has aspirations too . . . as a candidate. You know a few years ago he was flirting . . . *Opportunity Bloomberg!*" Senior program manager number 2, World Bank, Washington, D.C., interviewed by Jamie Peck and Nik Theodore, May 2009.

49. Senior program manager number 1, World Bank, Washington, D.C., interviewed by Jamie Peck and Nik Theodore, May 2009.

50. Remarks at the launch of the Inter-American Social Protection Network, Westin Hotel, New York City, September 22, 2009.

51. City of New York, "Mayor Bloomberg Speaks about the Opportunity NYC Conditional Cash Transfer Pilot Program at Launch of the Organization of American States' New Partnership to Fight Poverty," press release PR-412-09, September 22, 2009.

52. Presentation on Opportunity NYC at the Inter-American Social Protection Network Conference, Westin Hotel, New York City, September 22, 2009.

53. Organization of American States 2009.

54. See Henderson et al. 2002; Wright 1997.

55. See World Bank 2005a; Massey et al. 2006.

56. Levy 2006, 15.

57. Kaufman and Trejo 1997; Menocal 2001.

58. Dresser 1991.

59. Pastor and Wise 1998, 79, 61.

60. Levy 2006, 14.

61. Dresser 1998, 224; see also Babb 2001.

62. Teichman 2007, 562.

63. "The Lorenz curve for tortilla consumption is almost a 45 degree line," Levy (2006, 5) pointed out.

64. Ibid., 10–13.

65. Ibid., 11.

66. See Levy and Rodríguez 2004; Teichman 2007; social policy minister, Mexico City, interviewed by Jamie Peck and Nik Theodore, October 2008.

67. Lustig 1998, 210.

68. Pastor and Wise 1997, 2; see also M. Fineman, "Zedillo Touts 'New Era,' Targets Rebels," *Los Angeles Times,* September 2, 1996; and Dresser 1998.

69. Pastor and Wise 1997, 40; see also Lustig 1998.

70. Levy 2006, 14.

71. Levy 2006, 15; see also Yaschine 1999; Hall 2007.

72. Levy and Rodríguez 2004, 45.

73. Quoted in Luccisano 2004, 44.

74. Quoted in "Mexico's Oportunidades: Interview with Miguel Székely, Undersecretary for Social Development," *IDBAmérica* October, 2004, accessed at www.iadb.org/idbamerica.

75. P. Bate, "A Lean Machine," *IDBAmérica,* October, 2004, accessed at www.iadb.org/idbamerica.

76. P. Bate, "A Different Kind of Opportunity," *IDBAmérica,* October, 2004, accessed at www.iadb.org/idbamerica. In light of the PROGRESA experience, a requirement to evaluate all new social programs was later enshrined in Mexican law (Levy 2006).

77. Teichman 2007.

78. IDB 2003a, b; see also Rawlings 2004; Heinrich 2005.

79. IFPRI 2005.

80. Levy 2006, 35.

81. Senior program manager number 1, World Bank, Washington, D.C., interviewed by Jamie Peck and Nik Theodore, May 2009.

82. Each rural community was required to elect a *promotora communitaria,* usually a woman fluent in Spanish, to liaise with PROGRESA officials and to oversee the program locally (see Luccisano 2004). However, even though PROGRESA made use of such forms of decentralized service delivery, the finances and rules of the program were strictly managed from the federal level. As Levy (2006, 99–100) unapologetically explained, "There is no community participation in the running of the program. . . . [T]his is a federal program, applying federal criteria, funded with federal resources, and operated by federal bureaucrats." Community participation, which had been an unevenly realized feature of Salinas's Left-leaning approach, was eschewed (Yaschine 1999).

83. Levy 2006, 97.

84. Teichman 2007.

85. Levy 2006, 85.

86. Ibid., 88.

87. Parker and Teruel 2005, 213.

88. Parker and Teruel 2005; IFPRI 2005; Behrman et al. 2005; Behrman and Skoufias 2006; Caldés et al. 2006.

89. See Levy 2006, 113; Parker and Teruel 2005.

90. Molyneux 2007, 69; Rawlings 2004.

91. Wolfensohn Center for Development 2006, 4.

92. Ibid., vii.

93. Levy 2006, 114.

94. Teichman 2007.

95. See Moreno-Dodson 2005.

96. IBRD and World Bank 2004, 261.

97. P. Bate, "The Story behind *Oportunidades,*" *IDBAmérica,* October 2004, accessed at www.iadb.org/idbamerica.

98. Ibid.

99. Bouillon and Tejerina 2006, 42.

100. Bolsa Escola is credited to professor-turned-governor-turned-senator Cristovam Buarque, a Workers Party politician previously at the National University of Brasilia, whose work in the early 1990s was the immediate inspiration for the program in the municipality of Brasilia. José Márcio Camargo, an economist from the

Pontifical Catholic University in Rio de Janeiro had been making a parallel case for CCTs in a series of newspaper articles in the early 1990s, publishing what can claim to be the first extended exposition on the subject in 1994 (see Almeida and Camargo 1994). Bolsa Escola, which was launched in January 1995, was awarded a United Nations prize in 1996, after which it "became a model for the rest of the country" (Cardoso and Portela Souza 2004, 12). All of this occurred more than a year before the launch of PROGRESA in Mexico.

101. Bourguignon et al. 2003.

102. Cardoso and Portela Souza 2004.

103. World Bank 2004a.

104. See Lindert et al. 2007; de Janvry et al. 2006.

105. Soares 2012, 1.

106. World Bank 2005a, 5.

107. Following the introduction of IDB financing in 2002, "It is probably fair to say that the systematic analytical and operational involvement of IDB personnel in the program has been more important than the loan itself," Levy (2006, 115) later observed. "Mutatis mutandis, mechanisms of this sort can be extremely helpful in other countries experiencing similar political transitions, regardless of whether there is a need for external financing." Initially, it "was not deemed advisable" to request external financing, but by 2001 "the panorama [had] changed" (Levy and Rodríguez 2004, 139). Levy's longstanding connections to the World Bank and the IDB—where he currently serves as vice president—are also underlined in Yaschine 1999 and Teichman 2007.

108. Levy and Rodríguez 2004.

109. Ibid.; Levy 2006.

110. See Lindert et al. 2007, 12.

111. "Not Always with Us," *Economist*, September 17, 2005; "New Thinking about an Old Problem," *Economist* September 17, 2005, 38.

112. Levy 1991, 1.

113. Ibid., 32.

114. Ibid., 53, 85, 81, emphasis added.

115. See Yaschine 1999; Hall 2007.

116. Deacon 1999; Noël 2006.

117. See Williamson 1990.

118. UNICEF 1987; UNDP 1990.

119. See Levy 2006; Levy and van Wijnbergen 1995.

120. Levy 2006, 10; Lipton and Ravallion 1995.

121. Sen 1985; Killick 1991.

122. World Bank 1990.

123. Social policy minister, Mexico City, interviewed by Jamie Peck and Nik Theodore, October 2009; see also Lipton and Ravallion 1995.

124. Yaschine 1999, 56.

125. Rawlings 2004, 8, 2.

126. Ibid., 13, 16.

127. Remarks at the Launch of Inter-American Social Protection Network, Westin Hotel, New York City, September 22, 2009.

128. On the concept of experimentality, see Petryna 2009.

129. Michael Bloomberg, quoted in J. Bosman, "Disappointed, City Will Stop Paying the Poor for Good Behavior," *New York Times,* March 31, 2010.

130. Riccio et al. 2010, iii, ES-2, ES-6.

131. T. Ogden, "How Not to React to Rigorous Evaluation," *Philanthropy Action,* April 15, 2010, accessed at www.philanthropyaction.com, emphasis added.

132. One of the many conceits of randomized control trials, in fact, is that relationships measured, and ascribed causal status, at one scale or with one population are readily scalable to others, as well as transferable from place to place (see Reddy 2012).

133. Quoted in J. Bosman, "Disappointed, City Will Stop Paying the Poor for Good Behavior," *New York Times,* March 31, 2010. Qualitative follow-up work by MDRC researchers reiterated the party line that Family Rewards should "bridge the gap between the long-term pay off of education and the distraction created by the immediate attractions of street life," while at the same time recognizing that some parents were confused by the complex schedule of rewards and payments, no doubt compounded by their hasty induction into the program; others opting to shield their younger children, in particular, from what were interpreted as additional competitive pressures created by the incentive payments (Greenberg et al. 2011).

134. Aber 2009, 61.

135. See Peck 2010.

136. The initial group of partner cities included Cleveland, Kansas City, Memphis, Newark, San Antonio, Tulsa, and Youngstown (Ohio), as well as New York City itself.

137. Senior policy advisor, New York City, interviewed by Jamie Peck and Nik Theodore, December 2008.

138. Mayor's Fund to Advance NYC and Center for Economic Opportunity 2011, 8.

139. Ibid., 7–8, emphasis added.

140. Quoted in City of Memphis, "Mayor A. C. Wharton Unveils $12 Million "Family Rewards" Program to Combat Inner-City Poverty," press release, September 21, 2011.

141. M. Richens, "Linked to Memphis," *Commercial Appeal,* May 15, 2011; B. Warren, "Family Rewards Coming—Cash Incentives Offered Poor Teens, Parents for Achievements," *Commercial Appeal,* September 22, 2011.

142. B. Warren, "Family Rewards Coming—Cash Incentives Offered Poor Teens, Parents for Achievements," *Commercial Appeal,* September 22, 2011; W. C. Thomas, "Yes, It's a Gimmick, but Let's Just Try It," *Commercial Appeal,* October 6, 2011.

## 4. Globalizing Social-Policy Practice

1. Ayala Consulting 2003, 3.

2. World Bank official, program evaluation, Washington, D.C., interviewed by Jamie Peck and Nik Theodore, May 2009.

3. Ayala Consulting 2003, 3.

4. Ibid., 26.

5. Ibid., 33.

6. See Schild 2013.

7. Country program profiles, Second International Conference on Conditional Cash Transfers, accessed at http://web.worldbank.org/WBSITE/EXTERNAL/TOPICS /EXTSOCIALPROTECTION/EXTSAFETYNETSANDTRANSFERS/0,,contentM DK:20823929~isCURL:Y~menuPK:282766~pagePK:64020865~piPK:149114~theSit ePK:282761,00.html.

8. Ferreira 2004.

9. Ibid., 10–11.

10. See M. Sayagues, "Researchers Ponder Value of Cash Transfers," *Inter Press Service Africa,* May 12, 2009, accessed at http://ipsnews.net/africa/nota.asp?idnews= 46808.

11. See Datt et al. 2007; see also Garcia and Moore 2012.

12. Ellis 2007.

13. Senior economist and program evaluator, federal research agency, Brasilia, interviewed by Jamie Peck and Nik Theodore, February 2009.

14. Ministerial advisor with responsibility for social policy, Brasilia, interviewed by Jamie Peck and Nik Theodore, February 2009.

15. Ibid.

16. Samson 2009, 51.

17. Grosh 2006, original emphasis.

18. World Bank official, program evaluation, Washington, D.C., interviewed by Jamie Peck and Nik Theodore, May 2009.

19. Fiszbein et al. 2009, 1, 3.

20. Levy 2006.

21. Aber and Rawlings 2011, 3–4.

22. Senior economist, World Bank, Washington, D.C., interviewed by Jamie Peck and Nik Theodore, May 2009.

23. Ibid.

24. Ibid.

25. Senior evaluation manager number 2, IFPRI, Washington, D.C., interviewed by Jamie Peck and Nik Theodore, May 2009.

26. Ibid.

27. Aber and Rawlings 2011, 7.

28. Senior evaluation manager number 2, IFPRI, Washington, D.C., interviewed by Jamie Peck and Nik Theodore, May 2009.

29. Senior economist, World Bank, Washington, D.C., interviewed by Jamie Peck and Nik Theodore, May 2009.

30. Fiszbein et al. 2009, 46.

31. Ibid., 65–66.

32. Levy 2006.

33. Fiszbein et al. 2009, 47.

34. Ibid., 60.

35. Levy and Rodríguez 2004, 48.

36. Fiszbein et al. 2009, 197.

37. Ibid.

38. Felipe Calderón, quoted in Presidency of the Republic of Mexico, "United Nations Acknowledges Contribution of President Calderón's Oportunidades Program to Alleviating Poverty," press release, October 5, 2009, accessed at http://en.presiden cia.gob.mx/2009/10/united-nations-acknowledges-contribution-of-president-calde rons-oportunidades-program-to-alleviating-poverty/.

39. World Bank 2010 Mexico, "Proposed Additional Financing Loan for the Support to *Oportunidades* Project," Meeting of the Executive Directors, November 9, 2010, document 57825.

40. Social policy advisor, Brasilia, interviewed by Jamie Peck and Nik Theodore, February 2009.

41. Senior evaluation researcher, federal government research institute, Brasilia, interviewed by Jamie Peck and Nik Theodore, February 2009.

42. Lindert et al. 2007.

43. Evaluation manager, nonprofit research center, Washington, D.C., interviewed by Jamie Peck and Nik Theodore, May 2009.

44. Notable among these were the federal Bolsa Escola school grant and the Program for a Guaranteed Minimum Income, both of which had municipal predecessors, the Bolsa Alimentação health and nutrition grants, the cooking-gas subsidy, Auxilio Gas, and various complementary initiatives associated with President Lula's Fome Zero (zero hunger) commitment, which included a cash transfer for food consumption in low-income families.

45. A member of the World Bank's technical team recalled some of the challenges confronted in the early months of the Bolsa Família program: "If you take four programs that had already started, trying to merge their registries with some of our support, and IDB and DFID's support . . . thinking objectively, this is not easy! . . . That's not something you do overnight, it's slow. They had three million families [initially], but they were under pressure to scale up fast. And they started scaling up fast with what they judged was a good enough—but in need of improvement—registry. We all said that this is a pragmatic decision, and you've got to move with this. But there were problems, and they didn't have all of the oversight and control mechanisms in place. The registry wasn't as good as it is now. It's in much better shape now. They've done a fabulous job at turning it around. They dropped the monitoring of the conditionalities for a short time, partly because of practical reasons of just how do you get the kids' attendance records. [At first] you're just trying to see who is in the program." Senior program manager, World Bank, Washington, D.C., interviewed by Jamie Peck and Nik Theodore, May 2009.

46. Lindert et al. 2007, 3.

47. Senior research manager, federal evaluation agency, Brasilia, interviewed by Jamie Peck and Nik Theodore, May 2009.

48. Senior administrator, Bolsa Família program, Brasilia, interviewed by Jamie Peck and Nik Theodore, May 2009.

49. Evaluation manager, nonprofit research center, Washington, D.C., interviewed by Jamie Peck and Nik Theodore, May 2009.

50. Lindert et al. 2007, 13–14; see also F. Canzian and G. Athias, "Lula teve aula sobre plano social focalizado mexicano," *Folha de S. Paulo,* March 29, 2003, accessed at http://www1.folha.uol.com.br/fsp/brasil/fc2704200302.htm.

51. Senior manager number 1, World Bank Brasilia team, interviewed by Jamie Peck and Nik Theodore, May 2009.

52. Senior research manager, federal evaluation agency, Brasilia, interviewed by Jamie Peck and Nik Theodore, May 2009.

53. Senior evaluation researcher, federal government research institute, Brasilia, interviewed by Jamie Peck and Nik Theodore, February 2009.

54. Political advisor, federal government, Brasilia, interviewed by Jamie Peck and Nik Theodore; see also Morais de Sa e Silva 2011. Though see Lindert et al. 2007; Lustig 2011. Levy's only mention of Brazil in his otherwise definitive account of Oportunidades is an acknowledgement to World Bank president James Wolfensohn, for giving him the opportunity to participate in the Lula briefing.

55. Lindert et al. 2007, 14.

56. Political advisor, federal government, Brasilia, interviewed by Jamie Peck and Nik Theodore, February 2009.

57. Ibid.

58. Policy advisor, federal government, Brasilia, interviewed by Jamie Peck and Nik Theodore, February 2009.

59. Senior evaluation researcher, federal government research institute, Brasilia, interviewed by Jamie Peck and Nik Theodore, February 2009.

60. Policy advisor, federal government, Brasilia, interviewed by Jamie Peck and Nik Theodore, February 2009.

61. Manager, federal government research institute, Brasilia, interviewed by Jamie Peck and Nik Theodore, February 2009.

62. Senior manager number 1, World Bank Brasilia team, interviewed by Jamie Peck and Nik Theodore, May 2009, emphasis added.

63. Lindert et al. 2007, 10.

64. Ibid., 9.

65. Policy advisor, federal government, Brasilia, interviewed by Jamie Peck and Nik Theodore, February 2009.

66. Senior manager, federal evaluation agency, Brasilia, interviewed by Jamie Peck and Nik Theodore, May 2009.

67. Lindert et al. 2007, 6, emphasis added.

68. Fiszbein et al. 2009, 36.

69. Senior administrator, Bolsa Família program, Brasilia, interviewed by Jamie Peck and Nik Theodore, February 2009, emphasis added.

70. Ibid.

71. Senior program manager number 2, World Bank, Washington, D.C., interviewed by Jamie Peck and Nik Theodore, May 2009.

72. Senior manager, federal evaluation agency, Brasilia, interviewed by Jamie Peck and Nik Theodore, February 2009.

73. Senior program manager number 2, World Bank, Washington, D.C., interviewed by Jamie Peck and Nik Theodore, May 2009.

74. Evaluation specialist number 1, World Bank, Washington, D.C., interviewed by Jamie Peck and Nik Theodore, May 2009.

75. "Brazil always has this thing that they're the biggest and they're the first but nobody recognizes this," a World Bank official commented. "Please world, we're here!" Senior program manager number 2, World Bank, Washington, D.C., interviewed by Jamie Peck and Nik Theodore, May 2009.

76. Senior evaluation researcher, federal government research institute, Brasilia, interviewed by Jamie Peck and Nik Theodore, February 2009.

77. See Palma and Urzúa 2005.

78. Evaluation specialist number 2, World Bank, Washington, D.C., interviewed by Jamie Peck and Nik Theodore, May 2009.

79. Fiszbein et al. 2009, 39.

80. "PROGRESA was experimental, you know a real experiment. We didn't have that," a Brazilian economist conceded, "The IFPRI evaluation of PROGRESA is the gold standard evaluation." Senior manager, federal evaluation agency, Brasilia, interviewed by Jamie Peck and Nik Theodore, February 2009. On the "iconic" status of Oportunidades, see Fiszbein et al. 2009, 6.

81. Senior research manager, federal evaluation agency, Brasilia, interviewed by Jamie Peck and Nik Theodore, February 2009.

82. Evaluation specialist number 2, World Bank, Washington, D.C., interviewed by Jamie Peck and Nik Theodore, May 2009.

83. Peck 2001b; Handler 2004.

84. Senior evaluation researcher, federal government research institute, Brasilia, interviewed by Jamie Peck and Nik Theodore, February 2009.

85. Fiszbein et al. 2011.

86. Government of Chile, "Ethical Family Income Bill Comes into Force," accessed at http://www.gob.cl/english/government-information/2012/05/17/ethical-family-income-bill-comes-into-force.htm.

87. The UCT is limited to twenty-four months and is phased out through steadily declining transfer amounts beginning in the last five months of benefit receipt. The achievements program provides for a smaller transfer to families with children who rank in the second 15 percent of their class, while another transfer provides a wage supplement to low-income working women as well as a wage subsidy to employers.

88. Sumarto et al. 2010.

89. Hutagalung et al. 2009.

90. Sumarto et al. 2010.

91. See World Bank 2012b; SMERU Research Institute 2008; Alderman 2002.

92. Hutagalung et al. 2009.

93. Sumarto et al. 2010.

94. Senior policy analyst number 1, World Bank, Jakarta, interviewed by Jamie Peck and Nik Theodore, March 2011.

95. Senior government official number 2, government planning agency, Jakarta, interviewed by Jamie Peck and Nik Theodore, March 2011.

96. Program manager, international development agency, Jakarta, interviewed by Jamie Peck and Nik Theodore, March 2011.

97. World Bank 2012a; see also Hutagalung et al. 2009.

98. World Bank 2012a, 17–20. These results were achieved despite the fact that the transfer was not indexed for inflation "so by 2008, it was just 12 percent of the poverty line, which is really low for this region." Senior policy analyst number 1, World Bank, Jakarta, interviewed by Jamie Peck and Nik Theodore, March 2011.

99. Senior policy analyst number 1, World Bank, Jakarta, interviewed by Jamie Peck and Nik Theodore, March 2011. The analyst went on to explain, "If you are a poor household without work, you aren't going to be able to spend a day traveling . . . to look to see if there is a factory open. You are going to have to scavenge around your own area to make sure there is food on your table." The evaluation found no evidence of the types of employment disincentives that so often are hypothesized to occur whenever unconditional cash assistance is provided. An economist at the Bank added, "The direct effects on poverty are large. We've done some modeling on what it does to the poverty rate. It didn't perfectly target, but it represented large chunks in the decline in poverty at the time." Senior policy analyst number 3, World Bank, Jakarta, interviewed by Jamie Peck and Nik Theodore, March 2011.

100. Senior official number 1, government planning department, Jakarta, interviewed by Jamie Peck and Nik Theodore, March 2011.

101. Senior official number 1, government planning department, Jakarta, interviewed by Jamie Peck and Nik Theodore, March 2011.

102. World Bank, "Indonesia: Second Urban Poverty Project," accessed at http://web.worldbank.org/WBSITE/EXTERNAL/NEWS/0,,contentMDK:23195498~menuPK:141310~pagePK:34370~piPK:34424~theSitePK:4607,00.html.

103. Senior official number 1, government planning department, Jakarta, interviewed by Jamie Peck and Nik Theodore, March 2011.

104. Senior policy analyst number 2, World Bank, Jakarta, interviewed by Jamie Peck and Nik Theodore, March 2011.

105. Ibid.; senior government official number 2, government planning agency, Jakarta, interviewed by Jamie Peck and Nik Theodore, March 2011.

106. Senior policy analyst number 2, World Bank, Jakarta, interviewed by Jamie Peck and Nik Theodore, March 2011.

107. See Haarmann and Haarmann 2012.

108. "They mixed up gross and net costs, basically. You give everybody the money, but you take it back [through the tax system] if they earn above a certain threshold. And then there are the pensioners [who receive a different universal grant]. We always look at the net costs. . . . The IMF just took population times the grant. That's simplistic, but they did that." Civil society representative, Windhoek, Namibia, interviewed by Nik Theodore, October 2009.

109. Ibid.

110. Haarmann and Haarmann 2012; Senior manager, think tank, Windhoek, Namibia, interviewed by Nik Theodore, October 2009.

111. Haarmann and Haarmann 2012; D. Krahe, "A Basic Income Program in Otjivero," *Spiegel Online*, August 10, 2009, accessed at http://www.globalpolicy.org/component/content/article/211-development/48036-a-basic-income-program-in-otjivero.html.

112. Civil society representative, Windhoek, Namibia, interviewed by Nik Theodore, October 2009; Senior manager, think tank, Windhoek, Namibia, interviewed by Nik Theodore, October 2009; see also Haarmann et al. 2009; Haarmann and Haarmann 2012.

113. Senior manager, think tank, Windhoek, Namibia, interviewed by Nik Theodore, October 2009.

114. "Beyond aid." Speech by World Bank Group president Robert B. Zoellick, September 14, 2011, accessed at http://web.worldbank.org/WBSITE/EXTERNAL/NEWS/0,,contentMDK:23000133~pagePK:34370~piPK:42770~theSitePK:4607,00.html.

115. Transcript of opening press conference with World Bank Group President Robert Zoellick, April 19, 2012, accessed at http://web.worldbank.org/WBSITE/EXTERNAL/COUNTRIES/AFRICAEXT/0,,contentMDK:23175789~menuPK:2246551~pagePK:2865106~piPK:2865128~theSitePK:258644,00.html.

116. Quoted in PBS *NewsHour* transcript, December 29, 2009, available at http://www.pbs.org/newshour.

117. Fiszbein et al. 2009, 196, 200.

118. "Give the Poor Money," *Economist,* July 31, 2010.

119. Hanlon et al. 2010, 129.

120. Ibid., 43.

121. Ibid., 27, 47.

122. ILO 2001.

123. Cichon et al. 2011.

124. "According to ILO calculations, less than 2 percent of the global Gross Domestic Product (GDP) would be necessary to provide a basic set of social security benefits to all of the world's poor" (ILO 2008, 3).

125. Standing 2008.

126. ILO 2011, xxix–xxx.

127. Mahon 2013.

128. ILO 2011, 82; Samson 2009.

129. ILO 2011, xxxi.

130. See Peck 2011b for further discussion in relation to CCTs and the social-investment consensus.

131. Quoted from "Potential and Limitations of CCTs" at http://www.socialsecur ityextension.org/gimi/gess/ShowTheme.do?tid=2845, emphasis in original.

132. Skoufias 2005.

133. In the words of Nancy Birdsall, president of the Center for Global Development: "These programs are as close as you can come to a magic bullet in development. . . . Every decade or so, we see something that can really make a difference, and this is one of those things" (quoted in C. W. Dugger, "To Help Poor Be Pupils, Not Wage Earners, Brazil Pays Parents," *New York Times,* January 3, 2004). For further discussion, see Adato and Hoddinott 2010.

134. Rômulo Paes de Sousa, vice-minister of social development, Brazil, quoted in M. Bunting, "Brazil's Cash Transfer Scheme Is Improving the Lives of the Poorest," *Guardian, Poverty Matters* (blog), November 19, 2010, accessed at http://www.guard ian.co.uk/global-development/poverty-matters.

## 5. Reflections

1. B. Ozler, "Defining Conditional Cash Transfer Programs: An Unconditional Mess," *Development Impact* (blog), World Bank, May 13, 2013, accessed at http://blogs .worldbank.org/impactevaluations/defining-conditional-cash-transfer-programs -unconditional-mess, emphasis in original.

2. Ibid.

3. After Petryna 2009.

4. Léautier and Moreno-Dodson 2005, 7.

5. "[T]he effects of the impact evaluation of the Oportunidades program were felt beyond Mexico's borders," World Bank analysts have reflected. "In this sense, one can say that the impact evaluation of one program supported the expansion of the program in its own country but also a horizontal scale up across countries of an effective approach to reducing poverty" (Fiszbein and Gevers 2005, 196).

6. Fiszbein et al. 2009, 144.

7. Cf. Lindert et al. 2007.

8. See Peck et al. 2012.

9. Fiszbein et al. 2009.

10. Simmons et al. 2008b; Peck 2011a.

11. See Peck 2010.

12. Riccio 2013.

13. See Ferguson 2010; Peck 2011b.

14. Hanlon et al. 2010, 131.

15. Yaschine and Orozco 2010, 71.

16. See Samson 2009; Standing 2010; ILO 2011.

## 6. Porto Alegre as Participatory Laboratory

1. Porto Alegre hosted the inaugural meeting of the World Social Forum, in 2001, along with the two subsequent gatherings, and has hosted the event periodically ever since.

2. Hardt and Negri 2003, xvii, xvi. See also Chase-Dunn et al. 2009.

3. See Santos 1998; Fung and Wright 2003b.

4. Santos 1998, 464, 463, 467.

5. Ponniah and Fisher 2003, 5.

6. Avritzer 2009; Baiocchi 2005.

7. Santos and Avritzer 2007, xxxvi.

8. Ibid.

9. See Santos 2008.

10. See Avritzer 2009; Baiocchi et al. 2011; Gret and Sintomer (2002) 2005; Santos 2007.

11. See Fung and Wright 2003b.

12. See Davey 1993; Center for Urban Development Studies 2003.

13. Porto Alegre is featured on the UN-Habitat best practices database, www .bestpractices.org. See also UN-Habitat 1996.

14. Shah 2007b, 6.

15. Quoted in Karides et al. 2008, 70.

16. See Baiocchi 2003b, 2003c; Hunter 2010.

17. See Bruce 2004c; Baiocchi 2005.

18. Nylan 2000; Baiocchi 2004; Goldfrank 2004; Chavez and Goldfrank 2004.

19. Bruce 2004b, 5. See also Wainwright and Branford 2006.

20. See Baierle 1998, 2002.

21. Shah 2007a, 6.

22. Bruce 2004d, 23, 37.

23. Navarro 2004.

24. Goldfrank 2003, 29–31.

25. Bruce 2004b, 39; see also Avritzer 2009.

26. See Goldfrank 2007, 2003; see also Avritzer 2009; Baiocchi 2005; Baiocchi et al. 2011.

27. Baiocchi et al. 2011, 43. Baiocchi et al. (ibid.) go on to emphasize "the role [neighborhood-based social movement organizations] played in cultivating a new politics of citizenship and in promoting, through prefigurative actions and direct interventions, new institutions of participation."

28. Baierle 1998; Abers 2000; Goldfrank 2003, 2007; Wampler 2007b; Avritzer 2009; Ganuza and Baiocchi 2012.

29. See Alba 1968; Castañeda 1994; Roberts 1998; Santos 1998; Chavez 2004, 1–10; Goldfrank 2007.

30. See Baierle 2002; Baiocchi 2005.

31. Santos 1998, 466; Baiocchi 2005, Figure 1.

32. Baiocchi 2005, 37.

33. See Baiocchi 2003d; Marquetti 2001; Santos 1998; Abers 2000; Marquetti 2001; Baiocchi 2005; Bruce 2004b; Goldfrank 2007; Wampler 2007b; Avritzer 2009.

34. See the discussion in Santos 1998; Baierle 1998, 2002; Goldfrank 2003; Baiocchi 2005.

35. Dutra 2002, quoted in Goldfrank 2007, 95.

36. See Wampler 2007b, 2008. Wampler 2008 reveals that 100 percent of PT-controlled municipalities across Brazil those with populations of more than one hundred thousand adopted PB between 1989 and 2004. But the appeal of PB extended well beyond the PT's municipal strongholds. Sintomer et al. estimate that between 2005 and 2008, 41 percent of all Brazilian cities with more than one hundred thousand residents had a PB process in place (Sintomer et al. 2012, 7).

37. Goldfrank 2007, 2011.

38. Wainwright 2006a, 6.

39. Gret and Sintomer (2002) 2005, 4, 133.

40. See especially Baierle 1998; Santos 1998; Marquetti 2000; Baiocchi 2003; Goldfrank 2003.

41. Sintomer 2005.

42. E. O. Wright 2010, 160.

43. See chapter 1 of this work; with regard to PB, see Avritzer 2009; Baiocchi et al. 2011.

44. Goldfrank 2005, quoted in Goldfrank 2007, 100.

45. Baierle 2003, 32; 1998.

46. Gomes and Dutra, quoted in Wainwright 2006b, 37, 35.

47. Wainwright 2006a, 8.

48. Daniel and unnamed federal policymaker, quoted in Wainwright 2006a, 7; see also Baierle 2007.

49. See J. Petras, "Lula's 'Workers' Regime' Plummets in Stew of Corruption," *Counterpunch,* July 30–31, 2005, accessed at http://www.counterpunch.org/petras080 12005.html; Liby 2006.

50. Oliveira Dutra, quoted in Wainwright 2006b, 25, 37.

51. See Goldfrank and Schneider 2006.

52. Economist, Porto Alegre, interviewed by Jamie Peck and Nik Theodore, August 2009.

53. "It's really consolidated," a Fogaça appointee explained. "In Porto Alegre, there is no government that can eliminate participatory budgeting today. It has a really strong position in the organizations of the city." Senior official, City of Porto Alegre, interviewed by Jamie Peck and Nik Theodore, August 2009.

54. Political scientist, Porto Alegre, interviewed by Jamie Peck and Nik Theodore, August 2009.

55. Senior officer, City of Porto Alegre, interviewed by Jamie Peck and Nik Theodore, August 2009.

56. Chavez 2006.

57. Quoted in Chavez 2006.

58. Busatto, quoted in Baierle 2007, 70.

59. Busatto, quoted in Schneider 2007, 3.

60. Prefeitura de Porto Alegre 2008, 68–69.

61. César Busatto, Secretary of Political Coordiantion and Local Governance, City of Porto Alegre, quoted in Prefeitura de Porto Alegre 2008, 69.

62. Sintomer et al. 2008, 172.

63. Leubolt et al. 2008, 443, emphasis added.

64. Social activist, Porto Alegre, interviewed by Jamie Peck and Nik Theodore, August 2009; Chavez 2006.

65. Cidade analyses, conducted by Paulo Muzell and colleagues, summarized in Leubolt et al. 2008, 442–43.

66. Social activist, Porto Alegre, interviewed by Jamie Peck and Nik Theodore, August 2009.

67. See Baierle 2002, 2007. "From a Gramscian point of view, it seemed to have failed because it was not sufficiently radical: democratisation of the state was not systematically used as a step towards deepening social change . . . [As a result] dominant groups, historically hostile to popular participation and equal access for all, [were able to] challenge and finally defeat the counter-hegemonic strategy" (Novy and Leubolt 2005, 2034).

68. Léautier 2007.

69. Shah 2007b, 1.

70. Ibid., 2.

71. See Abers 2000; Baiocchi 2005.

72. Campbell 2003, 8.

73. See Stolowicz 2004; Naim 2000; Tulchin and Selee 1994; Campbell 2003.

74. Campbell 2003, 7–8.

75. Ibid., 9.

76. Political scientist, Porto Alegre, interviewed by Jamie Peck and Nik Theodore, August 2009.

77. Senior policy analyst, Porto Alegre, interviewed by Jamie Peck and Nik Theodore, August 2009.

78. See Campbell et al. 1995; Campbell and Fuhr 2004b.

79. Navarro 2004, 200; Campbell and Fuhr 2004a.

80. Campbell and Fuhr 2004a, 5.

81. See, respectively, Shah 2007a; Campbell and Fuhr 2004b; Wagle and Shah 2003.

82. See especially Fung and Wright 2003; Santos 1998; Wainwright 2004.

83. All of the PT-administered cities featured at the UN Conference were utilizing participatory methods of some kind, for which Porto Alegre had long been the party's emblematic model. See Goldfrank 2003, 2004; Baiocchi 2004. The PT poster is cited by Nylan 2000, n. 20.

84. Baiocchi 2005, 154.

## 7. Democracy on the Move

1. UNESCO 2010, 8, 29, 30, 32.

2. United Nations, Bureau International des Expositions and Shanghai 2010 World Exposition Executive Committee 2010.

3. Shanghai Expo 2010, "UBPA Welcomes Porto Alegre day," accessed at http://expo.southcn.com/en/newscenter/headlines/201006/t20100607_96677.htm.

4. Sintomer et al. 2010, 18.

5. Ibid., 7.

6. Ibid., 19.

7. Executive director, U.S. social advocacy network, interviewed by Jamie Peck and Nik Theodore, Chicago, May 2013.

8. Social researcher and policy evaluator, Porto Alegre, interviewed by Jamie Peck and Nik Theodore, August 2009.

9. Ibid.

10. The phrase belongs to Chavez 2006, in his skeptical commentary on the dilution of the Porto Alegre model under Fogaça.

11. Senior researcher and policy advocate, economic think tank, Washington, D.C., interviewed by Jamie Peck and Nik Theodore, May 2009.

12. Senior policy researcher, Porto Alegre, interviewed by Jamie Peck and Nik Theodore, August 2009.

13. UN-Habitat 2006, *The Habitat Agenda: Istanbul Declaration on Human Settlements*, accessed at http://www.un.org/ga/Istanbul+5/declaration.htm.

14. Sintomer et al. 2010, 25.

15. Cabannes 2004b, 27.

16. Cabannes 2004c.

17. Cabannes 2004a.

18. Tibaijuka 2004.

19. Cabannes 2004b, 35, 40, emphasis added.

20. Ibid., 46.

21. Ibid., 45.

22. See Santos 1998; Fung and Wright 2003a; E. O. Wright 2010.

23. Sintomer et al. 2010, 25.

24. Cabannes 2004c, 6.

25. Cabannes 2004b, 33.

26. URB-AL's Network 9 seeks to establish a "permanent process of exchange and enhancing experiences between local Latin American and European governments for socialization, systemization and implementation of the best experiences in the scope of local financing and participative democracy practices," including the "creation of common projects, attending capacitation courses," organizing seminars, publicity, and dissemination. Accessed at http://www2.portoalegre.rs.gov.br/urbal9_ing/default.php?p_secao=4.

27. Municipal Government of Porto Alegre 2003.

28. Chavez 2006.

29. Ibid.

30. Baiocchi 2003c, 207.

31. Fisher and Ponniah 2003a, 5.

32. World Social Forum: charter of principles, in Fisher and Ponniah 2003a, 354–57, 356.

33. Toussaint and Zacharie 2003, 31; Hardt and Negri 2003, xvii.

34. Fisher and Ponniah 2003b, 29.

35. Menser 2005, 103.

36. Hardt 2002.

37. See Wainwright 2003.

38. Menser 2005, 102, 107.

39. Santos 2005.

40. N. Klein, "A Fete for the End of the End of History," *Nation,* March 19, 2001.

41. Ibid.

42. Teivainen 2002, 629, 631.

43. Naomi Klein (2001, 10) complained that "the organizational structure of the forum was so opaque that it was nearly impossible to figure out how decisions were made or to find ways to question those decisions."

44. See Red FAL's website at http://www.redfal.org/en.

45. Yves Cabannes himself has been no stranger to WSF events, often occupying a Red FAL platform.

46. Sintomer et al. 2010, 26.

47. Menser 2005, 100–101.

48. Sintomer et al. 2010, 31.

49. On the Latin American left, see Sader 2011; Flores-Macias 2012; Webber and Carr 2012. On debates around the WSF and its futures, see Santos 2006; Sen and Waterman 2007; Conway 2012.

50. Baierle 2003, 28–29.

51. Navarro 2004, 252.

52. Cabannes 2003, 87–88.

53. Ibid., 87.

54. Cabannes 2004a.

55. Goldfrank 2012, 2.

56. PB advocate and social activist, correspondence with Jamie Peck and Nik Theodore, January 2014.

57. Ibid.

58. Sintomer et al. 2010, 25.

59. Mukhija 2006, 58; Davis 2004.

60. See the critical exposes in Wade 2001, 2002. The final version of the report itself was published as World Bank 2001.

61. World Bank 2002, ix, xvii.

62. Ibid., 9.

63. Ibid., 169–70.

64. Francis 2001.

65. See Goldfrank 2012 for perceptive reflections on this theme.

66. Gret and Sintomer (2002) 2005, 135.

67. World Bank, Participation and Civic Engagement website, accessed at http://web.worldbank.org/WBSITE/EXTERNAL/TOPICS/EXTSOCIALDEVELOPMENT/EXTPCENG/0,,contentMDK:20509380~pagePK:148956~piPK:216618~theSitePK:410306,00.html, emphasis added.

68. World Bank 2001.

69. Wagle and Shah 2003, 3.

70. See Goldfrank 2012.

71. Senior official, World Bank, Washington, D.C., interviewed by Jamie Peck and Nik Theodore, May 2009.

72. World Bank 2004b, 1; see also World Bank 2000.

73. Ackerman 2005, 3.

74. World Bank, Participation and Civic Engagement website, Participation and project, program & policy level, accessed at http://web.worldbank.org/WBSITE/EXTERNAL/TOPICS/EXTSOCIALDEVELOPMENT/EXTPCENG/0,,contentMDK:20507658~hlPK:1279660~menuPK:1278231~pagePK:148956~piPK:216618~theSitePK:410306,00.html.

75. Ackerman 2004.

76. Ibid., 39

77. Ibid., 32.

78. Ibid., 11.

79. Ibid., 34.

80. Barbone et al. 2005, vi.

81. World Bank 2005b, M-7, M-9.

82. Ibid., M-41, M-43.

83. Ibid., M-43, M-10.

84. See the ANSA website at http://wbi.worldbank.org/wbi/content/affiliated-networks-social-accountability-ansa.

85. Shah 2007a.

86. Wampler 2007a.

87. World Bank official, Washington, D.C., interviewed by Jamie Peck and Nik Theodore, May 2009.

88. Shah 2007b, 6–7, 11.

89. As Goldfrank (2012) quite rightly observes, the World Bank does not have a monolithic position on PB, and the model has its "true believers" here, as elsewhere. This said, PB itself remains "marginal" to the World Bank's dominant agenda and spending priorities, as Goldfrank also explains.

90. Governance specialist, World Bank Institute, Washington, D.C., interviewed by Jamie Peck and Nik Theodore, May 2009.

91. Senior researcher and policy advocate, economic think tank, Washington, D.C., interviewed by Jamie Peck and Nik Theodore, May 2009.

92. Senior official, World Bank, Washington, D.C., interviewed by Jamie Peck and Nik Theodore, May 2009.

93. Ibid.

94. Interviewed by Jamie Peck and Nik Theodore, Washington, D.C., May 2009.

95. Ibid., emphasis added.

96. See http://www.oidp.net/en/home/ and http://www.uclg.org/en.

97. Caddy et al., 2, 25.

98. Sintomer et al. 2010.

99. Sintomer et al. 2008, 174, 168.

100. Sintomer et al. 2008, 2010.

101. Sintomer et al. 2008, 179–83.

102. Senior researcher and policy advocate, economic think tank, Washington, D.C., interviewed by Jamie Peck and Nik Theodore, May 2009.

103. See Featherstone et al. 2012; Peck 2012a.

104. See Department of Communities and Local Government 2008.

105. Quoted in A. Pati, "Is Participatory Budgeting Losing Ground?" *Guardian Professional,* August 12, 2012, accessed at http://www.guardian.co.uk/local-government-network/2011/aug/12/participatory-budgeting-localism-big-society.

106. See Klages and Daramus 2007.

107. Herzberg 2011, 25–27.

108. Ibid.

109. See Metropolis 2011.

110. Herzberg 2011, 25–27.

111. Social-sector consultant, Amsterdam, interviewed by Jamie Peck, June 2011.

112. Independent policy advisor and consultant, Amsterdam, interviewed by Jamie Peck, June 2011.

113. Social activist, Berlin, interviewed by Jamie Peck, November 2009.

114. G. Baiocchi and E. Ganuza, "No Parties, No Banners," *Boston Review,* January/February, 2012, accessed at: http://www.bostonreview.net/BR37.1/gianpaolo_baiocchi_ernesto_ganuza_spain_indignados_democracy.php.

115. Sintomer et al. (2010, 34) report that EUR 14 million of the Seville budget was allocated via PB, of a total budget of EUR 862 million.

116. "Although in Brazil, PB is an instrument for achieving a more equitable distribution of public funds, and also for democratization (Avritzer 2006), in Spain, it has been mainly a tool for modernizing the state by improving relations between those who govern and those who are governed by increasing citizen engagement in public administration" (Ganuza and Francés 2012, 289).

117. K. Ainger, "Outrage of the Masses." *Guardian,* November 22, 2011.

118. See http://www.torontohousing.ca/pb.

119. Some thirteen thousand residents were involved in PB deliberations, the second round of which took place in 2013, across eight districts of New York City. See http://pbnyc.org/.

120. In Vallejo, residents are involved in the allocation of around one third of the funds derived from a newly introduced sales tax. See http://www.pbvallejo.org/.

121. White House, Office of Communications, "White House Highlights Open Government and Civic Hacking 'Champions of Change,'" press release, July 22, 2013, accessed at http://www.participatorybudgeting.org/wp-content/uploads/2013/07/Participatory-Budgeting-White-House-Release.pdf.

122. J. Byrne, "Ald. Moore Gets White House Award Same Day He Admits Talking to FBI Agents," *Chicago Tribune*, July 22, 2013, accessed at http://articles.chicago tribune.com/2013-07-22/news/ct-met-chicago-aldermen-ethics-report-0723-201307 23_1_fbi-agents-aldermanic-wrongdoing-city-council. C. Felsenthal, "See How a City Council Watchdog Ruined Alderman Joe Moore's Birthday," *Chicago Magazine*, July 25, 2013, accessed at http://www.chicagomag.com/Chicago-Magazine/Felsenthal -Files/July-2013/How-a-City-Council-Watchdog-Ruined-Ald-Joe-Moores-Birthday/.

123. International PB advocate and organizer, interviewed by Jamie Peck and Nik Theodore, Chicago, May 2013.

124. Sondra Youdelman, Community Voices Heard, speaking at PB Project conference, New York City, March 2012.

125. Rachel LaForest, Right to the City Alliance, speaking at PB Project conference, Chicago, May 2013.

126. Speaking at PB Project conference, New York City, March 2012.

127. Sondra Youdelman, Community Voices Heard, speaking at PB Project conference, New York City, March 2012.

128. Director, national social-movement organization, interviewed by Jamie Peck and Nik Theodore, Chicago, May 2013.

129. Community organizer, speaking at PB Project conference, New York City, March 2012.

130. Executive director, U.S. social advocacy network, interviewed by Jamie Peck and Nik Theodore, Chicago, May 2013.

## 8. Reflections

1. As in-depth investigations into the Porto Alegre experiment reveal, the context of local implementation plays a crucial role in both perceived policy successes and perceived policy failures. See Avritzer 2006, 2009; Baiocchi 2005; Baiocchi et al. 2011; Goldfrank 2011; Gret and Sintomer (2002) 2005; Wampler 2007b.

2. Sader 2011, 35.

3. Silva 2009.

4. Sader 2011, 37.

5. Ganuza and Baiocchi 2012, 1; see also Goldfrank 2011.

6. Goldfrank 2012, 2.

7. Social activist and PB advocate, interviewed by Jamie Peck and Nik Theodore, Chicago, May 2013.

8. Ibid.

9. Goldfrank 2012, 1, 8.

10. Data are from Goldfrank 2012.

11. Goldfrank 2007, 96; Shaw 2007a; Udall 1998. As an official at the World Bank explained, that was a "response to those criticisms [of development projects being imposed from above, without democratic input]. We want to have people engaged in the process, so that where the assistance goes [it] serves the needs of the people. The question is whether, by following this process, those needs are really satisfied." World Bank official, Washington, D.C., interviewed by Jamie Peck and Nik Theodore, May 2009.

12. Ganuza and Baiocchi 2012, 7, emphasis added.

13. World Bank official, Washington, D.C., interviewed by Jamie Peck and Nik Theodore, May 2009.

14. Social activist and PB advocate, interviewed by Jamie Peck and Nik Theodore, Chicago, May 2013.

15. Grewal 2008, 4, italics in original.

16. Sintomer et al. 2012.

17. Ganuza and Baiocchi 2012, 2.

18. World Bank economist, Washington, D.C., interviewed by Jamie Peck and Nik Theodore, May 2009, emphasis added.

19. Grewal 2008.

20. Ibid., chapter 1.

21. Patsias et al. 2013.

22. We recognize that the election of progressive mayors in a number of U.S. cities in 2013 may alter this pattern. At the time of writing, however, it is too early to say.

23. Sharzer 2012, 158–59.

24. Schumpeter 1918, 100.

25. Santos 2007.

26. Cabannes and Ming 2013.

## Conclusion

1. See Shah 2007a.

2. See DiMaggio and Powell 1983 and the discussion in chapter 1.

3. B. Ozler, "Defining Conditional Cash Transfer Programs: An Unconditional Mess," *Development Impact* (blog), World Bank, May 13, 2013, accessed at http://blogs .worldbank.org/impactevaluations/defining-conditional-cash-transfer-programs -unconditional-mess.

4. Goldfrank 2012, 7.

5. Sugiyama 2011, 264.

6. See the further discussion of model power in Peck and Theodore 2015.

7. Rodriguez 2008, 297.

8. Hall 2012, 26.

9. Cabannes 2004a.

10. Jez Hall, PB Unit, speaking at PB Project conference, New York City, March 30, 2012.

# Bibliography

Aber, L. 2009. "Experiments in 21st Century Antipoverty Policy." *Public Policy Research* 16:57–63.

Aber, L., and L. B. Rawlings. 2011. "North-South Knowledge Sharing on Incentive-Based Conditional Cash Transfer Programs." Social Protection Working Paper 1101, World Bank, Washington, D.C.

Abers, R. 2000. *Inventing Local Democracy: Grassroots Politics in Brazil.* Boulder, Colo.: Lynne Rienner.

Ackerman, J. 2004. "State-Society Synergy for Accountability: Lessons for the World Bank." World Bank Working Paper 30, World Bank, Washington, D.C.

———. 2005. "Social Accountability in the Public Sector: A Conceptual Discussion." Social Development Paper 82, World Bank, Washington, D.C.

Adato, M., and J. Hoddinott, eds. 2010. *Conditional Cash Transfers in Latin America.* Baltimore: Johns Hopkins University Press.

Alba, V. 1968. *Politics and the Labor Movement in Latin America.* Stanford: Stanford University Press.

Alderman, H. 2002. "Subsidies as a Social Safety Net: Effectiveness and Challenges." Social Protection Working Paper 1112, World Bank, Washington, D.C.

Almeida, H., and J. M. Camargo. 1994. "Human Capital, Investment and Poverty." Texto para discussão 319, Department of Economics, Pontifical Catholic University, Rio de Janeiro.

Avritzer, L. 2006. "New Public Spheres in Brazil: Local Democracy and Deliberative Politics." *International Journal of Urban and Regional Research* 30:623–37.

———. 2009. *Participatory Institutions in Democratic Brazil.* Washington, D.C: Woodrow Wilson Center Press.

Ayala Consulting. 2003. *Workshop on Conditional Cash Transfer Programs (CCTs): Operational Experiences.* Quito: Ayala Consulting.

Babb, S. 2001. *Managing Mexico.* Princeton: Princeton University Press.

Baierle, S. G. 1998. "The Explosion of Experience: The Emergence of a New Political-Ethical Principle in Popular Movements in Porto Alegre, Brazil." In *Cultures of Politics, Politics of Cultures: Re-Visioning Latin American Social Movements*, ed. S. Alvarez, E. Dagnino, and A. Escobar, 118–38. Boulder, Colo.: Westview.

———. 2002. "The Porto Alegre Thermidor? Brazil's 'Participatory Budget' at the Crossroads." In *Fighting Identities: Race, Religion and Ethno-Nationalism—Socialist Register 2003*, ed. L. Panich and C. Leys, 305–28. Winnipeg: Fernwood.

———. 2003. "The Brazilian Experience with the Participatory Budget: The Case of Porto Alegre." In Municipal Government of Porto Alegre 2003, 12–30.

———. 2007. *Urban Struggles in Porto Alegre: Between Political Revolution and Transformism*. Porto Alegre: Cidade.

Baiocchi, G., ed. 2003a. *Radicals in Power: The Workers' Party (PT) and Experiments in Urban Democracy in Brazil*. London: Zed Books.

———. 2003b. "Radicals in Power." In Baiocchi 2003a, 1–26.

———. 2003c. "The Long March through the Institutions." In Baiocchi 2003a, 207–26.

———. 2003d. "Participation, Activism, and Politics: The Porto Alegre Experiment." In Fung and Wright 2003a, 45–76.

———. 2004. "Porto Alegre: The Dynamism of the Unorganised." In Chavez and Goldfrank 2004, 37–66.

———. 2005. *Militants and Citizens: The Politics of Participatory Democracy in Porto Alegre*. Stanford: Stanford University Press.

Baiocchi, G., P. Heller, and M. K. Silva. 2011. *Bootstrapping Democracy: Transforming Local Governance and Civil Society in Brazil*. Stanford: Stanford University Press.

Bair, J., and M. Werner. 2011. "Commodity Chains and the Uneven Geographies of Global Capitalism: A Disarticulations Perspective." *Environment and Planning A* 43:988–97.

Barbone, L., S. Jorgensen, and K. von Ritter. 2005. Foreword. In *Institute Social Accountability in the Public Sector: A Conceptual Discussion and Learning Module*, vi. World Bank, Washington, D.C.

Behrman, J. R., P. Sengupta, and P. Todd. 2005. "Progressing through PROGRESA: An Impact Assessment of a School Subsidy Program in Rural Mexico." *Economic Development and Cultural Change* 54:237–75.

Behrman, J. R., and A. Skoufias. 2006. "Mitigating Myths about Policy Effectiveness: Evaluation of Mexico's Antipoverty and Human Resource Investment Program." *Annals of the American Academy of Political and Social Science* 606:244–75.

Benson, D., and A. Jordan. 2011. "What Have We Learned from Policy Transfer Research? Dolowitz and Marsh Revisited." *Political Studies Review* 9:366–78.

———. 2012. "Policy Transfer Research: Still Evolving, Not Yet Through?" *Political Studies Review* 10:333–38.

Blyth, M. 2008. "One Ring to Bind Them All: American Power and Neoliberal Capitalism." In *Growing Apart? America and Europe in the 21st Century*, ed. J. Kopstein and S. Steinmo, 136–69. New York: Cambridge University Press.

Bockman, J., and G. Eyal. 2002. "Eastern Europe as a Laboratory for Economic Knowledge: The Transnational Roots of Neoliberalism." *American Journal of Sociology* 108:310–52.

Bouillon, C., and L. Tejerina. 2006. "Do We Know What Works? A Systematic Review of Impact Evaluations of Social Programs in Latin America and the Caribbean." Working Paper, Inter-American Development Bank, Washington, D.C.

Bourguignon, F., F. H. G. Ferreira, and G. Leite. 2003. "Conditional Cash Transfers, Schooling, and Child Labor: Micro-simulating Brazil's Bolsa Escola Program." *World Bank Economic Review* 17:229–54.

Brash, J. 2010. *Bloomberg's New York*. Athens: University of Georgia Press.

Brenner, N. 2004. *New State Spaces: Urban Governance and the Rescaling of Statehood*. Oxford: Oxford University Press.

Brenner, N., J. Peck, and N. Theodore. 2009. "Variegated Neoliberalization: Geographies, Modalities, Pathways." *Global Networks* 10:1–41.

Brenner, N., and N. Theodore. 2002a. "Cities and the Geographies of 'Actually Existing Neoliberalism.'" *Antipode* 33:349–79.

———, eds. 2002b. *Spaces of Neoliberalism*. Oxford: Blackwell.

Brock, W. R. 1984. *Investigation and Responsibility: Public Responsibility in the United States*. Cambridge: Cambridge University Press.

Brookings Institution. 2007. "Poverty and Income in 2006." Center on Children and Families Briefing, August 28. Washington, D.C.: Brookings Institution.

Bruce, I, ed. 2004a. *The Porto Alegre Alternative: Direct Democracy in Action*. London: Pluto.

———. 2004b. "From First Steps to Final Stages." In Bruce 2004a, 38–53.

———. 2004c. "Introduction: From the PT to Porto Alegre." In Bruce 2004a, 1–5.

———. 2004d. "Participatory Democracy—the Debate." In Bruce 2004a, 23–37.

———. 2004e. "Prologue: The View from Below." In Bruce 2004a, 6–19.

Bulmer, S., and S. Padgett. 2004. "Policy Transfer in the European Union: An Institutionalist Perspective." *British Journal of Political Science* 35:103–26.

Burawoy, M. 2001. "Manufacturing the Global." *Ethnography* 2:147–59.

———. 2009. *The Extended Case Method: Four Countries, Four Decades, Four Great Transformations*. Berkeley: University of California Press.

Burawoy, M., J. A. Blum, S. George, Z. Gille, T. Gowan, L. Haney, M. Klawitter, S. Lopez, S. O. Riain, and M. Thayer. 2000. *Global Ethnography*. Berkeley: University of California Press.

Cabannes, Y. 2003. Proposals. In Municipal Government of Porto Alegre 2003, 82–88

———. 2004a. *72 Frequently Asked. Questions on Participatory Budgeting*. Nairobi: UN-Habitat.

———. 2004b. "Participatory Budgeting: A Significant Contribution to Participatory Democracy." *Environment and Urbanization* 16:27–46.

———. 2004c. "Participatory Budgeting: Conceptual Framework and Analysis of Its Contribution to Urban Governance and the Millenium Development Goals." Urban Management Programme Working Paper 140, UN-Habitat, Quito.

Cabannes, Y., and Z. Ming. 2013. "Participatory Budgeting at Scale and Bridging the Rural–Urban Divide in Chengdu." *Environment and Urbanization* 26:1–19.

Caddy, J., T. Peixoto, and M. McNeil. 2007. *Beyond Public Scrutiny: Stocktaking of Social Accountability in OECD Countries.* Washington, D.C.: World Bank Institute.

Caldés, N., D. Coady, and J. A. Maluccio. 2006. "The Cost of Poverty Alleviation Transfer Programs: A Comparative Analysis of Three Programs in Latin America." *World Development* 34:818–37.

Campbell, T. 2003. *The Quiet Revolution.* Pittsburgh: University of Pittsburgh Press.

Campbell, T., and H. Fuhr. 2004a. Introduction and preview. In *Leadership and Innovation in Subnational Government: Case Studies from Latin America,* ed. T. Campbell and H. Fuh, 6–7. Washington, D.C.: World Bank.

———. 2004b. "Selection of Cases and Methods." In *Leadership and Innovation in Subnational Government: Case Studies from Latin America,* ed. T. Campbell and H. Fuhr, 53–63. Washington, D.C.: World Bank.

Campbell, T., H. Fuhr, and F. Eid. 1995. *Decentralization in LAC: Best Practices and Policy Lessons.* Washington, D.C.: World Bank.

Cardoso, E., and A. Portela Souza. 2004. "The Impact of Cash Transfers on Child Labor and School Attendance in Brazil." Working Paper 04-W07, Department of Economics, Vanderbilt University, Nashville.

Carpenter, D. P. 2001. *The Forging of Bureaucratic Autonomy.* Princeton University Press.

Castañeda, J. G. 1994. *Utopia Unarmed: The Latin American Left after the Cold War.* New York: Vintage.

Castaneda, T. 1992. *Combating Poverty: Innovative Social Reforms in Chile during the 1980s.* San Francisco: International Center for Economic Growth.

Center for Urban Development Studies. 2003. *Assessment of Participatory Budgeting in Brazil.* Washington, D.C.: Inter-American Development Bank.

CEO (Commission for Economic Opportunity). 2006. *Increasing Opportunity and Reducing Poverty in New York City.* New York: CEO.

Chase-Dunn, C., R. Niemeyer, P. Saxena, M. Kaneshiro, J. Love, and A. Spears. 2009. "The New Global Left: Movements and Regimes." IROWS Working Paper 50, Institute for Research on World-Systems, University of California, Riverside.

Chavez, D. 2004. "Introduction: Local Left Politics in a Democratising Region." In Chavez and Goldfrank 2004, 1–10.

———. 2006. "Participation Lite: The Watering Down of People Power in Porto Alegre." *Red Pepper,* May. Accessed at http://www.tni.org/article/participation-lite-watering-down-people-power-porto-alegre.

Chavez, D., and B. Goldfrank, eds. 2004. *The Left in the City: Participatory Local Governments in Latin America.* London: Latin America Bureau.

Cichon, M., C. Behrendt, and V. Wodsak. 2011. *The UN Social Protection Floor Initiative: Turning the Tide at the ILO Conference 2011.* Berlin: Friedrich-Ebert-Stiftung.

Cochrane, A., and K. Ward, eds. 2012. "Researching Policy Mobilities: Reflections on Method." *Environment and Planning A* 44:5–51.

Conway, J. 2012. *Edges of Global Justice: The World Social Forum and Its "Others."* New York: Routledge.

Cramer, R. 2007. "Mayor Bloomberg Tackles Poverty." *Ripon Forum* 41:11–12.

Czarniawska, B. 2010. "The Uses of Narratology in Social and Policy Studies." *Critical Policy Studies* 4:58–76.

Datt, G., E. Payongayong, J. L. Garrett, and M. Ruel. 2007. "The GAPVU Cash Transfer Program in Mozambique: An Assessment." FCND Discussion Paper 36, IFPRI, Washington, D.C.

Davey, K. 1993. *Elements of Urban Management.* Washington, D.C.: World Bank.

Davis, M. 2004. "Planet of Slums." *New Left Review* 26:5–34.

Deacon, A. 1999. "Social Policy in a Global Context." In *Inequality, Globalization, and World Politics,* ed. A. Hurrell and M. Woods, 211–47. Oxford: Oxford University Press.

de Janvry, A., F. Finan, and E. Sadoulet. 2006. "Evaluating Brazil's Bolsa Escola Program." Working Paper, Department of Agriculture and Resource Economics, University of California, Berkeley.

de la Brière, B., and L. B. Rawlings. 2006. "Examining Conditional Cash Transfer Programs." Social Protection Working Paper 0603, World Bank, Washington, D.C.

Department of Communities and Local Government. 2008. *Participatory Budgeting: A Draft National Strategy.* London: Department of Communities and Local Government.

Desai, R. 1994. "Second-Hand Dealers in Ideas: Think-Tanks and Thatcherite Hegemony." *New Left Review* 203:27–64.

Dezalay, Y., and B. G. Garth. 2002. *The Internationalization of Palace Wars: Lawyers, Economists, and the Contest to Transform Latin American States.* Chicago: University of Chicago Press.

DiMaggio, P. J., and W. W. Powell. 1983. "The Iron Cage Revisited: Institutional Isomorphism and Collective Rationality in Organizational Fields." *American Sociological Review* 48:147–60.

———. 1991. "The Iron Cage Revisited: Institutional Isomorphism and Collective Rationality in Organizational Fields." In *The New Institutionalism in Organizational Analysis,* ed. P. J. DiMaggio and W. W. Powell, 63–82. Chicago: University of Chicago Press.

Djelic, M-L., and K. Sahlin-Andersson, eds. 2008. *Transnational Governance: Institutional Dynamics of Regulation.* Cambridge: Cambridge University Press.

Dolowitz, D., and D. Marsh. 1996. "Who Learns from Whom: A Review of the Policy Transfer Literature." *Political Studies* 44:343–57.

———. 2000. "Learning from Abroad: The Role of Policy Transfer in Contemporary Policy-Making." *Governance* 13:5–24.

Dresser, D. 1991. *Neopopulist Solutions to Neoliberal Problems: Mexico's National Solidarity Program.* La Jolla: Center for U.S.-Mexico Studies, University of California, San Diego.

———. 1998. "Post-NAFTA Politics in Mexico: Uneasy, Uncertain, and Unpredictable." In *The Post-NAFTA Political Economy*, ed. C. Wise, 221–56. University Park: Penn State University Press.

Dunn, E. 2007. "Of Pufferfish and Ethnography: Plumbing New Depths in Economic Geography." In *Politics and Practice in Economic Geography*, ed. A. Tickell, E. Sheppard, J. Peck, and T. J. Barnes, 82–93. London: Sage.

Dye, T. R. 1990. *American Federalism: Competition among Governments*. Lexington, Mass.: Lexington Books.

Eisinger, P. K. 1988. *The Rise of the Entrepreneurial State*. Madison: University of Wisconsin Press.

Eliasoph, N., and P. Lichterman. 1999. "'We Begin with Our Favorite Theory': Reconstructing the Extended Case Method." *Sociological Theory* 17:228–34.

Ellis, F. 2007. "Food Subsidy Program, Mozambique." REBA Case Study Brief 7, Regional Evidence Building Agenda, Regional Hunger Vulnerability Programme, Johannesburg.

Evans, M., and J. Davies. 1999. "Understanding Policy Transfer: A Multi-level, Multidisciplinary Perspective." *Public Administration* 77:361–85.

Evens, T. M. S., and D. Handelman, eds. 2006. *The Manchester School: Practice and Ethnographic Praxis in Anthropology*. Oxford: Berghahn Books.

Eyestone, R. 1977. "Confusion, Diffusion, and Innovation." *American Political Science Review* 71:441–47.

Fagnani, E. 2004. "Social Development Strategies to Combat Poverty." Paper presented at the Second International Conference on Conditional Cash Transfers, April 26–29. Accessed at http://web.worldbank.org/WBSITE/EXTERNAL/TOP ICS/EXTSOCIALPROTECTION/EXTSAFETYNETSANDTRANSFERS/0,,cont entMDK:20823929~isCURL:Y~menuPK:282766~pagePK:64020865~piPK:149114 ~theSitePK:282761,00.html.

Featherstone, D., A. Cumbers, D. Mackinnon, and K. Strauss. 2012. "Progressive Localism in the Age of Austerity." *Transactions of the Institute of British Geographers* 37:177–82.

Feigenbaum, H., J. Henig, and C. Hamnett. 1998. *Shrinking the State*. Cambridge: Cambridge University Press.

Ferguson, J. 2010. "The Uses of Neoliberalism." *Antipode* 41:166–18.

Ferguson, J., and A. Gupta. 2002. "Spatializing States: Toward an Ethnography of Neoliberal Governmentality." *American Ethnologist* 29:981–1002.

Ferreira, F. H. G.. 2004. "The Role of Conditional Cash Transfers in the Process of Equitable Development." Paper presented at the Second International Conference on Conditional Cash Transfers, April 26–29. Accessed at http://web.worldbank .org/WBSITE/EXTERNAL/TOPICS/EXTSOCIALPROTECTION/EXTSAFETY NETSANDTRANSFERS/0,,contentMDK:20823929~isCURL:Y~menuPK:282766 ~pagePK:64020865~piPK:149114~theSitePK:282761,00.html.

Fischer, F. 2003. *Reframing Public Policy: Discursive Politics and Deliberative Practices*. Oxford: Oxford University Press.

Fischer, F., S. Griggs, and N. Mathur. 2009. Editorial. *Critical Policy Studies* 3:1–2.

Fisher, W. F., and T. Ponniah, eds. 2003a. *Another World Is Possible: Popular Alternatives to Globalization at the World Social Forum.* London: Zed Books.

———. 2003b. "Key Questions, Critical Issues." In Fisher and Ponniah 2003a, 23–29.

Fiszbein, A., and C. Gevers. 2005. "Learning and Scaling Up through Evaluation." In Léautier and Moreno-Dodson 2005, 191–226.

Fiszbein, A., D. Ringold, and S. Srinivasan. 2011. "Cash Transfers, Children and the Crisis: Protecting Current and Future Investments." Social Protection Working Paper 1112, World Bank, Washington, D.C.

Fiszbein, A., and N. Schady, with F. H. G. Ferreira, M. Grosh, N. Kelleher, P Olinto, and E. Skoufias. 2009. *Conditional Cash Transfers: Reducing Present and Future Poverty.* Washington, D.C.: World Bank.

Flores-Macias, G. 2012. *After Neoliberalism? The Left and Economic Reforms in Latin America.* Oxford: Oxford University Press.

Francis, P., 2001. "Participatory Development at the World Bank: The Primacy of Process." In *Participation: The New Tyranny?* ed. B. Cooke and U. Kothari, 72–87. London: Zed Books.

Freidberg, S. 2001. "On the Trail of the Global Green Bean: Methodological Considerations in Multi-site Ethnography." *Global Networks* 1:353–68.

Friedman, M. 1962. *Capitalism and Freedom.* Chicago: University of Chicago.

Fung, A., and E. O. Wright. 2003a. *Deepening Democracy: Institutional Innovations in Empowered Participatory Governance.* London: Verso

———. 2003b. "Thinking about Empowered Participatory Governance." In Fung and Wright 2003a, 3–42. London: Verso.

Ganuza, E., and P. Baiocchi. 2012. "The Power of Ambiguity: How Participatory Budgeting Travels the Globe." *Journal of Public Deliberation* 8:1–12.

Ganuza, E., and F. Francés. 2012. "The Deliberative Turn in Participation: The Problem of Inclusion and Deliberative Opportunities in Participatory Budgeting." *European Political Science Review* 4:283–302.

Garcia, M., and C. M. T. Moore. 2012. *The Cash Dividend: The Rise of Conditional Cash Transfer Programs in Sub-Saharan Africa.* Washington, D.C.: World Bank.

Garrett, G., F. Dobbin, and B. A. Simmons. 2008. Conclusion. In Simmons et al. 2008a, 344–60.

Gilardi, F. 2005. "The Institutional Foundations of Regulatory Capitalism: The Diffusion of Independent Regulatory Agencies in Western Europe." *Annals of the American Academy of Political and Social Science* 598:84–101.

Gill, S. 2002. *Power and Resistance in the New World Order.* New York: Palgrave Macmillan.

Goldfrank, B. 2003. "Making Participation Work in Porto Alegre." In Baiocchi 2003a, 27–52.

———. 2004. "Conclusion: The End of Politics or a New Beginning for the Left?" In Chavez and Goldfrank 2004, 193–211.

———. 2005. "The Politics of Deepening Local Democracy: Decentralization, Party Institutionalization, and Participation." Paper presented at the annual meeting of the Midwest Political Science Association, Chicago, April.

———. 2007. "Lessons from Latin America's Experience from Participatory Budgeting." In Shah 2007a, 91–126.

———. 2011. *Deeping Local Democracy in Latin America: Participation, Decentralization, and the Left.* University Park: Penn State University Press.

———. 2012. "The World Bank and the Globalization of Participatory Budgeting." *Journal of Public Deliberation* 8:1–18.

Goldfrank, B., and A. Schneider. 2006. "Competitive Institution Building: The PT and Participatory Budgeting in Rio Grande Do Sul." *Latin American Politics and Society* 483:1–31.

Goldman, M. 2005. *Imperial Nature: The World Bank and Struggles for Social Justice in the Age of Globalization.* New Haven: Yale University Press.

González, S. 2011. "Bilbao and Barcelona 'in Motion': How Urban Regeneration 'Models' Travel and Mutate in the Global Flows of Policy Tourism." *Urban Studies* 48:1397–418.

Goodman, R. 1979. *The Last Entrepreneurs: America's Regional Wars for Jobs and Dollars.* New York: Simon and Schuster.

Gray, V. 1994. "Competition, Emulation, and Policy Innovation." In *New Perspectives on American Politics,* ed. L. C. Dodd and C. Jillson, 230–48. Washington, D.C.: Congressional Quarterly Press.

Gray, V., and D. Lowery. 1990. "The Corporatist Foundations of State Industrial Policy." *Social Science Quarterly* 71:3–24.

Greenberg, D., N. Dechausau, and C. Fraker. 2011. *Learning Together: How Families Responded to Education Incentives in New York City's Conditional Cash Transfer Program.* New York: MDRC.

Gress, F. 1996. "Interstate Cooperation and Territorial Representation in Intermestic Politics." *Publius* 26:53–71.

Gret, M., and Y. Sintomer. (2002) 2005. *The Porto Alegre Experiment: Learning Lessons for Better Democracy.* London: Zed Books.

Grewal, D. S. 2008. *Network Power: The Social Dynamics of Globalization.* New Haven: Yale University Press.

Grosh, M. E. 2006. "Lessons Learned." Paper presented at the Third International Conference on Conditional Cash Transfers, Istanbul, Turkey, June 26–30.

———. 2011. "CCTs: The Second Generation of Evaluations," Paper presented at the CCTs: The Second Generation of Evaluations workshop, World Bank, Washington, D.C., October 24–25.

Guillen, M. F. 2001. "Is Globalizing Civilizing, Destructive or Feeble? A Critique of Five Key Debates in the Social Science Literature." *Annual Review of Sociology* 27:235–60.

Haarmann, C., and D. Haarmann. 2012. "Namibia: Seeing the Sun Rise—The Realities and Hopes of the Basic Income Grant Pilot Project." In *Basic Income Worldwide,* ed. M. C. Murray and C. Pateman, 33–58. New York: Palgrave Macmillan.

Haarmann, C., D. Haarmann, H. Jauch, H. Shindondola-Mote, N. Nattrass, I. van Niekerk, and M. Samson. 2009. *Making the Difference! The BIG in Namibia.* Windhoek, Namibia: Desk for Social Development.

Haas, P. M. 1992. "Introduction: Epistemic Communities and International Policy Coordination." *International Organization* 46:1–35.

Hagerstrand, T. 1967. *Innovation Diffusion as a Spatial Process.* Chicago: University of Chicago Press.

Hall, A. 2007. "Social Policies in the World Bank: Paradigms and Challenges." *Global Social Policy* 7, 151–75.

———. 2012. "The Last Shall Be First: Political Dimensions of Conditional Cash Transfers in Brazil." *Journal of Policy Practice* 11:25–41.

Hall, P. A. 1993. "Policy Paradigms, Social Learning, and the State: The Case of Economic Policymaking in Britain." *Comparative Politics* 25:275–96.

Handelman, D. 2006. "The Extended Case: Interactional Foundations and Prospective Methods." In Evens and Handelman 2006, 94–117.

Handler, J. 2004. *Social Citizenship and Workfare in the United States and Western Europe: The Paradox of Inclusion.* Cambridge: Cambridge University Press.

Hanlon, J., A. Barrientos, and D. Hulme. 2010. *Just Give Money to the Poor.* Sterling, Va.: Kumarian Press.

Hanson, R. L. 1993. "Bidding for Business: A Second War between the States?" *Economic Development Quarterly* 7:183–98.

Hardt, M. 2002. "Today's Bandung?" *New Left Review* 14:112–18, 114–15.

Hardt, M., and A. Negri. 2003. Foreword. In Fisher and Ponniah 2003a, xvi–xix.

Hart, G. 2004. "Geography and Development: Critical Ethnographies." *Progress in Human Geography* 28:91–100.

Harvey, D. 1989. "From Managerialism to Entrepreneurialism: The Transformation in Urban Governance in Late Capitalism." *Geografiska Annaler* 71B:3–17.

Haveman, H. A. 1993. "Follow the Leader: Mimetic Isomorphism and Entry into New Markets." *Administrative Science Quarterly* 38:593–627.

Heinrich, C. J. 2005. "Demand and Supply-Side Cash Transfer Program Effectiveness: Improving the First-Generation Programs." Office of Evaluation and Oversight Working Paper 05/05, Inter-American Development Bank, Washington, D.C.

Henderson, J., P. Dicken, M. Hess, N. Coe, and H. W. C. Yeung. 2002. "Global Production Networks and the Analysis of Economic Development." *Review of International Political Economy* 9:436–64.

Herzberg, C. 2011. "Democratic Innovation or Symbolic Participation? A Case Study of Participatory Budgeting in Germany." Paper presented at the Sixth European Consortium for Political Research Conference, Reykjavik, Iceland, August.

Hughes, A., and L. Cormode. 1998, eds. "Researching Elites and Elite Spaces." *Environment and Planning A* 30:2098–179.

Hunter, W. 2010. *The Transformation of the Brazilian Workers' Party, 1989–2009.* Cambridge: Cambridge University Press.

Hutagalung, S. A., S. Arif, and W. I. Suharyo. 2009. "Problems and Challenges for the Indonesian Conditional-Cash Transfer Programme–Program Keluarga Harapan (PKH)." Social Protection in Asia Working Paper 4, Institute for Development Studies and Institute for Human Development, Brighton and Delhi.

IBRD (International Bank for Reconstruction and Development) and World Bank. 2004. "Mexico's Oportunidades Program." In *Reducing Poverty, Sustaining Growth: Scaling Up Poverty Reduction,* 260–62. Washington, D.C.: IBRD/World Bank.

IDB. 2003a. "A New Generation of Social Programs." *IDEA* 1:1–4.

———. 2003b. "A Pioneer Program: Mexico's Oportunidades." *IDEA* 1:6–7.

IFPRI. 2005. *Progresa and Its Impacts on the Welfare of Rural Households in Mexico.* Research Report 139. Washington, D.C.: International Food Policy Research Institute.

ILO (International Labour Office). 2001. *Social Security: A New Consensus.* Geneva: ILO.

———. 2008. "Can Low-Income Countries Afford Basic Social Security?" Social Security Policy Briefing Paper 3. Geneva: ILO.

———. 2009. "Social Security for All: Investing in Social Justice and Economic Development." Social Security Policy Briefing Paper 7. Geneva: ILO.

———. 2011. *Social Protection Floor for a Fair and Inclusive Globalization.* Geneva: ILO.

Jacoby, W. 2002. "Talking the Talk and Walking the Walk: The Cultural and Institutional Effects of Western Models." In *Postcommunist Transformation and the Social Sciences: Cross-Disciplinary Approaches,* ed. F. Bonker, K. Muller, and A. Pickel, 129–51. Lanham, Md.: Rowman and Littlefield.

Jessop, B. 2002. *The Future of the Capitalist State.* Cambridge: Polity Press.

———. 2008. *State Power.* Cambridge: Polity Press.

———. 2010. "Cultural Political Economy and Critical Policy Studies." *Critical Policy Studies* 3:336–56.

Jessop, B., and J. Peck. 1999. "Fast Policy/Local Discipline: The Politics of Time and Scale and the Neo-liberal Workfare Offensive." *Mimeo,* Department of Sociology, University of Lancaster.

Karides, M., J. Smith, M. Becker. 2008. *Global Democracy and the World Social Forums.* Boulder, Colo.: Paradigm.

Kaufman, R. R., and G. Trejo. 1997. "Regionalism, Regime Transformation and PRO-NASOL: The Politics of the National Solidarity Programme in Four Mexican States." *Journal of Latin American Studies* 29:717–45.

Killick, A. 1991. *A Reaction Too Far.* London: Overseas Development Institute.

Kingdon, J. W. 1995. *Agendas, Alternatives, and Public Policies.* New York: Harper-Collins.

Kingfisher, C. 2013. *A Policy Travelogue: Tracing Welfare Reform in Aotearoa/New Zealand and Alberta, Canada.* New York: Berghahn.

Klages, H., and C. Daramus. 2007. *Bürgerhaushalt Berlin-Lichtenberg.* Speyer: German University of Administrative Sciences.

Klein, N. 2001. "Farewell to the 'End of History': Organisation and Vision in Anti-corporate Movements." In *Socialist Register 2002: A World of Contradictions,* ed. L. Panitch and C. Leys, 1–14. London: Merlin Press.

Kogut, B., and J. M. Macpherson. 2008. "The Decision to Privatize: Economists and the Construction of Ideas and Policies." In *The Global Diffusion of Markets and Democracy,* ed. B. A. Simmons, F. Dobbin, and G. Garrett, 104–40. New York: Cambridge University Press.

Kong, L., C. Gibson, L-M. Khoo, and A-L Semple. 2006. "Knowledges of the Creative Economy: Towards a Relational Geography of Diffusion and Adaptation in Asia." *Asia Pacific Viewpoint* 47:173–94.

Knorr-Cetina, K. 1999. *Epistemic Communities.* Cambridge: Harvard University Press.

Krinsky, J. 2008. *Free Labor.* Chicago: University of Chicago Press.

Kuus, M. 2013. "Foreign Policy and Ethnography: A Sceptical Intervention." *Geopolitics* 18:115–31.

Larner, W. 2009: "Neoliberalism, Mike Moore, and the WTO." *Environment and Planning A* 41:1576–93.

Latour, B. 1987. *Science in Action.* Cambridge: Harvard University Press.

Lavinas, L. 2013. "21st Century Welfare." *New Left Review* 84:5–40.

Léautier, F. A. 2007. Foreword. In Shah 2007a, xiii–xiv.

Léautier, F. A., and B. Moreno-Dodson, eds. 2005. *Reducing Poverty on a Global Scale: Learning and Innovating for Development—Findings from the Shanghai Global Learning Initiative.* Washington, D.C.: World Bank.

Leitner, H., and B. Miller. 2007. "Scale and the Limitations of Ontological Debate: A Commentary on Marston, Jones and Woodward." *Transactions of the Institute of British Geographers* 32:116–25.

Lendvai, N., and P. Stubbs. 2007. "Policies as Translation: Situating Transnational Social Policies." In *Policy Reconsidered: Meanings, Politics and Practices,* ed. S. M. Hodgson and Z. Irving, 173–90. Bristol: Policy Press.

Leubolt, B., A. Novy, and J. Becker. 2008. "Changing Patterns of Participation in Porto Alegre." *International Social Science Journal* 59:437–50.

Levi-Faur, D. 2005. "The Global Diffusion of Regulatory Capitalism." *Annals of the American Academy of Political and Social Sciences* 598:12–32.

Levy, S. 1991. "Poverty Alleviation in Mexico." Policy Research and External Affairs Working Paper 679, World Bank, Washington, D.C.

———. 2006. *Progress against Poverty.* Washington, D.C.: Brookings Institution Press.

Levy, S., and E. Rodríguez. 2004. *Economic Crisis, Political Transition and Poverty Policy Reform: Mexico's Progresa-Oportunidades Program.* Policy Dialogue Series. Washington, D.C.: Inter-American Development Bank.

Levy, S., and S. van Wijnbergen. 1995. "Transition Problems in Economic Reform: Agriculture in the North American Free Trade Agreement." *American Economic Review* 85:738–54.

Liby, M. 2006. "Grabbing Hand: Corruption in Lula's Government." *Harvard International Review* 27:9–10.

Lindert, K., A. Linder, J. Hobbs, and B. Brière. 2007. "The Nuts and Bolts of Brazil's Bolsa Família Program." Social Protection Discussion Paper 0709, World Bank, Washington, D.C.

Lipton, M., and M. Ravallion. 1995. "Poverty and Policy." In *Handbook of Development Economics*, ed. J. Behrman and T. N. Srinivasan, vol. 3, 2551–657. North-Holland: Elsevier.

Luccisano, L. 2004. "Mexico's Progresa Program 1997–2000: An Example of Neo-liberal Policy Alleviation Programs Concerned with Gender, Human Capital Development, Responsibility and Choice." *Journal of Poverty* 8:31–57.

Lustig, N. 1998. *Mexico: The Remaking of an Economy*. Washington, D.C.: Brookings Institution Press.

———. 2011. "Scholars Who Became Practitioners." Working Paper 236, Center for Global Development, Washington, D.C.

Mac Donald, H. 2007. "Learning for Dollars." *Weekly Standard*, July 9, 17–19.

Mahon, R. 2013. "Initial Reflections on the Social Protection Floor Initiative." Paper presented at the symposium Toward a Global Social Protection Floor, University of Waterloo, April 24–26.

Mansfield, B., ed. 2008. *Privatization: Property and the Remaking of Nature-Society Relations*. Oxford: Blackwell.

Marcus, G. 1998. *Ethnography through Thick and Thin*. Princeton: Princeton University Press.

Marquetti, A. A. 2000. "Extending Democracy: The Participatory Budgeting Experience in Porto Alegre, Brazil, 1989–1999." *Indicator SA* 17:71–78.

———. 2001. "Participatory Budgeting in Porto Alegre as a Redistributive Policy," Proceedings of the Congress Marx International III, Nanterre, France.

Massey, D., R. Magaly Sanchez, and J. R. Behrman. 2006. "Of Myths and Markets." *Annals of the American Academy of Political and Social Science* 606:8–31.

Matin, I., D. Hulme, and S. Rutherford. 2002. "Finance for the Poor: From Microcredit to Microfinancial Services." *Journal of International Development* 14:273–94.

Mayor's Fund to Advance NYC and Center for Economic Opportunity. 2011. *Social Innovation Fund: Learning Network Kick-Off*. New York: Mayor's Fund to Advance NYC and Center for Economic Opportunity.

McCann, E. 2008. "Expertise, Truth, and Urban Policy Mobilities: Global Circuits of Knowledge in the Development of Vancouver, Canada's "Four Pillars" Drug Strategy." *Environment and Planning A* 40:885–904.

———. 2011. "Urban Policy Mobilities and Global Circuits Knowledge: Toward a Research Agenda." *Annals of the Association of American Geographers* 101:107–30.

McCann, E., and K. Ward, eds. 2011. *Mobile Urbanism: Cities and Policymaking in the Global Age*. Minneapolis: University of Minnesota Press.

McDonagh, E. L. 1992. "Representative Democracy and State Building in the Progressive Era." *American Political Science Review* 86:938–50.

McFarlane, C. 2011. *Learning the City: Knowledge and Translocal Assemblage.* Chichester: Wiley-Blackwell.

McVoy, E. C. 1940. "Patterns of Diffusion in the United States." *American Sociological Review* 5:219–27.

Menocal, A. R. 2001. "Do Old Habits Die Hard? A Statistical Exploration of the Politicisation of Progresa, Mexico's Latest Federal Poverty-Alleviation Programme, under the Zedillo Administration." *Journal of Latin American Studies* 33:513–58.

Menser, M. 2005. "The Global Social Forum Movement, Porto Alegre's "Participatory Budget," and the Maximization of Democracy." *Situations* 1:87–109.

Metropolis. 2011. *Integrated Urban Governance: The Way Forward.* Barcelona: Metropolis.

Meyer, J. W., J. Boli, G. M. Thomas, and F. O. Ramirez. 1997. "World Society and the Nation-State." *American Journal of Sociology* 103:144–81.

Mills, D. 2006. "Made in Manchester? Methods and Myths in Disciplinary History." In Evens and Handelman 2006, 165–79.

Mitchell, J. C. 2006. "Case and Situational Analysis." In Evens and Handelman 2006, 23–42.

Molyneux, M. 2007. "Two Cheers for CCTs." *IDS Bulletin* 38:69–74.

Morais de Sa e Silva, M. G. 2011. "Conditional Cash Transfers and Education: United in Theory, Divorced in Policy." PhD diss., Columbia University.

Morgan, M. S. 2008. "'On a Mission' with Mutable Mobiles." Working Papers on the Nature of Evidence 34/08. Department of Economic History, London School of Economics and Political Science, London.

Moreno-Dodson, B., ed. 2005. *Reducing Poverty on a Global Scale.* Washington, D.C.: World Bank.

Mörth, U. 1998. "Policy Diffusion in Research and Technological Development: No Government Is an Island." *Cooperation and Conflict* 33:35–58.

Mosse, D. 2004. "Is Good Policy Unimplementable? Reflections on the Ethnography of Aid Policy and Practice." *Development and Change* 35:639–71.

Mukhija, V. 2006. "Challenges for International Development Planning: Preliminary Lessons from the Case of the Cities Alliance." *Cities* 23:56–62.

Municipal Government of Porto Alegre. 2003. *Base Document: Launching Seminar of URB-AL Network 9, Municipal Finance and Participatory Budgeting.* Porto Alegre: Municipal Government of Porto Alegre.

Naim, M. 2000. "Fads and Fashion in Economic Reforms: Washington Consensus or Washington Confusion?" *Third World Quarterly* 21:505–28.

Navarro, Z. 2004. "Participatory Budgeting in Porto Alegre, Brazil." In *Leadership and Innovation in Subnational Government: Case Studies from Latin America,* ed. T. Campbell and H. Fuhr, 177–212. Washington, D.C.: World Bank.

Noël, A. 2006. "The New Global Politics of Poverty." *Global Social Policy* 6:304–33.

Novy, A., and B. Leubolt. 2005. "Participatory Budgeting in Porto Alegre: Social Innovation and the Dialectical Relationship of State and Civil Society." *Urban Studies* 42:2023–36.

Nylan, W. R. 2000. "The Making of a Loyal Opposition: The Workers' Party (PT) and the Consolidation of Democracy in Brazil." In *Democratic Brazil: Actors, Institutions, and Processes,* ed. P. R. Kingstone and T. J. Power, 126–43. Pittsburgh: University of Pittsburgh Press.

O'Connor, A. 2001. *Poverty Knowledge.* Princeton: Princeton University Press.

———. 2008. "The Privatized City: The Manhattan Institute, the Urban Crisis, and the Conservative Counterrevolution in New York." *Journal of Urban History* 34:333–53.

Offe, C. 1996. "Designing Institutions in East European Transitions." In *The Theory of Institutional Design,* ed. R. E. Goodin, 199–226. Cambridge: Cambridge University Press.

———. 1997. *Varieties of Transition: The East European and East German Experience.* Cambridge: MIT Press.

Ong, A. 2006. *Neoliberalism as Exception: Mutations of Citizenship and Sovereignty.* Durham: Duke University Press.

Organization of American States. 2009. *Social Protection in the Americas.* Washington, D.C.: Organization of American States.

Palma, J., and R. Urzúa. 2005. "Anti-poverty Policies and Citizenry: The Chile Solidario Experience." UNESCO Policy Paper 12, UNESCO, Paris.

Parker, S. W., and G. M. Teruel. 2005. "Randomization and Social Program Evaluation: The Case of Progresa." *Annals of the American Academy of Political and Social Science* 599:199–219.

Pastor, M., and C. Wise. 1997. "State Policy, Distribution and Neoliberal Reform in Mexico." Latin American Program Working Paper 229, Woodrow Wilson International Center for Scholars, Washington, D.C.

———. 1998. "Mexican-Style Neoliberalism: State Policy and Distributional Stress." In *The Post-NAFTA Political Economy,* ed. C. Wise, 41–81. University Park: Penn State University Press.

Patsias, C., A. Latendresse, and L. Bherer. 2013. "Participatory Democracy, Decentralization and Local Governance: The Montreal Participatory Budget in the Light of 'Empowered Participatory Governance.'" *International Journal of Urban and Regional Research* 37:2214–30.

Peck, J. 1995. "Moving and Shaking: Business Elites, State Localism and Urban Privatism." *Progress in Human Geography* 19:16–46.

———. 1999a. "Getting Real with Welfare-to-Work: Hard Lessons from America." *Renewal* 7:39–49.

———. 1999b. "New Labourers? Making a New Deal for the 'Workless Class.'" *Environment and Planning C* 17:345–72.

———. 2000. "Doing Regulation." In *The Oxford Handbook of Economic Geography,* ed. G. L. Clark, M. P. Feldman, and M. S. Gertle, 61–80. Oxford: Oxford University Press.

———. 2001a. "Neoliberalizing States: Thin Policies / Hard Outcomes." *Progress in Human Geography* 25:445–55.

———. 2001b. *Workfare States*. New York: Guilford.

———. 2002a. "Labor, Zapped/Growth, Restored? Three Moments of Neoliberal Restructuring in the American Labor Market." *Journal of Economic Geography* 2:179–220.

———. 2002b. "Political Economies of Scale: Fast Policy, Interscalar Relations, and Neoliberal Workfare." *Economic Geography* 78:331–60.

———. 2003a. "Fuzzy Old World: A Response to Markusen." *Regional Studies* 37: 729–40.

———. 2003b. "Geography and Public Policy: Mapping the Penal State." *Progress in Human Geography* 27:222–32.

———. 2004. "Geography and Public Policy: Constructions of Neoliberalism." *Progress in Human Geography* 28:392–405.

———. 2010. *Constructions of Neoliberal Reason*. Oxford: Oxford University Press.

———. 2011a. "Geographies of Policy: From Transfer-Diffusion to Mobility-Mutation." *Progress in Human Geography* 35:773–97.

———. 2011b. "Global Policy Models, Globalizing Poverty Management: International Convergence or Fast-Policy Integration?" *Geography Compass* 5:165–81.

———. 2012a. "Austerity Urbanism: American Cities under Extreme Economy." *City* 16:626–55.

———. 2012b. "Economic Geography: Island Life." *Dialogues in Human Geography* 2:113–33.

———. 2012c. "Recreative City: Amsterdam, Vehicular Ideas, and the Adaptive Spaces of Creativity Policy." *International Journal of Urban and Regional Research* 36: 462–85.

———. 2013a. "Explaining with Neoliberalism." *Territory, Politics, Governance* 1:132–57.

———. 2013b. "For Polanyian Economic Geographies." *Environment and Planning A* 45:1545–68.

Peck, J., and M. Jones. 1995. "Training and Enterprise Councils: Schumpeterian Workfare State, or What?" *Environment and Planning A* 27:1361–96.

Peck, J., and N. Theodore. 2000. "Work First: Workfare and the Regulation of Contingent Labour Markets." *Cambridge Journal of Economics* 24:119–38.

———. 2001. "Exporting Workfare / Importing Welfare-to-Work: Exploring the Politics of Third Way Policy Transfer." *Political Geography* 20:427–60.

———. 2007. "Variegated Capitalism." *Progress in Human Geography* 31:731–72.

———. eds. 2010a. "Mobilizing Policy—Theme Issue." *Geoforum* 41:169–226.

———. 2010b. "Mobilizing Policy: Models, Methods, and Mutations." *Geoforum* 41:169–74.

———. 2010c. "Recombinant Workfare, Across the Americas: Transnationalizing Fast Welfare Policy." *Geoforum* 41:195–208.

———. 2012. "Reanimating Neoliberalism: Process-Geographies of Neoliberalization." *Social Anthropology* 20:177–85.

———. 2015. "Paying for Good Behavior: Cash Transfer Policies in the Wild." In *Territories of Poverty*, ed. A. Roy and E. S. Crane. Athens: University of Georgia Press.

Peck, J., N. Theodore, and N. Brenner. 2012. "Neoliberalism Resurgent? Market Rule after the Great Recession." *South Atlantic Quarterly* 111:265–88.

———. 2013. "Neoliberal Urbanism Redux?" *International Journal of Urban and Regional Research* 373:1091–99.

Peck, J., and A. Tickell. 1994. "Searching for a New Institutional Fix: The After-Fordist Crisis and Global-Local Disorder." In *Post-Fordism: A Reader,* ed. A. Amin, 280–316. Oxford: Blackwell.

Peet, R. 2008. *Geography of Power: Making Global Economic Policy.* London: Zed Books.

Petryna, A. 2009. *When Experiments Travel: Clinical Trials and the Global Search for Human Subjects.* Princeton: Princeton University Press.

Piven, F. F. 1999. "Welfare and Work." In *Whose Welfare?* ed. G. Mink, 83–99. Ithaca: Cornell University Press.

Pollitt, C. R., S. Harrison, D. Hunter, and G. Marnoch. 1990. "No Hiding Place: On the Discomforts of Researching the Contemporary Policy Process." *Journal of Social Policy* 19: 169–90.

Ponniah, T., and W. F. Fisher. 2003. "The World Social Forum and the Reinvention of Democracy." In Fisher and Ponniah 2003a, 1–20.

Prasad, M. 2006. *The Politics of Free Markets: The Rise of Neoliberal Economic Policies in Britain, France, Germany, and the United. States.* Chicago: University of Chicago Press.

Prefeitura de Porto Alegre. 2008. *Revista da governança.* Porto Alegre: Prefeitura de Porto Alegre.

Prince, R. 2010. "Policy Transfer as Policy Assemblage: Making Policy for the Creative Industries in New Zealand." *Environment and Planning A* 42:169–86.

———. 2012. "Policy Transfer, Consultants and the Geographies of Governance." *Progress in Human Geography* 36:188–203.

Radaelli, C. M. 2000. "Policy Transfer in the European Union: Institutional Isomorphism As a Source of Legitimacy." *Governance* 13:25–43.

Rawlings, L. B. 2004. "A New Approach to Social Assistance: Latin America's Experience with Conditional Cash Transfer Programs." Social Protection Discussion Paper 0416, World Bank, Washington, D.C.

Rawlings, L. B., and G. M. Rubio. 2005. "Evaluating the Impact of Conditional Cash Transfer Programs." *World Bank Research Observer* 20:29–55.

Reddy, S. G. 2012. "Randomise This! On Poor Economics." *Review of Agrarian Studies* 2:60–73.

Riccio, J. A. 2010. "Early Findings from New York City's Conditional Cash Transfer Program." *Fast Focus,* no. 5. Institute for Research on Poverty, University of Wisconsin–Madison.

———. 2013. "New Findings on New York City's Cash Transfer Program." *Fast Focus,* no. 18. Institute for Research on Poverty, University of Wisconsin–Madison.

Riccio, J. A., N. Dechausay, D. Greenberg, C. Miller, Z. Rucks, and N. Verma. 2010. *Toward Reduced Poverty across Generations: Early Findings from New York City's Conditional Cash Transfer Program.* New York: MDRC.

Roberts, B. 1998. *Deepening Democracy? The Modern Left and Social Movements in Chile and Peru.* Stanford: Stanford University Press

Robertson, D. B. 1991. "Political Conflict and Lesson-Drawing." *Journal of Public Policy* 11:55–78.

Rodrik, D. 1997. *Has Globalization Gone Too Far?* Washington, D.C.: Institute for International Economics.

Rodriguez, E. 2008. "Beating the Odds: How Progresa/Oportunidades Became Mexico's Major Poverty Alleviation Programme." In *Poverty Reduction That Works: Experience of Scaling Up Development Success,* ed. P. Steele, N. Fernando, and M. Weddikkara, 287–302. London: Earthscan.

Rose, R. 1991. "What Is Lesson-Drawing?" *Journal of Public Policy* 11:3–30.

———. 1993. *Lesson-Drawing in Public Policy.* Chatham, N.J.: Chatham House.

Roy, A. 2010. *Poverty Capital: Microfinance and the Making of Development.* New York: Routledge.

Roy, A., and A. Ong. 2012. *Worlding Cities: Asian Experiments and the Art of Being Global.* London: Wiley-Blackwell.

Sader, E. 2011. *The New Mole: Paths of the Latin American Left.* London: Verso.

Samson, M. 2009. "Social Cash Transfers and Pro-Poor Growth." In *Promoting Pro-Poor Growth: Social Protection,* 43–59 Paris: OECD.

Santos, B. S. 1998. "Participatory Budgeting in Porto Alegre: Toward a Redistributive Democracy?" *Politics and Society* 26:461–510.

———. 2005. "The Future of the World Social Forum: The Work of Translation." *Development* 48:15–22.

———. 2006. *The Rise of the Global Left: The World Social Forum and Beyond.* London: Zed Books.

———. ed. 2007. *Democratizing Democracy: Beyond the Liberal Democratic Canon.* London: Verso.

———. 2008. "The World Social Forum and the Global Left." *Politics and Society* 36:247–70.

Santos, B. S., and L. Avritzer. 2007. "Introduction: Reinventing Social Emancipation." In *Democratizing Democracy: Beyond the Liberal Democratic Canon,* ed. B. S. Santos, xxxiv–lxxiv. London: Verso.

Schild, V. 2013. "Care and Punishment in Latin America: The Gendered Neoliberalization of the Chilean State." In *Neoliberalism, Interrupted: Social Change and Contested Governance in Contemporary Latin America,* ed. M. Goodale and N. Postero, 195–224. Stanford: Stanford University Press.

Schoenberger, E. 1991. "The Corporate Interview as a Research Method in Economic Geography." *Professional Geographer* 43:180–89.

Schram, S. F. 2000. *After Welfare: The Culture of Postindustrial Social Policy.* New York: New York University Press

Schram, S. F., and J. Soss. 2001. "Success Stories: Welfare Reform, Policy Discourse, and the Politics of Research." *Annals of the American Academy of Political and Social Science* 577:49–65.

Schumpeter, J. A. 1918. *The Crisis of the Tax State*. Graz: Leuschner and Lubensky.

Sen, A. K. 1985. *Commodities and Capabilities*. Amsterdam: North Holland.

Sen, J., and P. Waterman, eds. 2007. *World Social Forum: Challenging Empires*. Montreal: Black Rose Books.

Shah, A., ed. 2007a. *Participatory Budgeting*. Washington, D.C.: World Bank.

———. 2007b. Overview. In Shah 2007a, 1–18.

Sharzer, G. 2012. *No Local*. Alresford: Zero Press.

Shaw, A. 1887. "The American State and the American Man." *Contemporary Review* 51:695–711.

Shore, C., S. Wright, and D. Pero, eds. 2011. *Policy Worlds: Anthropology and the Analysis of Contemporary Power*. New York: Berghahn Books.

Silva, E. 2009. *Challenging Neoliberalism in Latin America*. Cambridge: Cambridge University Press.

Simmons, B. A., F. Dobbin, and G. Garrett, eds. 2008a. *The Global Diffusion of Markets and Democracy*. Cambridge: Cambridge University Press.

———. 2008b. "Introduction: The Diffusion of Liberalization." In Simmons et al., 1–63. New York: Cambridge University Press.

Simon, H. A. 1957. *Administrative Behavior*. New York: Free Press.

Sintomer, Y. 2005. Preface to the English edition. In Gret and Sintomer (2002) 2005, vi–x.

Sintomer, Y., C. Herzberg, and G. Allegretti. 2010. *Learning from the South: Participatory Budgeting Worldwide—An Invitation to Global Cooperation*. Dialog Global no. 25. Bonn: Inwent Ggmbh—Capacity Building International.

———. 2013. *Participatory Budgeting Worldwide—Updated Version*. Dialog Global no. 25. Bonn: Bonn: Engagement Global Ggmbh.

Sintomer, Y., C. Herzberg, and A. Röcke. 2008. "Participatory Budgeting in Europe: Potentials and Challenges." *International Journal of Urban and Regional Research* 32:164–78.

Sintomer, Y., C. Herzberg, A. Röcke, and G. Allegretti. 2012. "Transnational Models of Citizen Participation: The Case of Participatory Budgeting." *Journal of Public Deliberation* 8:1–32.

Skoufias, E. 2005. *PROGRESA and Its Impacts on the Welfare of Rural Families in Mexico*. Washington, D.C.: IFPRI.

SMERU Research Institute. 2008. *The Effectiveness of the Raskin Program*. Jakarta: SMERU.

Soares, S. 2012. *Bolsa Família: A Summary of Its Impacts*. IPC-IG One Pager no. 13. Brasilia: International Policy Centre for Inclusive Growth.

Soss, J. 2006. "Talking Our Way to Meaningful Explanations: A Practice-Centered Approach to In-Depth Interviews for Interpretive Research." In *Interpretation and Method*, ed. D. Yanow and P. Schwartz-Shea, 127–49. New York: M. E. Sharpe.

Standing, G. 2002. *Beyond the New Paternalism*. London: Verso.

———. 2008. "How Cash Transfers Promote the Case for Basic Income." *Basic Income Studies* 3:1–30.

———. 2010. *Work after Globalization: Building Occupational Citizenship.* Cheltenham: Edward Elgar.

Stolowicz, B. 2004. "The Latin American Left: Between Governability and Change." In Chavez and Goldfrank 2004, 169–90.

Strang, D., and J. W. Meyer. 1992. "Institutional Conditions for Diffusion." *Theory and Society* 22:487–511.

Stubbs, P. 2005. "Stretching Concepts Too Far? Multi-level Governance, Policy Transfer and the Politics of Scale in South East Europe." *Southeast European Politics* 6:66–87.

Sugiyama, N. B. 2011. "The Diffusion of Conditional Cash Transfer Programs in the Americas." *Global Social Policy* 11:250–78.

Sumarto, S., A. Suryahadi, and S. Bazzi. 2010. "Indonesia's Social Protection during and after the Crisis." In *Social Protection for the Poor and Poorest: Concepts, Policies and Politics,* ed. A. Barrientos and D. Hulme, 121–45. New York: Palgrave Macmillian.

SYDGM (Sosyal Yardımlaşma Ve Dayanışma Genel Müdürlüğü) and World Bank. 2006. 3rd *International Conditional Cash Transfers Conference.* Istanbul: SYDGM.

Teichman, J. 2007. "Multilateral Lending Institutions and Transnational Policy Networks." *Global Governance* 13:557–73.

Theodore, N. 2007. "New Labour at Work: Long-Term Unemployment and the Geography of Opportunity." *Cambridge Journal of Economics* 31:927–39.

Theodore, N., and J. Peck. 1999. "Welfare-to-Work: National Problems, Local Solutions?" *Critical Social Policy* 61:485–510.

———. 2001. "Searching for "Best Practice" in Welfare-to-Work: The Means, the Method and the Message." *Policy and Politics* 29:85–98.

———. 2012. "Framing Neoliberal Urbanism: Translating 'Common Sense' Urban Policy across the OECD Zone." *European Urban and Regional Studies* 19:20–41.

Teibout, C. 1956. "A Pure Theory of Local Government Expenditure." *Journal of Political Economy* 60:416–24.

Teivainen, T. 2002. "The World Social Forum and Global Democratisation: Learning from Porto Alegre." *Third World Quarterly* 23:621–32.

Thiem, C. H., and M. Robertson, eds. 2010. "Behind Enemy Lines: Reflections on the Practice and Production of Oppositional Research." *Geoforum* 41:5–25.

Tibaijuka, A. K. 2004. Foreword. In *72 FAQ on Participatory Budgeting,* Y. Cabannes, 12–14. Nairobi: UN-Habitat.

Toussaint, E., and A. Zacharie. 2003. "External Debt: Abolish the Debt in Order to Free Development." In Fisher and Ponniah 2003a, 30–37.

Tsing, A. L. 2004. *Friction: An Ethnography of Global Connection.* Princeton: Princeton University Press.

Tulchin, J. S., and A. Selee, eds. 1994. *Decentralization and Democratic Governance in Latin America.* Woodrow Wilson Center Report on the Americas no. 12. Washington, D.C.: Woodrow Wilson Center.

Udall, L. 1998. "The World Bank and Public Accountability: Has Anything Changed?" In *The Struggle for Accountability: The World Bank, NGOs, and Grassroots Movements*, ed. J. A. Fox and L. D. Brown, 391–436. Cambridge: MIT Press.

UNDP (United Nations Development Programme). 1990. *Human Development Report 1990*. Oxford: Oxford University Press.

UNESCO. 2010. *UNESCO at the World Urban Forum 5*. Brasilia: UNESCO.

UNICEF (United Nations Children's Fund). 1987. *Adjustment with a Human Face*. Oxford: Oxford University Press.

UN-Habitat. 1996. *The Habitat Agenda: Istanbul Declaration on Human Settlements*. Nairobi: UN Human Settlements Programme.

United Nations, Bureau International des Expositions and Shanghai 2010 World Exposition Executive Committee. 2010. *Shanghai Manual: A Guide for Sustainable Urban Development of the 21st Century*. Shanghai: Shanghai 2010 World Exposition Executive Committee.

Wade, R. H. 2001. "Making the World Development Report 2000: Attacking Poverty." *World Development* 29:1435–41.

———. 2002. "U.S. Hegemony and the World Bank: The Fight over People and Ideas." *Review of International Political Economy* 9:215–43.

Wagle, S., and A. Shah. 2003. "Case Study 2: Porto Alegre, Brazil: Participatory Approaches in Budgeting and Public Expenditure Management." Social Development Notes 71, Social Development Family, World Bank, Washington, D.C.

Wainwright, H. 2003. *Reclaim the State*. London: Verso.

———. 2004. Preface. In Chavez and Goldfrank 2004, vii–xvi.

———. 2006a. Introduction. In *In The Eye of the Storm: Left-Wing Activists Discuss the Political Crisis in Brazil*, ed. H. Wainwright and S. Branford, 6–11. Amsterdam: Transnational Institute.

———. 2006b. "Plural Visions." In *In the Eye of the Storm: Left-Wing Activists Discuss the Political Crisis in Brazil*, ed. H. Wainwright and S. Branford, 17–54. Amsterdam: Transnational Institute.

Walker, J. L. 1969. "The Diffusion of Innovations among the American States." *American Political Science Review* 63:880–99.

Wampler, B. 2007a. "A Guide to Participatory Budgeting." In Shah 2007a, 21–54.

———. 2007b. *Participatory Budgeting in Brazil: Contestation, Cooperation, and Accountability*. University Park: Penn State University Press.

———. 2008. "A difusão do Orçamento Participativo brasileiro: 'Boas práticas' devem ser promovidas?" [The diffusion of Brazil's participatory budgeting: Should "best practices" be promoted?] *Opinião Público* 14:65–95.

Webber, J. R., and B. Carr, eds. 2012. *The New Latin American Left: Cracks in the Empire*. Lanham, Md.: Rowman and Littlefield.

Wedel, J., C. Shore, G. Feldman, and S. Lathrop. 2005. "Toward an Anthropology of Public Policy." *Annals of the American Academy of Political and Social Science* 600:30–51.

Weyland, K. 2006. *Bounded Rationality and Policy Diffusion Social Sector Reform in Latin America*. Princeton: Princeton University Press.

Williamson, J. 1990. "What Washington Means by Policy Reform." In *Latin American Adjustment*, ed. J. Williamson, 5–20. Washington, D.C.: Institute of International Economics.

———. 2006. Foreword. In Levy 2006, vii–x. Washington, D.C.: Brookings Institution Press.

Wolfensohn Center for Development. 2006. *Wolfensohn Center for Development at the Brookings Institution*. Washington, D.C.: Brookings Institution.

Wolman, H. 1992. "Understanding Cross National Policy Transfers: The Case of Britain and the US." *Governance* 5:27–45.

World Bank. 1990. *World Development Report*. New York: Oxford University Press.

———. 2000. *Reforming Public Institutions and Strengthening Governance: A World Bank Strategy*. Washington, D.C.: World Bank.

———. 2001. *World Development Report 2000/2001: Attacking Poverty*. Washington, D.C.: World Bank.

———. 2002. *Empowerment and Poverty Reduction: A Sourcebook*. Washington, D.C.: World Bank.

———. 2004a. *Project Information Document: BR Bolsa Família 1st APL*. Washington, D.C.: World Bank.

———. 2004b. "Social Accountability: An Introduction to the Concept and Emerging Practice." Social Development Paper 76, World Bank, Washington, D.C..

———. 2005a. *Income Generation and Social Protection for the Poor*. Washington, D.C.: World Bank.

———. 2005b. *Social Accountability in the Public Sector: A Conceptual Discussion and Learning Module*. Washington, D.C.: World Bank.

———. 2012a. *BLT Temporary Unconditional Cash Transfer*. Jakarta: World Bank.

———. 2012b. *Protecting Poor and Vulnerable Households in Indonesia*. Jakarta: World Bank.

Wright, E. O. 2010. *Envisioning Real Utopias*. London: Verso.

Wright, M. W. 1997. "Crossing the Factory Frontier: Gender, Place and Power in the Mexican Maquiladora." *Antipode* 29:278–302.

Wright, S. 2011. "Studying Policy: Methods, Paradigms, Perspectives." In Shore et al. 2011, 27–31.

Yanow, D. 2007. "Interpretation in Policy Analysis: On Methods and Practice." *Critical Policy Analysis* 1:110–22.

Yaschine, I. 1999. "The Changing Anti-Poverty Agenda: What Can the Mexican Case Tell Us?" *IDS Bulletin* 30:47–60.

Yaschine, I., and M. E. Orozco. 2010. "The Evolving Antipoverty Agenda in Mexico: The Political Economy of PROGRESA and Oportunidades." In Adato and Hoddinott 2010, 55–77.

# Index

**JAMIE PECK** is Canada Research Chair in urban and regional political economy and professor of geography at the University of British Columbia. He is the author of *Work-Place: The Social Regulation of Labor Markets, Workfare States,* and *Constructions of Neoliberal Reason,* and the managing editor of *Environment and Planning A.*

**NIK THEODORE** is professor of urban planning and policy at the University of Illinois at Chicago. He is the coeditor of *Spaces of Neoliberalism: Urban Restructuring in North America and Western Europe* and the managing editor of *Antipode: A Radical Journal of Geography.*